OUT OF THE PAST

Spanish Cinema after Franco

JOHN HOPEWELL

First published in 1986 by the British Film Institute
127 Charing Cross Road
London WC2H 0EA

British Library Cataloguing in Publication Data

Hopewell, John
    Out of the past : Spanish cinema after Franco.
    1. Moving-pictures – Spain – History
    I. Title
    791.43'0946   PN1993.5.S7

    ISBN 0–85170–188–4

Set in Sabon
Cover design: Peter Virgo

Typeset by Fakenham Photosetting Limited, Fakenham, Norfolk
Printed and bound in Great Britain by W. S. Cowell plc,
London and Ipswich

CONTENTS

Cover: Carlos Saura's *Carmen*

Acknowledgments

The donkeys, duennas and desultoriness of Spain may be dying out, but the warm personal generosity of its inhabitants (both native and foreign) most certainly is not. I would like to thank the directors Pedro Almodóvar, Juan Antonio Bardem, Mario Camus, Celestino Coronado, Victor Erice, José Luis Guerin, Fernando Méndez-Leite, Francisco Regueiro, Imanol Uribe and Paulino Viota for patiently answering my questions; the critics Francesc Llinàs, Manolo Marinero, Zsi Zsi Markos, Carlos Mora, Juan Carlos Rentero and Agustín Sánchez Vidal for their insights; the staff of the Filmoteca Española in Madrid for their efficiency and good humour; Jane Hale for ordering my research; Pablo Devries for aid in documenting the later chapters; and Rocío Mesonero-Romanos Aguilar and María Jesús Díaz-Pinés for relaying vital information. Charles T. Powell allowed me to draw on his authoritative knowledge of contemporary Spanish history; Carmelo Romero, the Director of the Promotion Department at the Spanish Film Institute, answered my enquiries with his customary efficiency; and Fernando Lara and Eduardo Rodríguez very kindly invited me to the excellently organised 29 Semana Internacional de Valladolid.

This book could not have been written without the personal support of Juan Antonio Pérez Millán, the Director of the Filmoteca Española, who supervised my research there in 1984–5. I also owe an especial debt to Fernando and Beatriz Colomo, Elías and Chiruca Querejeta, Manolo and Alicia Gutiérrez Aragón, Luis Megino, and Carlos and Mercedes Saura for their aid and warm friendship; to María Jesús Maza and Ana Amigo for documentation; to Julio Pérez Perucha who disabused me of many *idées reçues*; to Nelson Modlin III who supplied the excellent English translations for Spanish film titles; and, above all, to Vicente Molina Foix who, as a teacher and friend, first awoke in me an interest in Spanish films.

In Britain I received valuable advice, information and encouragement from Don Dummer, Gwynne Edwards, Peter Evans, Robin Fiddian, Richard Hill, Clare Kitson, Sarah Lovett, Carmen Méndez, Peter Packer, Jenni Pozzi, Edward Riley, Stuart Urban and Sheila Whitaker; from Eduardo Garrigues and his staff at the Spanish Institute in London; from José Gallart at ESP Export who supplied video material; and, above all, from David Thompson and my former Spanish teacher Roger Hart. I learned a great deal talking ideas over with Nissa Torrents at University College, London; Paul Arthur suggested many improvements to my manuscript, and David Wilson edited it with much patience and skill. To all these people, and the many others who helped me, my gratitude.

John Hopewell, London, August 1986

INTRODUCTION

In the 1970s Spanish history had a great idea for a film. True to Sam Goldwyn's prescription, the story starts with a real earthquake:

> Morning, 20 December 1973, Madrid. Admiral Carrero Blanco has just attended morning mass. Prime Minister of Spain, Franco's closest collaborator for thirty-two years, he is the only figure in government with enough will and charisma to keep Francoism going when the aged dictator eventually dies. A massive explosive charge has been hidden beneath the road. An explosion. The Admiral's armour-plated Dodge rises fifty feet in the air, clears a parapet of the church of San Francisco de Borja and lands in a courtyard. Carrero Blanco is dead on arrival at hospital. An old problem is thrown wide open: after Franco, what?

The story has well defined characters, with something of a dark past:

> Waiting to succeed Franco as Spain's head of state is Prince Juan Carlos of Bourbon. Manly and large, limited in the main to walk-on parts, on state occasions he has stood behind the stubby Caudillo like a gentle giant. Juan Carlos has sworn fidelity to the principles of the Francoist Movement. He won't last, political pundits say. When Franco dies his reign will be remembered as that of 'Juan the Brief'.

There is a clear chronological progression:

> Carrero Blanco's successor is Arias Navarro. He attempts a timid liberalisation, an 'Opening'. He dithers between total immobility and cosmetic reform. Utterly devoid of inspiration, he sits at his desk with a face like a 'sphinx without a secret'.[1] Franco dies from peritonitis on 20 November 1975. Barcelona runs out of champagne. There is a perfume

1

of political putrefaction in the air. A political opposition gathers. The more radical press demands a clean break with the past. Politically apathetic Spaniards suddenly acquire a certain *mystique de gauche*.

Events work up to a climax:

> Franco's death is a sunset mistaken for a sunrise. Arias Navarro comes clean as 'a strict follower of Francoism'.[2] His successor, Adolfo Suárez, has youth, immense charm, equal ambition, and no democratic credentials whatsoever. But King Juan Carlos needs democracy to legitimise his throne, and Suárez needs democracy to legitimise his power. Before that he has to persuade the Francoist Cortes to approve a Law of Political Reform which would re-establish democracy in Spain. Two days of corridor negotiations...

And there's a happy massed finale; even the bit players get a look in:

> The yes-men in the Cortes refuse to take the onerous responsibility of saying no to a Law which the King, the Church, the majority of the Spanish people and the democratic world desire. In an act of calculated altruism the Cortes votes itself out of existence ... The first democratic elections for forty years take place in June 1977. Suárez's Union of the Democratic Centre gets home. The elections are a triumph of enthusiasm and moderation, a combination distinctly lacking in the past. Seventy-nine per cent of the electorate vote. Spain *grosso modo* is a democracy.

So ends the Spanish dictatorship-to-democracy melodrama.

Things do happen all of a sudden in Spain. When Alfonso XIII, Juan Carlos' grandfather, abandoned his throne in 1931, he took everybody by surprise. 'The fall of the monarchy,' wrote Alfonso's polo tutor, 'gave me a greater shock than any fall from a pony.'[3] The dissolution of Francoism has been far more dramatic, and deep-seated. There has been an attempt to rewrite the ending to the transition: on 23 February 1981 Colonel Tejero, a moustachioed blackguard with a three-cornered hat, burst into Parliament with a group of paramilitary Guardia Civil and held the assembly to hostage at gunpoint. Yet his coup ran up against the bedrock opposition of the King. Tejero got thirty years, and began them in a luxury apartment on the outskirts of Madrid studying the career of Napoleon. The socialists won a landslide in the general elections of October 1982. The moderation of their reforms had assuaged the fears of the right without alienating the support of the mass of their voters. Change had come to stay.

2

Spain's move towards change has also had artistic dividends. Since the early 1970s Saura, Berlanga and Borau have all made major works. A new generation of film-makers has emerged – Erice, Chávarri, Gutiérrez Aragón, García Sánchez, Franco, Martínez-Lázaro, Zulueta and Ungría – to take prizes at Cannes, Berlin and Venice. Garci won an Oscar in 1983 with *Volver a empezar* ('Starting Over'). There was a momentous and momentary spate of films with purported political commitment, a revival in comedies with films by Colomo, Trueba and Ladoire, co-productions with Spanish television and the United States, a dynamic Basque cinema, a vigorous film-funding practice under the socialist government.

By 1985 the Spanish cinema had never had it so good. There was also, earlier, one champagne event. In 1977 a 'rude Aragonian' came to Spain to shoot exteriors. Those famous bolting eyes were eclipsed by glasses; his frame had acquired the diminishing, dollish lightness of old age; like many great figures from Aragón, he was very hard of hearing. But still remaining was the provocative humour and black tobacco, the rite of the dry martini, and the unbothered and genial singularity of obsessions and experience. He had been contemplating his retirement for years. Each work from *La voie lactée* (1969) was regarded as 'the next last film' of Luis Buñuel. By 1977 Buñuel was feeling his age, was fascinated by terrorism, and had an enormous fear of death. The explosion which ends *That Obscure Object of Desire* (1977) was the truly last outrage of the imagination from the raconteur of Calanda.

The post-Franco cinema emerges most clearly with the reception, rather than the making, of Carlos Saura's *La prima Angélica* ('Cousin Angelica', 1974). One scene caught everybody's attention: the protagonist's uncle comes back wounded from the Civil War dressed in the uniform of the fascist Falange and with his arm permanently fixed by a plaster cast at the angle of a fascist salute. Saura's film had been seen and approved at a top-level meeting of six cabinet ministers, where it was programmed in a double bill with *Jesus Christ, Superstar*. The left raved; the right were left raving. *La prima Angélica* took just under sixty-three million pesetas by the end of 1974. Clear commercial and political precedents were set for the early post-Franco cinema. It was a cinema of ideological gratification, rather than escapist entertainment, a cinema of change, in change, and for or against change, a cinema which dealt in contemporary issues, vaunted (often hypocritically) its frankness on previous taboos, either to round-turn and declare that the liberal will always be libertine, or to see liberal reform as one bold step beyond the horizons of Francoism.[4]

Buñuel once sketched the arrant self-confidence of the Spanish: 'I have a fear of hell, but I'm good enough to spit on God.' Censorship was abolished in Spain by Royal Decree on 11 November 1977. The legendary individualism of Spaniards combined with new-found freedoms to favour, at least in

3

potential, a long-term post-Franco cinema where the film-makers work as *auteurs* endowing their films, perhaps unconsciously, with a recognisable persona, a constant permutation on a series of distinguishing if recondite motifs open to structural analysis. Saura, Berlanga, Garci, Erice, and Gutiérrez Aragón have all imbued their works with a sense of authorial personality. They invite some *auteur* attentions, if only to establish the continual discontinuities of their work, as in the case of Gutiérrez Aragón, and to suggest the consistent diversity of decisive influences on film-makers, which run from Freud to *film noir*, the rumbustiousness of Spanish farce, the structures of the folk-tale, the mechanisms of myth.

Yet the post-Franco cinema is a balancing act. The centrifugal forces of diverse influence and radical absorption in self are always crossed, checked, even obscured by the heavy weight of immediate necessities and the pull of the past. Rather than captains of their artistic fate, Spanish directors have often seemed deckhands of circumstance. 'For the Greeks, the implacable was Destiny; for us it is History,' Gutiérrez Aragón explains, speaking of the young fascist in *Camada negra* ('Black Litter', 1977) whose attempt to fly in the face of history wins him, in his director's eyes, the status of hero.[5]

A historical circumstance of crucial significance for the modern Spanish cinema has been its unrelieved industrial decapitalisation. 'The cinema in general is a mixture of art and industry, but the Spanish cinema is a mixture of art and a lack of money,' rasped the aphonic egghead and permanent *viejete* ('old boy') José Isbert, the amiable multiple murderer in Ferreri's *El cochecito* ('The Little Car', 1960).[6] No Spanish film-maker can afford to forget his market. *El sur* ('The South', 1983), Erice says, was not the film he really wanted to make. He would have preferred something more in the line of Wenders or Godard. But he accepted the project, and tailored its aesthetics for Gran Vía audiences, the Spanish equivalent of a West End or Broadway run. Erice's diffidence didn't entirely pay off. There were difficulties on the shoot and Spain's most prestigious film-maker wasn't able to finish his film. *El sur* still lacks its final and, Erice maintains, essential scenes.[7]

Erice's fate is repeated the world over. What marks out the Spanish cinema — in degree, not kind — is the contrary influence of its singular history. Few directors were able, for example, to turn their backs totally on the transition. It gave them urgent themes. It demanded some sort of stand, however discreet, at a time when Spanish intellectuals were opinion setters with an important voice in public debate. 'Don't footle, man!' critics cried at Carlos Saura, the political bother-boy of *La prima Angélica*. 'Say something!' Saura's intimist study of infancy, *Cría cuervos* ('Raise Ravens', 1975), was thought decidedly lacking in public-spiritedness.

Yet Gutiérrez Aragón's 'History' has meant, more than anything else, the Spanish Civil War. The film-makers of today were the children of the 40s

4

and 50s, a post-war period when perhaps 100,000 Spaniards were murdered in reprisals,[8] a Francoist 'peace' which left many, whichever side they had fought on, in a permanent state of evasion, of absence from reality, of withdrawal into fantasy, 'exiled within themselves' as Erice's telling phrase runs. History in Spain is often surrealist, grand guignol. It offers artists themes, contrasts, vignettes; but it also prescribes circumspection. Cupboards full of skeletons have still to be opened.

There's the rub. In 1986 Spain has entered the European Economic Community. The Spanish cinema will compete at home and abroad on equal terms with films from other Community countries. For forty years under Franco, each generation of film-makers and critics broke with the dominant film styles in an almost neurotic and thoroughly understandable attempt to start from scratch, to dissociate themselves from a damned and damning past. What Spanish film-makers lack in 1986 is, in part, a sense of identity. The Italian cinema has its tradition of neo-realism; a young French director will return to the *nouvelle vague* in the 60s if only to discover his own position in a national film-making tradition. A Spanish director has no such sense of filmic heritage and, because of this, few tags to act as selling points in the cultural supermarket of European cinema.

Yet there are traditions in Spanish film-making, and when they are drawn on by a director of ability the result may be an enormous success. Berlanga's *La vaquilla* ('The Heifer'), for example, was the box-office success of 1985. Yet it was scripted in 1957, its memorable music was first used in the Buñuel production *La hija de Juan Simón* ('Juan Simón's Daughter', Sáenz de Heredia, 1935), and its tradition in Spanish farce style, the *sainete*, dates back in cinema history to Spain's first ever fiction film, Gelabert's *Riña en un café* ('Café Brawl', 1897). Recent film studies and a television programme, 'Spanish Film Night', have opened up debate on Spain's film history. There is now, Victor Erice claims, 'a spirit of discovery' in the air. The future of the Spanish cinema will depend in part on its ability to approach, assimilate and, when necessary, break with the decisive influence of the past.

ROOTS AND REASONS
FOR REACTION

Spanish Cinema, 1896–1950

A Third World force: Spanish silent film, 1896–1929
For Luis Buñuel, holidays began like many of his films with a horse-drawn carriage ride. He was off to Calanda, the village on the dry plain of Aragón where he was born, and where 'the Middle Ages lasted until World War I':

> It was a closed and isolated society, with clear and unchanging distinctions among the classes. The respectful subordination of the peasants to the big landowners was deeply rooted in tradition, and seemed unshakeable. Life unfolded in a linear fashion, the major moments marked by the daily bells of the Church of Pilar.[1]

Few other sounds broke the quiet of Calanda: the arrival of the mail coach drawn by mules, the 'Song of Sunrise' sung by harvesters on their way to the fields, the call of the nightwatchmen: 'God be praised!' Calanda had enjoyed its moment of history: in 1640 the Virgin of Pilar appeared to the one-legged Miguel Juan Pellicer and transformed his stump into a limb. Snug in their fields and faith, the people of Calanda now let history pass them by.

Buñuel's Calanda was typical of turn-of-the-century Spain, a country of small towns, villages and hamlets, governed by a land-owning oligarchy. But Buñuel was an exception, the son of the fourth or fifth richest man in the provincial capital of Saragossa. 'Every night,' wrote Joaquín Costa, son of an Aragonese peasant farmer, 'half of Spain goes to bed hungry.' Spain had some of the poorest peasants in all Europe: the owners of handkerchief plots – the *minifundia* – in Galicia; the landless labourers on the vast estates – *latifundia* – of the south-west.

Spain had not yet experienced an industrial revolution. So it lacked the *grand bourgeoisie* of Britain or France which could capitalise a film industry, providing it with investments and moneyed audiences. The absence of

7 ·

true middle classes turned class differences into clear class divides. Cinema inherited the *submonde* stigmata of the popular theatre, whose actors were forbidden church burial in the nineteenth century. To the upper crust the film industry meant immorality, fatuity. Such attitudes died hard. In 1944, in Mervyn Le Roy's *Waterloo Bridge*, where Vivien Leigh takes to walking the streets after believing her fiancé to be dead, the word 'prostitute' was dubbed into Spanish by a meaningful equivalent: 'actress'.

Spain's fusty slumber was scarce disturbed by the arrival of A. Promio, sent by the Lumières to popularise their invention. The first public film-show in Spain took place in Madrid on 15 May 1896.[2] Promio projected eight to ten films, including *Workers Leaving the Factory* (1895). The Frenchman's exhibition provoked 'joy and astonishment' although, to be fair, he had packed the audience with presumably Francophile schoolgirls from a local French school.

The Lumières' first films were of people leaving factories, or of trains. Promio's first film was probably of his schoolgirls: *Salida de las alumnas del Colegio de San Luis de los Franceses*. In fine Pyrenean contrast, the first film shot by a Spaniard was Eduardo Jimeno Correas' *Salida de la misa de 12 de la Iglesia del Pilar de Zaragoza*. It showed a congregation leaving a church. In August 1897 Fructuoso Gelabert wrote, directed and acted in the first fictional short made in Spain: *Riña en un café* ('Café Brawl').[3]

The first Spanish films have features that survive in Spain's cinema up to this day. Jimeno's record shows that characteristic concern for a specifically Spanish reality. Gelabert's short, more importantly, connects with an indigenous theatrical genre of immense influence on Spain's films: the *sainete*. The cinema's early recourse to this tradition was perhaps inevitable. The *sainete* was immensely popular among Spain's lower orders; its *costumbrismo* – a rather rosy realism idealising popular customs – was the nearest the Spanish theatre got to the accuracy in depiction of scene which was the early cinema's stock in trade.

The *sainete*, like the first documentaries, delighted in its familiarity, which stirred a sense of complicity between fiction and audience. The location is normally the street, the tenement courtyard, the local fair; the characters in a *sainete* are types – the braggadocio ruffian, the young swain with a prickly honour, the old codger full of homespun philosophy; the stage bustles with action, and yet there is little plot; dialogue is localist, peppered with slang, malapropisms and sententious reflection. Themes vary with play and playwright. But in general they reflect the popular strain of the Belle Epoque (Ricardo de la Vega), essential human goodness in a romanticised Andalusia (the brothers Quintero), the happiness rewarding hard work and honesty (Carlos Arniches).[4]

Riña en un café draws on the *sainete* tradition in its scene, characters and plot, where rivalry in love provokes a fight. The copy at the Filmoteca

Española opens with an amiable old buffer facing the camera fiddling with his walking stick. Cut to idlers on a café terrace. One talks to a girl. She leaves. Enter the young swain. He approaches the same man, they exchange insults, fly at each other, are pulled apart.

The *zarzuela* rivalled the *sainete* in popularity.[5] Vernacular and comic operetta, part spoken, part sung, a full-length *zarzuela* could have an exotic, even biblical, setting. But the one-act *zarzuela* came much closer to the *sainete* settings and sentiments. Together with bullfights, melodrama and a nod to religious piety, the farcical strain of *sainetes* and *zarzuelas* bubbled together in the *pot-pourri* which nourished the first two decades of Spanish cinema. G. G. Brown, in *A Literary History of Spain: the Twentieth Century*, notes the anguish, the disillusionment with religion and rationalism, the despair at national decadence, common to some great early twentieth-century Spanish writers. The Spanish masses did not share, at least consciously, this angst. But their agrarian poverty meant that 'turning away from reality in search of something less depressing and distasteful', as Brown puts it, was 'the most characteristic response' not only of writers but also of film-makers from 1900 to 1939.[6] There are exceptions. But when the cinema turns back to popular reality, it will portray Spaniards (uncharacteristically, it could be argued) at rest. Or it will show labourers at that exceptional time of full employment: the harvest. The reaping scenes in *Nobleza baturra* ('Aragonese Nobility', Florián Rey, 1935) are an instance of this selective realism in an already mythicised vision of Aragón. Or, as in the first and immensely successful *zarzuela* adaptation of the 20s, José Buchs' *La verbena de la Paloma* ('Paloma Fair'), the hero will work at a printers, the cream of working-class trades.

Spanish films were popularist. But few were really popular. At first, already sated on a vibrant theatre, the Spanish masses could not take the cinema seriously. It was just a gimmick. For a year and a half in the early 1900s there was quite possibly *not one* cinema in Madrid. Those cinemas which existed were *barracones*, wooden booths at fairs where a film could be followed by 'The Woman Cannon Ball' or 'Malleu and his Tamed Lions'.

By 1910 there were cinemas in Madrid, but still no film-makers. And pictures which got made went to tortuous lengths to reconcile foreign genre models with a Spanish morality. *Lilian* (1922), for example, is a Spanish Western. But the conflict wasn't between cowboy and Indian, but between cowboy and pastor, in which the man of religion catechises the rude steersman aided by 'the sacrifice of an intrepid and loving young girl'.[7] Such was the preference for foreign cinema shown by Spanish exhibitors that *Lilian* was passed off as a British production, made by 'Good Silver Films', and hired to an exhibitor, the unfortunate Luis Pallares, who had claimed that Spanish films would be seen at his cinema over his dead body.

9

The publicity for the film *Boy* (Benito Perojo, 1925) was 'It's so good that it doesn't seem Spanish!' In emotional and industrial terms Spain was not far off a Third World country. Lacking skilled manpower, technology and finance, and being in no position to exploit her resources, Spain like any Third World country sold her raw materials abroad to companies who made profits by processing them and selling them back again. The Spanish cinema's 'raw material' included the sights of Spain which Lumière, Pathé, and Gaumont hired cameramen to film. They embraced contemporary events, and the traditions and history of Spain, as in the French super-production *Cristóbal Colón* ('Christopher Columbus', 1916), a great success at the Spanish box-office. Similar 'raw material' was the very fine talents of Segundo de Chomón and the young Luis Buñuel.

In 1925, Buñuel went to Paris. Behind him were his student days in Madrid: eight years of high jinks, friendships (Dali and Lorca especially), and studies in entomology which were to serve Buñuel for the whole of his film career. The douches and the abruptness of ending to *That Obscure Object of Desire* date from japes and literary games played when Buñuel was at the Residencia de Estudiantes over fifty years before. Buñuel went to Paris for the high-life, not for surrealism. 'Until 1927,' he has declared of the surrealists, 'I thought they were a load of poofs.'[8] But when Buñuel decided to make films, he stayed in Paris. It gave him technical facilities and assurance, finance (for *L'Age d'or*), and a sense, when he accepted surrealism, of tradition. The direction of *Un chien andalou* (1928), its script, and even the ants all came from Spain. But the film is normally counted in a history of the French cinema. A country's cinema is the corpus of films it finances, one argument runs. On this count, Buñuel's cinema is rarely Spanish cinema, for not one of his twenty-nine full-length features was wholly financed by Spaniards.

Buñuel's case was anticipated twenty years before by Segundo de Chomón (1871–1929). Chomón is dubbed 'the Spanish Méliès'; but such were the Spaniard's innovations that Méliès could be dubbed 'the French Segundo de Chomón'. What is so remarkable about Segundo de Chomón is the speed and ease with which he grasped and implemented in film *all* the premises of 'special effects'. He used models in *Choque de trenes* ('Train Crash', 1902), and combined images in the double exposure of *Gulliver en el país de los gigantes* ('Gulliver in the Land of the Giants', 1903) and *Pulgarcito* ('Tom Thumb', 1903).

Segundo de Chomón's major achievement was his *El hotel eléctrico* ('The Electric Hotel', 1905). This is the first example ever, it is claimed, of 'pixillation': the animation of objects by photographing frames individually and changing the position of the subject between frames. The result in *El hotel eléctrico* is a machine-age comedy. A couple check in at a totally mechanised hotel. Invisible, supposedly electric, forces unpack their cases,

10

serve dinner, comb the lady, shave the gentleman, untie the footwear. . . .
But a drunk gets into the control-room, leans against the panels and creates
chaos as objects fly all over the place in a good-humoured travesty of not
only a futuristic automation but Chomón's own ease of animation up to
that point in his film.

Segundo de Chomón is credited with the world's first cartoons (in a
sequence of *La maison hantée*, 'The Haunted House', 1907) and the very
first dolly travelling shot when he mounted a camera on a board with
runners to control perspectives in *La vie et la passion de Jésus-Christ* ('The
Life and Passion of Jesus Christ', 1907).[9] Chomón later arranged special
effects in *Cabiria* (Giovanni Pastrone, 1914), and *Napoleon* (Abel Gance,
1926). Chomón's legerdemain was such that when his *Atracción de circo*
('Circus Attraction') was shown in Spain it was banned at the behest of the
Society for the Protection of Animals because of a scene where the heroine
steers a horse across a highwire, only for both woman and horse to come
crashing to the ground. It was left to Chomón to explain that the horse (and
the acrobat) had been models.

Segundo de Chomón worked largely outside Spain from 1906. No
Spanish producer could afford the cost of his experimental films. The
Spanish film industry limped on without him in Barcelona, to collapse in
the early 20s amid the disruptions of strikes and a bloody labour war from
1919 to 1923 between the hired assassins of the retrograde Employers
Federation and the inspired assassins claiming allegiance to revolutionary
anarcho-syndicalism.

From the 1920s Barcelona still had far more cinemas, but Madrid had all
the film-makers and a growing industrial infrastructure.[10] José Buchs,
Fernando Delgado, Benito Perojo and Florián Rey emerged as directors
with artistic personality and, more crucially, industrial longevity. Buchs
made *zarzuelas* such as *La verbena de la Paloma* (1920, a huge success), or
La reina mora ('The Moorish Queen', 1922, originally written by the
Brothers Quintero). He also directed bullfight films and historical dramas.
Rey was equally popularist, by temperament as much as necessity, filming
zarzuelas such as *La revoltosa* ('The Mischievous Girl', 1924), and a rural
melodrama, perhaps the best Spanish silent film, *El cura de aldea* ('The
Village Priest', 1926). Perojo and Delgado gained 'cosmopolitan' reputa-
tions, the latter winning acclaim for a portrayal of middle-class hypocrisy in
Las de Méndez ('The Mendez', 1927).[11] *La malcasada* ('The Unhappily
Married Woman', Francisco Gómez Hidalgo, 1926) took this unusual
social concern much further, departing from a routine plot to arrive at a
screen debate on a contemporary issue: divorce. Writers, soldiers and
politicians appear together on the screen to give their opinions. One is the
soldier who in 1926, at the age of thirty-three, became the youngest general
in Europe since Bonaparte: Francisco Franco.

11

The legalisation of divorce was just one measure of the social reform contemplated under the lax dictatorship of Primo de Rivera (1923–30) and dashed by what his Finance Minister called 'the obstinate passivity of the conservative classes'.[12] The conflict between change and Castillian conservatism was to provide the background for the most acclaimed Spanish silent film: Florián Rey's *La aldea maldita* ('The Cursed Village', 1929).

Rey's film opens with a refreshingly disabused vision of peasant life in arid Castille. Juan Castilla is seen in the fields hacking at the soil. Meanwhile his wife Acacia croons cradle songs to their baby son; his ancient father sits nearby in happy dotage, proud of an unsmirched family honour. A hailstorm ruins the crops. Hunger, anguish; Juan in jail for threatening a storekeeper, Tío Lucas, who hoards his supplies; grandfather stays in the village and refuses to part with the baby who carries his name and is of his blood. Acacia, with the rest of the villagers, emigrates to the local town, and falls into prostitution. When released, Juan moves to the town, finds Acacia, and drags her home so that the grandfather can die with the illusion of an honourably united family. But Juan refuses to let his wife touch her child. With Juan's father on his deathbed, Acacia leaves the house to wander through a snowy landscape, return to the empty village, rock an empty cradle, and be discovered by Juan who, moved by her deranged maternal affections, grants her his pardon.

La aldea maldita is rampant melodrama, but also a provocative moral drama. As in the plays of the seventeenth-century dramatist Calderón de la Barca, an event external to the hero (here a crop failure, then emigration) presents him with conflicting moral and emotional demands to which his actions assign a hierarchy of importance. Juan is split between his love for his father, his love for his wife (professed throughout the film), his desire for external honour, and the Christian precept of forgiveness. Juan's first fidelity is not to a code of conduct, but to his love for his father who embodies that conduct – honour as a priceless family heritage – as the very fibre of his being. But with his father dead, Juan forgives the woman who has dishonoured him, partly at the prompting of Tío Lucas, who has pardoned Juan for attacking him.

Pardon brings pardon; love draws out love. The family survives one change (the emigration) because of another (the death of the grandfather). Rey's optimism and his faith in the regenerative value of simple Christian virtue is darkened, however, by a foreboding complexity. Honour finally yields to a desire for forgiveness. But even Juan's pardon presupposes a reactionary sense of the male as arbiter of moral right. Juan's sacrifice of principle (honour) confirms a deeper principle (male moral authority). Juan in Rey's fiction bends very little. Just how far real-life conservatives were prepared to accede to change was to be questioned by Spain's Republic of 1931–6, and answered with bloody unambiguity by Spain's Civil War.

La aldea maldita

A Hollywood exodus; a Republican revival

On 26 January 1929, face blacked as a negro, Ramón Gómez de la Serna presented *The Jazz Singer* to Spanish audiences. Gómez de la Serna's extravagance could not prevent the Spanish premiere of the first commercially successful synchronised sound film in the world from being a damp squib: the cinema had no sound system. But then no cinema in Spain had a sound system, and there were no sound studios either. Al Jolson's words, 'You ain't heard nothing yet', were truer than he could have imagined. The first sound film to be fully produced in Spain and have normal distribution was *Carceleras* ('"Carcelera" Songs'), directed by José Buchs in 1932.

Spaniards look back on the Second Republic (1931–6) with remorse and a hope for instruction from past mistakes. It was the last time that Spain was a democracy until 1977. But the Republic's failure to fulfil its promise helped precipitate a Civil War. For film-makers, the Republic has a twofold lesson: an industry needs talent; talent needs an industry. When the Spanish cinema achieved an industrial infrastructure, it boomed. In 1935–6, for the last time in its history, and under a democratic government, a Spanish cinema of indigenous themes and style won a lion's share of the national market. This enviable achievement ensures that the Republic remains a key period in Spanish cinema history towards which the attentions of modern film-makers frequently return.[13]

In 1930, the Spanish cinema lacked talent: most of it had gone to Hollywood.[14] Spain's influence on Hollywood has been significant, but sporadic. The Valencian realist writer Vicente Blasco Ibáñez had five major adaptations of his novels; *The Torrent* (Monta Bell, 1925) and *The Temptress* (Fred Niblo, 1926) were used by Metro to launch the Hollywood career of Greta Garbo. Another Spanish contribution to Hollywood came from the Sevillian *bailaor* (flamenco dancer) Antonio Cansino. Spearheaded by his children Eduardo and Elisa, his family flamenco spectacular acquired such prestige in the United States that when the Warner brothers wanted to test out their new Vitaphone system, a year before the premiere of *The Jazz Singer*, they thought of featuring the Cansino family in *La Fiesta*. For the film, Antonio got his seven-year-old granddaughter, Margarita, to strut a few steps and clack her castanets. 'Nobody could have imagined then,' writes film historian Emilio Sanz de Soto, 'that this would be the first screen appearance of Rita Hayworth.'[15]

In 1930, Hollywood was more interested in markets than individual artists. The transfer to sound had brought it to an impasse. Dubbing had not yet been perfected, and subtitled versions of its films could not be read by its largely illiterate world audiences. How could it penetrate the Hispanic market of 160 million spectators and, apparently, 6,000 cinemas in Latin America alone?[16] Hollywood's answer, a mixture of pragmatism and power, was to buy up the human potential of a still hypothetical Spanish sound cinema, transferring its writers and directors either to California or to the Paramount Studios in Paris. Hollywood films were then reshot, literally shot for shot, using Spanish dialogue and a Hispanic cast.

By 1931 the aristocratic Edgar Neville had introduced so many Spaniards into Charles Chaplin's set that Scott Fitzgerald called the comic's residence 'the Spanish House'. Excepting Neville's art direction on *El presidio* (a recast of George F. Hill's *The Big House*), the 'Spanish versions' won little praise, being low-budget productions made by Spaniards with theatrical rather than film backgrounds and tied to enslaving translations of American plots and sentiments which never rang true in Spanish. 'Original' films, adapted from the plays of Gregorio Martínez Sierra and Enrique Jardiel Poncela and made under the aegis of Fox from 1931, were markedly more successful. They included *Angelina, o El honor de un brigadier* ('Angelina, or A Brigadier's Honour', co-directed by Jardiel Poncela himself in 1935), a delicious burlesque of post-Romantic melodrama, distinguished by the ingenious ingenuousness of a dialogue written *totally* in rhyming quatrains and Jardiel Poncela's unbothered presentation of a world of utter absurdity. Perhaps Poncela's world view was influenced by his sojourn in Hollywood itself. The Hollywood majors may have been more interested in nipping a Spanish industry before its bud rather than cultivating a home-grown variety of its own, for most Spanish film-makers

14

in Hollywood were grossly underemployed and left to enjoy their own flippancies, such as Jardiel Poncela's concept of Hollywood beach behaviour where 'You can only do two things: lie on the sand and look at the stars, or lie on the "stars" and look at the sand.'[17]

'Spanish versions' include one of the most memorable films in Spanish history, produced by Paramount in Paris and co-directed by Florián Rey in 1931: Su noche de bodas. This version of Frank Tuttle's Her Wedding Night had its first night in Spain on the very first night of the Second Republic: 14 April 1931. For many Spaniards, Su noche de bodas would recall the immense enthusiasm for change provoked by the young Republic. Saura uses Imperio Argentina's lush rendering of a song from Su noche in El jardín de las delicias ('The Garden of Delights', 1970), an oblique lambasting of the conservative and Francoist classes which frustrated the Republic's ambitions for reform. The title of the song is Recordar: 'Remember'.

From 1932 to November 1933, the Republican-Socialist coalition under Manuel Azaña envisaged army reform, expropriation and redistribution of land, a lay system of education, an Autonomy Statute for Catalonia. Mauled by a fragmented Cortes (with twenty-six parties in 1931), these plans were then lamed for lack of money; the Autonomy Statute was the one substantial success of the new regime. During 'Two Black Years' (December 1933–February 1936) the reactionary governments of Alejandro Lerroux and José María Gil Robles set about systematically reversing the work of the Azaña government by appealing to what Gil Robles was later to call 'the suicidal egoism of the rich'.[18] Gil Robles' entry into government sparked a senseless rebellion by the socialists in October 1934; the armed revolt in the mining province of Asturias was put down with appalling brutality by government troops led by General Franco. The right was equally unprepared to accept the socialists in government. The nationalist authoritarian Falange founded in October 1933 by José Antonio Primo de Rivera, son of the dictator, began to make overtures to the army. By 1936 a conspiracy was afoot.

The divisions of the Republican years help explain the particular form taken by the production boom of 1934–6. Films were mass entertainment. The film fan became a figure of fun, immortalised with verve and Chaplinesque pathos by the buck-toothed and endearingly inept Patricio, the star-struck haberdashery assistant of Patricio miró a una estrella ('Patricio Looked at a Star', José Luis Sáenz de Heredia, 1934). Yet dubbing was not yet generalised. The Spanish preferred their own star, Imperio Argentina, speaking in Spanish, to a world star, such as Garbo, speaking in English. Spain remained predominantly rural, with an urban petit bourgeoisie being overtaken by a working class accounting for 70 per cent of Madrid's active population by 1930. Sensing that Spain was falling apart, Spanish audiences sought a cinema of national archetypes which were seemingly impervious to change and allowed Spanish spectators, through their identification with stock racial models, a sense of solidarity.

Produced largely by Cifesa (from April 1934) and Filmófono (from 1935), Spain now had its only truly national cinema.[19] Its foremost practitioner was Florián Rey, and one of his and Cifesa's first big successes was *Nobleza baturra*, which attempts to mythicise racial caste. It is also an honour drama. Pilar, daughter of a rich landowner, loves a labourer, Sebastián, and rejects his rival, Marco, who belongs to her own social class. Marco's revenge is to have a servant climb down from Pilar's balcony at night. Pilar is dishonoured, Sebastián distraught. He appeals to the local priest, who just tells him to 'think'. Sebastián's answer is for himself to be seen climbing down from Pilar's balcony but pretending to be a thief. Pilar's honour is restored. Discovering Sebastián's subterfuge, she grants him land to elevate him to her status. They marry.

Morena Clara ('Clara the Brunette', 1936) similarly takes its hat off to native wit, here the *gracia* or natural charm which allows a gypsy servant to win the heart and then the hand of her master, a young judge. Rey directs with utter conviction. Yet both films are exercises in evasion. They celebrate inter-class love; a few months later Spain's landlords and peasants would be shooting at one another. The films are located in a pre-capitalist era where man is seen in harmony with and influenced by nature, not history. They delight in the minor evasions of visual digression, and a rudimentary plot where conflicts are resolved by an individual act (such as Marco's repentance in *Morena Clara*) rather than by impersonal forces beyond individual cognisance and control.[20]

The keynote of Republican films is their sense of community. Under Franco, the essential social nucleus becomes the family and the most used setting 'the interior of a mansion belonging to the upper middle-class'.[21] Republican films are not nearly so bourgeois. Their tone is caught decisively by *La verbena de la Paloma* ('Paloma Fair', 1935), Benito Perojo's cosmopolitan adaptation of the one-act *zarzuela* composed by Tomás Bretón in 1894. The plot is minimal. Julián, a typesetter, argues with Susana, a seamstress. She decides to go to the fair with don Hilarión, a foppish old apothecary, and an ogrish Aunt Antonia. Julián flies at don Hilarión when they meet at the fair. But at the police station it is Susana's aunt who is arrested for her remonstrations. The apothecary flees, to leave Julián and Susana alone, and in love, at the fair.

The community in *La verbena* is not a village, but a *barrio*, a popular neighbourhood in the old parts of Madrid. It is the community which establishes character and regulates courtship: Julián's popularity comes through at the opening wedding where he is asked to give a speech; his evening at the fair with Susana will confirm the two as a couple. The community cuts through class divisions: outside work, Julián is the best of friends with his boss. *La verbena* excels in turbulent but joyous crowd scenes; films under Franco tended to equate mass turbulence with a rebellious rabble. The setting features nodal points in community life: a wedding, a tram-ride, the café-theatre, the tenement block, the street, the street-organ, the Big Wheel and boats at the fair. But Perojo insists on the coherence of his community, knit by the homogeneity of its setting, its idiom, its particular folklore, which allows a song to be taken up by Susana then echoed by the whole of her tenement.

Cifesa adopted Hollywood techniques: high-budget production; an attempted monopoly of star talent in Spain; publicity drives; a worldwide distribution network. Hollywood was also the touchstone for Filmófono, where Luis Buñuel produced, and virtually directed parts of, four films in 1935 and 1936. Their immense popularity not only influenced Buñuel's 'commercial' film-making in Mexico, but confirmed a style of Republican film-making whose distinctive popularism, for all the films' dross, makes the period an important reference for modern Spanish film-makers, hardpressed to conquer national markets.

Buñuel had already returned to Spain in 1932 to make *Las Hurdes* ('Land Without Bread'), a work of genius which no documentary film-maker in Spain could ignore. When Bunuel arrived at Las Hurdes, he turned to his travelling companions. 'Do you see this wonderful valley? Well, this is where hell begins.'[22] Las Hurdes, a mountainous region sixty miles from Salamanca, populated by the descendants of bandits and Jews who fled from the expulsions of the Catholic Kings in the sixteenth century, was one of the poorest areas in Europe. Bread was unknown in parts; there were few utensils, nor happiness nor songs nor windows to the squat shacks where the Hurdanos lived. Hunger, cholera, dysentery, goitre, incest, the mentally retarded, death, dwarfs – all are rife in Las Hurdes.

Las Hurdes has been called a surrealist documentary. This can be taken many ways. The reality recorded often resembles images found in dreams: at one moment we watch a goat miss its footing on a mountainside and tumble at nightmarish speed to death on the rocks below. An unspecified sexual symbolism is claimed for another event: grooms at a local festival galloping down a street, pulling the heads off chickens as they pass. The central irony of *Las Hurdes* (and its social indictment) derives from a 'surrealist' juxtaposition. 'Though its material civilisation is rudimentary and prehistoric,' Buñuel himself explains of the region, 'its religious and moral culture and ideas are like those of any civilised country.'[23]

The essential surrealism of *Las Hurdes* derives from Buñuel's sharp meditation on documentary types. As he wrote some years later in his autobiography:

17

Communities: *La verbena de la Paloma* ...

To my mind there exist two different kinds of documentary films: one
which could be called *descriptive* in which the material is limited to the
transcription of a natural or social phenomenon. For example: industrial manufacture, the construction of a road ... etc. Another type, much
less frequent, is one which, while both descriptive and objective, tries to
interpret reality.... Such a documentary film is much more complete
because, besides illustrating, it is moving.... Thus besides the *descriptive* documentary film, there is the *psychological* one.[24]

The commentary in *Las Hurdes* belongs to the descriptive mode, with an
apparent indifference to the suffering of the subject. The Hurdanos seem at
times the subject of an entomological rather than an ethnological study;
elsewhere the commentary sounds like a travelogue: 'The day of our arrival
we saw the women of the village in a great ceremony.'

Buñuel's film does not, however, share the essential indifference inculcated by most documentaries, where the cultured spectator is allowed to
feel no more than a passing pity for the subject portrayed quite simply
because logic soon takes us to more abstract questions whose answers may
be applied to the eradication of the problem under study. In a lesson which
Ricardo Franco was to take up in *Pascual Duarte* (1975) Buñuel presents us
with 'what is' and only twice suggests 'why'. We are left stranded watching

images from hell: hives strapped to a donkey's back break open, honey spills over the animal's back, it kicks blindly at the bees which attack it, stinging it to death. The musical background to *Las Hurdes* is Brahms' Fourth Symphony. It is sombre, sober. But it seems an unusual accompaniment to images of the Hurdanos' base poverty: it is 'high culture'; it is too grand. And it is our culture, that of the 'educated' middle classes who watch the film. This contrast between the 'almost prehistoric' material universe of the Hurdanos and modern culture implicates the spectator in the film's indictment of neglect. Our science (caught in the style of the commentary), our humanist ethos (reflected in the Brahms) have not eradicated the horrors of the Hurdanos' existence; they have never been enough.

'The artist describes authentic social relations,' Buñuel once insisted, 'with the object of destroying the conventional ideals of these relationships, of creating a crisis in the optimism of the bourgeois world.'[25] These ideals led him to play down his intervention in the four features he produced and partially directed for Filmófono: *Don Quintín el amargao* ('Embittered Don Quintín', Luis Marquina, 1935), *La hija de Juan Simón* ('The Daughter of Juan Simón', Sáenz de Heredia, 1935), *¿Quién me quiere a mí?* ('Who loves me?', Sáenz de Heredia, 1936) and *¡Centinela alerta!* ('Look out, Sentry!', Jean Grémillon, 1935). These films have aroused several misconceptions. Buñuel, it is said, directed them. 'Buñuel did everything,' cameraman José María Beltrán recalls: 'contracts, casting, script (in collaboration with Ugarte), rehearsals, lighting, corrections, camera angles and, naturally, direction and editing. We were no more than humble

... Buñuel's *Las Hurdes*

19

students.'[26] But Buñuel's directorial contribution varies from film to film. He was on set with Marquina shouting to lead actress Ana María Custodio to ham it up; he worked out shot movements for Sáenz de Heredia in *La hija de Juan Simón*, as can be seen in some Buñuelish frontal set-ups with lateral pans following character movements and belated cuts to close-up. But in *¿Quién me quiere a mí?*, Sáenz de Heredia was given 'almost complete control', and Buñuel only directed scenes from *¡Centinela alerta!* when Grémillon had toothache.

Buñuel was not pushed into producing. By 1934 he had 'a good salary' at Warner Brothers, supervising their dubbing operation in Madrid, and it was Buñuel who proposed going into partnership with his friend Ricardo Urgoiti, owner of an ailing 'art film' distribution company, not the other way round. Buñuel's motives, however, are clear. As his autobiography *My Last Breath* suggests, while in Hollywood Buñuel became fascinated by American work methods, how Americans raged too at a director like Sternberg who 'was notorious for basing his movies on cheap melodramas'.[27] Buñuel wanted to play at Hollywood in Madrid. Filmófono's *cine nefando* ('abominable cinema'), as Buñuel called it, was an experiment in production: punctuality, eight-hour days, lunch breaks, rehearsals before shooting, one take per scene, and all power to the producer. When Buñuel interfered with direction, he was only following a Hollywood precedent of the director as a hired hand.

Filmófono's productions compare with those of Cifesa in their radically popularist style. *Don Quintín* and *¡Centinela alerta!* are based on *sainetes* by scriptwriter Ugarte's father-in-law, Carlos Arniches. *La hija de Juan Simón* draws on two traditions: the *españolada*, a romanticised folkloric vision of Spain seen in *Carmen*; and the stock idealisation of rural life and portrayal of urban vice known as *alabanza de aldea/menosprecio de corte* ('praise for the village/scorn for the court'). The plot has Carmela, the daughter of gravedigger Juan Simón, seduced away to Madrid by a gentleman who leaves her pregnant. The noble-hearted if lowly born Angelillo follows her, becomes a famed flamenco singer, eventually rescues Carmela from prostitution and takes her to live with him on his sumptuous Andalusian estate.

The Filmófono productions are lax, lazy, unequal. But two things are very definitely Buñuel. There is a frankness in language and an honesty in characterisation shocking for any Spaniard brought up on Spanish film under Franco. A girl in a cabaret shakes her breasts at the audience in an atmosphere of sweaty sexuality recreated by Jaime Chávarri in *Las bicicletas son para el verano* ('Bicycles are for Summer', 1984). Characters are humanly cynical (cynics under Franco are inhumanly atheistic and rarely last the film out) — as in *La fe* (Rafael Gil, 1945) — and their diction is colloquial.

Bérlanga shows a similarly common touch in *La vaquilla* ('The Heifer', 1985), a film which borrows two of Angelillo's magnificent songs in *La hija de Juan Simón*. The first – 'I am a little bird, born to sing/And so I beg my liberty' – is a comic ditty sung in jail and accompanied by a chorus of prisoners, including one played by Buñuel. The second is Angelillo's emotional lament, on stage, when he believes that Carmela is dead: 'Like that Magdalene/Redeemed by Jesus/So good were you,/Carmela of my heart./The dastardly world/One day forced you to sin/And having thus injured you/This same world reviles you.'[28] *La hija de Juan Simón* turns on Angelillo's confusion, man's inability to control his own destiny, or his passions of anger (when Angelillo assails the gentleman), love (Carmela's infatuation) or melancholy (Angelillo's reaction to Carmela's apparent death). In *La vaquilla* the characters are similarly imprisoned, whether by being on the wrong side of the lines in a Civil War, or by a similar inability to control the chaos of their egocentric desires which turn a military expedition into a complete farce. Confusion, determinism, and consequent sorrow: these leitmotivs of the slight *La hija de Juan Simón* have become an insidious obsession of the modern Spanish cinema. The Spanish Civil War has taken care of that.

A Heart of Darkness: the Spanish Civil War

The hypnotic horror of the Civil War invites descriptions couched in the language of damnation, religion, or myth. Spaniards still regard the war as the origin of their contemporary evils, a historical Pandora's box which is also Spain's Fall, an event that endows the Republic with a sheen of innocence, and leaves Spaniards born in the *posguerra* – the post-war period – with an inalienable sense of distant and unmerited damnation. But since fewer than one in five of Spaniards alive today have had direct experience of the hostilities, the Civil War has become the 'Civil War', a myth in the sense given to the term by Joseph Margolis of 'a schema of the imagination capable of organising our way of viewing the world'.[29]

The Spanish Civil War hence has a decisive and diversified influence on modern Spanish cinema. Firstly, its events and films provide the background and documentary material for many post-Franco pictures. Secondly, liberal film-makers have consistently questioned the myths about the Civil War nurtured by Franco's Nationalists. Thirdly, it could be argued that the political consequence (if not purposeful intent) of films by Berlanga, Saura, or Gutiérrez Aragón transcends opposition to particular myths to challenge the very patterns of thought encouraged by the Francoist schema and the institutions which gave them solvency: a high and vacuous seriousness, Manichean divisions, a logocentric response to events encouraged by a church for whom history, like scripture, must yield an instructive meaning. 'The very end of myth,' Roland Barthes wrote, 'is to

21

immobilise the world.'[30] The major 'political' challenge of modern Spanish film-making is to shake up and break down a prevalent legacy of Franco-ism: a mental mediocrity, a sclerosis of the mind.

The origins of the Civil War derive from the nineteenth century. 'Much of modern Spanish history,' according to Raymond Carr, 'is explained by the tensions caused by the imposition of "advanced" liberal institutions on an economically and socially "backward" and conservative society.'[31] In the last century the doughty hillmen of Navarre had rallied to the cause of Don Carlos and his lineage to fight two civil wars of neo-Jacobite futility (1833–9; 1872–6) in an attempt to return to an intensely traditionalist agrarian society. The slow emergence of a proletariat in the twentieth century meant that the demand for reform from above was increasingly accompanied by the threat of revolution from below. To Carr, the Republic's loud-sounding political pronouncements but cautious social reform raised and frustrated the hopes of the underprivileged while convincing the land-owning oligarchies, the Church, and the military that they were faced by imminent social revolution. The army still thought itself the final arbiter of Spain's political life and guarantor of political order. The rebellion of mainly younger officers on 17–18 July 1936 aimed, ideally, at a quick coup. The opposition of more senior ranks in the Spanish army, and armed popular resistance, turned an abortive coup into a prolonged war.

Franco's wavering commitment to the uprising had twice driven its organiser, General Mola, to contemplate suicide. But the need for a single command, and Franco's crucial importance as Commander of the African Army, led the rebellious generals to elect him in September 1936 Commander in Chief and head of government of the Spanish state. The Republicans, in contrast, were fatally split. Anarcho-syndicalists and Marxist revolutionaries of the POUM pushed through a profound social revolution in many parts of Spain, especially Catalonia. The Communists toed Stalin's line of political ingratiation in the Popular Fronts of democratic Europe, putting the war effort before revolution. By May 1937 the two tendencies were fighting it out in the streets of Barcelona. The Communists then sought to destroy the POUM by a smear campaign. 'You had all the while a hateful feeling,' wrote ex-POUM militiaman George Orwell in *Homage to Catalonia*, 'that someone hitherto your friend might be denouncing you to the secret police.'[32] Orwell was to draw on the atmosphere of fear and suspicion within the Republican ranks for some of the best pages of *1984*.

In order to defeat the Republic, Franco brought hell to the rescue. The Messerschmitts, Heinkels and Junkers, as well as tanks, artillery and 92,000 men, supplied by fascist Italy and Nazi Germany gave Franco the superior equipment with which to win the war. His African Army cut through the Republican militia 'like a knife through butter', was held in the very suburbs of Madrid (November 1936), turned to conquer the north of

22

Spain from Spring 1937. The Republican counter-offensives failed. Franco turned and broke the Republican army in October and November 1938. His army advanced against disintegrating resistance to capture the last Republican position, Barcelona, on 31 March 1939.

The Nationalists had to win a war, but Franco did little to encourage a propagandist cinema. The major authorities on Civil War cinema, Ramón Sala and Rosa Alvárez Berciano, have suggested in the book *Cine español* that the Nationalists saw 'only the frivolous side to cinema'.[33] They were far more concerned with censorship and manipulation of Republican film material. The Supreme Board of Film Censorship, created on 18 November 1937, worked with such assiduity that the head of Nationalist propaganda, Dionisio Ridruejo, was prevented from seeing many of the Republican films he was meant to combat. Julio Pérez Perucha has unveiled the massive manipulation in *España heroica* ('Heroic Spain', Joaquín Reig, 1938), a Cifesa co-production made along with *españoladas*, romanticised visions of Spain such as *Carmen, la de Triana* ('Carmen, the Girl from Triana', Florián Rey, 1938), in Nazi Berlin. The best images, Perucha suggests, are from Republican films captured in Spain or pirated in Berlin on their way to Russia. *España heroica* also uses fictional techniques to give a (false) sense of documentary reality: the battle for Irún shows the Francoist assaults with dynamic editing, but resorts to much longer shots for the seemingly demoralised Republican evacuation.[34]

The Republicans also had to win over a people to more particular ideological or regional interests. Its film industry developed remarkable energies, shot several hundred films, used thirty or more producers, introduced new directors, and experimented with collectivisation in the Barcelona cinemas run by the CNT.[35] The anarcho-syndicalists made over one hundred short or medium-length films of often ingenious mixtures of revolutionary principles, formal experimentation and popular appeal. The CNT-FAI were also the only Republican film-makers to attempt continuous feature production, though they had to abandon the stricter ideological line of *Aurora de esperanza* ('Dawn of Hope', Antonio Sau, 1937), where the protagonist organises a hunger march and ends up leaving for the Front as a member of the anarchist militia, for the commercial style of *Nuestro culpable* ('Our Guilty Man', Fernando Mignoni, 1937), a film of pointed ambivalence which mixes the *sainete*, Busby Berkeley routines, a satire of bourgeois corruption and a revolutionary sentiment which hardly surpasses the popularist I'm-all-right-Jackness of the falsely accused hero.

By 1937 the anarchist CNT production was increasingly eclipsed by the Communist-inspired Film Popular, which produced a weekly trilingual newsreel: *España al día/Nouvelles d'Espagne/Spain Today*. International support was essential to the Republican causes. The one hundred or more shorts produced by the Commissariat for Propaganda of the Generalitat of

Catalonia stressed the vitality of Catalonia's culture and its contribution to the Republican war effort to ensure Catalan liberties in the hypothetical case of foreign intervention settling the Spanish War. *Sierra de Teruel* (*L'espoir*, for which the Spanish Max Aub must take joint credit with André Malraux) had the immediate aim of increasing foreign aid to the Republic. The image the Western world has of the Civil War derives more from *L'espoir* or from Joris Ivens' *Tierra de España* ('Land of Spain', 1937; Ivens' camera-carrier was Ernest Hemingway, who used the shoot to get close experience of fighting) than from the mediocre *España heroica*. So the Republic won a posthumous victory after final defeat. The world-worn idealism of the Republican exile suffuses one of the most influential role-models of the twentieth century: Bogart. His character in *High Sierra* (1941) and Rick in *Casablanca* were, after all, former Republican combatants.[36]

In his book, *Spain, Change of a Nation*, Robert Graham puts the number of people who fled from Spain in 1939 as high as 350,000 to 400,000.[37] The Republican diaspora hit Spain's film industry hard. Most, though not all, Spanish film-makers of liberal or left-wing sympathies fled for their lives. Filmófono's personnel disbanded with the war. Cameraman José María Beltrán accompanied Urgoiti to Argentina, where they made two films with Angelillo; Buñuel went to Mexico, where he was reunited with Ugarte to script the genial *Ensayo de un crimen* ('The Criminal Life of Archibaldo de la Cruz', 1955); fellow Spaniard Luis Alcoriza collaborated on nine more scripts in Buñuel's Mexican period. Filmófono's correspondent, Juan Piqueras, was unluckier: this tireless critic, editor of the Republican film magazine, *Nuestro cinema*, died early in the war, almost certainly shot. The momentum of the Republican film industry faltered. Filmófono had announced sixteen projects for the 1936–7 period, including adaptations of *Wuthering Heights* and works by Valle-Inclán and Pio Baroja which may have confronted a perennial bugbear for cinema in Spain: its lack of a middle class, an absence which opened up a cultural abyss between elitist and popular tastes. Breaching this gap has been a major concern and a partial achievement of Spanish film-making in the 1980s.[38]

Spaniards left in Spain could enjoy neither the self-righteous sympathy shown towards the defeated Republicans by many foreign observers, nor the prestige of some (not many) Civil War exiles. Historians Hugh Thomas and Gabriel Jackson reckon the death toll for both sides during and after the war to be between 500,000 and 600,000.[39] Spain was the scene of silent desolation, the landscape of Erice's *Spirit of the Beehive*, a land to which the narrator of Juan Benet's *Una meditación* returns in 1939: 'The wounds of the war were all still open, a good number of houses – those left standing – empty, abandoned or occupied by strangers, families were divided or dispersed, many names from my early youth pronounced with rancour,

24

others little less than unnameable if one wanted to sleep in peace.'[40] Like Erice or Saura, Benet uses physical scenery as a corollary for a mental landscape whose landmarks are enumerated in the title given to one of his essays: 'Uncertainty, Memory, Fatality and Fear'.[41] It is a crucial psychic legacy for modern Spanish film-makers.

Uncertainty: After the war many of the more sensitive Spaniards attempted to find reasons for it and their own actions in it. Their personal experience did not yield any easy sense. The 'difficulty' of many Spanish films (developed consciously in many of the films directed by Carlos Saura or produced by Elías Querejeta) may derive in part from a conviction, encouraged by the Civil War, that human motives are dense, difficult, obscure. The war did not mean an immediate division into two camps. Many Spaniards would have locked their doors, drawn their curtains, retreated into back rooms, put on their radios, and tried to decide, as Benet observes, 'not what kind of storm was threatening the country, but what kind of men they themselves were'.[42] The war offered Spaniards a clear existential choice; yet it deprived them of much freedom, serenity, or subtlety when choosing. Fear of execution, entrapment in an enemy zone, the *omnium gatherum* of allegiances on both sides, must have meant that many Spaniards co-operated with causes with which they did not identify, and saw themselves defined by actions which they could not always recognise as their own.

Fatality: Centuries of neo-feudalism had already deprived the Spanish peasantry of any confidence in individual initiative as an instrument for social change. The Civil War, like any other conflict, involved vast, impersonal forces; survival seemed a matter of chance. Fate, luck, accident absolved individuals from responsibilities for their actions and the Francoist government in the *posguerra* from the need to establish a welfare state. Bardem and Berlanga's *Esa pareja feliz* ('That Happy Couple', 1951) reproved Spaniards' beliefs in piecemeal godsends which distracted attention from the need for long-term economic improvements.

The Civil War predetermined thirty-five years of *posguerra* when a new generation of Spaniards suffered the consequences of events they had never experienced and, being in the historical past, could not hope to change. Doomed attempts to escape from the present, to shelter in childhood, to rewrite the past have been key themes of post-Franco cinema. Causation and consequentiality have also fascinated directors, leading to the comic plot patterns of mischance in *Habla mudita* ('Speak, Mute Girl', 1973, Manuel Gutiérrez Aragón) and the politically charged invitation, embedded in the Freudian apparatus of many of Saura's films (*Peppermint frappé*, for instance), to consider the remote causes of present psychic states. We are led back to the war and its multiple consequences, as sketched by Saura in 1974:

25

The war has had a decisive influence not only on those of us who lived it ... but also later generations born after the war who had to suffer its consequences. Consequences such as a total political system, a completely repressive education system, personal conflicts, family losses.... The Civil War undoubtedly weighs on the contemporary generations, on their behaviour and lifestyle, if only because it has had such a terrible effect on their parents.[43]

Memory: Writing of the volunteers who came to Spain to fight for the Republicans in the International Brigades, Pietro Nenni observed that they had, all unknowingly, 'lived an *Iliad*'.[44] For any Spaniard, the war would have seemed the decisive event in his or her life: the one event of undoubtedly substantial importance. Many, perhaps most, major Spanish film-makers working in the 80s were born in the 30s or 40s. They were to experience the most formative event in recent Spanish history – or its immediate aftermath – at the most formative time in their own lives. Saura's is the clearest case of influence. 'Infancy,' he has argued, 'is a particularly insecure period ... of great fear and all kinds of deficiencies. It leaves a deep, ineradicable mark on the individual, especially if he lives in the middle of a hostile environment.' Saura is explicitly speaking from experience: he spent some of the Civil War in Madrid only a few miles from the enemy lines. Ever since *La caza* ('The Hunt', 1965) Saura has been a self-styled *auteur*. 'I try to make sure,' he told Enrique Brasó in the early 70s, 'that my themes, story and narration are fundamentally my own.'[45] So the Civil War becomes immensely important not only for Saura's personal life but also for his films. The 'indelible' influence of past on present provides them with a theme and a familiar structure: the gradual dissolution of differences between two initial opposites. His own insecurity as a child may explain his present vulnerability to criticism, the covert battle he has waged against critics of his later work, often from inside the films themselves. And his 'fears' and 'needs' as a child would surely explain the importance of the parent figure, especially the Mother, in his fiction.

Fear: It was not the number of deaths in the Civil War but 'the manner of those deaths', Gabriel Jackson argues in *A Concise History of the Spanish Civil War*, 'which has burned itself into the agonised, if largely silent, consciousness of the Spanish people.'[46] Most deaths in the war and its aftermath were reprisals, executions. The Nationalist shootings were an act of policy calculated by Mola 'to spread an atmosphere of terror ... to create the impression of mastery' in areas where the Nationalists were outnumbered by a largely hostile working-class population. In Republican Spain, the killings were the result of anarchy, with investigation bodies, *checas*, or murder gangs, often stocked with ex-criminals, shooting anyone of right-wing leanings. The horror is numbing. Some *requetés* (the crack Navarrese

Nationalist troops distinguished by their red berets) told one man to extend his arms in the form of a cross and to cry 'Viva Christ the King!' while his arms were amputated. Forced to watch, his wife went mad when he was finally bayoneted to death.[47] The killings widened a river of blood, hatred and fear which had hardly run dry in Spain for centuries: 'Hatred distilled during years in the hearts of the dispossessed,' wrote President of the Republic Manuel Azaña, whose bedroom window faced the Casa de Campo where many of the killings took place. 'Hatred by the proud, little disposed to accept the "insolence" of the poor, hatred of counter-posed ideologies, a kind of *odium theologicum* with which one sought to justify intolerance and fanaticism.'

From July 1936 to the end of mass executions in 1944, Gabriel Jackson claims, the Nationalists shot 300,000 to 400,000 fellow Spaniards. The killings have endowed the modern Spanish cinema with a particular psychology, and a significant silence. The war produced 'a breakdown of restraint such as had not been seen in Europe since the Thirty Years War', Hugh Thomas observes in *The Spanish Civil War*.[48] Explanations for the war's atrocities hardly removed a sense of guilt. Film-makers return time and again to the brutality of Spaniards, their residual animality of conduct, with an insistence even on the same broad metaphor – human relations as a hunt – which runs from *La caza* to *Furtivos* ('Poachers', José Luis Borau, 1975), *Escopeta nacional* ('National Shotgun', Luis Berlanga, 1977), and *Dedicatoria* ('A Dedication', Jaime Chávarri, 1980).

When *Pascual Duarte* was shown at the National Film Theatre in London in 1985, many spectators left the screening, unable to stomach a scene where Pascual knifes a mule to death. The violence of Spanish films may seem tasteless, their hunting analogy overworked. Yet both have their justifications. Lacking international distribution, Spanish films have rarely accommodated international tastes. 'Those who do not remember the past are condemned to relive it,' Santayana wrote. The ultimate referent for much of the violence in Spanish cinema is the internecine savagery of the Civil War. Hunting also has specifically political connotations as the favourite sport-cum-slaughter of Franco and many of his ministers. And the high society hunt, a several-day shoot for bankers, businessmen, aristocrats and politicians, provided an important scenario for Establishment power struggles.

The psychological legacy of the killings goes beyond an insistence on violence. Firstly, the madness of reprisals has left an unforgettable lesson in the essential inscrutability of human actions. Spanish directors return to this point, and especially in contexts of potential violence, with a frequency which is surely no coincidence. Ana in *Cría cuervos* still can't explain to herself as an adult why she wanted to kill her father as a child. In *Demonios en el jardín* ('Demons in the Garden', 1982), a bull runs loose in a village. Is

The legacy of violence: *Pascal Duarte*

That could have been a result of the Western.

this a symbol of rampaging passions, or of Spanish manhood? No, its director Manuel Gutiérrez Aragón insists, 'I don't know how to explain it'; and symbolic explanations of his films 'make me retch'.[49]

Secondly, actions in many Spanish films seem undermotivated. The apparent cause of violence in particular seems hardly to justify the result. Carlos Saura's *Deprisa, deprisa* ('Fast, Fast', 1980) is a case in point. In one scene, its four delinquents rob a security van. The guard takes pot-shots at them as they make their getaway in a stolen car. The guard runs out of bullets, and starts to run off across a field. The girl gets out of the car, aims, fires, misses, then shoots the guard in the back. The guard dies like thousands of Spaniards decades before in a lonely field in Spain. Behind the Civil War killings were reservoirs of sullen rancour unlocked by any petty incident which could justify public retribution. Motivation in Spanish films seems equally petty at times, the driving force of conduct lying outside the film in Spanish history itself. Hence the extreme importance of background detail and secondary characters in Spanish films. They often establish the protagonist's experience as just one example of a collective condition within the fiction of the film; they inscribe that condition within a broader and enlightening historical framework.

The Spanish predilection to violence could hardly be related explicitly to the Civil War in films made under Franco. Even after his death a sense of wayward impulse, hidden passion, is insistently suggested in Spanish films by their frequent theme of incest. A sense of taboo, of covert dark forces underlying the Spanish character and Spanish history, is perhaps the last psychological legacy of slaughter in the Civil War. It is a dominant theme of post-Franco cinema, instanced in the alignment of violence and incestual desire with clear historical references in a remarkable number of key Spanish films: *Furtivos, Pascual Duarte, A un dios desconocido* ('To an Unknown God', Jaime Chávarri, 1977), *El corazón del bosque* ('The Heart of the Forest', Manuel Gutiérrez Aragón, 1978), and *Dedicatoria*, where the barriers to the revelation of historical or personal truths are grounded in the formal texture of the film.

To justify their actions in the Civil War both sides resorted to myths. However absurd, these could hardly be abandoned in the post-war period and many have survived until the 80s. The Nationalists, for instance, recreated the past in their image of the present. To Franco, his troops had fought a 'Crusade', a war of 'liberation' but never a civil war, to restore the true Spain epitomised by what he saw in a speech made in April 1937 as 'the most sublime and perfect moment of our history': Spain of the Catholic kings, Charles V and Philip II, which had been betrayed in the nineteenth century by the 'bastardised, Frenchified and Europeanised Spain of the "liberals"', and again in the Republic by communists, Jews, and Free-masons, whose lodges controlled, among others, Perón, the Gibraltarian government, and that 'bastion of international masonry', the *New York Times*.[50]

Francoists laid an almost mystical emphasis on national unity. José Calvo Sotelo, the monarchist leader whose assassination helped spark the Nationalist rebellion, once claimed to prefer 'una España roja a una España rota' (a red Spain to a broken Spain).[51] The hub of unity was Castille, a view fuelled by the writings of José Ortega y Gasset, who wrote that 'only Castillian heads had adequate organs' to understand the problem of Spanish unity.[52] Unity also paid practical dividends for Francoism, checking the centrifugal forces of Basque and Catalan separatism, ensuring the political dependence of these prosperous regions with their separate cultural traditions on the backward centre of Spain. Only an obsession with unity will explain the absurd sight, included in Diego Galán's television programme *Memorias del cine español*, of the Andalusian flamenco star Lola Flores being made to sing 'I hear the wind/The voice of Castille/Which is the voice of Spain/Placed on an altar./Castille, my Castille,/Night and day/Your memory accompanies me.'[53]

Franco, Carr and Fusi observe in *Spain: Dictatorship to Democracy*, styled himself as the providential saviour of Spain, ruling, he claimed in 1966, 'by the right of him who has saved a society'.[54] His constitutional lawyers also appealed to the legitimacy of performance: the maintenance of

29

a peace which, they argued, brought unparalleled prosperity. 'Time and again,' wrote the journalist Emilio Romero in 1962, 'those who want to demolish the present system forget the *ultima ratio* of the Spanish people – their refusal to sacrifice the peace they now enjoy.'[55]

When all else failed there was always the resort to the mythology of martyrdom, the gut appeal to old comrades. 'We did not win the regime we have today hypocritically with some votes,' Franco insisted in 1962. 'We won it at the point of the bayonet and with the blood of our best people.'[56] The martyrs were the Nationalist dead remembered by the monolithic and typically tasteless 150 metre-high cross constructed in the Valle de los Caídos ('Valley of the Fallen'). High up on the list of martyrs, buried in the basilica below the cross, was José Antonio Primo de Rivera, shot by the Republicans on 20 November 1936 in Alicante. Then there were the Moscardós, father and son. General José Moscardó held out in the Alcázar fortress at Toledo throughout the summer of 1936. Then the Republicans captured his twenty-four-year-old son, Luis, who was put on the phone to tell his father he would be shot if the Alcázar did not surrender. 'If that is so,' General Moscardó is said to have replied, 'commend your soul to God, shout "Viva España!" and die like a hero.' Luis was subsequently shot. When relieved, his father pronounced the famed understatement *sin novedad* ('nothing to report'), also the password for the uprising.

The vanquished in the war could at least feel a communion in suffering, a brotherhood in sensitivity. The remarkable double readings given to Spanish films by young dissidents derive not only from the genuine presence of oblique meanings in the films of Saura, Buñuel, or Berlanga, but also from a visceral need to establish their common bond of superiority with these directors whose secondary insinuations were too subtle for the boorish Francoist censor. Such superiority was easily established. 'Death to intellectuals!' the one-eyed, one-armed founder of the Spanish Foreign Legion, General Millán Astray, had shouted at an aged Miguel de Unamuno in 1936. Then there was Guernica, the event and the painting. Guernica was a small Basque town near Bilbao where the kings of Spain traditionally swore to respect Basque rights. On 23 April 1937, Guernica was bombed and strafed by German aircraft in the first Nazi essay at a blitz. It was a market day and the town had been full of refugees. Picasso's huge canvas brought Nationalist barbarism home to the world. It proved unequivocally which side Spain's greatest artist was on. 'Under the Franco regime,' Robert Graham writes in *Spain: Change of a Nation*, 'possession of a print of *Guernica* came to be a form of protest.'[57]

The modern Spanish cinema sometimes enrols the myths, legends and symbols of the war, as in Jaime Chávarri's subtle appeal to the political significance of the death of Lorca in *A un dios desconocido*. Equally it may react against the mentality or even the structures of Nationalist propaganda. Franco deliberately perpetuated the crude distinctions between victors and vanquished. When it was proposed in 1968 that ex-combatants for the Republic should get pensions, as did the Nationalists, Franco was outraged: 'You can't combine a glorious army,' he retorted, referring to the Nationalists, 'with the scum of the Spanish population.' 'I was just a boy then,' Emilio Sanz de Soto recalls of the *posguerra*, 'and I still remember how terrible I felt knowing I was the necessary enemy of other Spaniards and they, in their turn, were my necessary enemies as well.'[58]

Many modern directors have reacted against such Manichean distinctions. Borau and Gutiérrez Aragón coincide in their demythification of the traditional hero. In the largely misunderstood *Hay que matar a B* ('B Must Die', 1974), Borau contrasts key conceptions from the Western and the political thriller to suggest that the Western's model of heroism, the rugged romanticism of the social outsider, may in a different context involve a fatal failure of political consciousness and a betrayal of solidarity with others. Saura's films begin by presenting two opposites, bringing them together, and mixing them until they melt into one. In the climax of *Carmen* (1983), for example, neither 'This is fiction' nor 'This is reality' is an adequate explanation of the (anyway partially inexplicable) finale.

Characterisation in *Carmen* also exploits a further psychological legacy from Franco's victory in the Civil War: the dusting off of old archetypes. 'I remember saying to Arthur Koestler, "History stopped in 1936", at which he nodded in immediate understanding,' George Orwell wrote in *Homage to Catalonia*.[59] The reality – rather than the myth – of Francoism was that it attempted to put the clock back and restore an authoritarian, national Catholicism. Franco sought to justify his dictatorship in the eyes of Western Europe by claiming that 'Spain is different'. Spain, the Establishment argument went, was the land of *sol* and soul, an exotic, distinctive experience for the foreigner, the land of Don Juan and Don Quixote; amatory, amiable, but unfortunately anarchic Spaniards – even Spaniards were made to believe – needed a strong hand to govern them. Saura produces at least a triple distinction in *Carmen*. The pressure on the Antonio Gades figure to behave like a jealous lover is not only sexual (the attractiveness of Laura del Sol) but also artistic (the influence of his character in the ballet) and even sociological: the demand on the Spanish male to be *macho*.

In theory, *machismo* mixes a sense of male honour with shows of physical valour; in practice, it has become a hotchpotch of right-mindedness and wrong-headedness, unsophisticated male chauvinism, a petty and petulant insistence on getting one's own way, a tendency when challenged to round on your enemy, puff out your chest like a pouter pigeon, and dare your antagonist to throw the first punch. Franco encouraged *machismo*: sexual chauvinism went hand in hand with political and national chauvinism. When the United Nations boycotted Spain because of its association with the fascist powers during the Second World War, Spaniards were encouraged to pass this off with bullish pride: 'If they've got UNO ['one' in Spanish] we've got DOS ['two'],' the contemporary saying ran.

Machismo was a first cousin to the soldierly tenets of bravery, self-sacrifice, obedience and, once more, honour brought to prominence in Spain by the decisive role played by the Spanish armed forces in post-war Spain as the ultimate bulwark of Francoism. Notably lacking from these tenets is a sense of balance, of relativity, a sense, that is, of refined humour. In such a context frivolity could become a form of opposition, especially if it went beyond barrack-room broadness to achieve a sophisticated sense of irony. The insistent reverses and continual relativism of *Habla mudita* ('Speak, Mute Girl', 1973) hence possess an innate sense of subversion, confirmed by Manuel Gutiérrez Aragón's droll burlesque of the honour code: an idiot goes to shoot the man who has supposedly besmirched his sister's honour; but his gun misfires and he only succeeds in killing a cow.

Relativism was not encouraged by the mainstay of Francoist morality until the late 1960s: the Spanish church. It was the ecclesiastical authorities who were responsible for much of the moral and mental bigotry under Francoism. Hugh Thomas calculates that 6,831 priests were killed by the Republicans during the Civil War. With isolated exceptions, the Church threw all its weight behind the Nationalists. 'On the soil of Spain,' the Bishop of Salamanca proclaimed early in the war, 'a bloody conflict is being waged between two conceptions of life, two forces preparing for universal conflict in every country on the earth. . . . Communists and Anarchists are sons of Cain, fratricides, assassins of those who cultivate virtue. . . . [The war] takes the external form of a Civil War, but in reality it is a Crusade.'[60] Franco was not slow to reward the Church for its allegiance. Our Lady of the Fuencisla, the patron saint of Segovia, was appointed a Field-Marshal for her role in the city's defence in 1936. After the war, the Church was given control of the Spanish education system. Liberal teachers were liquidated: in Asturias, half the teachers were shot. Many others were reallocated or dismissed. Estrella's mother in *El sur* is a victim of these purges. In 1953, Franco signed a Concordat with the Vatican which allowed the dictator to nominate his own bishops and archbishops. The association of temporal and spiritual powers was nearly complete.

The obsession of so many Spanish film-makers with religion derives from its pervasive influence on their early education. Instruction at church schools has drawn Saura, Miró, Olea and Regueiro towards the mental legacy of Buñuel: the inescapable association of sexuality, sin, and religion; a fascination with sadism (forefronted in Miró's *La petición*, 'The Engagement Party', 1976); the close alliance of church and civil authority (denounced, for example, in *La prima Angélica*); a scepticism towards the practical results of intervention in lay affairs by the clergy, however well-intentioned (a theme taken up in 1985 by Francisco Regueiro's *Padre nuestro*).

The influence of the Church on modern Spanish cinema reaches beyond theme to film form. A Church education provided directors with a vast set of narratives, references, and images with instant meanings and moral associations for average Spaniards. Bible-reading ground into young Spaniards the patterns of parable, an instinct for allegorical exegesis which is equally visible in their readings of Spanish cinema. A Spanish film, like the Bible, normally subordinates style to 'message'; a Spanish 'art film' is often marked out by its themes rather than its pictorial values. Above all, a religious education will have given an insidious weight for the less enquiring to the idea of a single source of truth, a concept reinforced right up to the present by a state education system which relies, even at university level, on learning by rote from simplistic and dogmatic textbooks. The modern Spanish cinema is affected by contrary pressure. Film-makers have a near moral onus to produce texts which do *not* instantly cohere, which challenge, which encourage scepticism. Manuel Gutiérrez Aragón's filmography is, by these standards, a magnificent achievement. Yet unemployment and falling cinema audiences have meant that Spain's film producers have generally avoided difficult subjects. How far to go is still a large question for the Spanish cinema.

A cracked mirror: Spanish cinema in the 40s

In the summer of 1940 Franco visited Seville, the traditional point of departure for Spanish conquistadors. Signing his name in the golden book of the Archivo General de Indias, he wrote beside it, 'Before the relics of one empire, with the promise of another.'[61] The attempt at imperialist expansion, safeguarding the capitalist system by transforming the class struggle into a co-operative enterprise, has been regarded as the keystone of fascism.[62] Critics in *Primer Plano*, a film review founded by a Falange group in 1940, also made unequivocally fascist statements. José Luis Gómez Tello, for instance, campaigned for a film about Isabella the Catholic Queen; if one wasn't made soon, 'any day now some Jewish director will come along and film a version with no genius, no love, no passion, but rancour.'[63]

But the *Primer Plano* writers were to be disappointed. Fernando Fernández Cordoba had no illusions by August 1942: 'A falangist cinema, or one which responds to the principles of our National Sindicalist Movement, has still to be created.'[64] And, in a typical contradiction, Spain gave sanctuary to film-makers fleeing from the Gestapo: Abel Gance, for example, was in Spain from autumn 1943 to summer 1945 and shot part of a bullfighting project, *Sol y sombra de Manolete* ('Sun and Shade for Manolete'). Early cinema under Franco was, in fact, very rarely fascist, never monolithic, and not even 'Francoist' if the term is to suggest a large, homogeneous corpus of para-governmental production. 'When I was young,' Berlanga has confessed in a disarming disclaimer, 'I never saw any of that fierce direct control ('dirigismo') or horrendous repression that critics and historians claim characterise cinema in the 40s.' Then, Berlanga claimed, some Spanish films were remarkably popular. Their reconsideration in the 70s would help provide an understanding of 'the bases of an authentic popular communication'.

Francoist films were unlikely to be fascist since Franco was not a fascist.[65] The proof is *Raza* ('Race'), financed by the para-governmental Hispanic Council and directed in 1941 by Sáenz de Heredia, who adapted a novel written by one Jaime de Andrade, the pseudonym of Francisco Franco himself. Yet if *Raza* set the tone for films of the 40s (and indeed for much post-Franco cinema), it was not in style or ideology, but in its sense of an unconscious but consuming and structuring neurosis.

Franco seems to have felt inferior. Matching biography and film in *Raza, el espíritu de Franco* ('Race, the Spirit of Franco', 1977), Gonzalo Herralde exposes the gross simplicity, the radical egocentricism with which Franco attempted to pass off a wishful autobiography as exemplary racial conduct. It is all good *Boy's Own* stuff. Dubbed Franquito ('Frankie') at the Toledo Military Academy, ribbed for his diminutive size and treble voice, Franco created a fictional alter ego, José Churruca, played in *Raza* by the 40s heart-throb Alfredo Mayo. Franco's father was a hardly heroic paymaster lieutenant; worse, he was a rake who left Franco's mother to flirt with floozies in Madrid. Yet José Churruca's ancestors sport impeccably valiant offshore records: Admiral Damián Churruca dies at Trafalgar while engaging no less than five English ships; José's Captain father dies similarly overwhelmed in the Cuban War of 1898.

Raza justifies the Nationalist rebellion before God and History. José, for instance, must enjoy divine blessing. Standing before a Republican firing squad he thrusts out his chest, shouts '¡Arriba España!' and is shot. His girlfriend reclaims his body ... to find José still alive.

History takes two forms. There is the family precedent of patriotic sacrifice, but personal references are inscribed in a larger framework. *Raza* opens with scenes from Spain's imperial conquest of and commerce with the Indies; and ends with a victory parade followed by a vignette of galleons firing at sea. Success in war, the film's syntax implies, is part of a longer and glorious historical tradition. Yet the film breaks down when Franco isolates the racial denominator in this design. A racial ideologue in the 40s faced one major stumbling block: any accurate emphasis on Spaniards' racial distinctiveness led to an admittance of partial Moorish and Semitic origins unacceptable in a supposed essentially Christian culture. So Franco, recognising the part played by his Moorish African Army in the Civil War, has

34

Francoist fiction: *Raza*

José's father talk of 'elected warriors – the most representative of the Spanish race'. Their name bears a resemblance to the Almoravides, a Berber dynasty which conquered part of Spain in 1086, and their mantle is assumed in the film, but only very vaguely, by the Nationalist volunteers, unified in a flashback collage after the final victory parade which represents Spain's 'espíritu de raza'.[66]

Raza's theses are vapid. Most of the military films after 1939 hardly go beyond conservative patriotic platitudes. *Porque te vi llorar* ('Because I Saw You Cry', Juan de Orduña, 1941) is a lachrymose melodrama whose supposed arguments for a class alliance boil down to the pity a worker feels for the heroine, a young aristocrat raped by a Republican soldier and made an honest woman by the worker because, he tells her, 'I saw you cry'. *¡Harka!* (Carlos Arévalo, 1941) starts with a fascist appeal to the memory of the heroes and dead in the Moroccan War (1919–27) who 'opened up our imperial route'. Behind its jingoism a shadow of neurosis crosses the film. The readiness for self-sacrifice of the charismatic Captain Valcázar comes close to a death wish, and Arévalo endows his film with a heavy undertow of homosexuality when he uses the formal traditions of a love

35

scene – soft, partial lighting; the intimate reverse-field exchange of close-ups – for a fireside chat between Valcázar and his young (and handsome) lieutenant whose subject, however, is not their feelings for each other but their unifying, patriotic passion for danger.[67]

¡A mí la legión! ('The Legion Forever', Orduña, 1942) is equally delirious but more sinister. Mixing French barrack comedy, zarzuela mess songs, detective fiction, Viennese operetta, Duck Soup, and composed figure-scapes of religious inspiration, Orduña yet presents the Spanish Legion as 'an endogenous, enclosed collective',[68] a supra-national body, anti-semitic, and prepared, as one legionary puts it, 'to come to the defence, whether rightly or not, of any legionary who asks for assistance' (my italics).

No other Spanish film went as far as ¡A mí la legión!. That was unlikely. Far from fascist, historian Juan Linz claims, the Francoist state was a 'stabilised authoritarian regime' with 'limited, non-responsible political pluralism; without elaborate and guiding ideology (but with a distinctive mentality)'.[69] Franco ruled over a number of political 'families': Army, Church, Falange, monarchists of Carlist or Bourbon leanings, landowners, financiers, Spain's professional classes. The Caudillo played these factions off against each other, and jettisoned the Falange in 1937 when it threatened his personal power. 'In Germany,' write Raymond Carr and Juan Pablo Fusi, 'the head of the party took over the state; in Spain the head of the state, Franco, took over the party.'[70] Franco's clever Decree of Unification in April 1937 turned the Falange into a Movimiento which included the whole of the regime, so destroying its identity by diffusion and watering down the genuine social radicalism of the Falange which survived only in the quixotic ambitions of a few dyed-in-the-wool politicians, in the bureaucratic mastodons of state unions, and in the largely rhetorical Principles of the Movement. 'Fraga,' Emilio Romero wrote of the reformist minister of the 60s, 'is as much a Falangist as I am Bishop of Constantinople.'[71]

Franco's policy for the cinema was typical of his rule. Films were still a popularist phenomenon, smacking of sin and the Popular Front. Remarking that American films gave Spaniards 'a window on to the world' where they saw not only their 'first kiss' but their 'first strike', Gutiérrez Aragón remarks that 'cinema-going for us was not only entertainment ... but connected with a sense of sin.'[72] In Demonios en el jardín (1982), the boy protagonist discovers that his supposedly valiant father is just a waiter. Knowing his mother is a 'red', he decides to enter the world of the fallen. Breaking a family prohibition, he steals into the local cinema and watches a sexually steamy dance sequence from Lattuada's Anna. The ultimate father figure, Franco, had made few plays for the hearts of the vanquished who made up a large part of Spain's cinema audiences. A state film industry would have been out of character. As Felix Fanés observes, when Cifesa

36

appealed for government aid in 1946, Franco stood back and passed up a prime opportunity to use state investment to influence the film-making policy of the biggest film company in Spain.[73]

In cinema policy as elsewhere, Franco behaved like an old soldier. His strategy was not to interfere in the workings of the industry, but merely to ensure the established order. The cinema was farmed out among the victors in the war. The Church took charge of its morality; the state unions got its administration, racketeers and the rich the chance to make a buck. Between them, in frequent fits of absence of mind, these forces managed not so much to direct as to destroy a dynamic Spanish film industry. Three factors are crucial: censorship, compulsory dubbing, the subordination of national production to the importing of foreign films.

On its own terms, Francoist censorship can hardly be described as exorbitant. A faithful reflection of Establishment views, its incessant utilisation marks the mental chasm separating the regime's morality from normal popular tastes. The step-up in censorship from 1956 was a sign not only of the regime's cracking down but also of its cracking up. Censorship, predictably, was introduced when the regime was literally at war. The Supreme Board of Censorship, established in November 1937, began 'final censorship' – the viewing of finished films before their exhibition. The public use of Catalan was banned (from June 1939). Spanish scripts had to be approved before production could begin (from July 1939). Publicity was controlled (from November 1939). And non-fiction production was limited to the state-produced newsreel 'Noticiario Cinematográfico Español NO-DO' (begun in November 1942). What exactly the censor could proscribe was only defined in the Censorship Norms of 1963. Respect was to be shown to 'our institutions', 'historical facts, characters, and settings', 'the duty of defending the Fatherland', 'the Catholic Church, her dogma, morals and cult', 'the fundamental principles of state', 'the person of the Head of state'. Banned quite naturally by a regime which defined Spain in its Law of the Principles of the Movement (17 May 1958) as 'traditional, Catholic, social and representative Monarchy' were justifications of 'suicide', 'divorce', 'illicit sexual relations', and even 'contraception'.

Censorship laws, like the Movement, involved a declaration of principle; unlike the Movement they had a day-to-day importance in practice. This distinction may explain why Querejeta's patent disregard for prior censorship prohibitions in many of his productions was not always protested at in final viewings of the finished film.[74] The censor's strictures must not be underplayed, however. They were imposed by an executive without even the remotest approval of the people being censored. They were vague, and arbitrary in their application. They favoured foreign imports: Spanish audiences could see a film about police corruption in New York, but were barred from watching 'anything remotely contrary' to 'the internal ...

security of the country', which would include a film about police corruption in Madrid. Hence the proliferation of Spanish *film noirs* in post-Franco cinema. Censorship bans were also hypocritical, proscribing 'brutality' but allowing in practice a glut of Westerns and cop capers. They prohibited, moreover, the descriptive rather than the prescriptive depiction of sexual relations, disarming Spain's attempt to compete in a world film market of increasing erotica.

The obligation to dub all foreign imports, apparently introduced in April 1941 at the crass behest of the big Spanish film companies who owned dubbing studios, has commensurate consequences.[75] Dubbing allowed for appalling manipulation of original dialogue. The best example is still that vintage metamorphosis practised on John Ford's *Mogambo*, where the married couple (Grace Kelly and Donald Sinden) were transformed in the Spanish version into brother and sister to justify the wife's affair with Clark Gable.

Worse still, compulsory dubbing destroyed the main positive discrimination between Spanish and foreign films: the Spanish language. In 1942, only 28 American films entered Spain. This figure rose in successive years to 61 (1943), 121 (1944), and 138 (1945). American films were far more lucrative than national products, a fact recognised by the disastrous policy of the Board of Classification, founded in May 1943, which assigned import and dubbing licences to producers according to the quality of the Spanish films they made. 'Quality' entailed conformity. Up to five licences could be granted to a film. By 1947 an import licence fetched about 400,000 pesetas on the open market, rising to 700,000 pesetas by 1950. Production became an ancillary to distribution. 'Buying permits,' the film-maker Edgar Neville remarked in 1945, 'for one million pesetas you can get Greta Garbo films in Spanish which cost ten or fifteen millions to make; it's natural that businessmen should prefer this to making a Spanish film for half a million pesetas which, moreover, runs the risk of not being liked.'[76]

Pressures and prizes encouraged profit-seeking film-makers to make low-budget, ideologically orthodox films with an eye to import licences. This pulp, Neville claimed in 1946, destroyed the Spanish cinema: 'They were awful and the public took them as the norm. Now we're giving them good films but audiences have been left with a bad taste in their mouths and won't go to see them.'[77] This could have been written in the 80s. For most Spaniards in 1986, the only Spanish film is a bad film. American films, in contrast, are much better known in Spain than in, say, France. From the 1950s American cinema has practically dominated Spain's box-office. Only the peculiar moral demands made on Spanish film under Franco, the poverty of Spain's film industry, and the resilient survival of popularist Spanish film traditions will explain the failure of the American cinema entirely to dominate Spanish film styles.[78]

Given the many inducements to conform, cinema under Franco sometimes seems remarkable for the freedom it did achieve from Establishment
rhetoric. Several explanations are possible. Up to May 1943 the Spanish
cinema was still ruled largely by market forces. These were the 'years of
hunger', electricity cuts, black marketeering, rationing (until 1952), when
the struggle for existence sapped any interest in protest and cinemas offered
the cheapest form of escape. But the neuroses remain. Film after film traces
the same pattern. In Rafael Gil's *Huella de luz* ('A Sign of Light', 1943) and
El fantasma y Doña Juanita ('The Ghost and Doña Juanita', 1944) and in
Luis Marquina's *Malvaloca* ('Hollyhock', 1942), the victim of a loss in the
past tries to seek redress by rewriting the present. In Gil's comedies,
characters seek consciously to stop others from suffering their own past
misfortunes. In Marquina's melodrama, past trauma is repressed but wells
over into a series of associated symptoms.[79] 'Rose my mother has named
me for my own misfortune, for there is no rose in this world which does not
lose its petals,' Malvaloca recites at the beginning of the film. True enough,
in a world accustomed to deprivation Rosa/Malvaloca is soon deflowered,
allowing herself to be seduced so that she can support her hard-up family.
Desperately seeking 'wholeness', she meets Leonardo, a forge-owner obsessed to the point of neurosis by the recasting of a broken bell. Malvaloca's
ravaged virginity is a grossly sexual symbol for a country shattered by
poverty. Leonardo's obsession is left unexplained. But the village's desire
for salvation (embodied in the Christ figure in their religious procession),
and an old woman's act of throwing her dead son's war crosses into the fire
where the bell is cast, hint at a communal trauma to be healed by a purifying
fusion. Leonardo and Malvaloca will finally melt in embrace as he promises
to make her whole by giving her his name (so rewriting her name and her
destiny in the present); the recast bell tolls above them. The sense of a
neurotic need for renewal is only heightened by the air of near hysteria with
which *Malvaloca* reaches a climax.

For Felix Fanés, the *leitmotif* of assumed identity ('el equivoco de la
personalidad') runs through most of the comedies which made up nearly 80
per cent of Cifesa's production between 1942 and 1945. Its insistence may
reflect an attempt on a collective scale at a Freudian excision of the ego: in
role-play within a film a character could 'be who he was and pretend to be
someone else'.[80]

Steadily throughout the 40s, film-makers distanced themselves from the
regime: Edgar Neville and the falangist José Antonio Nieves Conde are the
best known examples. Ex-Republicans were also able to make features.
Again, their films were unlikely to be unambivalent endorsements of Francoist views. *El santuario no se rinde* ('The Sanctuary Refuses to Surrender',
1949), for example, was directed by Arturo Ruiz Castillo, who worked in
Lorca's 'La Barraca' travelling theatre company and made films during the

war for the Alliance of Anti-Fascist Intellectuals. Within the allegory of a sanctuary (read Spain) holding out against the International Brigades (read the United Nations during the diplomatic boycott of 1946–8), Ruiz Castillo takes a *moderate* Republican as his hero, shows how allegiance in the war could be a matter of circumstance, and arranges a discussion on the war between his hero and a Nationalist captain which patently echoes a famous confrontation between Don Lope and Pedro Crespo in Calderón's drama *El Alcalde de Zalamea* ('The Mayor of Zalamea', *c.* 1642), where, notably, neither speaker has a monopoly on right.

Edgar Neville had already made a similar plea for tolerance in his whimsical *La vida en un hilo* ('Life Hanging from a Thread', 1945). Claimed by Chaplin to be the best raconteur he had ever met, Neville was a friend of Buñuel and like him a product of the *tertulia*: the café get-together where banter sharpened a taste for paradox, irony, the anecdote which builds on itself to climb to the absurd. No doubt that *La fantôme de la liberté* was a product of *tertulia* training. Like Buñuel's film, *La vida en un hilo* turns on chance. The heroine walks out of a flower-shop into the rain. Two men offer her a lift home. She accepts one on impulse and ends up marrying him. He turns out to be a provincial bore. A fortune-teller reveals to the heroine what her life would have been like if she had accepted the offer of a taxi, then marriage, from the other man, a zany bohemian sculptor. The heroine's boorish husband in the 're-run' is discovered happily married to another (boring) girl. 'Everyone,' Neville concludes, 'carries within his soul the happiness of another.'[81]

In the late 40s the *telúricos*, a group of Barcelona-based film-makers centred round Carlos Serrano de Osma, began a movement of 'formal commitment', as associate Fernando Fernán Gómez put it. Their assimilation of foreign formal advances led to an occasional brilliant use of the sequence-shot (as in the banquet scene of Serrano de Osma's debut in 1946, *Abel Sánchez*),[82] and one sustained masterpiece which uses the reflecting mirrors of fantasy and reality to portray a film-maker's absorption by the film *Rebecca* and the reality of his wife's tragic death in the Civil War: Lorenzo Llobet Gràcia's *Vida en sombras* ('Life in Shadows', 1948).[83]

It is a mark – rather than a denial – of the latitude of film-making under Franco that from 1947, 'For the first time in the history of the regime, somebody attempted a coherently Francoist cinema.'[84] Establishment intervention in the cinema increased markedly from about 1945. The number of films receiving state credits rose from 8.5 per cent of production in 1943 to 87.5 per cent of production in 1945.[85] In June 1946 the new censorial body, the euphemistically named Supreme Board of Film Orientation, gave its ecclesiastical member virtual final say on all moral matters. Scandalised by such films as *La fe* ('Faith', 1947), in which a highly sexed parishioner attempts to seduce her priest, the Church drew up its own *cordon sanitaire*,

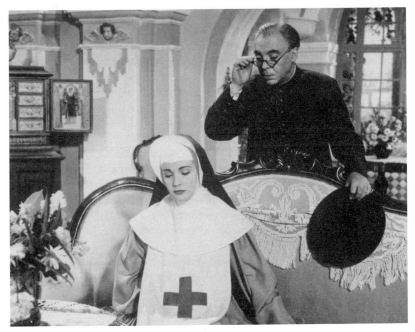

Church and cinema: *La hermana San Sulpicio*

the National Board of Classification of Spectacles, whose dictates were followed strictly by many cinemas, parents and teachers. The Board's rulings were extreme: Franco personally authorised *Surcos* ('Furrows', José Antonio Nieves Conde, 1951); the Board classified it as 'seriously dangerous'. Such decisions made cinema of any intellectual worth acquire an almost automatic stigma of dissidence.

Apart from trite hagiography and agit-prop for missionary endeavour (as in Juan de Orduña's trend-setting *Misión blanca*, 'White Mission', 1946), a religious tendency crosses much of film under Franco. Its key is its popularisation, as for example in the films of Luis Lucía. An event or insert completely extraneous to plot is used to establish the protagonists' religious credentials. The priest has the common touch: he is a bullfight fan (*Currito de la cruz*, 'Currito of the Cross', 1948); he plays billiards (*De mujer a mujer*, 'From Woman to Woman', 1949). The priest is a force for good: his charity drive prompts social regeneration (thus playing down the need for a social state: *Cerca de la ciudad*, 'Close to the City, 1951); he is a cuddly *deus ex machina* who doubles up with a Capra-ish cupid to unite the lovers of *La hermana San Sulpicio* ('Sister San Sulpicio', 1952); he merges with lay authority in the proximity of his presence, opinions, or even role, to the father figure (all the films cited above).

41

Coloured by Catholicism, the morality of the regime provided 'the keystone of Francoism', in the words of Gutiérrez Aragón, whose priest figure in *Maravillas* (1980) is pointedly a friend of the rich who destroys a romance. But when modern directors refer to or parody a 'Francoist cinema', they are most likely to be speaking of the six historical super-productions made by Cifesa in a doomed attempt to rival American cinema at home and abroad: *La princesa de los Ursinos* ('The Princess of the Ursines', Lucía, 1947), *Locura de amor* ('Madness of Love', Orduña, 1948), *Agustina de Aragón* (Orduña, 1950), *La leona de Castille* ('The Lioness of Castille', Orduña, 1951), *Alba de América* ('American Dawn', Orduña, 1951) and *Lola la piconera* ('Lola the Coal Girl', Lucía, 1951).[86]

These Francoist films are characterised by their contradictions. First, they aimed at historical lessons but denied their historical accuracy. 'We haven't aimed at recounting history,' the disclaimer in *La princesa* reads. 'Rather than giving names, dates and quotations we want to reflect the spiritual ambience of the eighteenth century.' The history in the films is very shoddy indeed. *Agustina* is set in the War of Independence (1808–13) but makes no mention of Wellington. But the omission was predictable. The films appealed through obvious allegories to the national self-righteousness created by the withdrawal of ambassadors from Spain by France, Britain, and the United States between 1946 and 1948 as a protest against its previous associations with the Axis powers. The films' structures vary little: true Spain embodied in Madrid (*La princesa de los Ursinos*), a Queen (*Locura de amor*), Saragossa (*Agustina de Aragón*), Toledo (*La leona de Castille*), or Cádiz (*Lola la piconera*), is under threat or siege from its foreign enemies. Politicians are revealed as ignoble intriguers; characters are responsible only to history; foreigners are ignoramuses – the French soldiers advancing on Cádiz are revealed as a gang of fops tossing each other up and down in blankets. Spaniards, it is implied, would never stoop so low. Spaniards, anyway, all pull together when it comes to the crunch: the defenders to the death of Saragossa even include a one-time reader of the *Oeuvres Complètes* of Voltaire.

Second, the style of the films is grossly vulgar but absolutely authoritarian. Dialogue is peppered with hurrah-phrases: resistance will continue, a character declares in *Agustina*, until 'not one Frog ('garbancho') is left in Spain'. Yet the Spanish spectator, groomed as a chauvinist new Numantian, is also encouraged to feel like a god.[87] Francesc Llinàs explains why in a key text on Orduña.[88] Three of the films begin with a flashback. The spectator knows the protagonists' destiny from the very beginning. The camera adopts and abandons point of view at will, manoeuvring to get the best view of events. We even view many scenes from above, from 'the Gods'. The films exude an insidious appeal to complicity with authority, to viewing the protagonists as inferior and their enemies as the lowest of the low. The only barrier to such an identification is our objection to the tendentiousness of the authorial declarations, especially the 'slogans'. The lesson, and attraction, is clear: acceptance of ideological 'goodness' is the pathway to Godness.

Post-Franco cinema often lies in inverse relation to the bizarre Cifesa super-productions. The Cifesa films are redundant beyond the duties of melodrama. Music, words, gesture and situation all work at often the same time to say exactly the same thing. Many modern Spanish directors, by contrast, are frequently elliptical, tending towards hermeticism. Cifesa has tainted the declaration in Spanish films for ever. When Fernando Fernán Gómez announces in *La noche más hermosa* ('The Most Beautiful Night', Gutiérrez Aragón, 1984) that 'Nothing is impossible for Spanish television', the Cifesa 'triumphalism' rears its head in the pointedly appropriate context of a supposed Francoist bunker – Spanish television.

What sticks in the mind like a bad tune is the tone of the historical films. It is sublime, hyperbolic, heightening, the language of high principles: the style which opens *Esa pareja feliz* ('That Happy Pair', 1951), the co-directorial debut of Luis Berlanga and Juan Antonio Bardem. In a clear parody of *Locura de amor*, a Queen confronts a noble who wants her to sign a scroll. 'Valencia demands it; God orders it!' the noble declaims. 'I shall never sign!' the Queen retorts, while a serried rank of courtiers follows the argument as if it were a tennis match. Hard pressed, the Queen throws herself over a balcony. The Fall of the Monarchy ends up with her dropping painfully on to two technicians holding a blanket below, but in the wrong place.

In general, the only way for the Spanish cinema after Cifesa's historical films was down. The Spanish super-production was often popular but never really economically viable in the 40s. With the introduction of neo-realist styles from the early 50s, Cifesa was systematically denied the enormous government funding which would have been necessary to keep it going. Its historical cinema remains, however, the most significant example in Spanish film history of the wider practice of Francoist idealisation. Without knowledge of this or other Francoist hostages to fortune, the post-Franco cinema will often seem to the uninitiated rather like the sound of one hand clapping.

THE MODERN SPANISH CINEMA

Mauling at myths

In 1939, Spain was a drab, sullen, agricultural state chilled by its recent past. In 1977, Spain had an urban, industrial economy. Industrialisation changed occupational structures more from the 1950s than in the previous hundred years. Spaniards moved in their millions to the cities. The tourist boom began: by 1973 Spaniards were almost outnumbered in their own country by the annual arrival of over thirty million holiday-makers. By the 60s economic growth was only outpaced in the capitalist world by Japan. Spain became one huge construction site giving on to 'the swimming pool of Europe'.[1]

The motive force for change was the move from the autarchy and state interventionism of the 40s to a capitalist market economy. The social transformation of Spain, many historians would argue, paved the way for the political transition of the 70s by enlarging Spain's middle class and creating, as historian Juan Pablo Fusi puts it, 'a social climate for democracy to prosper'. Change also lessened the likelihood of civil conflict on Franco's death by deflating arguments for a *ruptura*, a complete break with the past. Exactly, say critics of the transition: *plus ça change*.... Some of the best Spanish political films, such as Antonio Drove's *La verdad sobre el caso Savolta* ('The Truth about the Savolta Case', 1978), make precisely this point.

The modern Spanish cinema begins with the modernisation of Spain. Whether embodied in theme, background, or production limitations, it is the transformation of Spain which endows modern Spanish cinema with its pervasive sense of particularity. Characters in films are normally recognisable Spaniards with a concrete historical dimension. If symbolic, they often symbolise larger trends in Spanish history; if individualised, their personal experience will be a particular reaction to a collective Spanish reality. Most Spanish films are not immediately universal. But it is just this 'otherness' which gives them a vital authenticity, and an ability to snap the spectator out of his usual way of looking at things.

By the early 50s autarchy and interventionism had served their time. The Cold War brought a détente between Spain and other anti-communist powers which led to an agreement on defence and economic assistance with the United States in 1953. In 1955, Spain became a member of the United Nations. Seeking investment, the country attempted to liberalise its economy in 1951. It did not go far enough. Nationwide strikes provoked by the high cost of living forced government wage increases, which in turn created an inflation rate of 11 per cent by 1957, and a serious balance of payments crisis. However reluctant, however conscious of the possible political consequences of change, the Francoist regime had little alternative. A Cabinet reshuffle in February 1957 brought in 'technocrats' (apolitical advocates of economic progress who sometimes belonged to the powerful Catholic organisation Opus Dei) at key government posts. In 1959, 'technocrat' and Minister of Commerce Alberto Ullastres introduced a Plan of Stabilisation. Apart from belt-tightening, it attempted to stimulate investment, lifted tariff restrictions to facilitate cheap imports, and countered with a devaluation of the peseta which encouraged a more export-aligned economy. Three Development Plans in 1964, 1968 and 1972 aimed at sectoral growth through the creation of industrial estates.

Industrialisation fuelled mass rural immigration from the centre of Spain and its indigent south to the factories and building sites of Madrid and Barcelona. There the newcomers lived in *chabolas*, shacks in downtrodden working-class districts, seen in Saura's punchy debut, *Los golfos* ('The Hooligans', 1959). From the 60s an immigrant would probably end up in a high-rise apartment lost in a rampart of shabby drudgery and clothes-lines which Eloy de la Iglesia and Pedro Almodóvar stylise into urban precipices in *Colegas* ('Mates', 1982) and *¿Qué he hecho yo para merecer esto?* ('What Have I Done to Deserve This?', 1984).

Any surplus labour was absorbed by the European economic boom. By 1973 there were half a million Spaniards working in France and a quarter of a million in Germany. While their parents struggled to get by in the 40s, the 60s youth aimed to get on. The sternly Catholic and prolifically fertile professional classes were enlarged by new recruits: bank clerks, typists, secretaries, laboratory technicians, schoolteachers. Spaniards bought cars, refrigerators, washing machines. In 1979, General Motors decided to invest in Spain; they discovered that SEAT, Spain's own car manufacturers, had never done a market study on customer colour preference in cars.

A new era brought renewed 'official versions'. Their tone reflected a 'developmental triumphalism'. 'Franco,' wrote faithful Falangist minister José Solís, 'transformed a sandal-wearing Spain into one of the dozen most prosperous nations in the world.'[2] 'Europe and the world call us,' said

Ullastres on Spanish emigration, 'and if we go to them it is not to escape a possible deficit in the balance of payments but because it is our universal mission.'[3] This *zeitgeist* of national development got into songs. *Y viva España*, for instance, was not originally a tourist knees-up but a eulogy of Spanish emigrants presented as noble and illustrious adventurers setting out from a beloved homeland of fun and folklore. 'Life is a tombola,' chirped the girl star Marisol in Luis Lucía's *Tómbola* (1962). Rafael, millions of Spaniards' ideal son-in-law, aimed higher: 'You can achieve everything/You can reach everything/Nothing is impossible/If you struggle for it' (*Cuando tú no estás*, Mario Camus, 1966). Weened on Catholic miracle, Spaniards were now expected to believe in the Protestant work ethic. Traditions die hard: Spaniards still laugh at the workaholic Germans.

The new ethos affected the structures of films and soon created its emblems of progress. Saura's early, orthodox short film *El pequeño río Manzanares* ('Little River Manzanares', 1957) bears this out. Nowadays in summer Madrid's main river is reduced to a polluted trickle. The ducks reintroduced to the Manzanares in 1984 have acquired the status of folk heroes. Saura's Manzanares has more majesty. He also inscribes the river in a socio-economic development entirely coherent with Spain's historical traditions. On the Manzanares' banks, youths play at traditional throwing games; but busy lorries rumble across its old majestic bridges. The film embodies progress in its own development: it begins with a brook tumbling down a hillside; it ends with the Manzanares near Madrid flowing with measured dignity. Saura also presents a *leitmotif* of progress at a time when only one in a hundred Spaniards had cars. In a classic beside-the-tracks shot a train rushes towards us, past us, symbol of the ineluctable march of industry. Erice (*The Spirit of the Beehive*), Camus (*Los santos inocentes*, 'Holy Innocents', 1983), and Saura himself (*Deprisa, deprisa*) would all use different shot set-ups to subvert this icon of progress.

Yet many Spanish films chart not the course of change but its casualties and contradictions. Progress left many hostages to fortune – speculation rackets, bad housing, the once ravishing, now ravished coast, a level of involvement by multinationals in development which seriously questions Spain's economic independence. Urbanisation took place without the modern safety net of a social state. The poorer regions were left behind: in 1970, 70 per cent of Madrid homes had television sets, but only 11 per cent in the provincial district of Soria. Immigration sustained or worsened social inequalities. Franco boasted with cynical disdain that the Civil War was the only conflict which made the rich richer. The gap between rich and poor hardly narrowed in its aftermath: in 1975, the richest 10 per cent of the nation were nearly twice as wealthy as their counterparts in Britain.

Above all, material change outpaced moral and mental change, provoking a 'superficial modernisation', as Gino Germani puts it. 'By the 1970s,'

46

comment Carr and Fusi, 'Spain had become a curious mixture of traditional – largely Catholic – values and the behaviour thought proper for a consumer society.'[4] This juxtaposition saw surrealist expression in Franco's deathbed agony. Trailing away from one side of him were the coils of a life-support system; on the other, his constant travelling companion, the mummified arm of Santa Teresa; on his bed, the mantle of the Virgin of Pilar.

Modes of behaviour might change, but for many Spanish film-makers a bedrock morality remained. Flamenco singer, self-made *hombre* and immigrant idol Manolo Escobar knew where to draw the line. He achieves the Hispano-American dream by marrying an American millionairess in *Un beso en el puerto* ('A Kiss in the Port', 1965), and rises to stardom in *Mi canción es para tí* ('My Song is for You', 1965). But our Manolo is still a chip off the old Spanish block. 'If you ask me,' he volunteers in the smash-hit *Pero . . . ¡en qué país vivimos!* ('But What Sort of Country Are We Living In!', Sáenz de Heredia, 1967), 'a woman who doesn't go into the kitchen, doesn't sew and doesn't even pray isn't a woman . . . She's a Civil Guard.'[5] Despite progress, films insist that Spaniards are still different. The acid test is sex. For an unmarried woman it is a prelude to pregnancy or perdition, or both. Until the 70s it was only allowed a few perverse manifestations:

In rape. Such a plot cliché, so deprived by censorial circumspection of any possible verisimilitude, that Camus in *Esa mujer* ('That Woman', 1969) turns its depiction into an aesthetic event: big black men with white trousers contrasting with little white women dressed in black (nuns) struggling against a pale wall background. Artistic conventions expose the representation of rape in Spanish film as a plot convention, a falsehood.
In Spanish 'pasión'. Pasión is a particularly Spanish quality. In *La Tirana* (Juan de Orduña, 1958) *pasión* drives Goya to paint and inspires La Tirana, the best actress of her day. But *pasión* is also her tragic flaw, putting her at the mercy of a heart which acts with neither forethought nor restraint. And where the heart dictates, the body (implicitly) follows. *Pasión* needs the control of a strong hand, a dictator for instance. *Pasión* is temperament. Paquita Rico, who played La Tirana, suggested as much in 1976: 'My husband and I have a good time in bed. I am very temperamental.'[6]
In foreigners. If sex were to be practised it was best for the actress to be foreign, have a foreign name, or play a foreigner. The censor refused to let the character played by Spaniard Cristina Galbó sleep with the protagonist of Pedro Olea's *Días de viejo color* ('Days in Old Colour', 1967), observing that 'if she were French the act would be more comprehensible'.[7]
In an actress or artist. La Polaca, flamenco dancer and passionate, is the only one of the girls who has sex before marriage in *Las secretarias* ('The

Secretaries', Pedro Lazaga, 1968). But she goes straight to the Veronal tablets when she realises the awfulness of her act.

Cinema close to the Establishment under Franco very clearly created myths. The major political effort of the opposition to Franco went into exposing these delusions. Film-makers could isolate the political, social or economic interests under the myths they presented, and attempt to offer, as Elías Querejeta put it when characterising the films he produced under Franco, 'a vision of reality different from the official version'. Directors could similarly satirise Francoist myths by playing off different versions of reality within their fictions. A rich series of disparities could be set up between the old Francoist myths spawned by the war, the developmental 'triumphalism', Spain's actual social, economic or psychological reality, and a non-Spain of liberal Europe and America, whose vision of reality gave Spaniards, as novelist Francisco Umbral put it, 'a measure of our misery'.

Bienvenido, Mr Marshall ('Welcome, Mr Marshall', 1952, from a Berlanga-Bardem script) is a masterful instance of a director, Berlanga, slyly insinuating the interests at stake in Francoist myth. By the 50s, Spanish films had largely abandoned their morbidity for a less complicated attempt at religious drama of 'devout little believers, nice little saints, hagiography and schmaltz',[8] which was increasingly eclipsed by child stars – progeny of the rich, prodigies of song – who would slum with the poor for a few reels of film before being restored to the social status which they ignored but so plainly merited. Social position in the 50s was still a matter, it seemed, of predestination.

But the big genre of the 50s was the *folklóricas*, comedies or melodramas punctuated by folkloric Spanish song. The rise to fame of their stars, in and out of fiction, made such as Lola Flores and Carmen Sevilla 'missionaries of optimism', in Terenci Moix's phrase, ingenious advertisements for Europe of the ingenuous natural spirits and cultural distinctiveness of a Spain that was different, so pardonably a dictatorship, so worthy of subventions from the democratic West.[9]

What the regime saw as natural, *Bienvenido, Mr Marshall* exposed as artificial. A representative of the delegation in Spain for the Marshall Plan arrives at the dozy village of Villar del Río. His news, announcing the imminent arrival of American recuperation forces, brings myth pretty sharply into the film as the villagers describe their prospective benefactors by an appeal to archetypes. 'Indians, usurpers of Spanish conquests,' the local squire argues, referring to the North Americans. 'Major producers of wheat,' the spinster schoolteacher explains to a packed village hall, 'of petrol, pigs . . .' 'And sins!' interjects the local priest, striding to the front of the assembly, '49 million Protestants, 400,000 Indians, 200,000 Chinese, 5 million Jews, 13 million blacks, and 10 million . . . of nothing at all.'

Fabricating folklore: *Bienvenido, Mr Marshall*

Facts, then, rather than precluding myths, may be reorganised as their backbone and their source of verisimilitude. Myth's vehicle may be the apparently realistic medium of film. It is, after all, their watching a documentary on American aid to Europe which creates for the villagers the most potent myth of all, that the Americans are latter-day Wise Kings. This assumption is exploded when at the end of the film the Americans roar through Villar del Río without even stopping, frustrating the villagers' attempt to waylay them and milk them of presents by turning Villar del Río into a typical Andalusian village, dressing themselves up as *toreadors* and flamenco dancers. *Bienvenido, Mr Marshall* hence displays an economic motive for the fabrication of folkloric tradition. Interestingly too, the villagers' myth-making parallels film-making. The 'disguised' village acquires the artificiality of a film set; its decoration is organised by an artistic agent who brings in 'the number one star of Andalusian song', and directs the villagers in a scene designed by Berlanga as a homage to Pudovkin.

If *Bienvenido, Mr Marshall* associates film and myth it also indulges in demystification. Its butts are Francoist claims and unconfessed Spanish realities. The regime's historical assertion of concern for Spanish peasants contrasts with its bureaucrat who confuses Villar del Río with its bitter rival Villar del Campo, and assumes quite wrongly that it has some industry.

49

This is easy satire. To get at Spanish psychological reality discreetly, Berlanga also condenses the vision the villagers have of America (from films) with their subconscious sentiments, mixing the two in the characters' dreams. The squire's nightmare, for instance, begins as a parody of *Alba de América*, with him as a conquistador beaching on a newly discovered island. The squire dreams that he is immediately put in a cooking pot by some cannibals. His nightmare becomes an unconscious recognition of Spanish impotence when faced with American power. Yet the squire's patriotic chauvinism still allows him to represent the Americans as primitive Indians.

The representation of America in *Bienvenido, Mr Marshall* varies from one villager to the next. The perception held of larger realities by a character or community allows for incisive psychological comment. This technique is worked brilliantly in a cult film for many contemporary Spanish film-makers: Fernando Fernán Gómez's *El extraño viaje* ('The Strange Journey', 1964). The film's opening inscribes it in larger social realities: we cut from a newsstand festooned with magazines from Madrid and abroad to a disco where rural traditionalists watch Angelines, all tight dress and pert sensuality, dance the twist. Inside and outside Spain, Cristina Damieri observes, parallel the division in the village between the interior of Doña Ignacia's house where this repressed harridan tyrannises her siblings into cringing subordination, and the rest of the village where appearances are all.[10] Characters' conceptions of the symbolically open spaces of Madrid, the coast and abroad only emphasise, through their ingenuousness, just how enclosed is life in the village and its microcosm, Ignacia's house. 'You say that abroad we won't attract attention and I won't be thought old,' Ignacia reminds her lover, justifying their leaving the village.

Yet what lies outside the village, like off-screen spaces, remains largely hypothetical, being rarely discovered by entry or exit from frame or entry or exit from the village. Only one character escapes: Angelines, who goes off to work in a cabaret in Madrid. 'Perhaps we'll see you billed at the Pasapoga!' a villager says, referring to a fashionable night-spot in the capital. The implication is clear. Angelines' flight affects the village only as a potential addition to the mythical category 'Madrid'. It does not alter the village reality. Indeed, the film ends with one closed space, Ignacia's house, ceding to another. In a typical into-the-corner shot (practised throughout Fernán Gómez's magnificent *El mundo sigue*, 'Life Goes On', 1963), with camera-framing and wall adding to a sense of constriction, a girl falls weeping on to a bed having seen her boyfriend being led away by the police. Her sentimental horizons contract. A closed space opens up before her – her future of a room on her own.

Social myth and demystification run throughout the modern Spanish cinema. They survived 1975 quite simply because many myths have lived

50

on into democracy. Films after Franco have often returned to the *posguerra* and its myths. Furthermore, bitterness, irony, and the derision of delusions go way back beyond Franco to the dawn of Spain's decadence, the late sixteenth century, when high ideal began to separate from reality and the Spanish artist began to cultivate the art of clandestine scorn, ellipsis, bitter analogy, redirecting his anger since the real object of rage, the state, was protected from attack. Similar kinds of myth or reality may combine and contrast with richly varied results. Table 1 (overleaf) is an illustration, drawing on films made under and after Franco.

A Spanish realist tradition: neo-realism, the *sainete*, and *esperpento*

'I belong to a generation who believed in a revolution,' Mario Camus once admitted. 'Zavattini once said: "What we attempt is to move man to take an interest in the world around him. And particularly in what is happening today or in an immediate yesterday." The result for me was *Los farsantes* (1963) and *Young Sánchez* (1963).'[11]

A preoccupation with contemporary Spanish issues has given the modern Spanish cinema an essentially realist feel. Lacking international markets, film-makers have had little economic incentive to treat international themes. In the 50s, there was a hunger for reality in a nation starved of truth. In the 70s, Spaniards sated their appetites as censorship lifted. Economic crisis from the late 70s encouraged more of an escapist cinema. But from 1982 the socialist government has funded films which push Spaniards back to reality. Emile Faguet once said of Flaubert: 'Imagination was his muse and reality his conscience.'[12] So too for many a Spanish film-maker.

A history of the modern Spanish cinema is the history of its realisms. The narrative could begin with the Italian Cinema Week in Madrid in 1949. Zavattini and Lattuada attended. 'We were fascinated,' Berlanga recalls; and for Bardem, it was 'a window open on to Europe'. Neo-realism was acclaimed but never fully adopted in Spain. 'Things are there, why manipulate them?' Rossellini said in a *Cahiers du cinéma* interview.[13] The Francoist censor made manipulation inevitable under Franco; realism, in the sense of a straight transcription of reality, was impossible. While courting neo-realism Spanish film-makers married it to other styles. One stylistic partner was the *sainete*, the popularist realism preserved in 40s films by Edgar Neville, most notably in the rumbustious crowd scenes of *Domingo de carnaval* ('Shrove Sunday', 1945) and *El crimen de la calle de Bordadores* ('Crime on Bordadores Street', 1946). Having adapted Carmen Laforet's classic realist portrayal of middle-class moral squalor, *Nada* ('Nothing', 1947), Neville made *El último caballo* ('The Last Horse', 1950), 'the first Spanish film', Francesc Llinàs observes, 'to be influenced by a certain type of Italian cinema'.[14] The plot is very

51

TABLE I
Myth and Reality in the Modern Spanish Cinema

Film	Old Francoist Myth	Developmental Triumphalism	Spanish Reality	Outside Spain
Surcos (J. A. Nieves Conde, 1951)		Representative family emigrate to Madrid.		
			Finding unemployment, bad housing, black-marketeering, murder.	
	So the family returns to the wheatlands of Castille.			
		But the daughter slips back to the city.		
			Falangist moral: immigration divisive but inevitable and so should be controlled.	
Los golfos (Carlos Saura, 1959)		(Extra-filmic reality: Ullastres 'insisted that the new economic policy was to integrate Spain in the booming world of advanced Western capitalism.')[15]		

Film				
Nueve cartas a Berta ('Nine Letters to Berta', Basilio Martín Patino, 1965)	Spain's peasantry, bulwark of national traditions, the view taken by Lorenzo's right-wing cousin.	Second generation immigrants, living in shacks, working in non-mechanised jobs as market porters. The *golfos* have pre-capitalist ambitions (to be big in bullfighting), but no money and no hope. Peasants are emigrating to Germany and can't remember any traditional songs. makes protagonist Lorenzo think he's been 'living in a dream-land' in Spain.		Iconoclasm of London-based Berta
¡Vivan los novios! ('Long Live the Bride and Groom!', Berlanga, 1969)		Balding Leo from Burgos can't speak any foreign languages. (To a German girl: 'You looka ...*cordon bleu*, karate, *muy grande*, baby!')	Spaniards were 'new Europeans'.	

TABLE I (continued)

Film	Old Francoist Myth	Developmental Triumphalism	Spanish Reality	Outside Spain
(¡Vivan los novios!)		Spain was modernising fast.	Spain is still a medieval mixture of repressions, hypocrisy, the Church, and death. So…	
				while foreigners fornicate on all sides,
			Leo doesn't get anywhere on his stag night…	
				and while a couple make love on the beach…
			Leo's mother drops dead in a paddling pool.	
Los nuevos españoles ('The New Spaniards', Roberto Bodegas, 1974)		Advantages of a merger with a multinational…		
			are offset by exhaustion, stress, break-up of the family, and death…	
				leading to an American way of life exemplified by employment in the totalitarian company state, Bruster and Bruster.
			Moral: it's better to be an old Spaniard; neo-falangist(?) harmony preferred to capitalist competition.	

Film			
Camada negra ('Black Brood', Manuel Gutiérrez Aragón, 1977)	Heroism in a triumphal context.		Protagonist's heroism derives from his adherence to a dying cause: fascism in Spain.
¿Qué he hecho yo para merecer esto? (Pedro Almodóvar, 1984)	Catholic stereotype of woman as the mainstay of family.	Husband has worked in Germany. . . .	Heroine housewife maintains family at cost of personal drug addiction and sale of a son.
		Spaniards are modernising.	Three generations of Spaniards lead to surreal contrasts: granny harps on about her village, has a pet lizard; father still besotted by emigrant days; son is drug addict . . . who returns to his village with granny – superficial modernisation indeed.

but the European boom is over and only way he has of making money is to forge Hitler's diaries.

Chaplin, its Madrid background that of Arniches. Finishing national service, a private buys his horse to prevent it going to the knackers yard; he tries to find it employment in a Madrid where, in Neville's words, 'love, friendship, and goodness fall victim to the rush of modern life'. But schmaltz doesn't prevent some pretty sharp sideswipes at the mean-minded petit bourgeois girlfriend and at the dehumanised figures of authority.

Heralded as 'the first glance at reality in a cinema of papier-mâché',[16] *Surcos* ('Furrows', 1951) is in fact a curious graft of American gangster thriller and neo-realism. It is also a Falangist thesis drama, *hedillista* Nieves Conde[17] arguing for more control of immigration from above to compensate for a loss of control, symbolised by the destruction of family ties, from below. The family, to Falangists, was the basic nucleus of social order. In *Surcos*, its destruction prompts disaster. Jobless, a father loses moral authority over his children. His daughter goes to live with a gangster. His son moves in with the landlady's daughter, only for her old lover to murder him. His death on a railway line transforms him into a grossly symbolic victim, run over by the train of progress. Nieves Conde, like Mussolini, wanted this train to run to order.

Berlanga and Bardem's *Esa pareja feliz* is an equally cross-grained chronicle of working-class aspirations. Its influences run from the bonhomie of Capra (in a scene where the young married couple attempt to paper over their poverty by decorating their one-room flat) to 'the *sainete*, Arniches, and a film by Jacques Becker, *Antoine et Antoinette*'.[18]

One of the biggest obstacles to Spanish neo-realism was, however, commercial pressure. A cinema law of July 1952 had created new film classifications, linked to film subsidies, so separating production from the receipt of import licences and making films more market-oriented. The new subsidies only went up to 50 per cent of a film's budget; the old import licences could easily cover the cost of a film. In this context, Bardem's *Calle mayor* ('Main Street', 1956) is a high point of anti-Francoist film-making, a damnation of the society Franco created, a critique of empty provincial life where the only future for a woman is prostitution, the solitude of a spinster, or salvation through wedlock. Yet Bardem, in accordance with the 'realism of content' proposed in his celebrated article '¿Para qué sirve un film?', uses professional actors, a literary base (a text by Arniches), and carefully composed frames to put over his criticism.

If not fully feasible in practice, there were good reasons for demanding a Spanish neo-realism in principle. These reasons were political. By 1951 the Spanish Communist Party, the PCE, had abandoned its commitment to armed struggle in favour of a policy of 'national reconciliation'. Neo-realism attracted supporters right across the political spectrum of

Neo-realism: Bardem's *Calle mayor*

Spanish cinema. It was the perfect rallying call for a reconciliatory policy. Its origins in the aftermath of Italian fascism allowed militants to exploit the international belief that Spaniards, through their cinema, were fighting fascism in Spain. It is hardly surprising, then, that the film magazine *Objetivo* (founded by PCE collaborators Bardem and Ricardo Muñoz Suay in May 1953) should promote neo-realism, identifying realism as a 'national' style; declare itself a 'national window open to dialogue'; and mastermind the First National Film Congress at Salamanca in May 1955.

Salamanca was a Pyrrhic victory for the policy of reconciliation. It certainly initiated a broad base for dialogue, uniting a reformist Catholic of Falangist origins such as García Escudero with Communists. Bardem's pentagram delivered at Salamanca was the most memorable of all condemnations of film under Franco. The Spanish cinema, he said, was: '1. Politically futile; 2. socially false; 3. intellectually worthless; 4. aesthetically valueless; 5. industrially paralytic.' But the Salamanca Conclusions were inconsistent. They echoed the call of Falangist Arroita Jaúregui for the state to implement 'a film policy congruous with its true principles'. Yet, in obvious contradiction, the Conclusions attacked a cinema which was 'socially false'. All that the Salamanca Congress achieved in the short run was to bring anti-Francoist film-makers out into the open. *Objetivo* was suspended; Bardem and Berlanga became marked men. Bardem's *La venganza* ('The Revenge', 1957) and *Sonatas* (1959) and Berlanga's *Los jueves, milagro* ('Miracles on Thursdays', 1957) suffered multiple mutilations at the hands of the censor.

The Salamanca Congress anticipated general social disquiet: student troubles and nationwide strikes in 1956; new, illegal trade union movements in 1958; the foundation of the Basque separatist movement ETA a year later. 'From 1956 onwards,' writes David Gilmour in *The Transformation of Spain*, 'a regime whose principal boast was the preservation of peace and order found itself repeatedly declaring a state of emergency and suspending articles of its charter.'[19]

A new acerbity entered the cinema, as it discovered and annexed a realist tradition which is particularly Spanish, of immense possibilities, and a key influence on modern films such as *Maravillas* (1980), possibly Gutiérrez Aragón's best work to date, and García Sánchez's *La corte del Faraón* ('Pharaoh's Court', 1985), not the most interesting but easily among the most popular of the films sponsored by the socialist government after 1982. Yet the impetus for change may well have come from abroad: the arrival in Spain in 1955 of the Italian Marco Ferreri as a Totalscope lens salesman. Ferreri and Berlanga discovered their mutual scriptwriter, the dark-humoured Rafael Azcona, at very nearly the same time. Azcona co-wrote two of Ferreri's three Spanish films, all eleven Berlanga films from *Se vende un tranvía* ('Tram for Sale', co-directed with Juan Estelrich, 1959), five Saura films between *Peppermint frappé* (1967) and *La prima Angélica* (1973); and his less continuous collaborations include the script of Victor Erice's sketch in *Los desafíos* ('The Challenges', 1969), Juan Estelrich's *El anacoreta* ('The Anchorite', 1976), as well as *La corte del Faraón*. Cast as the *eminence noire* of the Spanish film industry, Azcona claims to be simply an *agent provocateur*: 'I've got nothing to say,' he has said, 'I just begin or conspire in something someone else finishes.'[20] Yet Fernando Lara's run-through of Azcona's 50s narrative fiction from *Cuando el toro se llama Felipe* ('When the Bull's Name is Felipe', 1954) to *Pobre, paralítico y muerto* ('Poor, Paralytic and Dead', 1960) reveals in incubation many of the grand themes of modern Spanish films: 'the tragedy of a character obliged by social circumstance to be what he doesn't desire'; 'criticism of the petit bourgeoisie, entrapped in their own peculiar mythology'; 'black humour'; 'an economic, physical, or mental deficiency – or that total deficiency called death – which serve as concave mirrors reflecting the far deeper and more damaging failures of a society which impedes the fulfilment, be it individual or collective, of human beings'.[21]

Azcona's black talent is best illustrated by a storyline. 'A man gets home and tries to kill his wife ... but the gun jams. He goes to the kitchen to grease it, he feels hungry so he makes himself a salad, eats it, uses the oil from it to grease the gun, and finally goes to the bedroom and kills her. Then he takes an immensely valuable stamp they had locked up, and leaves.' An Azcona/Muñoz Suay script; the film has still to be made.[22]

Through Azcona, the sheer aggressiveness of Marco Ferreri's hostility towards 'touching collective stupidity' probably rubbed off on Berlanga. The sourness of *Esa pareja feliz* stems from the impossibility of social advance. In *Plácido* (1959), *El verdugo* ('The Executioner', 1963) or *Escopeta nacional* ('National Shotgun', 1977) it is ambition itself which comes under ridicule. It's ignoble, narrow, consuming, morally compromising. In fact, in a pathetic reversal of Machiavelli, the ends just aren't worth all the effort the means to attain them involve. Apart from Ferreri's influence, however, Berlanga had his own cause for sarcasm. Among others, it had been Alberto Ullastres, Spain's Minister of Commerce and 'European Man' no less, who as Berlanga's head of production had made him add scenes to *Los jueves, milagro*, and then called in Jorge Grau to shoot more material for the film. This detail is normally excluded from Srs Ullastres and Grau's biographies.[23]

Radical directorial differences aside, it is essential to note that Ferreri, Berlanga and associate Fernán Gómez all appealed in their best work to the same tradition of Spanish black humour, *esperpento*, a concept defined and developed by Spain's greatest modern dramatist, Ramón del Valle-Inclán (1866–1936). 'The tragic sense of life,' says Valle-Inclán's mouthpiece, Max, in the play *Luces de Bohemia* ('Bohemian Lights', 1920), 'can be rendered only through an aesthetic that is systematically deformed.' And that is because 'Spain is a grotesque deformation of European civilisation'. *Esperpento* is the grotesque, the ridiculous, the absurd. Enrolled in the interests of an essential, historical realism, it points and derides the anomalous abyss between Spain's sublime tradition and her dismal reality. Characters in Valle-Inclán's *esperpento* grimace, gesture, grunt, performing mechanically like human marionettes. They are swept along by a tide of misunderstandings, imbecility, chaos. They struggle to transcend the crippling biological, social, psychological and accidental banality of life in general, their present predicament in particular. They fail. And 'No one,' comments Anthony Zahareas in his fine introduction to *Bohemian Lights*, 'seems to give a damn about anyone.'[24] Yet, though technically tragic, characters' defeats are too ludicrous, too insignificant, to rise beyond farce. Nothing, even death, is sacred. In *Rosa de papel* ('Paper Rose', 1924), for example, the wife of a blacksmith dies and is spruced up for her wake. The blacksmith has been indifferent to her death until he discovers that the little angel has been hoarding money for years. Piqued, he contemplates the corpse's beautiful whiteness. Shouting that he is within his rights, he tries to get under the covers as scandalised villagers look on.

59

Berlanga freely admits to *esperpento* as one of his trademarks. Fernán Gómez included Valle-Inclán among his literary models, along with 'Wenceslao Fernández Flóres ... the *sainete* and Arniches'.[25] And *esperpento* informs a magnificent series of Spanish films: Marco Ferreri's *El pisito* ('The Little Flat', 1958) and *El cochecito* ('The Little Car', 1960); Luis Berlanga's *Plácido*, his episode of *Las cuatro verdades* ('The Four Truths', 1962) and *El verdugo*; and Fernando Fernán Gómez's *La vida por delante* ('Your Life Ahead of You', 1958), *La vida alrededor* ('Your Life Around You', 1959), the outstanding *El mundo sigue*, and *El extraño viaje*.

Here, if anywhere, is an authentic Spanish film tradition. Its protagonist is a *desgraciado*, a social failure, a nobody. Being petit bourgeois, his needs extend beyond the instincts of hunger and sex to a social advance gauged by an acquisition of the emblems of the American Dream: a flat to bring up a family (*El pisito*, *El verdugo*, *La vida por delante*), a car (*El cochecito*, *Plácido*, *La vida por delante*, *El mundo sigue*), a respectable career (*La vida alrededor*), a holiday in an exotic country (*El extraño viaje*). Yet 'Spain is a grotesque deformation of European civilisation'. The car which old buffer Anselmo sets his heart on in *El cochecito* is a motorised invalid carriage so that he can go on outings with his disabled

The black humour of *esperpento*: Berlanga's *El verdugo* ...

60

... Ferreri's *El cochecito*

friends. Anselmo's tragedy is that he isn't a cripple. He feigns paralysis. His family are unmoved. His friends abandon him. 'I'm going to be left alone,' he wails. But nobody cares. Having murdered his family to keep the carriage, he makes his getaway in it and is arrested by the police. But his obsession remains: 'Will I be able to keep my car in jail?' he asks.

The icons of middle-class achievement come off no better elsewhere. A nice day by the swimming pool? Until, that is, a donkey begins to urinate in it (*Las cuatro verdades*). What about driving home in a big brash saloon car to show your family you've finally made it? Luisa does at the end of *El mundo sigue*. But the impression, and the car, are slightly dented when her sister launches herself from a top-storey flat and lands on top of it. And Doña Ignacia's romance in *El extraño viaje* is distorted in her brother and sister's infantile eyes (whose vision we share in the first part of the film) into the stuff of nightmare: doors creaking open, sinister noises in an old dark house on a stormy night.

The characters' inability to transcend their circumstances is best seen in their bodies. The brother in *El extraño viaje* looks like a retarded cherubim, his sister has a tiny face perched on a pumpkin of a body, and a book has been written on Isbert's dwarf-oak physique.[26] Physical deformation has moral correlatives. Frustrated, sometimes viscerally

61

obsessed by ambition, characters go to inordinate lengths just to gain a little dignity in life. Plácido organises a charity drive just to get a little money together; Rodolfo in *El pisito* schemes to marry an old woman with one foot in the grave (he thinks) in order to inherit her flat when she dies. Yet the characters will fail, and fail ludicrously. Chance, mishap, chaos and compromise sweep mild-mannered José Luis in *El verdugo* from being caught in bed with the executioner's daughter to being dragged to an execution chamber, as the state's official garrotte expert. José Luis has joined the system. State repression has far more insidious, and farcical, forms than pistols and rubber truncheons.[27]

The finest achievement of Berlanga and Fernán Gómez's films (Ferreri is rather a case apart) was to find a formal language, a series of resorts, seeping up from fictional circumstance, constantly delimiting their characters' freedom:

Deep focus photography but foreshortened interiors: The deeper the field, the greater the sense of constriction as whole screen areas are cordoned off by a tawdry environment. The family row scenes in *El mundo sigue* are shot on the axis of passageways to other rooms or using the corners of the living-room. But the sides of the frame are constantly cluttered by an ugly pot plant, a rough chair, bare walls. Free will, even in free movement, is minimal.

Foreground/background contrasts: to play off, in surreal conjunction, a damning contrast between two Spanish realities. A favourite Berlanga ploy: in *El verdugo* a rowing boat with two Civil Guards edges into the foreground as José Luis sits shrouded by tourists listening to Offenbach in a fairytale underground grotto. Fernán Gómez forefronts emblems of social condition, such as the luxury lady's handbag when Luisa first decides to sleep her way to social success in *El mundo sigue*, to relate motivation to a determining environment.

Sequence shot: Berlanga correlates character fate and audience viewpoint by extended tracking movements, the camera dodging this way and that at the beck and call of the convulsive chaos before us (*Plácido*; a technique hypertrophied by the time of *Patrimonio nacional*, 'National Patrimony', 1980, where Berlanga essays a seven-minute shot). In *El extraño viaje*, the sequence shot (as when Angelinès then other villagers leave the dance) again points to Spain's cross-grained reality within the confines of the same physical-geographical space. Tracking back in *El verdugo* from an initial framing to expose a new subject which the camera then follows creates a sense, Francesc Llinàs observes, of a constant aggression by a larger world on an original point of interest.[28]

Diminishing or denial of off-screen space: In *Se vende un tranvía* ('Tram for Sale'), Berlanga constructs 'an on-screen space with its own characteristics to which the characters are confined by framing. They struggle in the only space open to them, the depth of filmic field, flailing around in frenetic desperation, usually acting without sense or any historical perspective whatsoever.'[29] Those with sense cherish the off-screen spaces of liberty while they last. In *El mundo sigue*, for example, Luisa is asked out to dinner. At the table her boss tries to propose an affair. 'Leave it for after the dessert,' she replies. They dance. She looks up and off at the stars, opening up an immense off-camera space, unique in the film. 'You're very romantic,' he whispers. 'Perhaps.' She looks down. She has already agreed to be his mistress. They get into his car. The open space contracts to a closed context (the car) of social ambition. She hints that she wants to be kept in style. In the rest of the film she never looks up and off at the stars again.

Cinema and censorship

If the Spanish cinema is imagined as a relay race, it had pretty disastrous change-overs in 1929, 1936, and 1951. In 1961, it dropped the baton. Buñuel came to Spain, shot *Viridiana*, saw it banned. Its Spanish co-producer, UNINCI, was liquidated by the government in the wake of the film's scandal.[30] Ferreri's residence permit had been refused renewal in 1960. Berlanga and Fernán Gómez's careers were to be temporarily eclipsed by the work of younger directors. Perhaps it is just one more irony that from 1962 part of the Spanish regime attempted to rejuvenate the national film industry from above. The resultant 'New Spanish Cinema' was part of a cautious attempt at political liberalisation. The final goal of economic reform was always entry into the European Economic Community, a move most Spaniards seem to have disliked but, with characteristic historical fatalism, have seen as inevitable. But by 1961 the only thing Spain had entered was the Eurovision Song Contest. The EEC rejected its application because Spain was a dictatorship. An 'apertura' (opening) would further negotiations, and encourage tourism, up from 2.4 million tourists in 1958 to 6.3 million in 1962. One principal advocate of reform, Manuel Fraga Iribarne, may have had grander designs. By 1962 Franco was in his seventies and lacked an apparent successor. 'After Franco, what?' was the contemporary catchphrase. As Minister of Information and Tourism from 1962 to 1969, Fraga may well have encouraged reform as part of a long-term transition from Francoist immobilism towards democracy.[31] *La caza* (Carlos Saura, 1965), in this sense, acquires a large-seeming significance. It not only condemns Francoism but looks over the horizon by predicting its break-up. Its hunters, Saura commented, are 'marked by the way Francoism was going: they're tired, they don't really believe in it any more.'[32] *La caza* also marked out a space for Saura and producer Elías Querejeta as a permanent anti-Francoist opposition backed by a powerful international lobby. To this extent, *La caza* was the first film of the transition. Fraga's appointment in July 1962 as Under Secretary of Cinema was García Escudero. He had already held the same position from September 1951 to February 1952. His brave refusal to grant *Alba de América* 'national interest' status, despite common rumour that Franco had personally supervised the script, effectively cost him his job. García Escudero saw himself, with good reason, as the spirit of Salamanca incarnate. In September 1962 he brought fellow film critics of moderate reformist penchant into a reorganised Board of Classification. In November he remodelled the IIEC, the Spanish Film School, increasing its grants, changing its statute and professorship (relieving Carlos Saura). The School now became the EOC (Escuela Oficial de Cinematografía). From December fresh stimulus was given to films of artistic ambition when the terms of subvention were changed from 'national' interest to 'cinematographic' interest. Jorge Grau's Antonioni-style *Noche de verano* ('Summer Night', 1962) got the first new award in February 1963, the same month that new and explicit norms for censorship were established.

García Escudero's main measure, however, was the incisive Order of August 1964. Each Spanish film was granted one million pesetas in medium-term credit from a Protection Fund which the Banco de Crédito Industrial could increase to up to 50 per cent of the production budget.[33] All films received a grant equal to 15 per cent of their box-office takings. 'Special interest' films received 2 million pesetas credit, 30 per cent of box-office takings, and counted as two normal Spanish films for the purpose of distribution and screen quotas.[34] The state subsidy could be increased to 5 million pesetas (with a ceiling of 50 per cent of a film's budget), only repayable from the 30 per cent of box-office takings; and if commercial performance did not allow repayment, it was waived.

'Con Arias Salgado, todo tapado. Con Fraga, hasta la braga,' was a quip of the period ('With Arias Salgado, everything covered up. With Fraga, down to the panties'). Certainly García Escudero did liberalise film censorship. In October 1962, Elke Sommer appeared in *Bahía de Palma* ('Palma Bay', Juan Bosch) wearing the first bikini in Spanish screen history. The new legislation made an immense impact on film-makers. The Under Secretary made it clear in practice from 1962, and explicitly stated in his preamble to the 1964 Order, that special preference would be shown to projects which 'offer sufficient guarantee of quality, contain relevant moral, social, educative or political values', and 'facilitate the incorporation into professional life of the graduates from the Escuela Oficial de Cinematografía'.[35] Basilio Patino remembers the change: 'Suddenly I found I could chose between two or three producers and even ask for quite a lot of money, which was pretty remarkable considering that *Nueve cartas a Berta* was my debut.'[36]

64

Nothing has excited more polemic in Spain's film history than the 'New Spanish Cinema', the name soon given to the films García Escudero promoted. It was certainly an attempt to project a liberal image abroad, especially at festivals. 'A film is a flag,' García Escudero wrote in his diary. 'We must have that flag unfurled.'[37] But the 'New Spanish Cinema' was more than a promotion of new Spanish liberties, as García Escudero made clear in his *Cine español* (1962), where he sketched a virtual programme for reform which Fraga read just before appointing him. Spanish films had not been made by those who should have made them, 'intellectuals, university men'. Intelligence, to García Escudero, became a commercial policy: 'If you can't beat Hollywood on its own ground (a commercial cinema), you can, and Europe has actually done this, on Europe's home ground: intelligence.'[38] García Escudero placed high hopes on breaking into the Latin American market with Spanish art films. A sincere Christian, he believed in film-making as a means to save souls, and argued that the susceptibilities of the uneducated advised censorship. Above all, his legislation was an attempt to 'Europeanise' the Spanish cinema in accord with the general Europeanising tendencies of the Development Plan. If France had box-office control, so would Spain: Civil Guards were empowered to inspect box-office receipts from 1966. If France had *Cinémas d'Art et Essai*, Spain from 1967 had *Salas de Arte y Ensayo* ('Experimental Art Cinemas') in tourist areas and cities with more than 50,000 inhabitants. Subtitled foreign films and 'special interest' Spanish productions would be shown in the *Salas* in supposedly uncut versions. Subsidies of 15 per cent box-office takings was another measure copied from abroad.[39]

An attempt at box-office control; the relation of state subvention to box-office performance – these were revolutionary measures in 1965 and keystones of modern film laws in Spain. Here García Escudero was a pioneer. Yet one suspects that he never fully assimilated the contradictions of his film policies. He linked, for example, a costly protection system to an indigent Protection Fund. Spain could not afford the 15 per cent European level of film funding. As soon as the 1964 Law took effect, moreover, cowboys reined in, took their cheap credit, and left. Co-productions – many probably 'false' – rocketed from 25 in 1962 to 99 in 1965. By November 1967, when the Under-Secretariat for Cinema and Theatre was closed down as an austerity measure, the now jobless García Escudero was predicting a Protection Fund debt to producers. Augusto M. Torres puts this at 230 million pesetas by 1970, when 'special interest' awards were also discontinued.[40]

It was also a contradiction to encourage a 'social cinema' but discourage its social impact by consigning it to the cultural ghettoes of 'art' cinemas. The 'special interest' films, whatever their artistic values, were normally all-time flops. The ill-fated *Tinto con amor* ('Red With Love', Francisco Montoliu, 1968) took a total of 10,350 pesetas. Only *one* of the better-known 'new' Spanish films, *Fortunata y Jacinta* (Angelino Fons, 1969), got into the top hundred Spanish films screened between 1965 and 1969.[41] The 'new' films may have had commercial potential; but a country where only 5 per cent of the active population had had secondary education in 1965 hardly provided them with an audience. Worse still, Spanish directors were like Isaiahs crying not in a desert but in an oasis. By the 60s the economic boom had begun: 'The apathy of satisfaction replaced the apathy of privation.'[42] An opinion poll in 1969 suggested that more than three-quarters of young Spaniards had little or no interest in politics. Yet one major appeal of 'new' films was their ideological stand.

A Spanish cinema for Europe was as difficult as a European cinema for Spain. The nub of the problem was censorship. It was easy to improve on Arias Salgado, Fraga's predecessor, a man of such reactionary views that he prohibited close-ups of women on state television on the grounds that one never got that close to a woman in real life.[43] The sheer vulgarity of censorship in the 1950s begs credence. 'Prohibited,' it declared of *Some Like It Hot*, 'if only to continue our clamp-down on poofs' ('Prohibida, aunque sólo sea por subsistir la veda de maricones').[44]

Yet García Escudero's new line on censorship had its limitations. *La tía Tula* ('Aunt Tula', 1964) showed them up. Miguel Picazo's delicate adaptation of Unamuno's novel portrays repression not as opposition but as the consequences for self and others of a full acceptance of Establishment mores. Tula regards herself as a heroine of 'aunthood' (motherhood combined with virginity). Picazo sees this as a tragic contradiction and unwitting denial of self, in subtle scenes of disclosure such as Tula's susceptibility to a lazy summer's day when she goes down to a river and fans herself in the sun. In a film of such composed understatement every scene counted. García Escudero's cuts included a sequence showing Tula's spiritual meditations on virginity, which was crucial to an understanding of her 'aunthood'. With the cuts, Picazo claimed, his film lost much of its polemical force; which is exactly, one imagines, what García Escudero wanted.[45]

Basilio Patino's *Nueve cartas a Berta* (1965) tried to go beyond *La tía Tula*. The informing consciousness is now not Unamuno but Sartre, whose writings had a special relevance to an anti-Francoist cinema (as well as to Saura's studies of role-play, such as *Carmen*).[46] The whole moral onus of existentialism is towards demystification. Sartre's rejection of 'essences' countered the political and religious transcendentalism of the Francoist regime. Patino draws on Sartre in *Nueve cartas* for a study of how Spaniards washed their hands of responsibility for Spain's political condition. As Alvaro del Amo points out, Patino's protagonist illustrates the Sartrian distinction between an intellectual acceptance of the need for 'commitment' and a practical incapacity for action.[47] Lorenzo returns from London enamoured of Berta, daughter of a Republican intellectual, whom he met when they were on a student work camp. Romance with Berta and now her letters (which we never read but whose content is suggestively implied in Lorenzo's answers: 'I also want to embrace you,' he writes in an early letter, 'I'm ashamed you've had to find out my inhibitions') have changed Lorenzo: he now finds his home town of Salamanca absurd. Patino counters Lorenzo's letters to Berta, presented in voice-over, with sequences from his drab student life and a series of cutaways when the camera wanders over the shops and streets of Salamanca. It is this environment, established in all its cloying substantiality, which eventually wins out. Lorenzo's social and emotional condition – his love for his family who are so worried about how he has changed; his sentimental son-of-Salamanca syndrome – turns a rebellion at his city's complacent provincialism into a complaint to Berta about their ridiculous 'transcendentalisms' and the final thought that 'Maybe deep down I'm still a nice boy correctly brought up by his mummy and daddy.... But what can I do about it?'[48] In a symbolic act of historical fatalism, Lorenzo confuses a circumstance with a fate. He ducks a Sartrian

'New Spanish Cinema': Patino's *Nueve cartas a Berta*

Con el viento solano

'anguish': a recognition that man creates his own fate and is responsible for the world he lives in. Lorenzo emerges as a symbol of a whole generation of young Spaniards guilty of a collective act of 'bad faith'.

In a film of marvellous lyrical sweep, *Con el viento solano* ('With the East Wind', 1965), Mario Camus portrays a gypsy fleeing across Spain with a death on his hands, the police on his back, an eternal destiny of persecution before him. Francisco Regueiro achieves an incisive, good-humoured study of young Spaniards in *El buen amor* ('The Good Love', 1963). But no special pleading for individual cases can prevent a general agreement with Vicente Molina Foix's scrupulous verdict: 'the crisis of imagination', the 'pedestrian naturalism' of most of the 'new' films. Direct expression in depth was impossible in a censored state. 'Themes of current or political interest such as Opus Dei, the Civil War or the Republic were now mentioned *en passant* in some new Spanish films (Regueiro's *El buen amor*, for example) but were never actually dealt with or discussed.'[49]

The last years of film under Franco mark an evolving reaction to the limitations of a naturalist cinema restricted by censorial pressures. Some directors moved over into commercial production. In this context, Mario Camus' early films were rich parables for their times. *Los farsantes* ('The Actors', 1963) has a theatre troupe touring the provinces, living in squalid pensions, with no future, and no audiences. Camus did no better: his debut got a provincial showing, but was never screened in Madrid. So he made *Young Sánchez* (1963). In it an aspiring boxer sells out to a wealthy

68

manager to get into the big time. And Camus portrays this as a positive move: 'That's what I wanted to be understood – that it's important to face up to reality.'[50] Camus' facing up to his own reality took him from a Hitchcock spoof (*Muere una mujer*, 'A Woman Dies', 1964), a comic exposé of emotional infantilism (*La visita que no tocó el timbre*, 'The Visitor Who did not Ring the Doorbell', 1965), towards vehicles for pop stars where Camus' commercial compromise is countered by a sense of wry pleasure, running through his films with Rafael and Sara Montiel, at working in truly popular genres with outstanding technical facilities. A transparent delight in film-making itself in an industry of such difficult access is in fact a strong subtheme running through the modern Spanish cinema.

A second reaction to censorship, advocated by the so-called Barcelona School and its associate Gonzalo Suárez, was not to show how real things are, but how things really are. Or, in Joaquín Jordá's clipped version, delivered in 1967 when he took his indulgent *Dante no es únicamente severo* ('Dante is not only severe,' 1967) to the Pesaro Festival: 'Since we can't be Victor Hugo, let's be Mallarmé.'[51] The comparison is slightly facetious. But then facetiousness was an occasional plus of the Barcelona School. Durán's *Cada vez que ...* ('Each Time That ...', 1967), for example, has the winning morality of a Martini advertisement. For Durán, Madrid cinema of 'ugly women who after the slightest love scene get pregnant and go through terrible tragedies' was boring. In contrast, in *Cada vez que ...* 'Beautiful young bodies get together when they fall in love,' Joaquín Jordá comments, 'and split up without unnecessary agitation.' 'Making love,' Durán explained, 'is great. I thought it important that a sixteen-year-old girl should be told that.'[52]

The over-eighteen rating given to *Cada vez que ...* may explain its poor box-office. Its massed models did have a serious point. They reflected the development of an advertising industry in Barcelona supported by the middle class of the Catalan capital, whose very existence contrasted with the more backward Madrid. Durán's characters speak French, move from café terrace to boîte, or (in *Liberxina 90*, 1970) practise sub-Godard semiotics. But Durán's 'Frenchness' goes beyond snobbery. It is the assertion of a Barcelona culture not only separate from but also more sophisticated than that of Madrid, a claim to independence.

Unlike Mallarmé, the Barcelona School had in fact no intention of constructing self-sufficing artistic realities. Its most accomplished directors, Vicente Aranda and the slightly peripheral figures of Gonzalo Suárez and Pere Portabella, combined uncompromising political reflection, formal advances from the *nouvelle vague*, and censor-evading techniques best summarised as a resort to diffusion. Aranda recalls that when writing *Fata Morgana* (1966) he and Suárez sacrificed 'conventional coherence for the cinematographic and phenomenological possibilities of each action'.[53] *Fata Morgana* and Suárez's *Ditirambo* (1967) distract attention from covert political implication by the use of stock film genres, the sci-fi thriller and the *film noir* respectively. Portabella's *Nocturno 29* (1968) seems at first sight a sequence of vignettes taken from contemporary Spanish life. Yet all three films are unequivocally political works. In a clear contemporary reference, Aranda has *Fata Morgana*'s professor declare, with obvious relevance to Spain in the 60s, that 'only a desired fatality can truncate our existence, and that fatality is the daughter of fear. Fear, the authentic whip, the true epidemic, so contagious that all of a city, all of a country, can change into a victim.' So *Fata Morgana* returns, like *Ditirambo*, to Sartrian 'bad faith'. Murder and death result from a collective denial of responsibility for mass suffering; in this sense all the film's characters are victims and their fates are made symbolically interchangeable. Agent J.J.'s wild goose chase to save beautiful model Gim from murder ends with his falling into the trap supposedly awaiting her.

A further possible reaction to censorship was to use it as a principle of creation rather than just a barrier. Attempts at this were made in Madrid by so-called 'independent' film-makers whose only real links were their rejection of or ejection from the E O C; their dismissal of the New Spanish Cinema directors for their ideological compromise and stylistic limitations; their acknowledged influence by the films of Fernán Gómez and Ferreri; and their future, in the figures of Ricardo Franco, Alfonso Ungría, Emilio Martínez-Lázaro, Paulino Viota, and Augusto M. Torres, in the vanguard of post-Franco film-making.[54] The inscription of censorship into a film is seen clearly in *Contactos* ('Contacts', 1970). Director Viota systematically consigns action and dialogue to an off-screen space in a censorship of spectator viewpoint and knowledge. Characters walk out of camera view, leaving the drab walls and empty hallways of a pension where a girl hides her boyfriend from the police. The plot has a 'censor', the fusspot landlady who won't allow gentlemen in ladies' rooms, and the film is cut off (seemingly 'cut') at its end just as the boyfriend and his militant friends seem to be getting something organised. *Contactos* offers as few concessions to hope as it does to traditional entertainment.[55]

Ungría's *El hombre oculto* ('The Hidden Man', 1970) similarly advertises state censorship by cutting its narrative into discontinuous segments. Ungría's shabby realism combines with the shifting structures, the accumulation of disparate hints, which directors had moved towards by 1970.[56] *El hombre oculto* begins, for example, as a portrayal of a Spaniard who went underground during the Civil War to avoid possible execution (several Republicans were to stay in hiding places constructed in their own homes until 1969, when the Franco regime proscribed punishment for war crimes). As the hidden man's daily routine gradually moves towards that of a normal Spaniard, his condition emerges as a metaphor for all Spaniards whose life, to Ungría, was 'subterranean, agitated, dark, almost too terrible to be confessed'.[57]

Oblique stratagems always seem clever, but they risked being too clever by half. As Angel Fernández Santos observed in *Nuestro Cine*, 'new' films were pulled this way and that by contrary tendencies: their ideological rupture with the regime; the need for a surface appearance of conformity. The inevitable result was 'to situate any sort of rupture on a semi-hidden plain' with the danger of 'new' films becoming 'cinema for the initiated, an intellectual elite, a film-club cinema'.[58] These fears were well grounded. The penalty of sophistication for many young film-makers was to finesse themselves out of an audience. Only one director managed to transcend the stylistic crisis of the New Spanish Cinema while charming the censor and attracting a following in Spain and abroad: Carlos Saura. The key reference – as an illustration of oblique realism, as a source of style which lasts until *Elisa, vida mía* ('Elisa, My Love', 1977) – is *La caza*.

Getting round the censor: Carlos Saura and *La caza*
Saura never got over the failure of *Llanto por un bandido* ('Lament for a Bandit', 1963). He reckoned that he had lost control. The censor had cut an anthology sequence: Saura's friend Luis Buñuel playing a hangman in the execution of bandits, which was meant to open the film. Equally important, Saura felt he had lost economic control by being forced to shoot 'big' scenes (including a battle) with little finance and 'a hand-held Arriflex and five metres of tracks'.[59] *Llanto por un bandido* finished up neither fish nor fowl, a low-budget epic about nineteenth-century banditry.

Saura would not be fooled again. He met Elías Querejeta, and together they evolved a style of production, the 'Querejeta look': a fixed crew of outstanding talent, including Luis Cuadrado as director of photography, his assistant and successor from 1975, Teo Escamilla, editor Pablo G. del Amo, musician Luis de Pablo, Primitivo Alvaro as director of production, and art director Emilio Sanz de Soto; a single enclosed setting in or around Madrid (cutting down on transport fees, hotel costs and evening meals); a small cast but at least one star (lowering costs but maintaining commercial clout); a combative anti-Francoist stance challenging censorship threshholds; a stress on sex, violence, jealousy, questioning the superficial modernisation of Spaniards (developed in other Querejeta productions such as *Los desafíos*, 'The Challenges', and Anton Eceiza's *Las secretas intenciones*, 'Secret Intentions', both 1969); a delight in elliptical editing for insinuation, economy and wit, a style begun by *Los golfos* and continued up to Montxo Armendáriz's *Tasio* (1984); a similar desire to 'document' their films, which often start from *cinéma-vérité* material, relate to concrete historical contexts, and are sometimes 'fictionalisations' of contemporary problems.

Querejeta's style as a producer was tailored for Saura's own allegorical bent. Fewer locations and characters means that they have to become representative of larger historical realities if a film is to acquire a social relevance. And shooting in or around Madrid always located Saura's films in the symbolic heartland of the Francoist state: Castille. The main pressure for obliqueness came, however, from the censor, though Saura's natural inclination towards indirect strategies certainly helped him assimilate censorship's demands. 'The need to avoid mentioning facts without evading them,' Saura said in 1973, 'forces the director to explore narrative techniques and stories which gradually shape his personality.'[60] Such a 'detour' was sometimes beneficial. 'We couldn't use a linear structure or the ideas would be too clear. It often forced me to exercise my imagination.' But Saura has also claimed that working in oblique modes 'agrees with my personality'.[61]

Saura's style was defined by *La caza*. The film also had a large impact on Spanish cinema, setting new standards in formal elaboration. 'In terms of a well-worked language,' Gutiérrez Aragón observes, 'there is a cinema before *La caza* and a different one after it.'[62] Getting round the censor normally involved native wit; Saura made this part of his fine art, which in no way diminished the film's powerful immediacy. Obliqueness merely allowed it, at the same time, a rich overlay.

In *La caza*, three old friends drive into the country for a rabbit hunt in a desolate valley pock-marked by the caves and memories left over from the Civil War. Saura's crypticism begins in symbol. His hunters subsume the characterising traits of a generation which fought for Franco, and, as Saura puts it, 'did pretty well out of the war: there were fortunes made by people who were on Franco's side.'[63] All three hunters fought in the Civil War (the censor proscribed all explicit mention of a Spanish war, making the characters refer more abstractly to 'the war', and helping to push the film towards more general parable). Civil War memories and military modes mix with more general and very Spanish death fixations. José, the oldest hunter, organises the hunt like a military expedition, and is haunted by the suicide of a friend as well as by his own ageing. Paco is also typical of the Francoist classes in his vaunted *machismo* and firm belief in family life. All the hunters suggest the 'superficial modernisation' of Francoist Spain: Paco brings along a transistor and snazzy camping equipment; José has left his wife for a flighty young girl. Saura's opening shot of the hunters defines them: a jeep hurrying down a modern Spanish highway, a bizarre graft of old and new.

72

La caza: hunting as metaphor

Having established credentials, Saura proceeds to polemics. The supposed peacemakers of Spain slaughter rabbits for sport; an ineradicable memory taken away from *La caza* is rabbit after rabbit being shot. Saura wanted, however, to relate this violence to a collective psychology. He depersonalises the hunters' cruelty in the gun-loading episode and the hunt sequence: those eager fingers loading bullets or pulling barrel to stock are not always distinguishable. Such distinctions, the implication is, are not necessary. Any of the hunters – and, as far as they typify a class, any Francoist – could be capable of such cruelty.

In the end the hunters shoot each other. They fall like soldiers, as defenceless as rabbits. Insistent martial music also relates the hunt back to the Civil War, as well as to armed conflict in general. Here Saura moves from symbol to a kind of elliptical naturalism. Clearly influenced by the entomological aspect of Buñuel, Saura repeats the naturalist fantasy of the artist as scientist. Microscopic details of the hunters' bodies dehumanise them into the objects of a quasi-scientific inquiry. Long shots of characters set against landscape similarly diminish them to the perspective of insects. But *La caza* is like naturalism with some things missing. If the naturalists explained human behaviour in terms of heredity, environment and immediate circumstance, Saura's censorship-evading technique is to give us the immediate circumstances explaining the hunters' deaths and urge us to deduce for ourselves other contributing causes, such as historical environment or Spaniards' latent violence.

Again to avoid censorship, Saura aids us in our deductions by suggestion rather than statement. Metaphor and metonymy construct chains of association. The hunters, for example, find the carcass of a rabbit dead from myxomatosis. The rabbit compares to the suicide of José's friend, to the skeleton found in the wartime dug-out, and to the hunters themselves when they are finally killed. Victims merge with victors. Saura's schema opens up allusive spaces. If a dead rabbit is like a dead man, could not the cause of their deaths be similar? And might not these paradoxical associations point to wider contradictions?

The great quality of *La caza* is that complex associations are grounded in social and psychological observation. The hunters are indeed portrayed as victims; victims, like the rabbits they shoot, precisely of their own cruelty and their fatal indifference to the feelings of others. Their myxomatosis is Francoism, and more precisely its contradictions, which justify the paradox pointed in the film, that the Civil War's victors were also its victims. The hunters are riddled with contradiction. Francoism has allowed Paco economic prosperity; but it constantly denies him social respect, as José jibes at his origins as a lorry-driver. Modernisation allows José the *machista* coup of an affair with a much younger girl; yet separation from his wife implies a loss of the moral respect associated with being head of a family. Above all, Saura puts his finger on the animal defencelessness of the authoritarian temperament: that in 1965, 1936, today, it has to devalue or destroy what it cannot dominate.

In evading the censor, Saura also played on the particular ambiguities of film. In literature, comparisons can be pointed explicitly by metaphors and similes. In film, apparent similarities between, say, some hunters and the rabbits they hunt do not necessarily indicate that such a comparison was intended. Pure coincidence, the director can plead to the censor. Notably, too, in *La caza* such metaphorical associations are slyly delayed, and when made they are also diffused. The crucial connection between hunters and soldiers, suggesting the barbarity of war, is one example. Enrique, Paco's ingenuous brother-in-law who is brought along for the hunt, looks at the valley and asks the intellectual, Luis: 'Is this from the war?' (connection made). 'Lots of people died here,' Luis replies (connection emphasised). Cut to José and Paco. 'You knew this, didn't you?' José says, referring implicitly to the fighting which took place in the valley (connection confirmed, though diffused by the vagueness of 'this'). Paco assists, but deflates, the association. It was a long time ago, he replies, and anyway he fought 'lower down' (connection diffused: the war no longer marks him, the valley has no special connotations for him).

74

Saura also attacks the underbelly of censorship: its insensitivity to form. Nine of the thirteen prohibitions relating to the script of *La caza* were questions of dialogue. The censor suppressed four shots (of a priest and of the torso of a dressmaker's dummy, for example), but told Saura in much vaguer terms to 'be careful about the shots of the dead rabbit'. It was also no doubt far easier to decide that 'punetas' ('damn') was a swear word and should be cut out of the script than to decide the effect of a brief close-up of a dead rabbit. When viewing a finished version, the censor had either to suppress the shot or include it: there could be no intermediate decisions. In the formal aggression of the hunt scenes Saura no doubt exploited the reluctance of the reformist García Escudero Censorship Board to cut high quality, if highly subversive, film-making.

Film censorship in Spain may well have caused some misconceptions. It dominated Spanish cinema under Franco but it by no means totally determined it. The Censorship Board was probably less efficient and at times rather more intelligent than is often assumed. Censors in the 40s for example included the novelist Camilo José Cela – whose *La familia de Pascual Duarte* (1942) was a brutal indictment of rural deprivations – and Wenceslao Fernández Flóres, a writer with a strong realist streak much admired and adapted by such cultural non-conformists as Neville and Fernán Gómez. The greatest censorship caprices usually involved Franco

La caza: hunters as victims

and his ministers rather than the Censorship Board. Franco is reputed to have viewed and personally approved Carlos Saura's *Ana y los lobos* because he thought it was just nonsense. It is certain that part of a Cabinet meeting was dedicated to deciding whether the donkey urinating in the swimming pool during Berlanga's sketch in *Las cuatro verdades* was in fact a symbol of Franco performing similar functions over Spaniards.

What a film 'said' was probably not the only factor influencing Censorship Board decisions. Other elements, such as the picture's market and the consequences of prohibition, were also highly relevant. García Escudero seems for instance to have been aware of Saura's insinuations in *La caza*: 'That the film's got secondary intentions is evident,' he wrote in his diary. 'But whether that's enough to prohibit it is another matter. That it's got quality can't be doubted. The script was given "special interest" status.'[64] García Escudero's mention of 'quality' is significant. By the 60s Franco's government had become increasingly sensitive to foreign opinion and desperately wanted to retain top-flight directors in Spain, even, one suspects, if that meant giving them greater liberties. Saura's success with the censor also derived from the fact that he bargained from a position of strength. At a time when the Francoist regime was increasingly courting foreign opinion, Querejeta was attributed with far-reaching influence over the foreign media, which he did not go out of his way to deny. Of all Spain's producers he was the last a supposedly reformist regime wanted to disaffect.

By the 60s at least a film-maker's evasiveness served not only to distract attention from hidden themes but also to persuade the censor that the film's impact would be limited to an intellectual, dissenting minority whose existence the regime was resigned to. This market factor explains in part Saura's relative toleration by the censor. It is doubtful whether in Spain in political terms his films did much more than preach to an already converted minority. (For foreign audiences Saura's films may have been more illuminating: Sam Peckinpah once told Saura that seeing *La caza* changed his life.)

With a few exceptions, the fascination of Saura's films is not their politics but the psychological observations on which their political implications are based. Saura's importance was the fact that he was tolerated in Spain despite his clear opposition to its dictatorial regime. It is hardly surprising that when the Francoist government attempted to establish a wider, more liberal base for continuance in 1974, one of its most influential moves was to champion a Saura film, *La prima Angélica*, which made an acid attack on the extreme right. In this sense Saura's political importance was the opportunity which liberal censorship treatment of his films offered to part of the Francoist regime to express its desire for evolution from within.

How to get round the censor

'In the cinema you should begin by reading Machiavelli. It should be the bedside book of every film-maker – the edition with notes by Napoleon.'
Gonzalo Suárez[65]

The diffusion of sense, metonymy, metaphor, symbol, allegory, ellipsis, subjectivism (excusing subversive scenes passed off as the product of a supposedly imbalanced mind, such as the accident victim of *El jardín de las delicias*), subsuming sense in form – these were a few of the oblique stratagems favoured by Spanish film-makers. A few extra-filmic precautions came in handy too:

1. *Ignore the censor*: 'Suppress pan over figure in magazine,' the censor told Saura of a scene in *La caza*. He filmed it; and it was passed.

2. *Rewrite the script*, present it, get it passed, then film the original version. Querejeta's ploy at times; Saura left censorship bargaining to his producer.

3. *Bring in an adviser*, or be given one. Berlanga was sent censor Father Garau to help him rewrite the script of *Los jueves, milagro*. At first they didn't get on. 'You think I'm old-fashioned,' Garau complained one day. 'If only you knew ... I've had advanced ideas, I've had my problems with the hierarchy ... I swear to it on God, señor Berlanga, I was the first priest in Spain to wear a wrist-watch!' The partnership never really took off.[66]

4. *Base your film on a classic*, then subvert that classic's sense. Scriptwriter Antonio Drove, for example, claimed that his adaptation of Calderón's *El alcalde de Zalamea* drew on Lope de Vega's version of the same theme as a smoke-screen for his subversive reading of the Calderón original. In this, a mayor executes a captain who has raped his daughter, claiming that he was impartially carrying out his duty. In the Drove version, the king makes the mayor apply the same supposedly impartial sense of duty in the judgment of his son. Only a deus-ex-machina dénouement saves the mayor from either condemning his son to death or exposing the partiality of his decisions, and so his own culpability before law. Drove's script, directed by Mario Camus as *La leyenda del Alcalde de Zalamea* ('The Legend of the Mayor of Zalamea', 1972), was praised for its 'grace of style worthy of Lope de Vega'.

5. *Deny any particular relevance to Spain* in a prologue but confirm it in your film. So *Calle Mayor* begins with the censor-imposed claim that the story could occur in 'any city, in any province, in any country'. A pity that the obviously Spanish hero declares halfway through the film that 'the future, truth, is here in this city, in the main street. ... My country is here'.

SAYING A LONG GOODBYE
TO MOTHER

> I made *Ana y los lobos* because my mother, when I was young and wanted to talk about problems of politics, religion, or sex, would have none of that in the house. The Spanish Censor's the same.
>
> Carlos Saura

The protagonist of *El jardín de las delicias* is an industrialist who has lost his memory in a car accident. His family re-enact for him key scenes from his life. They are moved by money, not love: daddy can't remember the number of the secret bank account in Switzerland. His friends take him hunting. Having tied a bird to the end of his gun, they toss it into the air. The feathered corpse flops towards the ground. A once dictatorial head of the family, now a mental deficient, bangs away at the bird with infantile glee.

The one-off reference to Franco is clear. Hearsay had it that on his last fishing trips the old man would hold his rod while a frogman, hidden beneath the foam, attached a dead fish to the Caudillo's hook. By the 70s, Franco was 'like a piece of antique furniture in a new room'.[1] In 1969 Franco finally chose Juan Carlos to succeed him on his death as the Spanish head of state. Carrero Blanco acted as Spain's effective Prime Minister from October 1969. In 1972 Franco was obliged to attend the Victory Parade sitting down, and started to doze off at Cabinet meetings.

Yet as a member of Franco's last government wrote, 'While the protagonist of an epoch in Spanish history still lived, it was impossible to think of any real change.'[2] So the political transition to democracy is usually dated from Franco's death in November 1975 to 27 December 1978, when the new democratic constitution was enacted. The cinema of this transition obeys a rather difficult time-scale, however. Film-makers have kept discreetly silent over such topics as the role of the military or the multinational corporations during the political reform. The transition

78

(liberalisation, that is) of Spain's cinema is not quite the same as the cinema about the political transition. Films could not open up at the same rate as Spain's press, a 'paper parliament' by the early 70s, 'a true Fourth Estate where almost every opinion could find a place'.[3] Film censorship was far stricter. Films also took too long to make to register the minutiae of historical evolution. Censorship disappeared so quickly that film-makers had to rethink films in the middle of making them. *Camada negra* ('Black Brood', 1977) was originally 'highly esoteric' with a 'hidden political sense', according to director Gutiérrez Aragón. But 'then so many political films came out' that he and Borau 'decided to elaborate the elements with greatest ideological force'. Later he thought the film's most concrete contemporary reflections distracted attention from its true subject: 'the traits defining a fascist in any period, condition, or party'.[4]

In the highly market-oriented cinema of the early 70s, producers were concerned not so much with change as with what part of a changing society occupied cinema seats. Here was another drag on a rapid reaction to reform: the natural audiences for Spanish films were among the most conservative in Spain. The higher the per capita income of a province, the lower the number of Spanish films shown there.[5] The average Spanish film was a cheap pot boiler made for the Spanish poor who couldn't afford television, and shown at downtown or rural fleapits, which couldn't compete for the far more profitable Hollywood blockbuster. A report in 1973 claimed that Andalusia had the lowest living standards in Western Europe. Spain hardly looked the place for a burgeoning political cinema.[6]

Yet a cinema coming out of a dictatorship has vested economic interests in its own liberalisation. More nudes, more political scandal, more censorship rows meant more national audiences, and a sometimes patronising interest from abroad. Reformist pressures on a drag-heel industry led to immense contradictions. Considering the early transitional cinema as it debated the merits of liberalisation and squared up to Francoism, it is difficult to part true courage from good commerce. 'Reform' was as superficial as a starlet's satin skin. There were few political full-frontals.

First signs of a cinema transition

By the 70s the Francoist regime was in crisis. In December 1970, six ETA militants were put on trial at Burgos for belonging to an illegal organisation. Assailed by international protest, attacked even by his own church, Franco backed down. The activists' death sentences were commuted. But terrorist hold-ups and kidnappings still increased in the Basque provinces, there were serious strikes at Vigo, Ferrol and Pamplona between 1970 and 1974, and an initially Marxist urban guerrilla movement emerged: the Revolutionary Anti-Fascist Patriotic Front (FRAP).

79

The reaction of the regime was to try to tighten its grip. Universities were closed; political parties were outlawed by the 1969 Statute of Associations, which allowed 'associations of opinion' but only within the parameters of the Francoist Movement. Equally out of favour was the main champion for internal reform, Manuel Fraga. On 10 August 1969 the government admitted that credits of about £80 million granted to the textile firm, Matesa, for the export of machinery had in fact been used for private investment abroad. Fraga was slightly too keen to publish the involvement of three Opus Dei Cabinet Ministers in the affair. Franco sacked him.

The Minister for Information and Tourism between October 1969 and June 1973 was the preposterous Alfredo Sánchez Bella. As Ambassador in Rome when *El verdugo* was screened at Venice, he wrote an infamous letter to Castiella, Spain's Minister for Foreign Affairs, lambasting the Italian producer as an 'unscrupulous Jew' and dubbing Berlanga as 'a man who aspires to notoriety at any price'.[7] In January 1972, Sánchez Bella issued instructions for the Censorship Board to 'accentuate its rigour in classifying films'. The manipulations were legendary. At the end of Sam Peckinpah's *The Getaway*, for example, Steve McQueen and partner do get away, fleeing south to Mexico. In the Spanish version a narrator intones that the police caught the pair, and sent them to jail. And when Angelino Fons presented *Separación matrimonial* ('Matrimonial Separation', 1973) to the censor, he was told that 'If a Spanish woman separates from her husband she has either to take to religion or live in perpetual solitude.'[8]

Censorship was compounded by economic crisis. Founded in 1956, Spanish Television began to challenge cinema audiences by the late 60s. By 1970 it was running five films a week. Few of these were Spanish. By 1971 cinema audiences were 30 per cent down on two years earlier. Competition and market decline meant that the Spanish film industry needed state protection. Yet austerity measures, exacerbated by the Matesa scandal, led to a credit squeeze, with medium-term loans dropping from 325 million pesetas in 1968 to 94.8 million pesetas a year later.[9] With the Protection Fund in debt and 'special interest' awards halted, the industry reached rock-bottom when the subsidies on 15 per cent of box-office takings were discontinued by an Order of 12 March 1971.

Only a few forms of film-life survived and festered in such an economic climate. The Spanish horror genre, broken in by *La marca del hombre lobo* (Enrique Eguiluz, 1967), was able to undercut Hammer horror with a cheap *tremendismo* (graphic violence) satiated by sado-masochism and myth grafts (as in *El Dr Jeckyll y el hombre lobo*, Léon Klimovsky, 1971). So Javier Aguirre's *El jorobado de la morgue* (1972) has a hunchback, a Frankenstein-like scientist hell-bent on creating his creature, and an *esperpento* twist to the old cliché of a young man in hapless love with a terminally tubercular maiden: the humped Gotho only devils for the scientist in the hope of his master one day resurrecting his beloved, presently a putrefying corpse devoured by rats in a cellar.[10]

The most solvent of genres in the early 70s was, however, the 'sexy Spanish comedy'. A case in point is number twenty in the Spanish box-office table for 1965 to 1973, *Vente a Alemania, Pepe* ('Come to Germany', Pedro Lazaga, 1971). The hero is a *paleto*, a kind of village neo-idiot. One day his old mate Angelino comes cruising up the road in a Mercedes. Angelino has been working abroad. He enthuses about the easy money and even easier women to be made or laid in Germany. Pepe is soon on a train northwards. Yet Germany is no pushover: Pepe has to get up at five, wash dishes and windows, and ends up exhibiting his hirsute chest in a shop window as part of an advertisement for surplus hair removal. Humiliated, homesick, drugged and deceived by the German women, Pepe returns home to marry his Spanish fiancée and sit in the Spanish sun where he enthuses about the easy money and even easier women...

An 'extremely confusing conjunction of conformity and dissipation' was how José Luis Guarner summed up such hokum. According to the 'sexy Spanish comedy' any Iberian male worth his salt is uncommonly horny. His pan-sexualist brain gives almost everything a *double entendre*: froth from coffee, round objects, even dust ('polvo' in Spanish means not only 'dust' but also 'screw'). He is over-impatient and eternally open-mouthed. He becomes agitated. If sex is imminent he jumps up and down in excitement. Yet he never gets anywhere at all. For the structure of the sexy Spanish comedy, analysed in Alvaro del Amo's uproarious *Comedia cinematográfica española*, responds to a deep conservatism.[11] Change brings only meretricious benefits. All roads lead to the altar. The protagonist suddenly discovers inexplicit pleasures in a setting or wife that originally drove him abroad or towards desired adultery. And pre-marital or extra-marital sex is anyway impossible. So in *La descarriada* (Mariano Ozores, 1972) we find the bizarre case of a protagonist who is a prostitute but, being Spanish, is morally upright to the extent of still being a virgin.

In the 'sexy Spanish comedy', as in Spain's film industry at large, economic forces demanding greater sexual explicitness clearly clashed with the political conservatism of the regime – often shared by film-makers themselves. The archaic censorship controls not only cut out distribution abroad, but were cutting into audiences for foreign imports at home. Thousands of frustrated film enthusiasts hopped the French border to see the latest sex or political films. In an article entitled 'The Blue Pilgrims', *Time* magazine marvelled that in 1973 110,000 people had seen *Last Tango* in Perpignan when its population was only 100,000.

81

The attempt to reconcile economic and ideological pressures for reform with the political immobilism of the regime brought the first significant developments beyond the twilight horizons of cinema under Franco. A powerful lobby of independent but 'mainstream' producers such as José Luis Dibildos and 'progressives' such as Elías Querejeta sought to unite economic grievances with the pressure for ideological change by bringing their Film Producers Union (ASPC) closer to the more militant stance of the Film Directors Union (ASDREC) and activists in the acting profession. The regime responded slightly. Cinema prices were allowed to rise in 1971, and again a year later. Pronouncements changed. In 1972 the Ministry for Information and Tourism rounded on the 'out-and-out eroticism, pornography, and divisive, anti-social doctrines' of world cinema. In 1973 it declared that it backed 'an agile, flexible and dynamic censor moving in time with everyday events'.[12] Such declarations were not all flannel. A glimpse of Carmen Sevilla's bare torso in *La loba y la paloma* (Gonzalo Suárez) suggested as early as 1973 that the regime was more prepared to come to terms with the physical reality of the Spanish artist, symbolised for twenty-five years by the playful lustiness of *la Sevilla*, than it was with films pointing the political unreality of Francoism after Franco.

Pornography was, however, Carrero's *bête noire*. Censorship changes before his assassination in December 1973 were minor, if significant. The major victory achieved by the ASPC was the restoration in September 1973 of cinema protection equivalent to 15 per cent of box-office takings. Dibildos' reaction was to rush out *Vida conyugal sana* ('A Healthy Married Life', 1973), the prototype of a so-called 'Third Way' cinema, a halfway house between the 'sexy Spanish comedy' and the sobriety of Saura; a 'popular cinema with critical bite', as Dibildos himself explained, whose ultimate destination was foreign audiences. 'To conquer markets,' Dibildos argued, 'we must strengthen investment, improve film quality, widen thematic possibilities, including their film treatment. In short, only an "ongoing" Spanish cinema will break into foreign markets.'[13]

The protagonist of *Vida conyugal sana* is Vázquez, played by José Sacristán. Sunken-chested, large-nosed, myopic, Sacristán was especially adept at embodying the ordinary, brow-beaten Spanish *petit bourgeois*. Vázquez is such a man, but with a difference. He is an advertisement addict. Whatever they sell he buys: an Austin Victoria, soap which he stockpiles in the kitchen, dozens of bras and panties for his wife. But what really drops his defences is a billboard of a sexy model in lingerie. One glance and he'll put his workers in for more pay, tell his wife to become a 'new woman' – sexually liberated and independent – and recount at his boss' dinner how the firm of course originally expanded thanks to black-marketeering. His wife takes Vázquez to a psychiatrist, who diagnoses his condition and prescribes a cure.

Vida conyugal sana and its precursor, *Españolas en Paris* ('Spanish Women in Paris', Roberto Bodegas, 1970), mark the beginnings not only of the 'Third Way' but also of the emergence of a transition cinema. Gone for one thing is the simple dichotomy between films which submerge the spectator into their world and those which keep the audience at a distance. Spaniards will identify with Vázquez, whose education is typical for the middle-class post-war youth: a boarding school, then law studies at Salamanca University. Yet, while not directly stating its fictionality, the film often refers outside itself to a contemporary historical reality. In contradiction with the standard models, but in accord with so much Spanish transition cinema, identifying with its 'typical' protagonists allowed contemporary audiences a fluctuating sense of the film's reality and their own reality outside it.

The more contemporary the reference the better. So the model who turns Vázquez's head is played by the then Miss Spain, Amparo Muñoz. And Vázquez's actions, touched off by the sight of the model, find an immediate parallel in a 70s Spain of increasing wage demands, a more liberal attitude to sex, and a press now more inclined to criticise the authorities. Allegory? Yes, but director Bodegas no longer hides the reference, as in the New Spanish Cinema, but signposts the larger relevance of his fictional situations. 'Let's imagine,' the psychiatrist says in a metaphor which forces its contemporaneity, 'that your husband is a bottle.' Since the wife doesn't beg to differ, the psychiatrist goes on. 'His instincts, his bad instincts, that is his impulses, his bad impulses, have spent thirty years trying to get out of the bottle. They want to be free, to do just what they feel like. But the stopper on the bottle is preventing this from happening.' Thirty years was the rough span of Francoism. Behind the psychiatrist's metaphor is the familiar concept of a possible 'opening'. Audiences were once more pushed back to Spain 1973. Hesitancy between *apertura* ('opening') and immobilism had ended with Carrero's plumping for the latter. The unwanted gaucheness of the allusions in *Vida conyugal sana* becomes clear: Carrero, Franco and the rest are institutionalised bottle-tops.

The directness of *Vida conyugal sana* and other 'Third Way' films which followed was really a new blatancy. Other film-makers went much further. 'There's no question of an opening,' the regime's pronouncement had continued, 'just a determination to be more consequential with our constitution as a people and as men ... It's a question of authenticity, of speaking clearly.' These crass lines would seem to give a green light to the explicit portrayal of sex in all its (money-spinning) consequentiality: abortion (*Aborto criminal*, 'Criminal Abortion', Iquino, 1973); drugs (*El ultimo viaje*, 'The Last Trip', José Antonio de la Loma, 1973); separation (*Separación matrimonial*); prostitution (*Chicas de alquiler*, 'Girls for

Rent', Iquino, 1972); and loss of virginity, a boyfriend and a baby (*Experiencia prematrimonial*, 'Prematrimonial Experience', Pedro Masó, 1972).

The shadow crossing all these films is that of change. Transformation, transition was of course no new concern for the Spanish cinema. But in the 60s it was treated as an alienating ambition (*El verdugo*, for example), an impossibility (*El extraño viaje*), mere sheen (*La caza*), or as capable of complete assimilation with true Spanish traditions (most orthodox Spanish films). For the 'sexy Spanish comedy', change was a false allure. By 1973, change was far more challenging, a possible, imminent or actual option for a whole society. But above all most Spanish film-makers saw it as a rupture, and perhaps an irreversible rupture. In *Experiencia prematrimonial*, for example, the desire of a young girl to live with her boyfriend before marriage leads to the end of their romance and a dead baby. In a scene prescribed by the censor, *Separación matrimonial* ends with the husband suffering the ultimate consequences of 'rupture' with his wife: she shoots him. In *Vida conyugal sana* the prescription comes from another voice of authority, a psychiatrist. Vázquez's problems derive from the day, the analyst explains, when his father burnt his Marilyn Monroe photos. But repression in the past can only be cured by further repression in the present. Here the psychiatrist subscribes to the Carrero Blanco school of therapeutics. Vázquez has to be kept away from modernising elements which rupture his personality. The psychiatrist's cure is unintentionally hilarious. No sex; no reading ('The imagination never does anything good'); cold showers. Cinema? 'Yes, but very little,' and 'only Spanish films.' And careful with modern music: 'Its rhythms are terribly exciting.' The cure is naturally very successful.

Dibildos' developmental ethos suggests something of a halo effect, the result of collaboration with left-wing figures such as Bodegas and a move into high-quality technical values. But his films can't really be accused of dragging their feet. Rather, they caught something of the spirit of the time. As late as 1975 the dominant mood of the country was not a self-righteous hatred of Francoist fetters, but alarm at the lack of consensus within the government and between Establishment and opposition over Spain's future. According to opinion poll specialist Rafael López Pintor, what people feared for most in the mid-70s were their 'dearest values: physical security, social peace, and the maintenance of a material well-being which many were enjoying for the first time'.[14] The problem for Spaniards was to work out whether such values were best protected by immobilism, reform, or rupture with the past. The early transition cinema was merely reflecting the fears of a sizeable part of the Spanish population, by no means all reactionary, when it seemed to want as little transition as possible.

The 'Apertura' and *La prima Angélica*

The explosion which killed Carrero Blanco 'was so powerful', Robert Graham reports, 'that it ripped a hole in the street, Claudio Coello, ten metres by seven. Water from the burst mains which gradually filled this crater was symbolic of the tide closing in on the end of an era.'[15] Carrero's death put paid to immobilism; the new government experimented with reform. On 12 February 1974 President Arias Navarro made a celebrated speech, announcing 'the incorporation of new Spaniards – those whose age may be counted by the years of our peace – to the common task'. National consensus, hitherto expressed 'by way of adherence' to Franco, would now take the form of 'participation' in the regime. A new Statute of Association would allow the immediate formation of political associations.

The appointment of one of Fraga's associates, Pío Cabanillas, to the Ministry of Information and Tourism raised hope for reform in the government's film policy. Cabanillas' Under-Secretary for the Cinema, Rogelio Díez, liquidated Protection Fund debts, charged the Supreme Film Council (Consejo Superior de Cinematografía) with drawing up a film law, and announced that 146 films would be given a new, less stringent, censorship. Though the Censorship Board approved 70 of these revised films in August 1974, the reformists were looking for more outright proof, a decision on a *cause célèbre* perhaps, to confirm the Arias government's real readiness to endorse its *aperturista* intentions. The same government of the February 'opening' had, in sharp, brutal, near-medieval contrast, garrotted the Spanish anarchist Puig Antich a month later. 'Destroying books is bad,' declared Cabanillas, lamely, after yet another right-wing vandalisation of left-wing bookshops. A real sign of Cabanillas' commitment to reform came with the *Prima Angélica* affair; finally, the Spanish cinema behaved not only as a reflection of change, but as a vehicle for its achievement.

Like so many of his films, *La prima Angélica* (1973) derives at a distance from Saura's personal experience. During the Civil War Saura's mother packed him off to the provincial city of Huesca, in Aragón, to live with his grandmother and aunts. Saura has spoken of his bewilderment at leaving Republican Catalonia for the gloomy, family home:

> The Aragonese part of my family were very right-wing and very religious.... I was an exile, I felt like a foreigner: my infant universe, everything I learnt, the planes I sketched bombing Barcelona, my education in Catalan in a state school – all that had nothing to do with what was being forced on me now.... I remember these years with sadness, and I never fully understood why, in the space of a night, the 'good' became 'wicked' and the 'wicked', 'good'.[16]

Withdrawal: José Luis López Vázquez in *La prima Angélica*

Luis in *La prima Angélica* also remembers the war years with sadness. Now living in Barcelona in the 70s, he is a bachelor, the son of a Republican. He is played by José Luis López Vázquez, who endows Luis with a retiring manner, a receding hairline, a silence, and a slightly mechanised courtesy; sure signs of a withdrawal into self, a retreat into fantasy, hallucination or, as here, a melancholy attachment to memory, which Saura had already explored in *Peppermint frappé* and *El jardín de las delicias*, using the same actor to typify the post-war Spaniard. Saura returns in *La prima Angélica* to a cherished theme: the psychological legacy of the Civil War, what Erice calls Spaniards' 'exile within themselves'.

'In Huelva,' Saura said in 1979, 'I've just been given a homage, and one of the participants in the round table on cinema and literature . . . said that cinema was incapable of introspection. I disagree totally. A close-up of a face, with some antecedent, in a known context, can be as expressive, as profound, as tremendous and dramatic as five pages of literature explaining the state of mind of a character.'[17] A comparison between Saura's script and film does suggest that not all the uses of facial expression for psychological insight come off. With López Vázquez playing the character as a boy, gesture is often used to establish whether we are watching Luis as a boy or as a middle-aged man. Saura is caught in something of a double-take in this film: how can an actor express his sentiments externally when his personality – in terms of outward appearance at least – is so inexpressive? López Vázquez's acting achievement as the adult Luis is not so much to express a personality – the middle-aged Luis has the expressivity of a sphinx – as to suggest its destruction, in comparison with the spontaneity given to Luis as a bouncy and rather pugnacious pup of a boy.

Saura gains much of his insight in *La prima Angélica* by finding physical correlatives for a mental process. So Luis returns to his memories of the past when he goes back to Segovia, where he spent the Civil War with his Nationalist in-laws. He finds an aged and doting aunt and his cousin Angélica, once his childhood sweetheart, all pigtails and coquetry, now married, middle-aged, and mother of another Angélica who, bar the absence of plaits, is her mother's image thirty-seven years before. Luis' memories come flooding back: the night that war broke out, and Angélica's Falangist father paced round the living-room sweating like a pig, thinking that Segovia had fallen to the socialist militia, terrified at a bang on the door, believing (quite wrongly) that the militia has come to drag him off to a death in some lonely olive grove; young Angélica asking Luis what his daddy has done because granny says that when the Nationalists get to Madrid perhaps they'll shoot him.

'The power of his memories is so great,' Saura has said about Luis, 'that they end up by destroying the character.'[18] When Angélica (mother) makes a pass at him, he can only reply with tender pity, never passion. The last memory of the film has Angélica's father whipping Luis. He kneels cringing in a foetal position, a physical symbol of an arrested emotional growth which means that even thirty-seven years later Luis is still best able to relate to Angélica when she behaves like a child, or with Angélica the daughter who is a child. Given Luis' emotional sclerosis, the breezy tune accompanying the scenes hides a mordant irony in its title and theme, 'Change it all'. *La prima Angélica* emerges as the most sharply ironic of Saura's films. Luis comes to Segovia for a literal rehabilitation: to deposit the remains of his long-dead mother in the family vault. But his attempt to rehabilitate past memories proves far more difficult. When Luis finally leaves Segovia, it is more like a flight.

Saura's interests in *La prima Angélica* were similar to Erice's in *The Spirit of the Beehive*: what forces create a sense of identity, and how do these forces operate? Saura plays off an external influence – history – against an internal mechanism – memory. The key to the film's structure comes from a Valle-Inclán observation: 'Things are not as we see them, but as we remember them.'[19] To Saura, total recall is impossible: 'One day I looked in the mirror and said, My goodness, what did I look like as a child? I can't remember myself as a child in the mirror. I have photographs, but when I look at them I feel it's someone I don't know. ... That was one of the fundamental ideas that made this film – that you can't see yourself as a child.'[20] The scenes set in the past in *La prima Angélica* are not flashbacks to the past as it was but recollections of the past remembered. Luis constructs his own physical identity, and probably characteristics in the past, from his present appearance and desires. People met in Segovia also double as characters in the past; the most significant repetition is actor Fernando Delgado, who plays both Angélica's adulterous husband and her Falangist father.

Saura's abolition of the flashback was a fertile move towards portraying consciousness as an ambivalent flux of memory, fantasy, dream and sensation. In a crucial scene, for example, Luis and Angélica the mother climb out on to a roof overlooking Segovia. 'This is for kids,' Angélica says, perhaps inviting Luis to treat her as he did when they were child sweethearts. They sit down, and she snuggles up to him. An old convent bell rings, a reminder of the mellow passage of time. Luis remembers (and we hear) Imperio Argentina's wartime melody 'Rocío'. Looking towards Angélica, he feels (but does not yet see literally) the girl in the woman. Luis and Angélica kiss in the present but are interrupted by Fernando Delgado's voice calling 'Luis!' The tone is friendly, so it's probably Delgado as the husband. Nearly caught in a compromising position, Luis recollects (and we see) a similar occasion years before when Angélica's father caught the two on the same roof. In all other memories Angélica in 1936 is played by Ma. Clara Fernández de Loaysa, who also acts Angélica the daughter in 1973. For the first time in a recollection, Angélica assumes the appearance of Angélica the mother, played by Lina Canalejas, who frowns in childlike fear when she hears Fernando Delgado's voice. The possibility of a mature relationship with Angélica the mother – a relationship too mature, too compromising, too adulterous for Luis to handle – seems to be imposing itself upon Luis' memory of the past. In a typical Saura paradox, Luis kisses the girl in the woman in the present and can't help picturing the woman in the girl he remembers in the past. Luis' only emotional loophole, his idealised relationship with Angélica in 1936, seems to be closing. Neither remembered past nor present offers any promise to Luis; he leaves Segovia.

In Luis' case, memories of the past doom the present and fears from the present doom memories of the past. The Freudian model of suffering is used in Saura's films, as by Erice, as a rich metaphor for Spain's collective post-war psychology and, at least by implication, for its political development. Memories from the war, Marcel Oms suggests, are analogous to a 'primal scene' suppressed in Luis' consciousness. Repression (here emotional but in general political) leads to unrealised individuals. The problem in Luis' case is liberation from the father figure. Once more there is an obvious parallel in the subordination of Spaniards to years of patriarchal authoritarianism. Liberation and psychic health is gained by emotional independence, by the individual's formation of his own sexual relations which distance him from his parents. Political 'health' similarly derives from the individual's free choice of association without external control.

The broad parallels between models of psychic and political development allow many Spanish films about 'growing up' or parent/child relations to be interpreted as political allegories. This is one reason why many foreign spectators sense that there is more to Spanish films, especially historical dramas, than first meets the eye. There are three questions to ask. Does the Spanish film as a whole sustain, or indeed encourage, reading psychological detail as historical comment? Secondly, what sort of history can the film enlighten? The history of family structures under Franco? The regime as a dogmatic patriarch? Lastly, do the historical overtones offer any genuine new enlightenment about Spanish history or just confirm tired platitudes? In *La prima Angélica*, for example, Luis' attempt to achieve emotional maturity is frustrated when he and Angélica try to cycle to Madrid. They are stopped at the Nationalist line – the symbolic limit of Angélica's father's domain – and returned home, where Luis is whipped into a foetal position. Authoritarianism stunts emotional/political growth: but we knew that before. Angélica's development is, in terms of a more general psychology and with regard to Spanish history, as true and perhaps more interesting. Angélica has also lost that piquant spontaneity of youth, which is hardly surprising given her upbringing in the narrow confines of a staunchly Francoist family. And yet, according to Luis' way of seeing things at least, she has ended up marrying a man rather like her father. We know from photographs that the similarity is not physically exact; but there is some continuity in behaviour. Angélica's marriage, if the analogy holds, responded to a suppressed incestual desire. The political analogy here is more interesting: the most difficult suppression to root out is that which is both desired and not even seen as limiting one's freedom. The gallery of secondary characters in *La prima Angélica* who are slaves of their own complacency develops this implication into a major sub-theme of the film.

Such ruminations did not interest all of *La prima Angélica*'s first audiences. A hardening Right took immense exception to the film: to the Falangist's funk on the outbreak of war; to his return from the front with his arm strapped up at the level of a fascist salute; to his modern equivalent being put down as a dolt, an adulterer, and a land speculator. 'Only the Falangists made a stand in those times when Communist terror was in the streets of Spain,' proclaimed the Oviedo paper *Región*. 'Saura can't know that because he's too young. And that's his tragedy: to be young and stupid at the same time.' Days later the same writer was to go further: 'I've been phoned. People have said: "You should have given Saura a good beating for his bad intentions." Well I won't! That would be like killing maggots with

La prima Angélica: memories of the Civil War

shellfire. You don't even tread on maggots, because it's not worth dirtying the soles of your shoes.'[21]

Opposition went beyond words, however. In May 1974 four right-wing youths attempted to steal the film from a Madrid cinema. In July, a bomb explosion set fire to the Balmes cinema where *La prima Angélica* was having its Barcelona run. The incidents formed part of a ragged attempt by right-wing elements to destabilise the *apertura*. In May 1974 the leader of the ultra-right Fuerza Nueva, Blas Pinar, slated infiltrators in the Arias government as 'dwarfs' and declared the Civil War not yet over. Yet the Right lacked bite. At a time of great uncertainty about Spain's future or the regime's true intentions, the government's refusal to withdraw *La prima Angélica* from circulation, or censor its offending sequences, marked a significant defeat for the Right. Its voice had been ignored, and the censorship ceiling had gone up a few flights.

With *La prima Angélica*, an opposition cinema of distinctly non-Francoist traditions came out into the open. 'The Civil War has been a disaster,' Saura told critic Enrique Brasó, 'the post-war too: the rooting of the Spanish culture in its past has stopped dead. This past is not the glorious, idealised past that we've been taught, but a fantastic, critical, and realist past, a realism which often goes beyond a strict acceptance of the term.'[22] Saura's partnership with Azcona was a conscious attempt to resurrect such an authentic Spanish style of critical realism by means of satirical distortions based on psychodrama (*El jardín de las delicias*), role-play (*Ana y los lobos*) or a subjective memory (*La prima Angélica*).

Though not the first Spanish film shot from the point of view of the losing side in the Civil War (Julio Pérez Perucha gives that distinction to Ferreri's *Los chicos*, made in 1959), *La prima Angélica* appeals to pre-Franco Republican traditions. Imperio Argentina, though she supported the Nationalists in 1936, was the star of the cinema in the Republic. Luis' parents were Republicans, and he, even as a young boy, very consciously a Republican's son. Luis also talks of the poet Antonio Machado (1875–1939). The reference in fact splits Angélica's family along a division mirrored in 1974 at a national level: the cultured (the Angélicas, Luis/liberal Spain), the uncultured (Angélica's husband Anselmo/the apathetic majority). The mention of Machado is hardly casual on Saura's part; it is tantamount to an admission of influence and allegiance. Machado wrote and lectured in the Republican cause, and died an exile having crossed the border to France already ill one bitter January night in 1939. In his poetry Machado moved from deep meditations on time and memory where the poet seeks to recuperate a past joy (*Soledades*) towards a more strident

La prima Angélica: rooting out the past

91

criticism in *Campos de Castilla* of Castillian culture, written in Soria, a town on the same austere, windy plateau which Luis contemplates at the beginning of *La prima Angélica*. The influence on Saura also extends to what many regard as Machado's greatest poetry, written on the death of his seventeen-year-old wife. Here is the same nagging, corrosive melancholy as in many of Saura's films, as the thread linking the lover in the past and the poet in the grey present is found to be subtly, and irreparably, broken.

'Historical events,' Querejeta said at the time of *La prima Angélica*'s release, 'do not have just one reading, just one meaning, and I think it's permissible, convenient, positive, for them to be contemplated from different perspectives.'[23] *La prima Angélica* is not only Republican but also pointedly democratic. It satirises the mental paralysis of the fascist Falange by presenting a ridiculous physical equivalent in the plaster-cast scene. Saura also notably abandons an omniscient and authoritarian viewpoint to identify with a figure whose recollection of the past will be one version among many. The only way characters reconstruct the past with any kind of certainty is by pooling their memories, or by technical aids, such as Angélica's photographs, to achieve a more balanced account by collaboration.

The Spanish opposition, however disunited and amorphous in 1974, was equally interested in using *La prima Angélica* as a war cry. 'I don't mind if things get political,' Querejeta said after the attempted theft of the film.[24] From 1974 and throughout the transition, such film-makers acquired a clear political function: to produce films of firm democratic credentials and demonstrate by their box-office that such films – and the values they promoted – had a massive following in Spain. *La prima Angélica* had taken 25 million pesetas by September 1974, becoming one of the top-selling films of the year. 'Given the incidents,' Diego Galán writes in his account of the film and its effects, 'Saura's film is carrying out a kind of referendum at least on some cultural aspects of national life.'[25] And films of political consequence were shown to have commercial clout. Politically and industrially, *La prima Angélica* was a film for change.

Running out of dope

'My distinguished colleagues were smoking the hashish of liberalisation and *apertura*.'

Journalist Emilio Romero, on early 1974.[26]

In a suggestive essay, 'The Children of Franco', Marsha Kinder examines films by Erice, Saura, Borau, Chávarri, Armiñan, and Gutiérrez Aragón. In them she finds 'precocious children who are both murderous monsters and poignant victims, and the stunted childlike adults who are obsessed with distorted visions of the past, both placed in the social context of a divided family that is fraught with sexual deviations and that functions as a microcosm for the corrupt state.'[27] 'Growing up' is a central concern for all these film-makers. None sees the process as easy. It entails withdrawal from a horrific reality (*The Spirit of the Beehive*), a capitulation to normality (*Cría Cuervos*), confrontation with authority (Borau's *Furtivos*), hesitant regeneration (Chávarri's *A un dios desconocido*), disillusion with the father figure (*Demonios en el jardín*).

'We film-makers of artistic ambitions are like winter flowers in the pastures of Ozores, Lazaga, etc.,' Gutiérrez Aragón once remarked.[28] While possibly acknowledging the political analogues of 'growing up', most Spanish film-makers sought to treat the tentative liberalisation of 1974 at a far more expedient level: maturity meant sexual initiation or acquiring sexual knowledge. *El amor del capitán Brando* ('The Love of Captain Brando', Jaime de Armiñán, 1974) is a case in point.[29] There is more than an echo here of *The Spirit of the Beehive*. Like Ana in that film, the protagonist Juan lives in the Spain of the oppressive provinces, this time a country village in the early 70s. A similar lack of a strong father-figure pushes Juan into personal myth. But Juan's fictional creation, Captain Brando, is not only a figure of authority (as the monster was for Ana) but also a fantasy *alter ego* for a boy in his early adolescence. Brando's squaw, for whom he confesses an undying and impossible passion, is modelled on Juan's pretty schoolteacher, Aurora. She in turn is fascinated by an ex-Republican, Fernando, who has returned from exile and still lives in the past. Aurora, who needs an escape from the constricting village environment, is willing to be in Juan's fantasies but unwilling to be his girlfriend. She is obviously too old for Juan, and Fernando says he is too old for her. So Juan ends up discovering a father-figure in Fernando and a kind of older sister in Aurora: these are the 'good' family figures which any child needs to establish so as to grow. Armiñan's film ends with Juan's imaginary execution of Captain Brando. The outlaw Juan-Brando has become a healthy part of society.

The novelty of *El amor del capitán Brando* was that it was not only about changes but also for change. It hints, with a censor-demanded diffidence, at the extraordinary backwardness of provincial Spain. A schoolmistress tells her pupils that the Roman aqueduct of Segovia was built by religious miracle; the local mayor is coarse, full of empty neo-falangist platitudes. The film's opening shots do not so much establish social environment as announce the transgression of former moral norms for the cinema – an 'opening'. Night. The light goes on in an upstairs window, whose curtains have been left open. As Aurora (Ana Belén) moves across the window, she takes off her shirt and we have a brief glimpse, in long shot, of her breasts. The first few scenes put Spanish audiences firmly in their place, suggesting that they were like children badly in need of sexual education. The view of

93

Aurora is a subjective shot seen through the eyes of some village urchins: voyeurs hiding in the dark. Next day an indignant Aurora decides it is time for her pupils (who include the voyeurs) to have a sex-lesson. She makes them draw the figures of a naked man and woman on the blackboard; but her pupils can't get any further than naive details. Armiñan's allegorical comments on Spanish immaturity were apposite: *atraso*, backwardness, was still a source of embarrassment for many young Spaniards at the time.

The film's emphasis on contemporary reference echoes a problem common to any cinema at a time when history upstages fiction: the inclusion of scenes, comments or characters justified more by Spanish history than by the dramatic reality of the film itself. Here, for example, former exile Fernando leaves his parents' grave and meets an old woman he has not seen for thirty-five years. Their brief, elliptical conversation includes a passing reference to the Civil War ('Do you remember my boyfriend? Too many people died in the war.'). With so many significant allusions to make, there is little time for detailed construction of character. While so many filmmakers during the transition period showed their characters trying to assert their individuality in a constrictive environment, characterisation here is hardly individualised at all. Aurora, for instance, is a *progre*, a Spaniard who favours progress: a character whose naturalness (not bothering to close her windows when she undresses) runs up against the starched provincialism of the village. The contrast runs through the film. The final, brief affair of old Republican and young *progre* is a vaunted substitution of sexual act for voyeurism, a coupling of old and new democratic traditions clearly distinct from the fusty village status quo.

Armiñan and Saura's films stand out at a time of near bankruptcy for innovative Spanish film-making. Taking its title from the 12 February 1974 speech by Arias, Bodegas' *Los nuevos españoles* (1974) wrote off modernity, which it represented as the totalitarian subjection not of citizen by state but of Spanish worker by American multinational. In another 'Third Way' film, Antonio Drove's *Tocata y fuga de Lolita* ('Lolita's Toccata and Fugue', 1974), Lolita leaves home to live with her boyfriend just as her father is standing for the Francoist parliament as a respectable, if liberal, head of family. But her rebellion is short-lived. She soon returns to her father, who is duly elected and then starts an affair with her flatmate; her boyfriend goes off to do military service. Drove, one of Spain's most talented film-makers, sought to steer his material away from contemporary reflection, and stylised the film along the lines of American comedy. The results are unequal.

Another Drove film, *Mi mujer es decente dentro de lo que cabe* ('My Wife is Decent as far as that's possible', 1974), was a disappointment. According to statistics, there were half a million prostitutes working in Spain in 1974,[30] a consequence of a strict sexual morality which has left Spanish men with a sexual dilemma: a woman who is decent cannot be sexually attractive because a woman who is sexually attractive is not socially decent. But Drove's film treats this paradox with a sexist complacency, despite a noble attempt to sabotage his script, 'making the actors speak . . . panting or with their heads down, hoping that way the dialogue wouldn't be heard'.[31]

The box-office revelation of *La prima Angélica* would take years to work through the industry. Meanwhile the bane of an adventurous film-maker in Spain was distribution. Since the American film industry's boycott of Spanish imports between 1955 and 1958, distribution in Spain had effectively become an appendage of American multinationals, whose films were distributed either through subsidiary companies or through exclusive rights agreements. With the complacent connivance of a supposedly nationalist regime, foreign capital was allowed to call the shots in the Spanish cinema. Pre-production deals allowed the distributors to dictate terms to Spanish producers, whose less profitable films they were required to buy by law (the 4:1 distribution quota) but could release in the worst cinemas at the most unpopular times of the year. Even if better Spanish films were making more money in 1974, the distribution network largely did not care. All Spanish films risked the fate of *Hay que matar a B*. ('B. Must Die', José Luis Borau, 1973), released in the summer of 1975 with very little publicity when most of Madrid was on holiday. Borau's film had picked up national awards. Debuts such as Chávarri's *Los viajes escolares* ('School Trips', 1974) or Herralde's accomplished film-within-a-film *La muerte del escorpión* ('The Death of the Scorpion', 1975) took, respectively, two years and eighteen months to be released.

Industrial indifference was matched by continuing government opposition. By late 1974 the '12 February spirit' was a phantom at best. It had established an uneasy press freedom and the right of a moderate opposition to exist in Spain, but little else. Cabanillas was sacked in October 1974 because of alleged press pornography. Arias' Statute of Associations in December 1974 still only allowed for groupings within the Movement, so excluding the whole of the democratic opposition. But the anti-Francoist forces were in no position to press for more. Mutual suspicions, dogmatism and internal jockeying for power meant that the Spanish Left was to greet Franco's death as divided as they had his rebellion nearly forty years earlier. The Socialists, the most viable opposition party, had a dynamic new leader by 1974 in Felipe González, but only 2,000 members in Spain.

'We can't take a leap in the dark,' Under-Secretary for the Cinema Rogelio Díez protested after banning eighteen of the films rescued for censorial revision in 1974. By the end of 1974 the Administration had fallen back to pussy-footing. One test case was the 'religious' cinema which appeared that year. Church–state relations deteriorated drastically in Franco's last years; so much so that in September 1971 a clear majority at the first joint assembly of bishops and priests approved a resolution declaring that 'we humbly recognise and regret the fact that we did not play our true role as ministers of reconciliation among our people when they were divided by a fratricidal civil war'. The push for reconciliation made the liberal Archbishop of Madrid and President of the Episcopal Conference, Cardinal Tarancon, the *bête noire* of the ultra-right. Some residual fascists thought he should be shot.

Here then was an excellent opportunity for a revisionist cinema which re-examined the role of the Spanish church under Franco. The Church might have accepted such films; but the government it was at odds with certainly did not. *La regenta* ('The Regent', Gonzalo Suárez), *Pepita Jiménez* (Rafael Moreno Alba), and *Tormento* ('Torment', Pedro Olea) all broke new ground in 1974 by showing priests who break their vows of celibacy. But all three derived from classic nineteenth-century novels (by Leopoldo Alas, Juan Valera, and Benito Galdós) and the censor proscribed hints of contemporaneity.

Tormento is the most galling case, since the Galdós original had intriguing possibilities as an allegory for the 1970s. In book and film a maid (the oppressed Spaniard?) is courted by a Spanish nabob back from the Americas (liberal capitalism?), despite the opposition of the nabob's staid and reactionary Catholic cousins (Francoist petit-bourgeoisie?) and the maid's past affair with a priest (Spain's compromising past endangering its capacity for change?). Yet these parallels are hardly exploited, and Galdós' acute attack on middle-class hypocrisy and his sensitivity to social change is diluted into an anecdotal period piece, 'a distant yellow daguerrotype where everything is more beautiful, more intense, and comforting'.[32]

'I don't believe in the *apertura*,' a disillusioned Pedro Olea told *Fotogramas* in November 1974. 'Current problems can't be treated in Spain. *Tormento* was made because it was set in the past. One of the censor's suggestions – one of those which never get on to official Ministry notepaper – was not to make the story contemporary.'[33] In February 1975 the government announced another way of deflecting criticism, when it passed New Norms for Censorship. They were 'very similar to the last lot', Carlos Saura complained. There was one novelty: Item 9 admitted 'the presentation of the nude body' but only, it added, 'if the intention is not to arouse the passions of the normal spectator'. The *apertura* had been sidetracked into a *destape* – an 'opening' became an 'uncovering'. Or, as *Posible* deftly put it: 'Sex, yes; politics, no.' Film-makers were allowed to show – and still compelled to condemn – 'prostitution, sexual perversions, adultery and illicit sexual relations'. The result, as Fernando Méndez Leite observes, was a spate of 'hybrid products, pure smut for the most part, which justified what they had shown with singular complacency during ninety minutes by five minutes of condemnation at the end.'[34]

1975: Borau and *Poachers*

In the summer of 1974, the newly formed Democratic Junta of the Communist Party, the independent Socialists under Tierno Galván, and the Workers' Commissions began to call for a 'democratic break' (*ruptura*) as the only road forward to democracy. In October 1974, González committed his Socialist Party to the same formula. In the spring of 1975, Catalan leaders in Barcelona also demanded a full democracy. Both Fraga, now Ambassador in London, and the *Tácito* group of reformists disowned Arias' Statute of Associations to campaign for a 'democratic evolution' of the regime from within. Arias tried to unravel a Gordian knot. How could he create a democracy which would satisfy the opposition and still be Francoist? 'Oligarchy for the people!' the comic Máximo cried, summing up the problem. Arias had no answer; and in the brutal year of 1975 his ingrained Francoist loyalties were to tell.

Opposition to Arias had an intriguing parallel in the Spanish cinema. There an opposition – which, like its political counterpart, was increasingly vocal but for the most part impotent – clamoured for a democratic cinema and chided a reticent industry for still refusing to uncover the dirt beneath the supposedly spotless Francoist carpets. 'Where,' film critic Fernando Lara was to ask later, 'are the films on ... the revival of the nationalities, or the corruption during the dictatorship, or the five executed in 1975, or torture?'[35] Ironically perhaps, it took longer to change a film industry than a regime. An essential continuity in the administration's economic policy for the film industry gives Spanish cinema a sameness in production standards which political change tends to belie. Until the very late 70s 'art' films were made despite the Spanish industry, not because of it.

The director who was to go most against the grain in 1975 was José Luis Borau. To apply a description of Pablo Neruda, Borau is a 'motionless traveller'. His wide-angled vision of industrial possibilities has led to a co-production with Sweden (*La Sabina*, 1979), to a film in the United States (*Río abajo/On the Line*, 1984), to fund-raising in Peru and a death threat from a general, and to becoming Spain's most significant 'independent' producer after Querejeta in the cultural scrubland of the early 70s. Hardly surprising for such a peripatetic, Borau's main theme, since the emergence of a distinctive creative voice with *Hay que matar a B.*, has been the bases of allegiance, whether to a cause, a country, or a person. *Furtivos* ('Poachers', 1975) in this sense is something of a hiatus in Borau's career.

Marsha Kinder relates Borau's 'humanistic realism' that focuses on 'facts, actions, and people' to Renoir and Rossellini: Borau 'avoids excessive camera movement, beautiful photography, non-diegetic music, clever dialogue, and scenes designed to reveal character.'[36] Yet Borau's aim is to create a reality, not to use the camera 'like the veil of Veronica pressed to the face of human suffering' as Bazin described the realist mission of film.

Limited perspectives: José Luis López Vázquez as the 'spinster' in *Mi querida señorita*

Borau's style model is the American cinema. 'I can't stand films where nothing happens in the image, and everything in the plot. American cinema achieves a sense of action even in situations where there's no physical movement at all.' At his best, Borau achieves images of far greater ambition and tautness than any other director in Spain.

A key factor with Borau has been his age. Turning thirty by the time he graduated from the EOC, he was about the oldest 'young director' in Spain. Borau's first films were a loving pastiche of the Western, *Brandy, el sheriff de Losatumba* (1964), and 'a brooding psychological thriller set in an unusual and almost magic Madrid',[37] *Crimen de doble filo* ('Double-edged Murder', 1965). Two films were enough for Borau to realise that artistic freedoms entailed far greater economic independence. In 1967, and while a teacher at the EOC, Borau founded his own production company, El Imán, to finance the projects of his ex-students. Its first feature, Ivan Zulueta's *Un, dos, tres ... al escondite inglés* ('Hide and Seek', 1969), was a perhaps over-ambitious musical satire of the gaudy psychodelia, outdated modernity and powerful commercial interests behind the Spanish pop world.

Mi querida señorita ('My Dearest Señorita', Jaime de Armiñan, 1972) proved more controlled. A parody of the 'sexy Spanish comedy', its protagonist changes not only environment but also sex: a frumpy old maid in her forties with an inexplicable gift for football suddenly becomes a cowed

98

bachelor looking for a job in the city. In an eloquent twist the protagonist's new manhood allows for good-humoured but incisive commentary on the exceptionally limited perspectives open to Spanish women. As a spinster the protagonist does 'spinstery' things, like sit at home alone. As a man, the protagonist's former life as a spinster leaves him virtually unemployable and ludicrously bereft of male worldly confidence. With or without a sex-change, the capacity for change of women in a changing Spain seems decidedly limited. The bachelor, for example, forms a relationship with his ex-maid whose life and work as a waitress still carry the mental habits of a life in service. At the end of the film the ex-maid calls her ex-mistress 'señorita'. Perhaps she knows his identity. Or perhaps she equates her ex-mistress with the bachelor because she regards him, as the man she will marry, as her new master. Servitude or solitude emerge as the only two options confronting Spanish women.

The endearing thing about Brandy was that he was a rotten cowboy and a thoroughly nice guy; the two things are probably related. In *Hay que matar a B.*, protagonist Pal's downfall is to try to be a hero. He lives in an archetypal banana republic. Chaos reigns; strikes and demonstrations demand the return from exile of a charismatic politician, B. An immigrant, Pal blacklegs the strike, driving lorries to get money to return to his native Hungary. Pickets wreck his lorry, he is tempted into a blackmail plot, and falls in love with the mistress of his victim. But she is a set-up, the plot backfires, and an implicated Pal is forced by government agents, who have kept an eye on him because of his superb marksmanship, to assassinate B.

Critical reaction to Borau's film was that it was a not particularly original variation on the theme of an individual victimised by the secret state. Yet it was designed to be exactly the opposite. Scripted in 1966 by Borau and Drove, *Hay que matar a B.* reflects a common concern of Spanish cinema in the 60s: a call for collective action, for a new political consciousness in self-satisfied Spaniards. The butt of the film's criticism, Drove has explained, is the adventurer of such films as Anthony Mann's *The Far Country* and King Vidor's *Man Without a Star*. A second influence was a Borges poem, 'Labyrinth', which begins, 'There will be no door. You are inside. And the fortress covers the universe.'[38] Borau's direction insists on Drove's points. In a nice detail, Pal's naive nationalism, seen in his belief that things will be better in his native land, is reflected in the enthusiasm he shows for collecting coloured stickers of national flags. In a more obvious detail, as a crowd moves up a road towards a demonstration Pal and the girl, self-styled romantic outcasts, push their way in the other direction to find a hideaway where they can make love. Pal ignores the reality of his country, as he is ignorant of the fact that the girl is only faking her feelings for him. Yet the source of both private deception and public discontent is the same – the country's present political regime.

Hay que matar a B. was originally set in the Basque country, but the censor forced Borau to relocate the story in an unspecified Latin American state. For *Poachers*, the censor demanded forty cuts. Borau refused to make them. 'The director,' he wrote, 'will always be guilty if he makes a pact or renounces his rights and obligations.' For film reformists, 'Censorship is the first target.'[39] The censor prevaricated. 'Every time I get the tribunal to decide what they're going to do,' Borau complained, 'they suddenly want more information and there are further delays.' Borau then effectively took the issue to the country. Private projections to critics and intellectuals brought glowing reviews (as well as pointing the gap between press and cinema as regards censorship). 'Let us pretend,' *Fotogramas* announced, 'that *Poachers* has opened, although this is not the case. We will talk of this extraordinary Spanish film as though you could see it at your local cinema.' Even the patrician brows of the Spanish Academy were ruffled. 'I have heard,' wrote Julián Marías, 'that *Poachers* might be cut to pieces. That would be lamentable.'

The kinds of cut demanded included 'erotic scenes, swear words and authentic details, like the Civil Governor's use of his official car to go shooting.'[40] But the number of cuts demanded pointed up the relevance of *Poachers* to Spain of 1975. A ferret-faced mother lives with her downtrodden son in the heart of a forest. The mother is played by Lola Gaos, whose character name (Saturna) in Buñuel's *Tristana* reminded Borau of Goya's painting of Saturn devouring his children. Late in the film Martina, the mother, undresses her son and says mischievously, 'I can see your willy …' 'One supposes,' Borau comments, 'that every night this mother, like Saturn, devours her son.' The mother symbolises 'Spain itself, who wants her children only for herself, who loves, crushes, and devours them.'[41]

One day the son, Angel, goes down to the local market town to buy some traps and nooses. A girl, escaped from a reformatory, flirts with him; he buys her a dress to disguise her; she sleeps with him in the nearest hotel. Come home with me, he urges. Milagros, the girl, resists: 'You've done me a favour. I've done you one back. We're at peace.' Milagros' words (as everything else in *Poachers*)·are hardly casual. Already Borau's film has presented its principal thesis: politics, in the sense of the struggle for and use of power, is not the monopoly of states but found in ordinary, personal relations. Milagros has the power to please Angel; he has the power (sexually/economically) to cover her. The quality of *Poachers* is in fact its ability to produce metaphors for Spain's political systems without straining a story of love, sex and petty power play. Two initial metaphors stand out. The mutual benefits pointed to by Milagros reflect what has been thought a Spanish illness. 'Everything in Spain,' wrote Dionisio Ridruejo, 'a telephone, a business concession, a flat, the most insignificant bureaucratic favour, is obtained because you have a friend.'[42]

Licence to shoot: Borau as the Civil Governor in his own *Poachers*

The other metaphor, the film's title *Furtivos*, has two meanings, Borau has explained: 'illegal hunters or poachers, and also those who live their lives in a secretive way. Both meanings apply here – I wanted to show that under Franco, Spain was living a secret life. Virtually everyone in this film is a *furtivo*.'[43] Most critics took the furtive goings-on in the film to refer to contemporary corruption: the hush-hush export of Spanish capital to bank accounts in Switzerland; building speculation scandals such as the Sofico affair, where a company took hard-up Spaniards' life-savings and left them with half-finished holiday homes. 'Is this country,' asked Francisco Umbral in Barcelona's *La Vanguardia*, 'not full of poachers?'

The pay-off involved in poaching itself gave an equally incriminating meaning to Borau's film. A poacher's minor benefits distract his attention from a restrictive system which reserves its major benefits for the privileged few. So Angel is allowed to poach by his Civil Governor foster-brother and in return leads the Governor to the best game. But only the Governor (perhaps an assistant, but never Angel) is allowed to shoot the best stags in the forest. Poaching emerges as a brilliant political metaphor for the Francoist regime.

The political allegory soon widens. The Civil Governor, mid-forties, podgy, surrounded by yes-men, arrives for the open season. Neither his childishness nor his fecklessness inspires much confidence in Francoist officialdom. Milagros' tearaway boyfriend El Cuqui, for example, has just run rings round the Governor's forces. Once in the woods, the Governor breathes deep and remarks 'What peace!', the words echoing Franco's comparison of Spain to a 'peaceful forest'. By 1974 in fact Spain was experiencing more social unrest than at any time since the 40s. The incest, intrigue, murder and above all violence hidden beneath the surface of the woods in *Poachers* are a pointed retort to official Spanish rhetoric.

The kernel of *Poachers* shows a transition from a system of unequal benefits to a kind of freedom, and the different but equally inadequate attempts by the figures of authority – Martina and the Governor – to destroy this development. Angel brings Milagros home. Borau draws the political parallel: 'He has fallen in love and known a true woman and for a moment has enjoyed happiness, or something like it. . . . It's like when a man tastes liberty.'[44] Freedom for Angel is not an abstract right, but a concrete, humanising experience: 'a superior enslavement', as Mario Vargas Llosa described it, 'wherein he discovers sexual pleasure, exalted feelings, and even humour'.[45] In one scene Milagros, with childlike insouciance, offers to do a striptease for Angel in the middle of the forest. The scene is comic rather than erotic, as the censor maintained. The characters exchange pleasures freely, spontaneously.

Milagros still has one trade-off left. One day El Cuqui turns up to claim her. Surprised by the Governor's guards, he flees. Angel is enlisted to track the delinquent down, but Milagros persuades him to allow El Cuqui to escape; in return she will stay with Angel for ever. The poacher carries out his side of the bargain, only to discover on his return that Milagros has left. Next morning Angel shoots the magnificent 'Governor's stag', an instinctive destruction of the major local benefit in a system whose falseness Angel has brutally discovered. Events now move apace. Under arrest, Angel is forced by his foster-brother to become a Civil Guard. In town he runs into El Cuqui, who demands to know where Milagros is. The shadow of a suspicion crosses Angel's mind. Back home he finds Milagros' memento box still in its hiding place, and forces Martina to admit the girl's murder. After confessing in church, the mother is taken by Angel to the snowy woods. A shot, heard off-screen, sounds over the sierra.

Poachers emerges as a parable on repression and a critique of Francoist policies. The Governor's reaction to Angel's insubordination is either to ignore it, hurrying away to the city when he suspects his foster-brother of helping El Cuqui to escape, or to institutionalise it, as when he makes Angel a Civil Guard. Likewise in Spain at large the Francoist rearguard either passed off democratic demands as Communist subversion ('Everything,' Franco said in his last public appearance, 'is part of a masonic leftist conspiracy of the political class in collusion with Communist-terrorist

Poachers: the 'hard hand' of authority

subversion in the social sphere'[46]), or attempted to emasculate an opposition by allowing it to participate in an enlarged administration. The Governor changing Angel from poacher to guard proves as feckless as Arias' 'opening'.

To Borau, the most important scene in the film is the one when Angel pushes a crudely insinuating Martina away from his bed after she has told him that Milagros has left him. 'When a person has known liberty,' Borau comments, 'he cannot return to former oppression.' We suspect that Angel will go on poaching even as a guard.[47] More importantly, the irreversible experience of freedom makes Martina's policy of repression equally misguided. Her *mano dura* ('hard hand') tactics had plenty of contemporary advocates. Lieutenant General García Rebull promised to take his tanks 'wherever necessary', even into subversives' houses. *Poachers* reveals such ploys as leading to a bloody retaliation; Spanish history – murder and revenge in the Basque provinces, for example – bore this out with precision.

Poachers presents individual versions of widespread political practices. It is also one of the most tightly constructed of Spanish films. Dialogue is sparse, an expression of characters' immediate circumstance, not a signpost to their sentiments. Crucial actions occur off-camera, allowing other scenes to stand in for them: the violence presumed in Martina's murder of Milagros (which we never see) has a brutal equivalent in Martina battering a she-wolf to death with a hoe. The film is finely cut, favouring 'abbreviated' shots. 'It's hard for an image to be extended when its extension makes it less pure,' Borau commented. 'It's very hard for a character's scale or his actions to take on sufficient interest to warrant an extension of the shot, unless the actors or the director begin to do things for the *camera*. I hate that.'[48]

Besides political allegory, *Poachers* is also a fairy tale. 'Old fairy tales are still living,' Borau says, 'because they respond to the eternal needs of the soul. So in this film we include the elements of a very old tale – the primeval forest, the King (in one scene Martina even calls the Governor "my King"), the witch, the old mother, the two innocent children lost in the woods.'[49] As Marsha Kinder observes, the fairy tale Borau refers to is Hansel and Gretel, which ends in the murder of the witch 'who doubles for the bad stepmother. Thus the desire for matricide is at the centre of the tale.' But the fairy tale receives a sceptical recasting. Imagery in *Poachers* repeatedly lowers characters to the level of beasts: Milagros in her death and Martina in her ferociousness compare to the she-wolf which Angel traps. Camerawork (Luis Cuadrado) is sombre, a dark visual style related by Borau to 'the forest and the suffering. When characters are searching for something they are in the darkness.'[50] And, unlike in fairy tales, there is no happy final marriage or miraculous resurrection.

In tension in *Poachers* are two key axes of fiction: myth (here the fairy tale base) and history (the analogues with Spanish reality, and 'how things really are'). In the end only one cut was forced on the film: a shot of the Civil Government building in Segovia. Borau's film anticipated not only further freedoms for Spanish film, but also – in its contrast of myth and history – a central, provocative and thoroughly modern concern of the post-Franco cinema.

DICTATORSHIP TO DEMOCRACY, 1975–1977

'Parkinson's Disease ... Acute digestive ulcers ... massive haemorrhage ... Peritonitis ... Bronchial-pneumonia ... Cardiac arrest ...'[1] When Franco died in 1975 many Spaniards wondered whether his final medical report presaged the disintegration not only of his body but also of his regime. The forces for its survival seemed legion. Hardliners in the army like Iniesta Cano had said they would fight another Civil War if necessary, to ensure that 'Francoism continues after Franco, that it lasts for centuries'. Major institutions – the Cortes, the Council of the Realm – were Francoist strongholds. And Franco had groomed his successor as a Francoist monarch.

What observers had not reckoned for, and the average Spaniard could not know, was that King Juan Carlos backed democratic reform, and the Armed Forces as a whole, though vetoing *ruptura*, would not oppose 'whatever option which can be contained in the institutional order and its legitimate development'.[2] Since the Nationalist Airforce Commander, General Kindelan, had attempted to change Franco for a King in the 40s, the Caudillo had carefully depoliticised the Armed Forces. By 1975, riled by Spain's ignominious withdrawal from the Spanish Sahara, the Spanish military was more interested in technological overhaul than the incumbency of running a country.[3]

Juan Carlos' succession polarised public opinion. Right up to 1977 many older Spaniards remembered the chaos, divisions, demagoguery of the Republic and feared that with elections it would be like 1936 all over again.[4] But far more people – 37 per cent in 1972 – favoured democratic evolution than the 10 per cent behind traditional authoritarianism. Backed from below, Juan Carlos could impose reform from above. His stumbling-block was Arias. In April 1976 the King, ever the bluff soldier, told *Newsweek* that his Prime Minister was a 'complete disaster', 'the flag-bearer of the bunker', an 'immobilist' standing in the way of reform. Arias'

evements by summer had been nugatory. In a comedy of contradictions, for example, the Cortes passed a law in June 1976 recognising
political parties, but rejected a reform of the article in the Penal Code which
penalised party activities. Arias had to go. However ineffectual, his last
government had at least set important precedents. 'It established,' Charles
T. Powell comments, 'that the transition to democracy would be a process
directed by the successors of Franco, not their adversaries.' It encouraged
the opposition to abandon its call for *ruptura* and 'political francoism ...
began to recognise the inevitability of change and even to organise itself
politically for the new era.'[5]

The good news for democrats on 1 July 1976 was Arias' resignation; the
bad news, apparently, his successor, Adolfo Suárez. Young, handsome,
smooth, Suárez seemed more a Francoist *apparatchik* than the helmsman of
a democratic transition. He had made his way from origins in provincial
Avila to become a Civil Governor and head of Spanish Television, by acts of
legendary grovelling. Suárez, who was a new member of the Francoist
old-guard, was to spawn a prototype, the opportunely reformist Francoist,
complacently parodied by Rafael Gil's *De camisa vieja a chaqueta nueva*
('From an Old Shirt to a New Jacket', 1982). Suárez's policy was to start
with a few significant acts – a partial amnesty in July 1976; allowing a
Catalan national day – to announce his intention of transforming a 'social
reality ... however vague ... into a political conscience,' as he later put it,
by engineering a 'peaceful change to democracy'.[6]

Suárez had two political mountains to climb. In November 1976 he
managed to persuade the Francoist Cortes to approve a Law of Political
Reform which created a bicameral system based on universal suffrage. In
December, Suárez appealed, over the head of the opposition, to public
opinion via a national referendum which overwhelmingly supported democratic reform. 'A majority of the opposition,' Carr and Fusi record, 'recom-
mended abstention.'[7] Wildly at odds with consensus opinion, the opposition accepted a *ruptura negociada* ('negotiated break').

There was only one item of business still worth negotiation – the legalisation of the Communist Party, without which no democracy would be
complete. Many Spaniards would never forgive the Communists for their
cold-blooded sectarian murders – Trotsky's secretary Andrés Nin was just
one victim – or their implication in Civil War slaughters such as the
shooting of 2,400 Nationalists at Paracuellos del Jarama. Henry Kissinger
advised Arias not to legalise the Communists. Suárez did, but very cleverly.
Solos en la madrugada ('Alone in the Early Hours', José Luis Garci, 1978)
pictures the scene: Easter Saturday, 1977; a broadcaster sits like the last
man on earth in an empty Madrid and announces that the Communist
Party is now legal. Suárez's decision took Spaniards by surprise, but an
immediate military coup was impossible: the barracks were closed and

many generals outside Madrid. In a meeting a few days later the Armed Forces merely registered their absolute and abiding disgust at Suárez's action.

Spain's first general elections for forty years took place two months later.

The political boom

The transition to democracy had its victims. 'We do not feel,' declared the ultra-right *El Alcázar* in December 1976, 'that we have been defeated in the referendum. We did our duty and now we shall go on to the offensive.'[8] In January 1977 assassins shot down five labour lawyers in Madrid. The Communist Party and Workers' Commissions turned the funeral into a massive show of contained strength: 100,000 Spaniards attended. Suárez took note; and Juan Antonio Bardem made *Siete días de enero* ('Seven Days in January', 1978) whose title, with its echo of the 1963 Frankenheimer film, located the murders in a larger attempt at political takeover.

The interest of Bardem's film goes beyond its testimonial value. Life at the top had been brief for Bardem in the 50s: after *Muerte de un ciclista*, Doniol-Valcroze wrote in *Cahiers du cinéma* of the 'birth of Juan'; having seen *Sonatas*, Truffaut issued a brief valedictory: 'Bardem est mort.' Not dead, merely dormant, Bardem was to reply, and he insisted for the next fifteen years that only political liberty would allow true expression of his talents. Politics could best be pursued outside films; until censorship went he would make pot-boilers.

By 1976 Bardem's hour seemed to have come. From January NO-DO newsreels were no longer obligatory in film programmes; prior censorship ceased a month later. Taboos were disappearing. The test case, as ever, was the Civil War. The allusions to it in *El amor del capitán Brando* increase in number and directness in Armiñan's next film, *¡Jo, papa!* ('Oh, Daddy!', 1975), where Civil War memories are consigned slightly too easily to the baggage of reminiscence of an old war veteran who drags his far more forward-looking family round his old battle-grounds. *Pim, pam, pum ... fuego* ('Bang, Bang, You're Dead', Pedro Olea, 1975) recreated the sordid atmosphere of post-war Madrid; *Las largas vacaciones del 36* ('The Long Holidays of '36', Jaime Camino, released late 1975) was a wartime film, set on the Republican side, though the conflict remains for the most part out of sight, a distant thunder of guns. Finally, in one scene at least, *Retrato de familia* ('Family Portrait', 1976) actually becomes a war film as the hero takes to driving trucks behind the lines.

Bardem's *El poder del deseo* ('The Power of Desire', 1975) also suggested a return to more demanding film-making in its attempt, however raw, to equate emotional manipulation – the pulp plot has a guileless hero set up by a seductress to murder her uncle; she then abandons him – and various forms of political oppression, such as the media. But it was with *El puente*

('The Long Weekend', 1976) that Bardem claimed to have shed his shackles: 'Making it, I felt new, happy,' he said. 'Everything was easy, direct. I wanted to say some things and I said them.'[9]

On the whole Spanish film-makers adapted to their new freedoms only with difficulty. Several problems, or temptations, proved for the most part insurmountable. A first danger was to be too overt, too direct, after years of scheming obliqueness. In *El puente*, for example, Alfredo Landa, the protagonist of so many 'sexy Spanish comedies', plays a Madrid mechanic looking for a bit of fun during a long weekend. With a quick rebuff to his workmates' attempt at union action, he jumps on his motorbike and heads for the coast. He meets some foreign girls who lead him on and then zoom off in their sports car. He later encounters unemployed labourers, exploited farmers and toreros, immigrants far happier with Germany than with Spain, *progre* actors victimised by the police, the family of an imprisoned trade unionist. He drives back to Madrid a changed man. Unionism has won a new convert.

El puente is ideologically sound rather than artistically interesting. It was presumably meant to change the way people thought about Spain during the transition, but what it misses is a sense of spontaneity: little details whose lack of a larger meaning would signify a sense of things as they really are rather than a transparent embodiment of Bardem's political principles. *Siete días de enero* falls foul of a second obstacle: Spanish film-makers, for all their new freedom, still had to make concessions to commerce, and in doing so they often courted incoherence.[10] After Franco's death the key draw for audiences was still sex, with politics a close second. 'The colourful newspaper kiosks were flooded with images from a denied past – like La Pasionaria and Carillo – which appeared side by side with photographs of splendid females, defiant and a little surprised in their total nudity,' as Nissa Torrents remembers.[11] But by 1978 Spanish audiences were perhaps a little satiated with sex. The commercial clout in *Siete días de enero* is its subject – a political scandal – and its thriller format.

These two elements clash. On the one hand, the film delves into the assassins' background, which Bardem invented, for lack of information. One of them has a dimwitted girlfriend and a domineering mother who urges her son to be more like his father. The assassination becomes 'men's work', as the son puts it, a defence of the Crusade of 1936, and an attempt to destabilise Spain and justify a coup. The rest of the film is a detailed reconstruction of events. Bardem insists on techniques connoting objectivity: a historical summary, newsreel footage, a teleprinter. Such apparent neutrality is vitiated, however, by the manipulation for dramatic effect of both the murders themselves and the funeral of the victims. They are shown out of chronological order, the murder is seen in slow motion, and the funeral has an epic musical backing suggesting in its final crescendos a

Bardem shooting *Siete días de enero*

combination of sorrow and hope. The memory most Spaniards took away from the actual funeral, however, was its silence.

Curiously, the strongest impression left by *Siete días de enero* is not of its events but of its maker, and a resilient confidence in his convictions which makes Bardem, as the critic José Luis Guarner describes him, so *entrañable* ('loved for his courage').[12] Bardem's problems are perhaps endemic to any small film industry confronting large historical events. It desperately needs markets, so entertainment ploys sometimes overrule historical truth. It runs on minuscule budgets (£500,000 as a rough average for a current 'art' film), which means that part of history – the 'vast impersonal forces' – has to be forgotten, or caricatured in a battle which seems a skirmish (in the ambitious *La Conquista de Albania*, 'The Conquest of Albania', Alfonso Ungría, 1983), a decade reduced to a few representative scenes or key events (*La ciutat cremada*, 'The Burnt City', Antoni Ribas, 1976), or a demonstration which, in *Siete días de enero*, looks more like a street scuffle.

Liberalisation, it might seem, did little to advance Spanish film-making. But even if, paradoxically, the pressures of censorship did produce better films, this would of course be a poor justification for the censor's retention. In the case of Spanish film-making, moreover, it was the legacy of past restrictions, rather than the innate disadvantages of freedom, which bedevilled transition period films, in at least two ways.

Firstly, with greater freedom of expression, Spanish film-makers began to talk of the past. The relative ease of the transition belies the fact that most Spaniards only knew where Spain was going when it got there. Even in 1977 many observers seriously doubted Suárez's ability to carry off the general elections. Transition films drawing parallels between past and present found deep analysis difficult partly because they lacked present coordinates to work out their own historical conditions. Secondly, for the moment, mere recall served a therapeutic function. Interpretation could be left until later. So Spain's historical cinema became, as J. E. Monterde puts it in *Crónicas de la transición*, one of 'recognition' not 'cognition': 'It doesn't attempt reflection so much as adhesion.'[13] Olea's *Pim, pam, pum ...fuego* works with typical zeal. It charts the ill-fated romance of a man on the run with a cabaret star, burdened with a ruthlessly possessive protector who has made a fortune from black-marketeering. Discovering the affair, he kills both the lovers. Olea achieves a splendid period reconstruction in shabby blues and browns of the hunger, cold, rationing, war cripples and defeatism of Madrid in the 40s. The film does prompt reflection: most dramatically, the ready recourse of the extreme Right to violence when subtler means of persuasion failed. Yet the Manicheism of so much earlier cinema remains, only this time the hero is a Republican and the villain a Francoist black-marketeer. For an authentic political cinema, as Pere Portabella observes, 'It's not enough to make those who used to be bad now seem good.'[14]

Many Spanish films about and for change showed, in style and structure, very little change at all. Some directors, such as the 1983 Oscar winner José Luis Garci, perhaps could not change. His *Asignatura pendiente* ('Pending Exam', 1977) has been called 'the key film of the transition'.[15] The plot captured the frustrations of a whole generation of Spaniards. José and Elena were sweethearts as children. He was always talking, recounting films, telling jokes, Elena remembers. Now she meets him again in the heady days of late 1975. 'They've robbed us of so many things,' José muses in that verbose, maudlin spirit typical of Spaniards speaking out about the *posguerra*. 'The times you and I should have made love and never did, the books we should have read. . . . It's as if there's still something pending, like those exams left over from one course to the next.' Predictably perhaps, José and Elena begin an affair. Garci relates the romance to a generational experience by repeated reference to events or personalities which focused popular consciousness in Spain: Arias Navarro, Franco's death, the police killings of five demonstrators at Vitoria in 1976; the Workers' Commissions, the arrest of Communist intellectuals such as Bardem or the economist Tamames.

'Generational' films made up much of the Spanish cinema in the 70s. They were often criticised. The keys for the film's interpretation are outside the text, and those who miss the references will miss out on the film's sense. The generational experience of most influence in *Asignatura pendiente*, however, is Garci's typical Spanish adolescent experience of the local picture palace. Every day Garci travelled from a destitute Madrid to a heroic Hollywood.[16] Hardly surprisingly, the hallmark of Garci's style is the Hollywood master-shot: the establishing shot, perhaps an aerial view of Madrid with 'supermarket jingle' music, as his critics put it; followed by a staggered approach to the scene's subject through a series of intermediate shots. 'A filmic field, then the reverse-field with references,' Garci says, 'has all the magic of the American cinema.'

Asignatura pendiente is an uncomfortably cross-grained film. On the one hand, it is an accurate and at times sensitive portrait of a failed attempt to resurrect the past. As Elena explains, José sees her as a chance to return to a younger self when he dreamed of taking on the world. But as adults they fail to sustain the spontaneity of young love; their romance soon gathers the monotony of a marriage. Like Spain as a whole, they can never return to the past. On the other hand, as in all Garci's films, there is also a large element of wish fulfilment. Elena's description of José as a child fits Garci himself almost perfectly. But while Garci became a bank clerk, José becomes an important labour lawyer, whose only perceived client is a union activist seemingly modelled on the renowned Workers' Commission organiser Marcelino Camacho. José in fact is a latter-day Wild West hero. And when political protest picks up, it is clear, as Elena recognises, that his hour has come. In a contradiction typical of transition films, a 'progressive' act of political commitment is cast in the most conservative of 'classic' film traditions. Like John Wayne leaving his girl behind as he rides out to war, José rides off to rejoin the democratic advance guard. He never asks Elena to be part of the transition with him. She – like the Hollywood woman – remains historical flotsam, left in the wake of the history-makers.

Women and love
Relative freedom of speech by 1976 did, however, have its benefits. For the first time in thirty-five years, for example, film-makers could portray an adult love story in an adult manner. As critic César Santos Fontela has observed, film-makers under Franco either elided the sexual dimension of a relationship, or lamented the 'coldness, the impossibility of love in a repressive society ... erotic repression'.[17] In *Peppermint frappé*, for instance, Saura departs from the parti-pris that repression is itself erotic since it pushes the repressed – here a respectable doctor in provincial Cuenca – towards sexual fantasy. As ever, there has been no total escape from the past. Only two major Spanish films – *Opera prima* ('A Cousin at Opera'/ 'First Work', Fernando Trueba, 1979), and Borau's *Río abajo* (1984) – centre on a successful and protracted love relationship.

111

In the transition, environment still eclipses romance. Camus' *La joven casada* ('The Young Married Woman', 1975) explores, somewhat tentatively though with magnificent photography of the wild northern Spanish landscape, a marriage where sexual success contrasts with a social incompatibility stemming from class difference. Closed Catholic minds in Gonzalo Suárez's adaptation of Valle-Inclán, *Beatriz* (1976), cause a family to interpret the daughter's nascent sexual longings as a diabolical curse. *Emilia ... parada y fonda* ('Emilia ... Roadside Motel', Angelino Fons, 1976) is a delicate portrait of a young girl's attempt to escape from a constrictive, provincial world.

Other films marked a more decided step forward by laying claim to a feminine sexuality no longer subjected to a derogative caricature. *Caperucita y roja* ('Little and Red, Riding Hood', Luis Revenga and Aitor Goiricelaya, 1976), for example, was an unashamedly scabrous recasting of the original folk tale. With a hotchpotch narrative of songs, skits and gags, its directors sketch a satirical vision of a Spain peopled by police cretins, dwarf megalomaniacs, and a 'Juan Wolf' who is a cheery playboy stud wanted by the police as a public menace, wanted by almost everybody else — including Granny, Mother and Little Red Riding Hood — for his unslayable sexual prowess.

Equally iconoclastic was Eloy de la Iglesia's *La criatura* ('The Creature', 1977). Believing that the presentation of sexual perversion was one way to drag Spanish audiences out of their chronic stupor, this highly original director crossed *esperpento* and role-reversal in a portrayal of a woman's extreme reaction to marginalisation and what de la Iglesia saw as machisto 'phallocracy'. In the film's upper-class couple it is the husband who goes to church, the wife who has the money and remains sexually unsatisfied. But rather than with her politician husband — whose right-wing Alianza Nacional Española is clearly based on Manuel Fraga's Alianza Popular — she prefers to slake her idle desires in a sexual relation with her dog. She ends the film pregnant, and barking.

However tasteless, de la Iglesia's films avoided both the predictability and the elitism of much Spanish cinema. Pilar Miró's *La Petición* ('The Engagement Party', 1976) also shocked the censor. Miró is one of the very few woman directors in Spain. The first was the eclectic Rosario Pi, Catalan, producer, scriptwriter (of Fernando Delgado's *Doce hombres y una mujer*, 1934), who because of a limp rode to shoots on her horse. Pi's directorial debut, *El gato montés* ('The Wild Cat', 1935), was a considerable, if disjointed, achievement. Based on an operetta by the composer Penella, it was an *españolada* narrating the tragic fate of a gypsy girl torn between a bullfighter and her childhood companion, an outlawed bandit. Pi's direction varies radically from populist broad humour to an exultant high romanticism.

112

Pi's career reflected the increased freedoms and opportunities for women under the Republic. In 1936, for example, the Catalan Parliament approved a bill legalising abortion that was among the most advanced in Europe. With Franco, the position of women was seemingly set back centuries: if a woman wished to work in the 40s she had to obtain a certificate from her husband granting his permission. The demands of a growing service sector incorporated women into the workforce at an unprecedented rate from the 1960s. Nevertheless, the image of woman has not entirely evolved from the 40s role of home-maker and child-bearer.

Apart from actress Ana Mariscal, who made some competent films in the 50s and 60s, Pilar Miró and Josefina Molina were the only women directors to work under Franco, Molina making a rather lame Gothic horror story *Vera, un cuento cruel* ('Vera . . . A Cruel Story', 1973). 'The singular career of Pilar Miró,' Vicente Molina Foix comments, 'says a great deal about the familiar difficulties women face in the film industry.'[18] Even in 1985 Spanish Television is still regarded as one of the last bastions for democracy to storm. Miró recalls a long apprenticeship at TVE from 1960. A woman, it was claimed, distracted the men from their work, and the idea of a woman actually directing a film was thought quite simply 'a stupidity'.[19] A finally successful if fraught career as a director in the TVE drama department left various hostages to fortune: a television style; an adeptness for period reconstruction; a strong belief in the need for widespread reform in Spanish film-making practices. Miró's films also clearly reflect a backlash against a severe Catholic upbringing: a father who was a Lieutenant-Colonel in the Spanish army; education at a religious school — a youth not so different from Ana's in Saura's *Cría cuervos*. 'We have all been educated — but especially we women — in the principles of good intentions, good etiquette, good manners,' Josefina Molina said once. 'The result is a fascination with evil.'[20]

Miró's debut, *La petición*, combines personal and professional backgrounds. A free adaptation of a Zola short story, it is a highly ambiguous study of evil, embodied in the daughter of a wealthy and respectable family. Teresa's social position in a nineteenth-century world allows her to seize the initiative in an affair with her housekeeper's son. She uses the relationship to indulge her clearly sadistic impulses, and her lover dies in their violent love-making. Teresa enlists the aid of a deaf-mute gardener, and together they dispose of the corpse; Teresa then batters the mute to death with an oar. She returns to her engagement party to dance with her fiancé . . . with whom, one suspects, she will soon have, or has already started, a sadistic sexual relationship.

The censor banned *La petición* outright. But Miró refused to negotiate, and a press campaign with support from fellow directors ensured the film's final release. It was a mark of the remarkable change in Spain by 1976, as

113

well as the effective irrelevance of the 1975 censor Norms, that a film could be released which makes no apology for necrophilia (Teresa, consumed in her own passion, fails to notice her lover has died), sadism, murder, and miscellaneous amorality.

La petición responds to Miró's provocative stand on male/female contrasts: 'Women,' she has said, 'have a much greater capacity for evil than men.' Man is 'more stupid' in the sense of being 'more ingenuous'. So Teresa manipulates the men in all three of her relationships. And evil, as critics Hernández Les and Gato point out, becomes 'a kind of creative power informing ... human acts.'[21] Material in *La petición* is spread rather thin. Yet the film is distinctly unnerving. There is no ambivalence in actress Ana Belén's excellent performance as Teresa: she is evil, pure and simple. The sequence of the mute being battered to death is played out far beyond its dramatic needs to reveal an unequivocal emphasis on the infliction of pain. Equally subversive is the clash between blunt brutality and exquisite period detail. Miró has said that the formal orthodoxy and historical re-creation were designed to counterpoint the film's more modern psychology. But the period gloss generalises the heroine's surface charm into a social condition. What malevolence, what other intrigues, one is tempted to ask, lie hidden behind the fastidiously ordered surface of Miró's world? *El crimen de Cuenca* ('The Cuenca Crime', 1979) and *Hablamos esta noche* ('Let's Talk Tonight', 1982) were to answer this question, continuing Miró's disturbing portraits of abused power, and pain.

'D'un silenci': the Catalan cinema

'Jo vinc d'un silenci' ('I come from silence').

The Catalan protest singer, Raimon

Liberalisation was a pre-condition of the resurgence of a nationalist cinema in Catalonia, Galicia, the Basque country, Valencia and the Canaries. The earliest and most emotive revival came from Catalan film-makers.[22]

Much more than a geographical entity, Catalonia could claim a distinct language dating from at least the ninth century and an autonomous culture with a fine tradition in troubadours and a thirteenth-century religious writer of European stature, Raimon Llull. Backed by an independent legal system and their own political institutions, the medieval Catalans conquered Sardinia, Sicily, and even Athens. Associated in unequal partnership with the Crown of Castille from 1469, excluded from trade with the New World, Catalonia had its residual independence dismantled by Philip V in 1716 as a result of the same War of the Spanish Succession which gave Britain Gibraltar.

At its birth and again in the 1930s Catalonia took the lead in the Spanish cinema. An early industrial revolution had given Catalonia a propitious base for a film industry in Barcelona, which had the most significant working class and *grand bourgeoisie* in Spain. Exactly the same factor of industrial growth explains the emergence of Catalan nationalism in the late nineteenth century. 'There is no surer recipe,' Carr and Fusi write, 'for the mutation of regional tensions into full blown nationalism than the political dependence of a prosperous region with independent cultural traditions on a capital located in a poorer backward region.'[23] Apart from common origins, nationalism and cinema in Catalonia coincide in broadly contemporary gains. 1932, for example, saw Azaña grant Catalonia its Statute of Autonomy, and the new Catalan government – the Generalitat – responded to the overtures of film entrepreneur Francisco Elías by creating the Orphea studios where the first six Spanish talkies were shot in 1932. Cinema spoken in Catalan began a year later with the ribald *sainete*, *El fava d'en Ramonet* ('That Clodpole Ramonet', directed by Lluís Martí, Berlanga's uncle), and the Catalan version of *El café de la Marina* (Domènec Pruna d'Ozerans), a militant attempt at an indigenous cinema by the Catalan intelligentsia which was left virtually unfinished and unsung.

The four film studios in Barcelona and its 525 sound cinemas (as opposed to 147 in Central Spain) suggested a promising future for a Catalan cinema under the Republic. Regional autonomy was anathema to Franco. His regime tended at best to subsume Catalonia in a vague pan-Mediterranean culture, a concept encouraged by Franco's token and complying Catalan genius, Salvador Dalí. 'Catalonia is a country of artists,' Berlanga's Falangist minister observes in *Escopeta nacional*. 'Some people think it's just got industry. I love Barcelona's Mediterranean feel – Greece, Italy.' Franco's real-life ministers sometimes quite forgot their Catalan origins.

With the Catalans Franco attempted cultural extinction. Guidelines published in the first *Primer Plano* made 'Castillian dialogues' obligatory and explicitly proscribed nationalist 'dialects' save for bit-players. Yet as ever repression came as much from economic forces and the regime's self-interested *laissez faire* policies as from any direct intervention, such as the four import licences dangled before Paramount to entice it to move from Barcelona to Madrid in 1966. Such encouragement was hardly necessary. As Juan Antonio Pérez Millán observes in his 'La provincia española y el cine', dependency on home markets and state finance gave Spanish cinema an innate centrist and supra-regional slant.

The film image of Catalonia was very unflattering. Regional differences, Pérez Millán writes, were either denied or played up for commercial ends – in tourist backgrounds, folkloric pot-boilers and satires of provincial dunderheads. Or differences were admitted in analyses which failed to lay the blame for regional or rural deficiencies at the feet of the central powers. The Francoist concept of the Catalan – which many Spaniards in present-day Madrid would still accept – is illustrated by the yokel of *Agustina de*

Aragón, ludicrous in his bumpkin accent and one-track fidelity to the Catalan shrine of Montserrat, and humbled in his exemplary conversion to centrist thought by his dying gesture of kissing an image of the Virgin of Pilar, the patron saint of Saragossa. By no coincidence, the besieged city of Saragossa was used in the film to symbolise the fatherland Spain.

A nationalist renaissance began in the 1960s. In books in the vernacular, in a folk protest movement (the *nova cançó*), in a thriving publishing industry, cultural nationalism became a vital surrogate for banned political nationalism, a channel for Catalans' separatist desires. A few films focused on specifically Catalan problems such as the Barcelona bourgeoisie (*Brillante porvenir*, 'Brilliant Future', Vicente Aranda and Román Gubern, 1964), emigration (*La piel quemada*, 'Burnt Skin', Josep María Forn; and the more achieved look at second-generation disorientation, *El último sábado*, 'The Last Saturday', Pedro Balañá, 1967), industrial relations (Antoni Ribas' light comedy *Medias y calcetines*, 'Stockings and Socks', 1969). The Catalan version of *María Rosa* (Armando Moreno, 1965) was the first of six adaptations of films originally shot in Castillian. Limited distribution, uneven artistic standards, and the need for a literary antecedent limited the impact and number of Catalan-version films.

By the mid-1970s repression had taken its toll. Catalonia had only one film studio and accounted for only 11 per cent of Spanish production in 1976. But repression had only invigorated Catalan nationalism. No pressure group entered the transition with as clear an idea or as strong a consensus about what they wanted as the Catalans. Catalan demands, exemplified by the 75,000 people who demonstrated for amnesty and autonomy in Barcelona in February 1976, proved a powerful motor for change during the transition.

In the Civil War the Catalans had been barbaric 'red' fanatics duped by international Communism, sowing disorder and death. That at least was the official Francoist version. Jaime Camino's *Las largas vacaciones del 36* was the first film in the 70s to redress Spaniards' collective memory from a Catalan viewpoint. In exact contrast to Francoist myth, Camino's protagonists – the members of two Catalan families – are not 'reds' but fastidious champions of domestic order distinguished by that most humanising of traits, cowardice. Rather than support the Republic, the families prefer to remain in the relative seclusion of their holiday chalets in the hills around Barcelona, where the Nationalist rebellion was quickly quelled by anarchist militia and a loyal Civil Guard. One father is a shop-owner who commutes to work every day down the local funicular railway. The other is a doctor. The Republic needs him, but he puts his family, and biology experiments with guinea-pigs, before the possibility of work in a Barcelona war hospital. The war brings only minor changes at first. The maid insists on being called 'comrade', but remains the maid. The village electrician,

The intrusion of war: *Las largas vacaciones del 36*

who should be making repairs on a house, is found playing a trumpet at a revolutionary dance. But while the parents flee from reality their children follow an opposite course. The war at first means an extension of the summer holiday. The children abandon a Catholic education for a growing political morality. Games are a step towards understanding the reality of war. The gang leader, Quique, first plays at being a soldier, then acquires a real gun but still plays, then becomes a real soldier. A mild-mannered and starving Communist tutor begins the children's political education by explaining that poet Antonio Machado was a 'red'.

Most important for the children's conversion, and the film's political point, is their sentimental education. Quique's father dies fighting the Nationalists. That, and sexual baptism courtesy of the maid, produces Quique's commitment which he conveys to Alicia, his formal girlfriend. Quique then fights and dies. The other children are too young to follow, and anyway the Republic's cause is lost. At the end of the film the children bury their possessions, including Quique's revolver, 'for the next holidays'. These, Camino implies, were to be in 1975 when the film's children had become adults who were once more enjoying new liberties. The quiet message of *Las largas vacaciones* is that abstentionist apathy, however

117

comprehensible, must be abandoned for a growing sense of political responsibility if freedoms are to last more than a few high summers.

Camino's film had a mixed international reception, in part perhaps because the original script (by Camino and Gutiérrez Aragón) seems broken-backed. There is a suggestion that domestic ties weigh heavier than political ideology – a political lesson is cut short, for example, by the sound of a newborn baby crying. Yet the children's growth contradicts the film's scepticism. It was left to Gutiérrez Aragón's magnificent *Sonámbulos* ('Sleepwalkers', 1978) to develop fully and freely the theme of political commitment *and* family life as forces for alienation.

The drawback of Camino's film may be its attitude to the way film treats memory. Camino was born in 1936 and so lived the Spanish Civil War through family memories, used as the base for his film: 'I only had to close my eyes and compile the family memories.' Faithful to these memories, Camino overlooks the fact that memories are often not faithful. Pain, especially the hunger of the last years, is only remembered as a provenance for the ironic anecdote: one family sets out in a luxury car to a farm to buy food with a bracelet (wealth is sometimes meaningless); the family, tired of a diet of lentils, eagerly opens a food parcel from Switzerland to find it contains negligible delicacies and a large tin of lentils (even hunger, when you look back on it, had its funny moments).

In a sense *Las largas vacaciones* paid for its directness. With no veil of allegory to shield it, the film (which was shot at the end of 1975) could not touch, let alone tackle, such subjects as the actual fighting in the war. The censor sought in fact to decontextualise the film entirely. Cuts included a shot of the Republican flag, a banner saying 'Down with fascist killers', and a superb finale, a telephoto long shot of the Moorish cavalry from Franco's African Army approaching Barcelona, whose mixture of perceptible movement but no perceptible progress sums up the nightmarishly prolonged inevitability of the Republic's defeat.

Catalanism was to benefit from the slightly more liberal climate brought by Franco's death. In December 1975 seventy film professionals founded the Institut de Cinema Català (ICC), a limited company aimed at promoting Catalan cinema as 'the vehicle for the culture of a people', as a film industry, and as 'a cinema which fights for democracy both through its content and its means of production'.[24] Internal debate and lack of finance delayed ICC production until 1977. Meanwhile Francesc Bellmunt shot two pioneering documentaries, *La nova cançó* ('The "New Song"', 1976) and *Canet Rock* (1976).

Bellmunt, like Ribas and Forn, found his vocation with the Catalan film renaissance. His previous career was patchy – an episode in a four-part chronicle of 'terror across the centuries', *Pastel de sangre* ('A Blood Cake', 1972); a run-of-the-mill children's movie, *Robin Hood nunca muere*

('Robin Hood Never Dies', 1974). But from the mid-70s Bellmunt emerged as the most significant voice of Catalan youth in film.

La nova cançó was the earlier and better of Bellmunt's folk-rock documentaries, a film which 'fights for democracy' – as the ICC demanded – in its very style. Gone, for instance, is the NO-DO use of a commentator to deliver an official version of events; instead of a voice-over, Bellmunt interviews politicians, writers, singers and artistic agents to establish a pluralistic, and not always complimentary, view of the Catalan folk-rock movement. Counterpointing the interviews are recordings from concerts of the 'new songs' themselves with their protest themes, elemental music, see-through political allegories, and lyrics which forefront the Catalan language in words sung slow and clear and with a sharp sense of irony.

No other Spanish film documents better that exhilarating moment of a nation emerging from forty years of dictatorship. There are some anthology sequences: the old campaigner Raimon intoning his rallying song 'Jo vinc d'un silenci' ('I come from silence/ancient, so long/from a people that arises/from the depth of centuries'); the finest Catalan song-writer, Lluís Llach, singing 'L'Estaca' at the Palau del Sports in January 1976. The sense of a clear Catalan conscience, of being part of history, is caught in a series of shots from the stage towards the audience. The lit matches which it waves bob like little beacons of light in a sea of darkness.

By 1976 many Catalans began to feel the same heady joy not only at the dawn of national freedom but in a sense of their own transcendence. 'Participation' and 'commitment' were no longer a duty but a sense of belonging to a movement which, in a century of chaos and suffering, was going to achieve something positive. Under Franco, history for the Catalans had seemed an unchanging slough of oppression. Now history meant forward movement. There is nothing more natural for a culture coming out of a dictatorship than to attempt to set the past – even defeats in the past – in the mould of a vast nationalist design given meaning and direction by a halting, but never quite halted, process of politicisation which would receive its absolute fulfilment in autonomy. *Las largas vacaciones* responded to this design; so did the most significant Catalan-language film to date, Antoni Ribas' sprawling historical fresco, *La ciutat cremada* (1976).

Ribas' film begins pointedly at a key moment of the modern Catalan nationalist revival: the loss of Cuba in 1898, which closed off Latin American markets to Catalan investments and convinced Catalans that their Madrid government was irredeemably incompetent. Ribas' narrative is then ribbed with historical vignettes: Catalan soldiers on the boat back from Cuba in 1899, feverish with disease and the desire to get home; the conservative separatists and leaders of the autocratic Lliga Regionalista, Cambó and Prat de la Riba, discussing how to exploit discontent with the centrist regime; factory workers in 1901 debating the social reform

119

proposed by Radical Republican Alejandro Lerroux; the Lliga's sweeping election victory in 1902; Lerroux lambasting the Spanish church, urging young Catalans to 'destroy the convents, tear aside the veils of novices and elevate them to the category of mothers'; Cambó, speaking before Alfonso XIII in 1904, demanding Catalan liberties; finally, the 'Tragic Week' of 1909, a muddled affair of church-burning and a few discontents manning the barricades in a purposeless act of rebellion.

Despite its epic scale, *La ciutat cremada* was very much a film made for, by, and about Catalans. Outsiders will understand but never fully feel the joy felt by Catalan audiences at the way the film addressed specifically Catalan problems. Ribas even indulges in typical Catalan humour, mocking the *seny* – the sharp common sense – of the Catalan businessman. A Barcelona shopowner thinks of breaking a curfew to make a sale and asks himself: 'To sell or not sell? That is the question.' The 'human interest' is provided by the strapping figure of Josep, a worker who marries the daughter of Pere Palau, a wealthy industrialist. *La ciutat cremada* emerges, in fact, as a mordant critique of the Catalan middle classes who stood aside and shrugged at the revolutionary movement they had helped foster. Lerroux's deputy Iglesias, for example, appears in the film too ill to take any firm stand in support of the rebels. He was alleged in fact to have taken a laxative to incapacitate himself for the barricades.

The Palau family's performance is equally shoddy. As the Catalan national anthem plays on the soundtrack and barricades go up in the street below, the Palaus play parlour games. Josep has wavered about joining the rebels. But when he sees a sniper firing at the barricades from a rooftop, he crawls out and shoots him. He is pursued by his sister-in-law Roser, who seduces him there and then, pushing his rifle out of reach so that it falls into the corpse-festooned street below. The moral of Ribas' film is clear: the Catalan middle classes, and even the working class, lacked a firm political and national consciousness. But Ribas does hold out some long-term hope for the Catalans. Roser's seduction of Josep is more than gratuitous lust: she wants him to father her child (her husband is an upper-class fop), so transforming his vocation for class revolution into that *grand bourgeois* enterprise, the creation of a family. Ribas' montage of the rebels dying in the street as Roser and Josep make love above them is, however, ambivalent. Blood is spilt but new blood is being created; and as Roser points out, her baby will have 'street blood' because of father Josep. The Tragic Week at least has a positive product in the invigoration of Roser's line. Pointedly, the film's favourite image is of dawn.

La ciutat cremada lacks the sweep of a similar historical fresco, Visconti's *The Leopard*. But it was an ingenious attempt at a vital political cinema, a manifesto of Catalan rights and culture. Many of the minor parts were taken by leading Catalan personalities, and the dialogue includes phrases which were cheered by Catalan audiences, and which were perhaps more relevant to 1976 than to the turn of the century. Rankled by Suárez's prevarication over the Statute of Autonomy, Catalan audiences enthusiastically applauded such lines as Cambó's complaint to Alfonso XIII about the regime's foot-dragging on reform: 'In Madrid they are never in a hurry.'

By 1978 the Catalan cinema seemed to be losing its initial dynamism. From June 1977 the ICC began a fortnightly newsreel, *Noticiari de Barcelona*, which spoke up with a bravely independent voice on such issues as land speculation, education, and sanitation. But the ICC soon fell foul of internal tensions within the provisional Catalan government, and Catalan cinema suffered accordingly. Josep María Forn's *Companys, Procés a Catalunya* ('Companys, Catalonia on Trial', 1979), for instance, is a conventional and too uncritical biography of Lluís Companys, President of Catalonia from 1933 to 1940, who became a tragic symbol of his nation's dignity in martyrdom when he was handed over by the Gestapo to Franco and, when facing the firing squad, took off his shoes and socks so as to die touching the soil of Catalonia.

Ribas continued his fresco approach to history in the three-part, six-hour *Victoria!* (1983–4), which marshals events on three days and nights in June 1917 when Barcelona was a hotchpotch of anarchists, bohemians, men grown rich on arms smuggling with the Great Powers, and a dissident army officer class, the *junteros*. Here Ribas' historical set scenes appear long-winded and tangential. The relationship between an anarchist and a *juntero* is used to convey the inability of supposed army rebels to cooperate with the Catalan people – the *junteros* were even to help crush the anarchist rising of 1 August 1917. The result is a romantic trivialising of a complex historical process.

Apart from Ribas and Forn, the only director committed to a cinema of Catalan themes – here in a regional variety – was Carles Mira. His work shows a consistency of subject and an individuality of focus, all his features starting from the same opposition: a repressive, death-obsessed, Judaeo-Christian centrist power counterpointed by an earthly delight in vulgarity, sex and spectacle. Mira relates these qualities to his Valencian origins and especially to the riposte to good taste proposed by the Valencian *sainete*, the yearly festival of the *Fallas* (bonfires) and Valencia's strong Moorish influence. Mira's literal transcription of the miracles of a Valencian saint in *La portentosa vida del Padre Vicente* ('The Miraculous Life of Father Vicente', 1978) reduces them to pure *esperpento*. In *Con el culo al aire* ('Caught With Your Pants Down', 1980) Mira portrays Francoist Spain as institutionalised lunacy, presenting a madhouse whose completely sane inmates are forced to mimic the inspirational figures of Francoism such as Columbus and Isabel the Catholic. *Jalea Real* ('Royal Jelly', 1981) insists on Castillian austerity and intransigence as seen in the intrigues surrounding the

121

impotence of Charles the Bewitched, during whose reign (1665–1700) Castille reached the nadir of decadence.

Mira's problem is to raise his black humour beyond mere vulgarity. He is noticeably happier celebrating sybaritic sensuality in *Que nos quiten lo bailao* ('No One Can Take Away Our Good Times Together', 1983). Here Moorish Spain, at a time when the Caliphate of Cordoba rivalled the Abbasid dynasty of Baghdad, is revealed as a land of sensual delight and irremediable scatology. In comparison the dank castle of Christians seems locked in a Dark Age mentality; which was not so far from the historical truth.

Three film-makers working on Catalan themes hardly adds up, however, to a vital film industry. Other directors do shoot Catalan-language features, but they prefer to connect with larger traditions in Spanish or international film. Francesc Bellmunt is a central figure in the so-called 'New Spanish Comedy'; newer directors have made police thrillers, as in a slightly insipid mix of *film noir* and black comedy, *Barcelona Sud* ('South Barcelona', Jordi Cadena, 1980), or *Putapela* ('Filthy Lucre', 1981), Jordi Bayona's low-budget account of prostitution in a somewhat folkloric Barcelona underworld.

'For there to be a Catalan cinema,' Ricardo Muñoz Suay argued in 1978, 'Catalonia must be autonomous.'[25] Catalonia's Autonomy Statute, ceded by the UCD government in 1979, may however have snuffed the potential for a vigorously nationalist cinema by effectively ending the Catalan question as a serious political issue. The film industry in Catalonia is still not self-supporting in finance, markets, or jobs. Catalonia is known, for example, for discovering excellent actresses who then become familiar faces in Madrid films: Assumpta Serna (the mother and girlfriend in Saura's *Dulces horas*), Isabel Mestres (the sister in *Elisa, vida mía*), and Silvia Munt (the walk-out wife of much 'New Spanish Comedy'). Catalan investors are notoriously cautious. 'In Madrid,' Forn has complained, 'you'll find a financier who, if nothing more, might think a film will lead to an erotic adventure. The Catalan in this case will use the money to buy his mistress a flat.' Forn is one victim of this economic caution, not having directed a film since *Companys*. A Catalan cinema also seems at times a rather academic cause. The Generalitat prizes for 1983–4, for example, were reserved for films shot in Catalan. Policy is then to dub these pictures into Castillian, leaving them indistinguishable from many films shot in Catalonia, but in Castillian. Like any minority cinema, the major stumbling-block for Catalan film is the smallness of its natural market: the 6½ million Catalan speakers (37 million Spaniards speak Castillian). Lacking international markets, Spanish film-makers need to win all of their national market. So an enterprising Barcelona producer such as Pepón Coromina uses national stars who don't speak Catalan and non-Catalan directors such as Eloy de la

Iglesia (a Basque), for whom he produced the excellent *Navajeros* ('Knife Fighters', 1980).

Co-financing deals struck between Catalan Television (TV-3) and Catalan producers point a way forward for films promoting a sense of regional identity. Meanwhile the curiously cross-grained nature of production in Catalonia is illustrated by the most attractive of Catalan films: Francesc Betriu's *La Plaça del Diamant* ('Diamond Square', 1982). Betriu is a *maldito* (a 'damned' director): numerous abortive projects, short shooting schedules which force a *feísta* ('ugly'), throwaway style, pigeon-holed as a popularist because of the pulp novel influence on his celebrated short *Bolero de amor* ('The Love Bolero', 1970). But Betriu's main theme is alienation. In *Furia española* ('Spanish Fury' – the 'virile' do-or-die surge towards goal which embodied, supposedly, the Spanish style of soccer), made in 1974, Betriu portrays the Barcelona Football Club as a popular opiate sublimating his characters' frustrations. *Los fieles servientes* ('The Faithful Servants', 1980) is subtler. Servants on a farm, conditioned by their employees, use their liberties to mimic the very class that exploits them. Betriu's film is both a perceptive parable on the ironies of power and a satire of Spain's transition.

La Plaça del Diamant had a long history of abandoned treatments of an original novel (by Rodoreda) thought too 'literary' for the cinema. Betriu's solution was to use a voice-over for sustained interior monologue, and even to have the heroine Colometa turn to the camera (in a scene deliberately rendered dreamlike by an unnatural blue-and-orange ambience) to inform the audience that her husband Quimet and his best friend Cincet both died in the war. The use of interior monologue is crucial. First, Betriu is the only Spanish film-maker not just to shoot in Catalan but to exploit the distinctive quality of the language, its relative softness which endows much of its poetry with a lilting melancholy of tone. Rodoreda's 'poetic' prose, preserved in the film, is seductive. Second, the interior monologue allows a rich and clear idea of Colometa's sensibility. We first see her as a young girl in a Barcelona buzzing with excitement at its fiesta. Dragged out to dance by a girlfriend, she meets Quimet, who is young, handsome, ebullient. He wants her to dance, she resists, then surrenders. Colometa is one of those people, she says, 'who could never say no'.

La Plaça del Diamant returns to a grand theme of Spanish cinema: the difficulties of gaining a true sense of self in a Spain whose history encourages alienation. Colometa duly marries Quimet and dutifully has his children. There is one moment of happiness, when the Republic is proclaimed in 1931, but for Colometa it never returns. Colometa, as Juan M. Company writes, remains only a latent personality, 'a popular conscience which could have been and never was'.[26] Betriu's film adroitly suggests how Colometa, as a housewife without much education, actually attempts to find an identity for herself. She 'has to cling to domestic objects, to everyday details as the only referential item which makes the surrounding world natural and partially comprehensible,'[27] such as when she runs her thumb along a groove in a table to extract the breadcrumbs, or plays her hands across a wall engraving of musical scales as she climbs her stairs. Yet, as with so many Spanish film heroines, her sense of identity never really coalesces. The root cause of her later alienation is the Civil War. Quimet goes to fight for the Republicans. He comes back on leave a changed and nearly broken man. 'When all this is over,' he says, 'I'll stick at home like woodworm sticks in wood and nobody will ever get me out. Never!' (A very similar sentiment is expressed by the father in *The Spirit of the Beehive*.)

Quimet is killed. Colometa stays in Barcelona dizzy with hunger, dragging herself to shop for her children, although there is very little she can buy. Always dreamlike, she is now an automaton. Again Betriu uses an object to signal Colometa's condition: a little mechanical bear with a drum which has perched for years in the window of a local toyshop. Colometa first sees it during the Republic, when a subjective shot establishes her as doing something active, if only looking. By the 1940s the bear has come to symbolise 'an artificial palpitation ... a mechanical movement comparable to the blind and instinctive action of bees in a beehive.'[28]

The film ends in 1952. Barcelona has once more been in *fiesta*, as Colometa wanders into a huge tent where a party has long since finished. She looks up at the awning and sees a small opening to the sky. Finally, in her dark well of alienation, Quimet and the Republican illusions lost for ever, Colometa's sense of self briefly and intuitively materialises. Looking up at the opening, she lets out a scream.

Dark intuitions: Patino, Ricardo Franco, Chávarri

'With a dark intuition of what could have been happiness.'
Calvert Casey, quoted in *El desencanto*.[29]

In the 60s a main bugbear of opposition film-makers had been 'developmental triumphalism'. By the mid-70s a new 'transitional triumphalism' proposed a view that everything could get better, that the past was past, and Spaniards must cooperate in building for the future. But the film opposition would not say goodbye to the past: 'Not forgetting the past,' wrote Jorge Semprun, Civil War exile and scriptwriter of *La guerre est finie* and *Z*, in 1976, 'one better understands the present. Knowing where we came from, we don't walk blindly into a future dominated by pragmatists and amnesiacs.'[30] Spaniards looked back at their past with as much sarcasm as anger. The pragmatism Semprun refers to, for example, was part of a transition to democracy which allowed the victors in the Civil War, including war criminals, to age gracefully, some of them still enjoying the fruits of the fortunes they made from the war. 'The worst thing,' wrote Carlos Sempelayo in *Los que no volvieron* (1975),'wasn't that they beat us in the war; they also won history'.[31]

The past explained the present; it was also a convenient symbol when discretion was still advisable. During the transition, for example, the Spanish police organisation with its Policía Armada, Guardia Civil and Municipal Police was proportionally the largest in any Western country. In September 1975 five militants of ETA and FRAP were executed. Such institutionalised violence often reached bizarre levels: the anti-riot police are alleged to have attacked Spaniards merely for carrying a copy of *El País*. 'In hell,' the *Economist* once remarked, 'it is reliably reported, the cooks are English, the journalists are Russian and the policemen are Spanish.'[32] A direct description of police violence was hardly feasible in 1975; though Ricardo Franco's *Pascual Duarte*, by being set in the past, was allowed to describe a general violence in unremitting detail. Its very generality and distance in time saved it from censorship: Spanish audiences caught contemporary allusions with ease.

Few Spanish films dealt more sensitively with the past than *Canciones para después de una guerra* ('Songs for after a War'). Made in 1971, its release in 1976 was another benefit of liberalisation. Since *Nueve cartas a Berta*, Basilio Patino's career had floundered like that of so many new directors in the censorship crackdown of the late 60s. His *Del amor y otras soledades* ('On Love and Other Solitudes', 1969) was a 'description of marriage problems in Spain, the version demanded by a Ministry of Information and Tourism when the government was in a state of emergency.'[33] The result, not surprisingly, was laboured, and Patino emerged by the early 70s as Spain's most eloquent critic of collaboration with the regime. *Canciones* became the censorship scandal of the 70s. Approved by the Censorship Board as suitable for all audiences, denounced in the ultra-right *El Alcázar*, personally viewed and banned by Carrero Blanco, its very existence was denied by the Under Secretary for Cinema when a representative of the Academy of Motion Pictures expressed his interest in it.

Was *Canciones* really that subversive? The film is a highly elaborate melange of newsreel, newspaper clippings, extracts from comics, advertisements, documents, film clips – from for example *Morena Clara*, *El gato montés*, *Agustina de Aragón*, *¡A mí la legión!* – and a soundtrack which includes occasional voice-overs and songs of the 40s. Patino had the last laugh on the censor: his film's final approval in 1976 was the beginning of the end for the Francoist censor. From then on prohibitions were rarer, and a source of embarrassment for new President Suárez, whose Under

Canciones para después de una guerra

Secretary for the Cinema, the bureaucratic survivor Rogelio Díez, took to telephoning *Fotogramas*, Spain's main cinema weekly, to inform them which film had just been approved.

On its release, parts of Patino's film pleased audiences of all political persuasions. In Valencia, for example, when the Falangist anthem 'Cara al sol' ('Face to the Sun') began in the film a group of old Francoist diehards stood up with arms raised in fascist salute and sang along with the hymn; more liberal spectators replied by joining in the chirpy 'Se va el caimán' ('The Alligator's Going') but, with obvious reference to Franco, put the verb in the past tense. What right-wing audiences may have missed is Patino's editing. With a train of one-off ironies, shibboleths of hope and faith for the 40s are played off against insinuations, which seep up often from the Francoist newsreels themselves, of a reality which was falsified, darker or completely hidden from the Spanish people. *Canciones* cuts from Spanish football to Auschwitz (perhaps not a NO-DO newsreel: Franco naturally played down his former political associate's genocide); a newspaper headline, 'Tuberculosis should not scare you!' – implying of course that it did – gives way to refreshingly non-tubercular film stars at the first night of *La fe*. Similarly, 'Lili Marlene' plays over newsreel of the Franco-Hitler meeting at Hendaye in 1940. The music is inaptly romantic; but so was the Francoist version of the interview according to which Franco out-talked Hitler and avoided Spain's entry into the Second World War. In reality neither leader desired Spanish entry.

The film's appeal lies in its gently nudging sarcasm, the songs themselves, and Patino's jazzy montage. Patino cuts snappily, image and music grating slightly as they change with different rhythms. *Canciones* is in fact cut like a commercial with a 'vertiginous montage rhythm where one glimpses rather than sees; juxtapositions to elicit smiles, or surprise.'[34] Patino's film returns to the theme of alienation. The songs and scenes from the 40s of football, bullfighting or mass rallies portray, Marcel Oms observes, 'the cultural elements which conditioned the collective imagination of a people, showing, therefore, the mechanisms of power: preliminary infantilisation of citizens, carefully elaborated to create false needs and false desires, alienated relations with figures of authority.'[35] Patino also points, however, to the natural wish of Spanish audiences in the 1940s for escapism. The film's first song, 'Cara al sol', calls for commitment; its last song is the much later and significantly titled 'A lo loco se vive mejor' – 'You live better being mad.'

Canciones taunts its Spanish audience with their alienation from the past. Its montage style could be seen as a metaphor for history, where the past, like an advertised commodity, is only our interpretation of it. Patino had some frames of the film coloured, suggesting that the past can never be known objectively. There are few better vehicles for a journey to the past than photographs backed by melodies from the period (a device frequently used in Saura's films); but Patino frustrates the illusion of being back in the past by intruding into these songs and films of the 40s in a way that changes them. And his quick-fire montage has another implication: the ephemerality of the past as remembered in the present. 'In thirty years,' a rueful voice declares at the end of *Canciones*, 'nobody will remain: what will be left, taking its revenge on us all once more, is time.'

Canciones began a trilogy on 'Spanish fascism – its emblems, figures and ideological framework.'[36] *Caudillo* (1974–7) was a straightforward documentary biography of Franco. The earlier *Queridísimos verdugos* ('Dearest Hangmen', 1973–6) is remarkable. Its subject is garrotting – capital punishment by strangulation – institutionalised, the film's commentary tells us, by Fernando VII in 1832 to celebrate his wife's birthday. Patino's coup was to get two state executioners under Franco very drunk and then interview them. They demonstrate on each other where to put the strangling apparatus. Anecdotes flow: one executioner's first client was his own niece; another victim took twenty minutes to die. Patino counterpoints the executioners' garrulousness with an ironic setting for the interview – a cellar in a bar with a background of flamenco dancers and folk song. Finally, reportage follows up the crimes committed by the garrote victims. Most of the murderers seem clinically ill and their murders often acts of desperation. One man strangled a woman for sixty-five pesetas. Garrotting emerges from Patino's film as an integral part of Spanish tradition, 'like the bulls or flamenco'; and a brutal reminder of Spain's 'black legend' for violence.

Ricardo Franco's *Pascual Duarte* (made in 1975 and approved by the censor in April 1976) tackles a similar theme from a vastly different angle. Few Spanish films are so carefully thought through; no Spanish film shocks so greatly.

The literary base to Franco's film was Camilo José Cela's *La familia de Pascual Duarte*, a novel which took Spain by storm in 1942. Particularly arresting was its *tremendismo*, the brutal realism with which the peasant Duarte recounts a series of crimes against a background of sordid rural misery at complete variance with the official version of countryside life where the Spanish peasant was to be called, by Franco's Agricultural Minister in 1952, 'probably the noblest and most worth aiding of all creatures populating the globe'. José Cela begged to differ from government rhetoric. Scriptwriters Ricardo Franco, Emilio Martínez-Lázaro and Elías Querejeta not only echoed Cela, but were among the first Spanish film-makers to adapt material to accentuate its political relevance rather than diminish it out of fear of censorial reprobation. Born in 1902, Pascual goes to school and learns by heart the passage from the Bible about Abraham and Isaac. An early memory is of his father reading about the execution of Ferrer, an anarchist involved in the Tragic Week of 1909. Now a young man, Pascual goes hunting with his little sister Rosario, who scampers off to retrieve the fallen birds. Grown up, Rosario goes off to become a prostitute in the local town. Pascual kills his hunting dog; hacks a mule to death with a pocket knife when it kills his young wife; shoots Rosario's pimp when he comes to collect her from the family home. He is imprisoned, but the victory of the Popular Front in the 1936 elections leads to an amnesty. Against a background of growing rural unrest – labourers being killed; farms set on fire – Pascual shoots his mother and his landlord, and is finally executed by garrotte.

Why does Pascual kill? The only clues are a suggested sexual passion for his sister, his own violent, psychotic character, and the barren rural environment. Possible explanations might be that Pascual pictures himself as a man who desires his sister. That desire makes him bad, so every 'bad' action – like Abraham's willingness to kill Isaac – will confirm his own supreme love. Or that Pascual kills everybody responsible for his frustrated bad love: obstructions, such as the pimp; figures of authority who give him his sense of 'badness'. Or Ricardo Franco's own interpretation: Pascual's victims are all substitutes for Rosario.[37]

Yet Franco's direction discourages psychological interpretation. He avoids close-ups and significant facial expressions, using an immobile

128

camera, slow protracted sequences, empty sets, and a vast expanse of desolate plateau separating character from camera to create and emphasise a harsh, pre-cultural environment. The setting is a symbol for the characters' 'psychological desolation', Franco argues. It is also another partial explanation of conduct: 'Pascual ... is almost a pre-cultural being who can't distinguish between good and bad and lacks a normal family, a normal school or a normal religion.' In such circumstances violence becomes 'the expressive language of beings who have no other means of expression'.[38]

The shock delivered by *Pascual Duarte* comes from how such violence is shown. Cela's *tremendista* style is, if anything, accentuated in the film. The original novel describes the mule's death in six quite casual lines. In the film there is no filtering conscience, just actor José Luis Gómez ripping into a heaving mass of hide and blood. The shot of Pascual being garrotted is held in a forty-second freeze frame. Why is there such cruelty to animals in so many Spanish films? 'Daily news of assassinations numbs our capacity for horror, even if – as in most cases – the victim is a man,' Borau said in *Fotogramas*, defending his faking the death of a she-wolf in *Furtivos*. 'I chose to use a dog because violence is, paradoxically, more startling.'[39] Ricardo Franco was appalled in particular by the equanimity with which

Pascual Duarte: the garrotte

129

Spaniards had taken the death of Puig Antich. If reality can't shock Spaniards, perhaps a film could.

Pascual Duarte was an offshoot of the success enjoyed by *La prima Angélica*. In the 70s Spain's most enterprising producer, Elías Querejeta, had twice tried to enlarge his stable beyond 'New Spanish Directors' Regueiro and Eceiza, who had never really caught the public's attention, and Saura, who could only make a film every eighteen months. Gutiérrez Aragón and Erice were brought in in 1973. In June 1974, seeing greater opportunities for film production, Querejeta called in the Madrid 'independent' film-makers Augusto M. Torres, Emilio M. Lázaro, Alvaro del Amo, Ricardo Franco, and Jaime Chávarri. Querejeta proposed a series of shorts. Franco made the black-humoured *El increíble aumento del costo de la vida* ('The Incredible Rise in the Cost of Living', 1974), then *Pascual Duarte*. Jaime Chávarri developed a short film, found he had too much material, and shot *El desencanto* ('Disenchantment', 1976), a landmark in Spain's transition cinema.

The theme of *El desencanto* is 'the family as an instrument for filicide', or so one of the affected sons in the film claims.[40] The prominence of the family in Spanish cinema reflects the traditional importance of the family in Spain. 'No one was ever born a member of a political party,' José Antonio Primo de Rivera said in a famous speech. 'On the other hand we are all born members of a family.'[41] The family under Franco became the minimum political unit, a fact recognised explicitly in 1967 when heads of families were allowed to elect deputies directly to the Cortes. Fathers were expected to control their children. In *El nido* ('The Nest', Jaime de Armiñan, 1980), for example, a kindly father is forced by a domineering wife to punish their daughter. He takes her into a room, makes her lie on a bed, gets out his belt, and thrashes the bedcover beside her. Other Spanish fathers were not so yielding. Above all fathers were meant to be fertile. Under Franco, 'an abundance of children was almost a promotional necessity for the ambitious servant of a state that made the "numerous family" the centre of its demographic policy.'[42] The ten ministers in Suárez's first Cabinet had fifty children between them. With no welfare state to speak of, the family proved the only safety net for Spaniards caught by the vicissitudes of industrialisation. Spaniards still usually live at home until marriage, so preserving family unity beyond the children's adulthood. The Spanish family still challenges the democratic nature of Spain by its denial of economic and emotional independence in the name of those most tyrannising of forces: parental domination and filial love.

Jaime Chávarri comes from a Spanish equivalent of the Mitfords. His family financed his first film, *Los viajes escolares* ('School Trips', 1973), ironically a dystopic vision of family life. The teenage hero's mother (played by Lucia Bosé) is dominating, doting, and unnervingly beautiful for any

130

son; his grandparents are in dotage; one aunt has been in prison; another aunt has a weak heart and a pacemaker which she insists on showing to all and sundry; another relation flagellates the grandmother. Hero Oscar ends up, not surprisingly, a schizophrenic.

Los viajes escolares is in fact a tragi-comic dramatisation of R. D. Laing's hypotheses on schizophrenia. The family to Laing was a collective 'phantasy system'; if someone 'begins to wake up from the family phantasy system, he can only be classified as mad or bad by the family since to them their phantasy is real and what is not their phantasy is not real.'[43] Oscar is called both mad and bad and ends up a schizophrenic because he challenges his family phantasies. He insists for example that he had a horse when he was a child, but his family deny all knowledge of it. (Oscar is right: his mother shot the horse, thinking it made her son too independent.) Still pining for his horse, and for a father (his real one ran off when Oscar was a child), Oscar persuades his mathematics teacher to spend some of the holidays at his family home. The teacher soon discovers the family 'phantasy system'. As an example, when Oscar tried to run away as a child his shoes were taken away to stop him; but all the family took off their shoes so that it would seem quite normal to go around shoeless.

Laing compared the family to a box. As soon as someone realises he is in the family-box, 'he can try to get out of it. But since to them [schizophrenics] the box is "the whole world" to get out of the box is tantamount to stepping off the end of the world, a thing that no one who loves him could sit by and let happen.'[44] So Oscar is told to grow up, made head of the family, and yet encouraged to lay his head in his mother's lap while she tries to guess what he is thinking – a game they played when Oscar was a child. Oscar's final gesture is typically ambivalent. Having started an affair with his grandmother's young nurse, he goes off to get her some honey – an attempt at last at an adult relationship. But the honey is to be found at the place where he thinks his horse was buried, and it is a spot which only his mother knows. Lévi-Strauss, in *Mythologiques*, famously related honey to menstrual blood. So Oscar's very gesture of independence marks his continuing absorption by the past and a fairly obvious return to the mother-figure. The fact that the bees sting Oscar to death may symbolise just how untenable his position has become: he can neither escape from his family nor live with it.

The problem with *Los viajes escolares* is that it uses myths obscurely (one has to know the reference), unlike for instance the use of the Frankenstein myth in *The Spirit of the Beehive*. In *A un dios desconocido* and *Río de oro* ('Golden River', 1986), Chávarri connects with more expressive myths: the garden of innocence, the river of time. In *El desencanto* he retains Laing's ideas but develops them more clearly, bringing out the political resonance of family structures.

131

Like Laing in *Sanity, Madness and the Family*, Chávarri interviews members of a family in varying combinations – a mother and son; two sons – to get different visions of a central person, here Leopoldo Panero, dubbed by some as the official poetic voice of Franco's regime. The film begins with the unveiling of a statue to Panero in his local town twelve years after his death in 1962. His widow records that a few days into their honeymoon Panero asked his cronies to stay with them. Elder son Juan Luis recites a poem calling Panero a drunkard and a frequenter of brothels. Juan Luis quickly exposes the vacuousness of Francoist rhetoric by recounting that the 'sleepy frenzy of my flesh, word of my silent depths' (Panero about his son in a poem) never got on very well with his father. The irony is obvious; more interestingly, the shadow of the father still falls across the son. He worries about continuing the family line; he still writes with a pen his father gave him. He concludes with maudlin satisfaction that, 'In the final count, as a man I love so much, old Ernest Hemingway, once said: "The son of nobody is a son of a bitch".'

Whether in opposition or as a successor, Juan Luis' conception of self is still dominated by his father. In a film where direction is rarely gratuitous, Juan Luis pronounces his flat, sarcastic paean to his father ('Your drinking has given a lot to talk about.... Comments have been made about your heroic exploits in the brothel') beside his dead father's statue. In the Don Juan legend it is the statue of a dead father which drags Don Juan off to hell. Even when dead poet Leopoldo Panero still represents a reproach, Juan Luis' predicament may be symbolic. The ultimate father figure in Spain was of course the regime and Franco himself. The death of a leader or the fall of a regime would not mean the immediate end to their influence. Even Spaniards' struggle for freedom from their father-figures was a compromise of their freedoms. Rebellion from, opposition to, hatred of the father-figure is a subtle form of slavery. As Gutiérrez Aragón said of Franco, 'Deep down I detest Franco because he makes me go on detesting him.'[45]

A new member of the family appears: Leopoldo María, second son, alcoholic, self-confessed schizophrenic, his words strangled into barely comprehensible gurgles. Chávarri's point in *El desencanto* is gradually to leave Panero senior to focus on the family as a repressive institution which endows members with an identity rather than with any individuality. 'The Paneros are always acting,' Chávarri says. 'They never act as independent beings but as Paneros.... They accept the family as every moment.'[46] The attraction of the film is in part the characters' own awareness of their alienation. Leopoldo is exemplary. He is a self-styled remnant: 'In infancy we live; afterwards we survive.' His problem is that he has never totally controlled his own acting performance. Who decided he was mad? His uncle and mother, he says. Leopoldo's version may not tell all the truth. Chávarri's direction is discreet, neither exposing his characters' true selves (though he knows the family quite well) nor intruding to explain that the Paneros are acting. But his two-shots subtly place commentary, including what many spectators take to be disarmingly honest confessions, in a larger family context which supplies all declarations with a histrionic function. And he cuts away from straight interview to voice-over against symbolic backgrounds, as when the mother is seen wandering through the melancholy ruins of the summer house where she spent her honeymoon: 'I had so many hopes, and little by little they have gone.'

The Paneros' role-playing and their disenchantment with the father-figure is not just social or political allegory. Repression, Spanish directors often emphasise, begins at home, and the family is the earliest, the strongest, and perhaps the most inevitable instance of repression facing Spaniards under – or indeed after – Franco. The results – alienation, capitulation, unnatural loves, infantilism – are key themes of post-Franco cinema as it charts the legacies of repression in a world where they run deep.

CARLOS SAURA

The case of Carlos Saura is unique. He was the only director to claim under Franco, for example, that he controlled his films, and that, from *La caza*, 'at every moment I have done what I thought I could do'.[1] Saura insisted that he was an *auteur*.[2] The claim seemed unlikely, even dangerous, when the Francoist censor so clearly interfered with personal expression in Spain. Yet Saura's career under Franco did suggest a consistently personal voice surviving from one film to the next, which could be matched in Spain only by Edgar Neville and Luis Berlanga.

The key to Neville and Berlanga's independence was their personal wealth, which allowed them to avoid pot-boilers, pick and choose their projects, prepare them with care, and ride out the censor's opposition. Such patience was very necessary: Berlanga claims to have had more than thirty scripts rejected by Spanish producers or the censor. Saura once claimed he would not know how to make commercial cinema.[3] His cohabitation with Geraldine Chaplin, the great comic's daughter, from, in film terms, *Peppermint frappé* (1967) until *Mamá cumple cien años* (1979), saved Saura from such contingencies. Indeed, when asked how he saw his rather difficult future, fellow director and friend Francisco Regueiro declared in 1973: 'There's one solution I've been plannning ... which is to kidnap Geraldine Chaplin, not to muck up Carlos but because she earns a lot of money and so I'd have more creative liberty.'[4]

Saura's singularity derived not only from his secure economic base but also from the fact that in international terms he was Spain's only famous director. Fame, in turn, brought Saura's films a special treatment in Spain. Thanks to the Silver Bears won at the Berlin Film Festival in 1966 and 1968 for *La caza* and *Peppermint frappé*, he and Querejeta acquired, in his own words, 'a kind of "aureola" of quality in Spain. The censor said "Careful with these two: they can't be harmed too much." And they were right: no sooner would any serious problem come up

134

than we would mobilise our contacts in France and Germany so that they would protest.'[5]

Such skilful manoeuvring has caused some critics to claim that Saura's international prestige was based on an 'excellent publicity operation'.[6] Yet Querejeta may be said to have done good business because he made good films, not the other way round. Saura's international appeal under Franco was, moreover, perfectly explicable on a number of counts. First, Saura's films clearly responded to the assumptions of Freud. 'Nothing in my films is casual,' he once said. 'The most minimal detail has a sense.'[7] Saura was not always sure what these senses were. He attributed to his characters multiple motives for actions, he delved into their past and present, and he saw sexual repressions prompting jealousy (La caza; Stress es tres, tres, 'Stress is Three', 1968), fantasy (Peppermint frappé), role-playing (Ana y los lobos, 'Ana and the Wolves', 1972) and emotional immaturity (La prima Angélica). Saura's characters freely associate and condense fantasy, hallucination and memory, as in Freud's theory of dreams. They suffer Oedipal complexes (La madriguera, 'The Den', 1969), fetishism (Peppermint frappé), regressions, and a transference of parental figures (El jardín de las delicias, 'The Garden of Delights', 1970). Few directors have attempted with such conviction or consistency to show what Saura calls 'the most important thing ... what someone thinks, what he imagines, the ghosts inside his head.'[8]

Another aspect of Saura's international appeal was his particularity, the palpable presence of Spain. Los golfos ('The Hooligans', 1959) has a bull-fight and a flamenco music score; Llanto por un bandido ('Lament for a Bandit', 1963) has a garrotte execution, portrays the rise to power of a nineteenth-century Spanish bandit, and draws for its compositions on the work of Goya and the drawings made after a journey in Spain by Gustave Doré. Equally though less obviously Spanish is Saura's insistence on characters' theatricality (La madriguera), his confluence of fantasy and reality, and a critical realism which uses allegory and distortion (El jardín de las delicias). Though such techniques were developed in part to evade the Francoist censor, Saura traces them back through esperpento and Goya to such 'Golden Age' seventeenth-century writers as Gracián, Quevedo, Calderón and Cervantes who took to 'transfiguring reality in the imagination ... because of the weight of the Inquisition on the intellectual life of the age.'[9]

It was a sense of Spanishness, added to an assimilation of Freud, which linked Saura to Buñuel. His discovery of Buñuel took place at the Rencontres de Cinéma Hispanique at Montpellier. 'At the time I was toying with a kind of realist cinema in the wide sense of the word, but I didn't know what kind that meant.' At Montpellier, 'I saw the cinema of Buñuel, El and Subida al cielo. It was a fantastic solution for me: on the one hand it connected with a whole pre-Franco historical and cultural process; on the other, there was a man who worked on reality and a Spanish reality at that. Thirdly, and above all, he had a personal world to express and a critical sense, even a moral sense ... of looking at things.'[10]

Saura's description of Buñuel was a prescription for his own career. The moral sense of Saura's early films made him a leading voice of Spain's internal anti-Franco opposition. In a number of interviews he has denied a primary political concern for his work, claiming (in 1972) that 'If I were essentially political I wouldn't make films but dedicate myself to another activity where politics could play a greater part.' The political elements in his cinema remain 'a reflection of what I see in my life every day, a fundamental element, an always present backcloth.'[11] Yet the sophisticated naturalism of Saura's plots breaks the rather simple foreground/background dichotomy. In all his films under Franco a repressive background not only provides a particular context but also explains the characters' outbursts of passion, their intimate fantasies. There is no such thing in Saura's cinema as a pre-social being. The traumas suffered by his characters are an indirect but often caustic indictment of the society Franco had created.

Saura's anti-Francoism was yet another reason for his international appeal. Foreign critics indeed played up Saura's political allusions to the detriment of his subtler psychological implications. Yet Saura's opposition to Franco did give his cinema its most immediate cultural context. The questions which arise from Saura's post-Franco career are not only 'What happens to an artist when he suddenly finds his freedom?', but 'What happens to an artist when he suddenly loses some of his co-ordinates?'

Cría cuervos

Title sequence: The initial credits appear. We see photographs from a family album: a mother (Geraldine Chaplin) in bed laughing, beside her a newborn baby; the baby, Ana, being fed; Ana, a child in a white dress, at the seaside, in a square with pigeons; a close-up of Ana, her round face unnaturally pale, boyish fringe cut, slight nose, large dark impenetrable eyes; Ana with her mother, Ana with her parents, mother in a black dress with flowers, father mounted on a magnificent white steed in his officer's uniform; Ana running in the garden with her two sisters.

Sequence 1: The light of dawn filtering into a room of sober portraits, large sofas, drab wallpaper, high ceilings, the sombre lounge of a traditional Spanish middle-class family. Ana walks down the staircase, a phantasmagoric eight-year-old in a white nightgown. She hears whispers of pleasure, then a gasp. A half-dressed woman scurries out of the father's bedroom. Ana finds her father dead on his bed, an empty glass of milk on his bedside table.

136

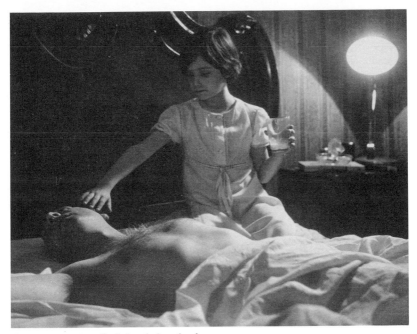

Cría cuervos: Ana finds her father dead

Sequence 2: Ana washes her glass in the kitchen sink. Her mother steals up behind her, and gently scolds her. Ana smiles at her mother, who kisses her and bundles her off to bed.

Sequence 3: Mother combs Ana's hair in front of the mirror. She kisses Ana and pretends to nibble her neck. She withdraws. The children go downstairs to pay their last respects to their father. Ana tells a sister that she heard him gasping 'and then mummy appeared'. 'But mummy's dead,' her sister tells her.

Cría cuervos ('Raise Ravens') records the memories, hallucinations and perceptions of eight-year-old Ana as they are recalled by her adult self (in 1995), who occasionally appears in the film to reflect to the camera on her infancy and especially a summer spent in Madrid in 1975. So the mother's appearances in Sequences 2 and 3 are 'a reconstructed memory of a hallucination based on an earlier reconstructed memory.'[12]

Though the film was conceived in 1974 and shot in 1975 with Franco still alive, Saura was more or less convinced when making *Cría cuervos* that 'Francoism was dead before Franco died.'[13] *La prima Angélica*, he remarked in 1977, 'ended completely my cycle of films with a sense of commitment to myself and perhaps – why not? – to others. An ethical and

137

moral compromise.'[14] Following the break-up of his scriptwriting partnership with Azcona,[15] Saura's work found a new subtlety, a greater complexity, an abandonment of the sarcasms and coarse parabolic style of *El jardín de las delicias* and *Ana y los lobos*. Saura no longer saw the need to be so accessible. Extending a trait of *La prima Angélica*, his new film enlists a number of personal allusions such as his own mother's promising piano career and the Thumberlina story, the only bedtime tale he says his mother ever knew.

Characterisation also changes. There is no longer a one-to-one equation between character and Francoist institution (as in *Ana y los lobos*) or character and sociological type (as with the secondary characters of *La prima Angélica*). Ana's family in *Cría cuervos* is located precisely in the traditionalist middle classes who gave Franco his main social support and were distinguished by their 'Catholicism, an abundance of children, sexual hypocrisies ... a rigid ethic ... ritualised, conventional boredom'.[16] Yet these cultural currents are never subsumed by just one individual, and character portrayal is never banal. Ana's father fought for Nazi Germany on the Russian Front as part of Spain's volunteer *División Azul* ('Blue Division'); but he is distinguished in the film not for his fascism but for his adultery, the prerogative of the Francoist *pater familias*. 'I am what I am,' he tells his reproachful wife.

The father's words are not a gratuitous detail. Saura's political thesis in *Cría cuervos* is that Francoism as a political force could pass away, as Ana's parents literally pass away, but its psychological legacies would remain. One reason for this is that in any complacently conservative society such as Ana's family the reason for things is their very existence. Because nothing is explained, Ana lives prey to traumatising confusions, misconceptions and unrecognised terrors which, the film suggests, are repressed rather than resolved with growing maturity. Ana's mother, María, becomes a source not only of affection but also of horror. Though Ana thinks her mother loves her, she pictures her in her hallucinations and memories as a kind of vampire who bites her neck, is deathly pale and bleeds copiously when ill. Nobody seems to have explained to Ana that vampires don't exist and dead people can't be summoned back to life.

A Francoist upbringing traumatises; it also represses. Ana's predicament in *Cría cuervos* is very similar to Leopoldo's in *El desencanto*: the struggle to be oneself in a society which grooms its members in social roles rather than developing their individuality. Ana's rebellion is muddled, wishfully murderous and seemingly doomed. Mistaking a box of bicarbonate for poison, she slips some into her father's milk (she blames him for her mother's illness and death) the very night he dies from a heart attack. Ana makes up stories, she dreams of flying, she summons up her mother by shutting and opening her eyes as if the two are playing a private game, and

138

she tries to poison Aunt Paulina, a chic martinet who drills her nieces in etiquette. But Paulina naturally survives Ana's bicarbonate dose and Ana's rebellious world of fantasies collapses. The school holidays are over. When her sister Irene recounts a dream which included her mother and father, it is Ana's turn to remind her sister that their parents are dead.[17]

Rarely has repression – its domestic scene, its mechanics and consequences – been so well portrayed. As Peter Evans observes, at the lunch where Paulina introduces herself to the children, 'Only twice . . . is Paulina framed with the other characters, and on each occasion this is done in long shot, so that any lingering impression of intimacy with any members of the family can be eliminated.'[18] Saura also plays with the characters' 'look'. In most films a shot of a character's eyes will cut with an eye-line match to another person's look, so establishing a relationship of some intimacy. In *Cría cuervos*, in contrast, a shot of Ana's face is likely to introduce some reverie which isolates her in the solitude of her own imagination. Ana's stare, moreover, is opaque, completely neutral, fixed in a wax-like pallor, a blank look designed more as a passive defence against inquisition than a means of making contact. 'Raise ravens and they'll peck your eyes out.' The most obvious reference in the title is to Ana's rebellion against her upbringing (Paulina calls the sisters 'crías' – literally 'young creatures'). Equally, however, the children's domestic education denies them their eyes as a faculty for communication. Paulina first appears in the film, as Peter Evans points out, disguising her eyes with a touch of eye-shadow.

Words are equally seen as a vehicle of repression. As Vicente Molina Foix observes, for Ana 'the ghosts of the thought world vanish with the end of the holidays and contact with the school uniform. Restored to reality is the verbal world through Ana's pact with words which "say the truth".'[19] Ana's final assertion to Irene that their parents are dead marks a capitulation. But Ana gives in less to reality (her parents can, after all, 'really' appear in Irene's dream, even if dead) than to convention, to saying what is expected of an orphan, to drawing, possibly, a line between what she thinks and what she says. Ana has learnt the lesson of a repressive education: words are not to communicate but to command or concede in relationships based not on affection but on hierarchies of power. This at least is how Paulina uses words: 'If we all make an effort we'll get along fine together,' she says, but 'From now on the disorder must stop.' Rather than affection, Paulina offers an authoritarian political order combining communal effort with a strict hierarchy.

After portraying Francoist repression in *La prima Angélica* by having a Falangist whip a child, Saura surprises in *Cría cuervos* by the delicacy (and greater accuracy) with which he now shows the mechanics of social conformity. In the girls' acting games, where Ana plays her mother but calls herself Amelia and treats her little sister like a maid, we can see them rehearsing and contrasting the various social roles they will adopt in maturity. Resting unobtrusively in the background, or placed on a secondary plane of action, are details which promote stereotypes of femininity: woman as mother, wife, housewife, virgin, or sex object.[20] And repression and solitude are conveyed by a sense of physical stasis, as Saura multiplies enclosed, isolated or cold spaces: the women are all housebound (granny is confined to a wheelchair); much of the action takes place behind closed doors; Ana erects a make-believe house in the empty swimming pool, and little sister Maite summons the image of a cold-fish existence when she reads aloud from a comic strip whose leading character is a 'Mrs Hake'.

Though insisting on the repressive elements in a Francoist education, Saura is by no means dogmatic. There is in fact a move to greater ambiguity in *Cría cuervos* when compared to earlier films. The double-casting of Geraldine Chaplin as Ana's mother and Ana as an adult leaves us, as Marsha Kinder comments, 'uncertain as to whether the cherished image of the mother has shaped the development of the daughter, or whether Ana's own image has been superimposed over that of the absentee.'[21] Ana's memories of her own past are perhaps none too reliable in other ways. If her memories are anything to go by, then her commentary to the camera is too forgiving to her father, a sign, Peter Evans observes, of the *embourgeoisement* of the post-1975 Ana. Yet if Ana is too forgiving to her father, her memories are perhaps not fully reliable and so can't be used to damn him, or could suggest that he was even more contemptible than she recalls. But the father's remembered cruelty towards the mother is slightly too stereotyped. The parents' quarrel is pointedly shot, moreover, against a simply contrasting background of dark brown and white curtains, as if to point a tendency to black and white reductionism in Ana's memories. The source for the scene may in fact be the maid Rosa, an avid listener to radio novels in 1975, who tells Ana that all men are the same and one day she'll tell her what her father was really like.[22]

Cría cuervos leads the spectator into circles of uncertainty. Saura's film runs in fact on a series of tensions whose tenor is caught by its opening sequence of the family album. 'On taking a photograph,' Saura has said, 'reality automatically becomes the past.' So the family snaps, seen as we listen to piano music, are a source of nostalgia for a past which the very same photographs suggest to have been rather dreary. The photographs are a record of repression – suggesting the same stereotyped images of femininity which *Cría cuervos* laments – and a source of mystery: the emotions behind the poses remain inscrutable. Rather than diffusing the protest implicit in *Cría cuervos*, its ambiguities distance the film's political passions, so rendering them both more subtle and more convincing.

Searching for values: *Elisa, vida mía* and *Los ojos vendados*

Unlike most Spanish directors, Saura enjoyed relative freedom under Franco from about 1973 when *Ana y los lobos* was approved without a cut by the censor. Again unlike most directors in Spain, Saura made no attempt to take advantage of increasing liberties from 1975 to deal with more political issues. In 1975 he could still make a film with a clear anti-Franco stance, but after mid-1976 such a stance became increasingly difficult. For Saura, as for many other directors, the crucial event in Spain was Adolfo Suárez's accession to power in July 1976 and the hope of a rapid transition to democracy. By September 1976 Saura could say that 'the things that bother me in Spain are less clear than under Franco'.[23] Saura now faced a typical predicament for post-Franco film-makers. His films, like much Spanish cinema, had always shown a great moral sense: but what now was 'worth' filming?

Saura's immediate answer was that filming was a 'worthy' activity in itself. *Elisa, vida mía* can be seen as an elaborate metaphor for the mechanisms and values of filming. And the film's more overt theme is the search for values in a world of shifting complexities. Saura sets this theme within the Spanish traditions of *desengaño* (literally, 'disillusionment') – the seventeenth-century emphasis on turning away from worldly distractions towards essential values. Such a search has taken Luis, twenty years before the film begins, from the plush comfort of an upper-class home in Madrid to an isolated farmhouse where he lives alone. He has no social security or property of value, so the doors and windows of his farmhouse are left open.

To suggest the difficulties involved in Luis' search for values Saura enrols another Spanish literary reference: Calderón's play *El gran teatro de este mundo*, which Luis gets some of his students to act at the school where he teaches. In this seventeenth-century allegory life is compared to a play, men to the actors, God to the producer, and the parts to the social status or profession allotted to every man according to his individual capabilities. Since there was no written text, men possessed the free will to comply with or disobey the producer's initial instructions.[24]

Not limited by any religious belief, Luis' freedom in *Elisa, vida mía* is all the greater, as in consequence is his uncertainty. He reads Gracián's *El criticón* (1651–7), a treatise on *desengaño* through the teachings of experience and reason.[25] He also writes a journal which he attributes to his daughter Elisa, who becomes the 'I' of the text. But the only 'absolutes' suggested by the text are uncertainty ('This man doesn't even possess the security they say one acquires with age') and a preoccupation with death. In the longest sequence dramatising a section of Luis' text, he pictures himself back in the family home in Madrid, on his deathbed dreaming of bloodied horses' heads being swung down a rack at a slaughteryard, a surrealist *memento mori*.

141

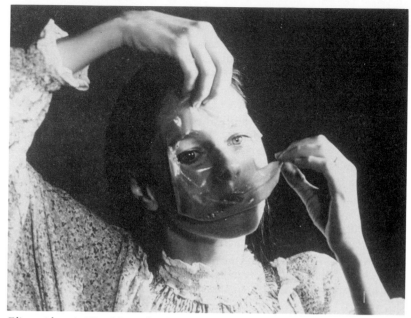

Elisa, vida mía (Geraldine Chaplin)

The narrative of *Elisa, vida mía* is slight. Luis is visited by his two daughters and his son-in-law. He invites Elisa to stay for a few days, and since her marriage is in crisis she welcomes the chance to get away. Elisa and Luis discover an imaginative affinity, and start telling each other stories. Elisa attends her father's Calderón class and takes it over when he falls ill. When he dies, she takes over his journal, writing as her own the words which open the film – Luis' journal account of Elisa's marital crisis, which he reads over an image of his visitors' car approaching the farmhouse. This same image, accompanied by Elisa's words, now closes the film, whose structure has described an elegant spiral.

One of the many pleasures of *Elisa, vida mía* is its effective use of symbolic space, characteristic of Saura's cinema. Enclosed in a conventional marriage, Elisa is often pictured enclosed in conventional spaces – a telephone box, a car – when she speaks to her husband.[26] Breaking with him, she gets out of the car to walk alone over the great open space of the Castillian countryside, an image both of her new freedom and of her new solitude. Open spaces in the film, as elsewhere in Saura, suggest mystery, paradox, and death. It is while out walking, for instance, that Luis drops to the ground in pain as his final attack begins. Behind him a new dawn breaks over Castille.

142

The film stands or falls, however, on its ability to portray and communicate a sense of pleasure and value in art itself. Such a project may not have been Saura's conscious aim, but it is as a film on film, art and imagination that *Elisa, vida mía* acquires its originality.[27] On the simplest level Saura's film includes some fine writing, such as the Calderón allegory or the poetry by Garcilaso de la Vega which gives the film its title.[28] Narrative events and declarations also suggest the value of art. Elisa's re-encounter with her father, his teaching and his journal leads to her spiritual regeneration. At first she adopts a passive position, listening to a story told by Luis in which a man kills his lover and returns each year to the scene of the murder to lay flowers. But soon Elisa begins to recount experiences to stimulate Luis' imagination, and when he dies she becomes his active, creative successor.

Luis' imaginative tutorship of Elisa breaks his solitude. His journal also affords him a sense of authenticity. 'I've spent all the night writing,' Luis says on his last walk, 'and now I feel liberated. I'd like to prolong these moments of plenitude, when I feel alive, alive.' In writing, as in his relationship with Elisa, Luis himself becomes something like a director figure. He draws on his environment to produce a work in which he transfers his own views into other, fictional, characters' mouths. He then persuades real people to take on these roles. His 'direction' becomes an act of mutual self-definition and enrichment. Saura has in fact admitted that 'One thing which I'm passionate about is to seize the chance ... to show an actor how he is.'[29] And his insistence on shooting a film in sequence gives a particular importance to the development of an actor's role as a film progresses. Elisa's imaginative growth, Luis' discovery of human contact and deep pleasure in writing stand as metaphors for the satisfactions of the film-making process in general.

As a film on film, *Elisa, vida mía* explores some of the less researched possibilities of the medium. Luis' constant voice-over, heard as he reads his texts, gives the film a gentle, musical rhythm. Saura sometimes contrasts voice-over and accompanying image to show film's duality: what is heard, what is seen.[30] And, rebelling against film as denotation, Saura sometimes hones down images to the bare minimum – often just a character and an undifferentiated background – so as to make film work as connotation, one image allowing a variety of interpretations.

Elisa, vida mía not only portrays but also proffers some values of art. Luis' journal does not explain reality totally; but it at least marshals its uncertainties. Luis calls his writing 'occupational therapy'. The appeal of much 'difficult' art – whether in its creation or its interpretation – would seem to be the promised discovery of a semblance of order in a simulacrum of reality. Such a promise is suggested in *Elisa, vida mía*, where characters' stories, fantasies and memories and Luis' texts are mixed in highly involved ways. Elisa's memory of childhood at the family home flows freely into a

143

visual embodiment of one of Luis' texts, where he pictures his abandoning that home. But there are no editing indications to suggest where memory ends and text begins, or indeed that this one sequence must be attributed to two separate imaginations.

In an essay on the film, Raul Beceyro shows that Saura fulfils the contract entered into by any 'difficult' film-maker of supplying the means for at least a partial resolution of his film's surface confusions. While *Elisa, vida mía* convincingly suggests the intellectual and aesthetic values of film, one aspect is slightly underplayed: the moral value of the creative imagination. Saura seems slightly uneasy about the domination exercised by Luis as director/father-figure over Elisa. There are some suggestions of an unresolved and returned Electra complex in the relationship. When Luis remembers making love to his wife, for example, he pictures her as Elisa.[31]

Though a lesser work, *Los ojos vendados* may be seen as responding to some of the ambiguities or inadequacies of *Elisa, vida mía*. The film drew immediate inspiration from events in Spain in 1977: the Atocha killings; a right-wing attack on Saura's sixteen-year-old son Antonio, to whom the film is dedicated; a symposium on torture in Latin America where one testifying victim made Saura reflect on the role of representation in an act of political protest: 'I asked myself if she wasn't acting out the role of torture victim which had been assigned to her. And if I, seated at the presidential table – an ideal vantage point – wasn't part of the same theatrical work which was taking place with my role being the spectator and actor at the same time.'[32] *Los ojos vendados* developed these speculations. Its theme is not torture but the portrayal of torture. 'Saura shows,' comments critic Marcel Oms, 'that it isn't physical pain that awakens or kills conscience but the imaginative reaction before such a horror.'[33] *Los ojos vendados* returns, then, to the question of value and an issue of great importance to any director fluctuating between political and more purely 'artistic' expression: the moral and political worth of the creative imagination.

Los ojos vendados begins with Luis, a theatrical director, attending a symposium on torture. Like Saura, he conceives the idea of re-creating the symposium in a play which he will direct. His problem is to imagine the horror of torture, to represent it to himself. He does this simply by analogy, fantasising that the torture victim is Emilia, the wife of a dentist friend and the woman he loves. At the dentist's he imagines her being kidnapped by torturers, then experiences pain himself when the dentist touches a nerve. Bored, trapped in a conventional marriage, Emilia begins attending Luis' acting classes. Luis persuades her to play the torture victim in his play, and the film finishes with Emilia on stage, looking identical to Luis' original vision of her at the symposium as the testifying victim. 'I hope,' Emilia concludes, 'that my testimony will help alert public opinion against military, authoritarian and repressive regimes to stop such events recurring.'

144

Suddenly two youths stand up and spray the audience, Emilia and Luis with machine-gun bullets.

The mass slaughter is its own condemnation. It also conforms to Saura's attempt to represent torture to the spectator. 'Almost without realising it,' Saura has said, 'we live in a world dominated by a violence which, visible or hidden, restricts our freedom.'[34] Torture and terrorism become extreme points on the film's scale of violence: Luis is beaten up by extremists, Emilia is hit by her husband, and their relationship contains its 'tortures' of remorse and fear. Saura also cleverly involves the spectator in the mechanisms of 'commitment'. He encourages us to identify with Emilia and Luis, feeling their suffering as our own. He creates in Luis a spectator surrogate, confronting him with problems similar to those of any spectator watching a film.

The final mass slaughter may be real, or part of the play, or imagined by Luis either during the play or during the original symposium. Such ambiguities are hardly gratuitous. The greatest interest of *Los ojos vendados* is its reflection on the role of representation and imagination, not only in politics but also in art and everyday reality. In *Elisa, vida mía* a 'normal' relationship served as a metaphor for an artistic process; in *Los ojos vendados* the reverse occurs. At Luis' acting classes Emilia learns that to understand a character one must search for analogous experiences in one's own life. She also finds out how to represent the emotions of her character to an audience.

The mechanism of the couple's relationship is not so different. Luis is first attracted to Emilia when he collapses with an attack of colic and she bends over him in sympathy. And when Emilia arrives at Luis' apartment, seemingly distraught at her husband's attack, she suddenly interrupts her tears to ask 'How's my performance?' The problem Saura points to runs like an undercurrent through the whole of his work: the self's knowledge of another's experience, conscious or unconscious, may well be based entirely on inference. Relationships come to involve a double act of 'representation', of one's own feelings to others and their representation of these feelings to themselves. Symbolism in Saura's work – here seen in the torture victim's dark glasses, Emilia's acting gestures, Luis' play, the symposium and so on – becomes not just a censor-avoiding stratagem but an observed feature of normal life.[35]

Modernism: *Mamá cumple cien años* and *Deprisa, deprisa*

One major conclusion suggested by Saura's post-Franco career is how difficult it was for established Spanish directors to change. Saura declared that his political commitment ended with *La prima Angélica*, yet *Cría cuervos* was a sharp if subtle attack on Francoist conventions, and *Los ojos vendados* repeated important features of Saura's cinema under Franco: an attack on an obvious political evil (a repressive society, torture and violence); an oblique treatment; close psychological observation.

Saura's slowness to change reflected a general uncertainty on the part of Spanish film-makers as to just how they should change. Saura's own uncertainties were compounded by his mixed feelings about the transition: he felt that there were still issues to be resolved, but that despite everything much had changed in Spain by 1979. Saura did have, however, one unique advantage over most Spanish film-makers – the particular character of his films to date. By charting his distance from his previous work, Saura would be able to suggest Spain's evolution and announce his own changes as an artist. At a time of dislocation such self-reflections provided a valuable means towards definitions of self and of Spain.

Saura's first film to refer back to his own work was *Mamá cumple cien años* ('Mama Turns a Hundred', 1979), a variation on his earlier *Ana y los lobos* ('Ana and the Wolves', 1972). This earlier film was a sharp critique of some of the attributes of the Francoist Establishment – militarism, lechery, religious hypocrisy – as embodied in the sons, José, Juan and Fernando, of an effusive, epileptic and ultimately tyrannical mother. A new governess, Ana (Geraldine Chaplin), comes to teach Juan's daughters in the family's isolated, rambling house. Ana provokes the men, causing Juan to declare his attraction to her, José to swagger round in his military uniforms, and Fernando to try to turn her into a religious recluse. With the sons increasingly competing for Ana, Mamá intervenes to insist that the girl must leave. As Ana walks away from the house, she is trapped by the three men: Fernando cuts her hair, Juan rapes her, and José shoots her dead.

Ana y los lobos paints a double-sided allegory: Francoism as the orchestrated alliance of competing interests, Spain as a country warped by its frustrations. At a time when Spain was seeking to present a modern image to the outside world, Saura's *esperpento* reflected Valle-Inclán's statement that 'Spain is a grotesque deformation of European civilisation'. The film's deformations may be literal, as in the grotesquely large scissors Fernando uses to cut Ana's hair. Another source of distortion is the film's irrealities – such as Fernando's levitation, a hallucination which he shares with Ana – which are shot realistically, as if they really occur. The greatest deformations are supplied by the characters' frustrations: José is not actually a soldier but just collects uniforms; Juan never seduces Ana; Fernando's mysticism is just a ploy to attract her. As Enrique Brasó suggests, all the brothers' actions may be staged, performances from the past: characters speak of 'other girls', 'other times'.[36]

After *Los ojos vendados*, Saura says, he felt 'dried up': 'I needed to do something more open, more extrovert, even more amusing.' Planning a short feature homage to Luis Cuadrado, he decided to take some characters from a film Cuadrado had shot, *Ana y los lobos*, and 'see what happened to

146

Mamá cumple cien años

them'. The idea developed into *Mamá cumple cien años*, where Saura
'resurrects' Ana who returns to Mamá's house with her husband Antonio.

The initial scenes of *Mamá cumple cien años* enlist most of the same
characters, move them on fifteen years and construct an allegory of the
newer Spain. In an essay on the film, Susan Tate has listed most of the
changes Saura points to.[37] There is, for example, a symbolic passing of
authority: Ana is now an ex-governess: José is dead and his uniforms sold
to the Spanish Salvation Army. Juan has left his wife for the cook, an event
which marks the loosening of marriage ties and the near disappearance of
domestic service in post-Franco Spain.[38] Eldest daughter Natalia has grown
up into a sexually reckless woman who seduces Antonio, smokes hashish
and lives in a 'sultan's tent' of a bedroom: she characterises Spain's new
liberalised youth, who were socially 'progressive' but tending politically
towards abstentionism.

The only merit in such allegory is its enjoyable predictability. *Mamá
cumple cien años* suggests that Saura, like Spain, has changed. The film is
Saura's first comedy. Fernando, for example, has become a hang-gliding
enthusiast and flaps round the garden like an ungainly bird before laun-
ching himself into space to nose-dive into the ground. Actor Fernando
Fernán Gómez's balding pate and stringy frame and Fernando's technical
jargon (about readjusting his glider's centre of gravity) turn him into a
latter-day Don Quixote. Saura's shooting style has also changed. An often

147

hand-held camera, wide-angle shots, and fluid sequences give a new spatial liberty to his direction. Lighting is warmer, airier, even sensual. The *huis clos* of earlier films (the valley in *La caza*, the industrial engineer's house in *La madriguera*, the family home of *Ana y los lobos* and *Cría cuervos*) establishes careful delimitations between the interiors and the world outside. In *Mamá cumple cien años*, however, the frontier between interior and exterior (here the walls of the house) is continually crossed by movement or characters' looks. A sunrise is presented, implicitly viewed from the house; Antonio regards the estate from the balcony while lazily smoking a joint; next morning Natalia leans out of a window to greet Antonio, who looks up at her from outside. Equally new, space inside the house is split up into what in terms of decor and behaviour are like autonomous areas, of which Natalia's bedroom is only the most obvious example.[39]

Most critics were only willing, however, to admit non-essential changes in Saura's vision of new Spain. Marcel Oms points out that the grown-up daughters inherit the vices of their father and their uncles: the second daughter dresses up in a military uniform which she finds in a trunk, the youngest mopes dreamily round the house reading *The Brothers Karamazov*. Mamá prohibits the sale of family land to housing developers, pushing Luchy, Fernando and a returned Juan to scheme to kill her. 'The faithful soldier is gone,' comments Julio Pérez Perucha, and 'Mamá is betrayed by the venal civilians she has nurtured and who are driven by mercantile interests to abandon her immutable principles which she inculcated in them. Mamá could well be the spirit of Francoism in person.'[40]

The problem with wholly allegorical interpretations of *Mamá cumple cien años* is that they lead to what in historical terms is an absurdity: the 'spirit of Francoism' enlisting 'Foreign Aid' (one allegorical interpretation of Ana) to withstand its final destruction by the capitalist classes. Such glosses also ignore Saura's intriguing emotional changes from the late 70s, when he begins to respond far more to the southern Spanish side of his family. 'I was very much at ease with *Mamá cumple cien años*,' Saura has said. 'It has something Levantine-Andalusian about it: the Levant attracts me, the mother, the sons....'[41] Any comparison between *Ana y los lobos* and *Mamá cumple cien años* is made difficult by the fact that the families of the two films suggest clear social differences: that in the first film is purely Francoist, that in the second is typical, as Saura has said, of the southern Spanish bourgeoisie.[42]

As was natural in a film-maker who viewed Francoism as forty years of cultural aberration, Saura's vision of Spain in 1979 reflected not only the country's temporary state as it came out of a dictatorship but also its more essential nature. Saura sees this as embodied in Spain's most enduring cultural traditions, which he uses to regulate the events and tenor of his film. The cultural references in the film are legion. The scene where Ana

148

hears Mamá's voice in the grotto was inspired by Saura's reading of the Spanish mystic writer San Juan de la Cruz; Mamá's birthday treat of being lowered from the ceiling in her chair recalls the re-enactment of the miracle of Elche.[43] And the scene where Mamá appears to die but revives following a gust of supernatural wind was inspired by Spain's grandiloquent theatrical designer Rambal.[44] But the trouble with Saura's observations on both Spain's temporary state and its essential condition is that a reference to one – such as Mamá's revival – could be taken as an implication about the other.[45] *Mamá cumple cien años* reflects the problematic attempt by a post-Franco film-maker to abandon an anti-Francoist tradition for a wider cultural context. The reference back to *Ana y los lobos* confuses rather than points this transition. Saura's self-reflection in his next film, *Deprisa, deprisa* ('Fast, Fast', 1980), a return to the world of his first feature *Los golfos*, was pointedly more successful.

An important influence on Saura's later career has been the fierce opposition of Spain's film press. By the late 70s Saura was being accused of an 'exacerbated, useless narcissism', of being too serious, 'monotonously repetitive', pretentious. Such criticism hurried Saura along a road he was already taking: a change in his film-making personality.[46]

Deprisa, deprisa marked a short-term departure in subject and characters' social class by depicting the lives of four Madrid delinquents who pull robberies, snort heroin and steal cars, moved by a vague but visceral sense of 'liberty' and a scorn for middle-class conventions. Saura's work methods also changed: he abandoned an original script and took to wandering the bars, cafés and discos on the working-class periphery of Madrid, looking to base his characters on real-life delinquents.[47] The film documents the delinquents, recording their flamenco-pop music, their ignorance of the Civil War, their racy diction – a mix of slightly archaic homespun wisdom and demi-monde slang. Saura's dialogue rings true.

The other source for *Deprisa, deprisa* is also external to Saura: the format of the American crime movie. The delinquents' crimes become more complicated and violent; small details predict their doom – the blood-red car which the leader, Pablo, buys for the girl, Angela; the social background which drives the delinquents into crime is not examined, but there is a vague desire for escape, symbolised by the trains which rush by Angela's flat but which she and her friends will never catch.

Saura plays documentary and fictional modes off against each other. In the first robbery, for instance, Angela is left watching the security guard at the industrial compound entrance. Her false moustache begins to slide; the guard says her friends have obviously abandoned her. Such dramatic tension is accentuated by formal conventions from documentary film such as hand-held shots, off-centre framing, Pablo's slang as he delivers a pre-robbery briefing. Saura transforms his documentary material into striking film forms. 'These characters,' he said of Madrid delinquents, 'who are at certain times absolutely violent, are in normal life very calm. They spend hours and hours doing nothing.' This contrast is systematised in the film's montage, which balances narrative back-waters with sudden violence. Frame composition varies according to mood from a normal background of urban industrial decay to a dark blue sky against which the delinquents talk of driving to the sea. Here, chat about an implicit escape from environment is matched by one rare moment of disengagement from the familiar visual background.

The reference point for these techniques was *Los golfos* ('The Hooligans', 1959), Saura's debut, 'a sort of documentary and feature', as he puts it, detailing the attempts of a group of working-class youths to escape from their drab surroundings by forming a bull-fighting team and scraping together enough money to pay for their torero's professional debut. Destitute, unemployed, or poorly paid as market porters, they end up stealing. One is recognised, pursued by bystanders, throws himself down a manhole and drowns in the sewers. When it comes, the final fight is a shambles.[48]

Deprisa, deprisa drew on *Los golfos* for its portrait of social dissent. Saura's first film begins, as Brasó suggests, 'already in gear'. It presents the catalyst for action – the need for money to launch a torero – rather than its larger social causes: the late-50s economic crisis as Spain abandoned autocracy; a mismanaged urbanisation in a country lacking a social welfare system. The causes of delinquency in both films are implied by a few subtle but significant details. When Pablo and Angela take a television into his grandmother's home, for instance, the camera pulls away from the television up to the church tower. The sequence at the memorial site El cerro de los Angeles opens with the monument's cross foregrounded, and the delinquents diminished in the background – a typical Saura composition suggesting the domination of characters by their environment.[49] A police car arrives and the boys are lined up against a wall and frisked. 'What a democracy!' one comments. 'I'll do the talking round here!' a policeman retorts. The implication is that though traditional religious repression has disappeared in Spain, new comparable forms have taken its place such as the police and the mass media where only the voice of authority is allowed (television in Spain is entirely state-run). Back at her flat with Pablo, who is mortally wounded from a police bullet, Angela turns on the television. The state news now does the talking. A positive report on the Pope's involvement with Catholic schools is followed by an item on the delinquents' bank raid. The newscaster's Spanish is the otiose 'officialese' of Spanish television. But the facts given are wrong, and eye-witness accounts from 'normal citizens' describing the delinquents as 'monsters' contrast pointedly with our knowledge of them. Spaniards, the state and the average citizen are seen to condemn what they do not know.

150

Saura drew on *Los golfos* to chart Spain's change and his own distance from his previous work. At a time when he was increasingly ostracised by Spain's critical establishment he also drew on *Los golfos*, one senses, for its romantic sympathy towards social outsiders, a mood encouraged by the obvious analogy between the delinquents of *Los golfos* and Saura and his crew, who were also attempting in 1959 to break into the entertainment industry. *Deprisa, deprisa* shows a similar sympathy for social rejects. It is in fact a double love story. There is Pablo's relationship with Angela, caught in moments of stilted declarations and quiet scenes of unselfish affection. There is also Saura's own relationship with his characters, especially Angela. The key to Saura's new mood is the delinquents' music, songs of gutsy flamenco pop. The music gives the film its sense of drive and emotion. Most of the romantic melodies are, moreover, accompanied by close-ups of Angela. These shots are 'unlocated'. The one time when a close-up of Angela can be linked to Pablo's adoring gaze is when he drives her to the coast, singing along with the words of 'Me quedo contigo' ('I'd Stay With You') and turning to look at Angela as he does. *Deprisa, deprisa* announces a new romantic Saura. It is a mood which, though sometimes distanced by ironies, has remained with him up to the mid-80s.

Spanish musical: *Bodas de sangre* and *Carmen*

Ever since Fructuoso Gelabert, Spanish film-makers have attempted to make a 'national' cinema, one which expressed Spain's 'true' character and style. The drawback for foreign audiences of any purportedly 'Spanish' film was its many lost references, its sometimes irritating suggestion of a self-possessed and self-obsessed Spanish nation. In Saura's early films the essential cultural references remain external to the plot. Allusions – often very important insinuations – are lost on the uninitiated. Those spectators who do not perceive the *esperpento* style of *El jardín de las delicias* and *Ana y los lobos* will miss their *esperpento* conclusion: 'Spain is a grotesque deformation of European civilisation.'

In his cinema under Franco, Saura played off two levels: his characters' fantasies, and their reality. In *Bodas de sangre* ('Blood Wedding', 1981) and *Carmen* (1983) Saura dramatises his films' cultural influence by adapting Lorca's play and Mérimée's novella. Instead of two levels we now have three: the social reality of the original texts reflected in their dance adaptations; the world of ballet; the reality of the dancers external to the ballet rehearsals. Instead of being a barrier to international comprehension, Saura's specifically Spanish texts form the base of a richly nuanced art.

Alfredo Mañas' dramatic adaptation of Lorca's play *Bodas de sangre* omits the supernatural characters, dramatises the final knife-fight, but reproduces Lorca's melodramatic story-line with an economy of means echoed in Antonio Gades' eloquently simple choreography. A mother

151

dances with her son as she dresses him to go and ask officially for his fiancée's hand. She reacts in horror when he prepares to take a knife: her husband and other son were killed in blood feuds and she doesn't want the same thing to happen to her remaining son. In the second duo, a mother rocks a cradle; her husband Leonardo returns; she clings to him but he pushes her away with haughty disdain. The third dance duo tells us why: Leonardo and the bride-to-be dance together, separate to writhe in agonies of self-repression on the floor, come together again to melt in passionate embrace. Musicians arrive to announce the morning of the wedding; Leonardo prowls round the wedding dance and the new bride only has eyes for him; later, Leonardo's wife rushes in to say that Leonardo and the bride have eloped; the vengeful mother urges her son to pursue them. In the final scene Leonardo and the groom kill each other in a knife-fight, leaving the bride to lament.

Saura adapts Gades by filming a rehearsal not a performance, and adding a prologue where we see the dancers making up, warming up, and then changing for their full dress rehearsal. Saura adapting Gades adapting Lorca allows for rich insights into the way effects are transcribed from one medium to another. 'Drama,' Lorca said, 'is poetry which gets up from a book and becomes human.'[50] Lorca's 'poetic' theatre used colour contrasts, the supernatural, and verse of rich imagery often drawn from nature. Gades' 'poetry' is his balanced movements of 'classical' flamenco ballet and a sometimes surrealist choreography, which Saura captures in the prologue: a general shot shows Gades' dancers lifting their hands and turning them in unison, producing the effect of a forest of arms seemingly bending in the same direction, as if in a wind. Saura's 'poetry' is to place the camera in a ballet relationship to the dancer, the movements of one determining the possibility of the other. Movement in frame encourages a fixed camera; the camera tends to move if a dancer keeps to one spot. There are other eloquent transcriptions. Snapping fingers create tension in the ballet, and Saura achieves a similar effect by sometimes emptying his frame of figures, then having the dancers burst into shot.[51]

Bodas de sangre's greatest quality is its visual impact; the key to its more cerebral undercurrents is its use of mirrors. In an establishing sequence Gades dances in front of a mirror and then in front of his troupe, looking beyond the camera to the mirror in which he can see the reflection of his dancers behind him. The placement of the camera in front of the mirror equates it, as Saura has said, with 'a mirror in front of which the dancers are rehearsing, or the public which in some ways is an imaginary mirror'.[52] Later, the dancers again pose in front of the camera but this time for a wedding photograph. For a moment they freeze into conventional positions, the groom for example setting his hands on his knees in an act of imposing *machismo*.

152

Bodas de sangre: blood feud

There is an obvious physical similarity between the dancers' artistic pose and the social pose of the characters in the drama. Ballet and social ceremonies are both rites which involve restrictions. Gades' characters dress up for the wedding; his dancers dress up for the ballet. Ballets repeat exactly the same steps; so almost does society. Gades tells his dancers to 'hold in' their bodies; as characters Leonardo and the bride try desperately to hold in their emotions. A point made by *Bodas de sangre*, however, is that art is *not* necessarily a mirror to reality. Events or figures differ substantially in their artistic and social significance. Self-control and discipline in the dancers leads to ballet of great beauty; the self-repression of Leonardo and the bride leads to great self-torment. A similar ambivalence affects the key figure of *Bodas de sangre*: the circle. The groom lifts up his mother and dances circles with her in his arms; the film turns full circle, beginning and ending with a freeze-frame of the wedding photograph. Aesthetically, such repetitions are pleasing. Yet the social meaning of such circles is highly negative: the groom's world turns unhealthily around his mother; with the rebel Leonardo eliminated, *Bodas de sangre* ends on an ironical image of social harmony.

A key technique of *Bodas de sangre* is its use of out-of-frame space. Lying out of shot are repression (the pursuers of Leonardo and the bride), 'reality' (the dancers not involved in immediate scenes of the ballet), or a figure restricting individual freedom (Leonardo at the wedding dance, where Saura cuts from a general shot to a close-up reverse-field exchange of Leonardo and the bride directing 'significant' glances at each other). Equally out of shot is the source of the clapping and shouts as the groom and Leonardo sink their knives into each other. The soundtrack converts an act of individual vengeance into a social act which meets with society's approval. But what of the dancers' social reality? It lies in a great 'out of shot' space to which the make-up and changing rooms act like anterooms. Saura at times insinuates restrictions. The stage manager assigns each dancer a space to make up, in a carefully observed hierarchy, a nice echo of the producer-God in *El gran teatro de este mundo*. The dancer playing Leonardo's wife (who reproaches Leonardo for his indifference to his family) slots photographs suggesting her own strongly Catholic family beliefs into the side of her mirror: a photograph of a boy (her son?), an image of Christ, and a saint with a boy. These good-luck symbols form part of an artistic ritual; their exact social significance is more ambiguous.

It was left to *Carmen* to systematise these suggestions into a theme. Here dance and the social reality of the dancers reflect each other sufficiently to suggest that male-female relations have not evolved substantially beyond the Spain which Mérimée found in the nineteenth century, a country, Saura says, which was 'traditionally Catholic, still dominated by external appearance and honour, where crimes of passion were justified by irrational jealousy and a sense of "possession" which seems to have marked men-women relations for centuries.'[53]

Carmen begins with choreographer and director Antonio (played by Antonio Gades, who shared scriptwriting and choreography with Saura) searching for a girl to take the lead in his Spanish dance version of *Carmen*. He finds her: her name is Carmen (of course); she is an independent, strong-willed young dancer at a flamenco nightclub. Antonio falls in love with her and their subsequent affair allows Saura to make ironic comment on present-day *machismo* in Spain. Like his fictional counterpart Don José, Antonio chafes with jealousy if he suspects any other man of being involved with Carmen: he won't even speak, for example, to Carmen's agent. He abuses his professional position as ballet troupe director and the dancer playing Don José to urge Carmen to caress him in their dance rehearsals. He idealises Carmen, treating her as the embodiment of an archetype rather than an individual. He also puts pride before love. In the final scene in his ballet, he and the torero quarrel over Carmen. Each man tries to outdance the other, and Carmen is soon forgotten in what becomes a duel of dancing in which the essential thing is not to lose face in public.

Machismo impedes communication. It is also quite simply a lie. One of the Doré engravings used for the title sequence shows an Andalusian girl

154

dressed as a bullfighter, a bull dead at her feet, the girl's masculine air making her look like a transvestite. The detail is significant since Antonio, for all his manly pretences, is forced to take a subordinate role in his relationship with Carmen. He takes the woman's role in the rehearsals to show Carmen how to dance. She initiates their sexual relationship both in the fiction of the ballet and in reality, going to Antonio's studio one night when he has stayed behind to dance.[54]

Carmen and Antonio's first night together is a watershed in the film. Before that Saura has accumulated various elements or effects which suggest that the scenes before us are or tend towards fiction, in the sense of being rehearsals or Antonio's subjective visions. *Carmen* begins, for example, with flamenco dancing girls strutting some steps before Antonio. They are on a stage, the lights are low and soft-focus camerawork and subjective shots from Antonio's viewpoint suggest that Antonio is already 'subjectivising' the scene before him, imagining the girls as his mythical Carmen. Other elements – mirrors, editing, camera placement, lighting, props – also help fictionalise the reality before us.[55]

After Carmen has seduced Antonio and left, he goes back to his studio and dances in front of a mirror, confirming his artistic, fictional and social personality as a magnificent dancer, a Don José character, and a sexual conqueror. His *macho* reaction, having gained Carmen, is immediately to fear her loss. Drinking from Carmen's half-empty glass, he imagines Carmen going to jail to visit her husband, whom Antonio depicts as a member of his dancing company.[56] One explanation for the remaining scenes in *Carmen* is that they are all Antonio's imaginings. In that case Carmen would suggest how a *macho* male, when challenged by an aggressive woman, will divert her threat by turning her into a fictionalised archetype. Carmen the girl he has gone to bed with, Antonio imagines, will die like Carmen the myth. It is at once a sublimation and a revenge. It is equally plausible to see the final scenes of Carmen as mixing Antonio's fantasies (such as when he sees Carmen's husband, played by a dancer, arrive at his studio accompanied by her manager, who seems to have no notion of the husband's 'fictionality'), staged parts of Antonio's ballet (such as the torero/Don José duel) which are influenced by reality, and real happenings (such as Antonio discovering Carmen making love to the dancer 'Tauro') which mirror the fiction. Or, thirdly, we can conclude that reality and fiction mix inextricably. A constant flux between different realities again makes a point: the impact on Spanish reality of 'fictions', of which *Carmen* and the still prevalent code of *machismo* would be two examples in modern Spain.

The flow of fiction and reality in *Carmen* has other interpretations. *Carmen* was a conscious attempt by Gades and Saura at a Spanish musical. Saura declares his intentions in an early scene: Antonio listens to Bizet's

Carmen: mirrors of fiction

Carmen; his friend Paco, played by the world's leading flamenco guitarist
Paco de Lucía, translates the opera music with off-the-cuff brilliance into
flamenco guitar music. 'Bizet's *Carmen*,' Saura comments in his script, 'the
music of his universal opera, returns to the country of origin of the myth.'[57]
The dances in *Carmen* include the *pasodoble*, *sevillanas*, flamenco ballet,
and the *farruca*, a flamenco dance of hard, austere movements which
Antonio dances to express his love for Carmen. Saura's film not only
embodies Spanish culture but isolates some of its major features. The film
ends with Antonio knifing Carmen to death in a corner of his studio. In his
fantasies, in his ballet production, or in reality he prefers to kill her rather
than cede her to another man. The fact that fictional or possibly 'real'

events in *Carmen* follow closely the Carmen myth gives them a familiar Spanish air of inevitability. Saura and Gades include another ritual of blood, passion and inevitable death: the bullfight. Both Bizet's *Carmen* and the bullfight are parodied at the dance company's party, suggesting their centrality to a culture grounded in fatalism.

The sheer mystification resulting from the mix of fiction and reality in *Carmen* combines with its visual appeal in a way typical of Mediterranean Catholic culture: a sense of spectacle, a delight in the sensual representation of events, an air of mystery. Saura's *tour de force* is Carmen's fight with another girl at the tobacco factory, where he mixes soft focus, warm or brilliant colours, a continually tracking camera, dramatic diagonals in shot composition, quick cuts from general shot to medium close-up, and repeated foregrounding of secondary action – the dancing of other girls – to create two ebullient centres of dance action. Equally effective, and more mysterious, is the film's opening scene where the vivid turquoise, mauve and red clothes of the dancers paint an atmosphere of perfumed sensuality, a garden of swaying figures.

Carmen, writes Vicente Molina Foix, 'becomes the reflection on the danced life of some characters for whom music and dance are the only signs and the most certain language'.[58] In a world of dissimulation, warped passions and failed communication, what better way to symbolise a beautiful sentiment than through a gesture of beauty? Dance also captures the tenor of Carmen's sentiments, extrovert passions felt and expressed immediately as sensation in the present. A moving sequence in *Carmen* is the bedroom scene, when Antonio and Carmen are in love as people as well as characters. She dances for him and he watches; he dances for her and she watches. Pleasure is given for pleasure.[59]

Carmen also delivers a pessimistic and very Spanish verdict on freedom. Carmen, in fiction and reality, prefers to die rather than stay with Don José/Antonio. That has not changed from Mérimée's novella; nor has the suggestion – seen in the sad look in Carmen's eyes as she promises to stay with Antonio – that Carmen knows how her life will end. In a post-Franco Spain the characters still bear the marks of centuries of authoritarian government: 'freedom' for them seems less a right than a vicarious form of escape. 'Let's take away the ladder,' Antonio says as he prepares the stage for his bedroom dance with Carmen. 'We'll put the mirrors in their place, close the curtains slowly, and leave all of this space empty for me.' Disembodied from a dross and treacherous reality, Antonio dances with Carmen. As he embraces her the camera slowly approaches, leaving even such a reminder of reality as the stage-light out of shot. Antonio's arms encircle Carmen; they close their eyes and dance. Their escape from reality may be an illusion. Art at least gives this illusion an 'empty space' in which to breathe.

157

Dulces horas; Antonieta; Los zancos

Saura returned to the Spanish musical and collaboration with Gades in 1985 with *El amor brujo*, based on the ballet whose music was written by Manuel de Falla. His dance trilogy apart, Saura's cinema in the 80s has produced interesting rather than major works. *Dulces horas* ('Sweet Hours', 1981) reflects Saura's consistent search for a new voice. Its protagonist is Juan, a theatrical director and owner of an art gallery, who acquires his parents' correspondence written after his father had left his mother to escape with a lover to South America in the wake of a financial scandal. The letters inspire Juan to stage a play featuring his middle-class family life as a child in the 40s. Rehearsals spring memories: Civil War bombings, his mother's domineering attentions, her suicide which Juan thinks he witnessed and unwittingly aided. Juan falls in love with and marries Berta, the actress who plays and (he thinks) looks like his mother. At the end of the film, now pregnant, she sings 'Recordar' (a song from Saura's childhood) as she bathes Juan and asks maternally, 'And how is my baby?'

In *Dulces horas*, Saura says, he wanted to tell the same story another way.[60] Old forms remain; their identities change. Saura's dialectic is now one of memory contrasting and fusing with fiction. Since Juan plays himself at his rehearsals and their dramatic nature remains unannounced far into the film, we first think that his fiction is memory. Both fiction and memory are eventually shown to be inaccurate, hence 'fictions' of another kind. Juan, for instance, remembers his mother taking an overdose; yet he admits elsewhere that nobody knows when his mother died. In his play, Juan slopes homes from watching *Gilda* to find his uncle reading about Germany's invasion of Russia; but *Gilda* was premiered in Spain, to utter scandal, in 1947.

The major novelty in *Dulces horas* is its tone. It is a clear parody of earlier films. When Juan remembers his childhood, for instance, music swells and the camera rises to float ethereally in the trees. Juan also sees his idealising of his mother as quite unjustified: it was his mother's 'total domination' which drove his father away. Juan's obsessions may be misguided and ridiculous; the film's acerbic conclusion is that this does not make them any the less consequential. Juan may distance himself from his past intellectually, but its emotional legacies remain. One reading of the plot would indeed be that Juan, discovering from the letters that his mother loved his father more than him (the letters thus acting as a kind of epistolary 'primal scene'), marries a woman he persuades himself to be his mother's double so as to re-establish his position as his mother's lover.[61] Suggesting catalysts such as the mother's possessive love for Juan, *Dulces horas* encourages us to think about the real roots of Juan's obsessions: the enclosed horizons for an abandoned woman in the 1940s, loveless marriages of incompatible

158

couples common in any country which discourages expression of genuine feelings.[62]

Dulces horas confirmed Saura's modernist trait of reflecting on the past art of Spain and his own past as a director. Its reviews in the Spanish film press were so vitriolic that he was to abandon this latter option altogether.[63] In 1983 he filmed *Antonieta*, in which a researcher (played by Hanna Schygulla) investigates the life and suicide of Antonieta Rivas Mercadé (Isabelle Adjani), a beautiful Mexican patroness of the arts who broke with social convention to abandon her husband for the Mexican politician Vasconcelos. For the first time Saura filmed abroad, and didn't write his own script. The result is an unadventurous historical film: a large production bereft of any intellectual pretensions; a formally conventional portrayal of an individual's rebellion; a de luxe illustration of poverty. Saura's normally acute sense of female psychology and his fertile comparisons of past and present are largely missing.[64]

Saura's authorial personality disappears in *Antonieta*. It re-emerged in *Los zancos* ('The Stilts', 1984) enriched by Fernando Fernán Gómez, who collaborated on the script and whose acting performance is the film's major pleasure. Fernán Gómez plays Angel, a university professor and writer who, depressed and lonely after his wife's death, contemplates suicide, to be rescued by a pretty young neighbour, Teresa. Smitten, Angel writes a fable for the theatre troupe for which Teresa works, a play called 'The Melancholy Knight' which is rehearsed and performed on stilts. Teresa wants to comfort Angel but rapidly withdraws from an affair. Rejected, Angel attempts to gas himself in a shed, but he can't go through with it. At a distance, Angel sees Teresa and her husband relaxing in the glow of their sitting room, their mutual love, and their youth.

Though a minor work, replete with Spanish references, *Los zancos* suggests some evolution. Ambiguities about the status of scene before us – is it fiction or reality? – are replaced by uncertainties about motives: does Angel pull out of suicide because he is too deflated? Or does he still entertain a perverse hope of reconciliation with Teresa? Surreptitiously, but successfully, old ideas find new forms which modify meanings. Angel, for example, has a video camera. The video film replaces the photograph as a record of a human face, so mysterious beneath its tangibility: Angel magnifies a freeze-frame of Teresa's face until it is reduced to a full-screen blur. Yet it is far less easy to strike a pose before a video camera than for a still camera: Angel's video clips of himself show his advancing old age unequivocally.

What remains of Saura's earlier style in *Los zancos* is a sometimes acute sense of human psychology and a continuing preoccupation with the legacy of Spanish culture. The young actors in the theatre troupe set Angel's play to Judaeo-Spanish medieval music which gives its equation of love and suffering, which Saura's film only echoes, a timeless dimension. Embracing Teresa, Angel quotes a series of paradoxes from a poem by the Spanish metaphysical poet Quevedo which portray love as an ineffable mystery. Behind *Los zancos*, sharpening Angel's predicament, is the seventeenth-century emphasis on solitude and *desengaño*, the need to recognise one's true condition, in Angel's case the cold truth that he is too old ever to attract a young girl again. Saura gives such traditions a further twist: love may be paradoxical but some paradoxes won't endure. One of them is the relationship between a young girl and an old man, whose physical incongruities are brought home by Saura's use of reverse shot exchanges or two-shots contrasting Teresa's fresh-faced youth with Angel's wrinkled age.[65]

For the very first time in *Los zancos* Saura shows his own age. 'Reality' is no longer the repressions of Franco's dictatorship, or the long-term legacies of contradicting social conventions, or just 'what someone thinks ... the ghosts inside his head.' 'Reality' is also the skull beneath the skin, man's mortality. Once more Saura draws on Spanish culture to frame this preoccupation. He echoes Quevedo's double-sided vision: men as they seem, men as they essentially are; death the great exposer of man's true state, youth as a kind of ephemeral disguise. Notably in *Los zancos* all Teresa's friends are young, and mostly actors who perform with histrionic sound and fury and whose stilts – to Saura a symbol of the physical advantage of youth – give them an artificial and suggestedly temporary superiority over Angel. More morbid is Angel's magnifying of Teresa's face on his videotape recorder by which a beautiful young girl is reduced to 'nothingness'. The richness given to *Los zancos* by pre-Franco traditions suggests that Saura will return to them in the future. To the painter Joan Miró, Francoism was an aberration. His image of Spanish culture is of a carob tree, deep-rooted and evergreen. It is an attitude, one suspects, which a cultural regenerator like Saura would share.

STOCKTAKING: 1977–1981

On 15 June 1977 Spain held its first free elections for forty years. The streets were littered with handbills, posters plastered the walls; there were daily mass meetings. The month-long election campaign made Spain and Spaniards unrecognisable. Even the *pijas* (daughters of the rich) were to be seen elegantly dropping handbills for the neo-Francoist Alianza Popular as they cruised round Madrid in their cars. As Spain's politicisation peaked, there was even an attempt to pass off a burgeoning pornography trade as a mark of democratic tolerance. 'My own democratic position,' Susana Estrada, the ineffable authoress of *Wet Sex*, announced in September 1976, 'is to show everything so that the public can vote as it wants.'[1]

In general the June elections were a defeat for extremism and the past. The extreme right of the 18 July National Alliance collected less than 0.5 per cent of the vote, the PCE 9 per cent and Alianza Popular a low 8 per cent. Mindful of Spain's last elections, whose divisiveness helped precipitate a Civil War, Spanish voters converged on Felipe González's social democrats, the PSOE, and on Suárez's centrist UCD, who received 28.5 and 34.3 per cent of the vote respectively. The election results also reflected a widespread desire for a political breathing-space. A regime which had ruled for forty years had disappeared in sixteen months: Spaniards needed time to assimilate the consequences of change, which soon showed themselves. When that same summer the UCD government announced that bank accounts could be inspected for tax purposes, a *frisson* ran through Spain's rich.

From 1977 Spanish film-makers also entered a period of stocktaking. They began to count the personal cost of Francoism, the limitations to change, and, most important, the literal cost of film-making as Spain's film industry, like the country at large, entered its worst economic crisis in recent history.

The return of a native: Luis Buñuel and *That Obscure Object of Desire*

No feature of Spain's return to democracy was more moving perhaps than the return of its old democrats, its surviving Civil War Republicans. Among them was Luis Buñuel. Buñuel's treatment at the hands of the Spanish government from the time he first set foot again in Spain in 1960 is a testimony to the limitations of its liberalism.

By the late 50s, Buñuel's communist sympathies appeared to be waning. 'I've never been one of Franco's fanatical adversaries,' he was to admit in *My Last Breath*. 'As far as I'm concerned, he wasn't the Devil personified. I'm even ready to believe that he kept our exhausted country from being invaded by the Nazis.'[2] While the Francoist government thought Buñuel ripe for a symbolic act of rehabilitation, the young Spanish film-makers, such as Saura and Portabella, who met Buñuel at Cannes in 1960 saw in him a bridge with Spanish film-making of the 30s and the one director who, working in Spain, could prompt a renaissance in a truly national cinema.[3]

Buñuel returned to Spain somewhat warily to film *Viridiana*. A Spanish location was in part made necessary because of the film's thoroughgoing Spanish themes and settings, like the convent of the opening scenes, which the novice Viridiana leaves to visit her uncle Don Jaime. Reminding him of his wife, who died on their wedding night, Viridiana is made to dress up in the dead wife's trousseau. He drugs her and prepares to rape her, but pulls back at the last moment. Rejected by Viridiana and unfaithful to his dead wife's memory, Don Jaime commits suicide. Jorge, his virile and pragmatic illegitimate son, takes Don Jaime's place, and begins to modernise the estate; Viridiana meanwhile sets up a communal home for a motley group of beggars. When Jorge and Viridiana are out one day the beggars get drunk, fornicate, and try to rape Viridiana when she returns. Her mission in ruins, the ex-novice yields to her awakening sexuality, joining Jorge and the maid Ramona in a card game which hints at the beginnings of a *ménage à trois*.

Viridiana created the greatest film scandal of Franco's Spain. The censor accepted Buñuel's rewritten script, which incorporated the highly suggestive ending, and *Viridiana* was nominated as Spain's entry to Cannes. The Under-Secretary of Cinema, Muñoz-Fontán, personally collected the Palme d'Or and the French critics' prize. But the next day the Vatican newspaper *L'Osservatore Romano* exposed in apocalyptic terms the film's anticlericalism. Muñoz-Fontán was dismissed, *Viridiana* banned in Spain, UNINCI, its producer, liquidated.

It is normally assumed that with *Viridiana* Buñuel in some way 'put one over' on the Spanish censor. This seems uncertain. Buñuel himself wanted *Viridiana* to be seen in Spain and had planned a special 'soft' version for release there. The scandal suggests rather the essential incompatibility of Buñuel and the Francoist regime. The government valued Buñuel's reputation as a great film-maker but could not be associated with many of the legends on which this reputation was based, like Buñuel's supposedly diabolic atheism. Secondly, Buñuel was by no means as discreet as other Spanish film-makers under Franco. *Viridiana*, for instance, contrasts Francoist values and a new, developing Spain, and debunks an 'official version': the supposed lack of sexual interest attributed to 'pure' women in Spain. Yet Buñuel systematises these references with a near sarcastic obviousness, so that the very stridency of his ironies becomes laughable. As the beggars recite the Angelus, for example, the sound of a nearby dump-truck drowns their prayers.

The main problem with Buñuel for Franco's regime, however, was that he had the personality and genius to found a school of film-making in Spain. A country whose moral standards were set by the Church could hardly have its film standards set by its most famous atheist. Franco's government practically recognised this by allowing the production of *Tristana* to be set up almost in its totality in 1963, and then banning the script on a technicality, its supposed justification of duelling.

Buñuel eventually made *Tristana* in Toledo in 1969. Scenes from *The Phantom of Liberty* (1974) and *That Obscure Object of Desire* (1977) were also filmed in Spain, and yet key Buñuel films remained banned: *Un chien andalou* (until 1968), *L'Age d'or* (first shown in 1974), and *Viridiana* (premiered in April 1977). One crucial, calculated and abiding legacy of Francoist film policy was that, as Katherine Kovács wrote in 1983, 'It would be difficult to find direct evidence of Buñuel's influence on contemporary cinematographic trends.'[4] Most 'new' Spanish directors had finished their film formation by the time they got to know Buñuel's work fully. There are flashes of influence in Aranda, Camus, and, much later, Uribe, but only Saura and, to a lesser extent, Regueiro suggest an essential contiguity of preoccupations.[5]

Pedro Almodóvar's *Matador* ('Killer'/'Torero', 1986) suggests a possible recuperation of Buñuel by leading younger Spanish film-makers attracted by Buñuel's profound 'Spanishness'. Buñuel's films are replete, for example, with memories of a Spanish childhood. The great precipice and eagle seen below the lavatory bowl in *The Exterminating Angel* recall the peculiar toilet facilities of houses perched on the edge of a steep cliff in the Spanish town of Cuenca. Even a word in Buñuel's films, such as 'discreet', means so much more in Spanish, harking back to the great Golden Age stress on *discreción* which went beyond 'circumspection' to mean the capacity for correct decisions in practical matters where the mind is guided – not necessarily for good – by reason rather than passions.[6]

Buñuel's obsessive atheism is quite typically Spanish, reflecting his own father's obsession (he determined to build his house higher than the local church) and that peculiarly Spanish mixture of anticlericalism and a visceral fear of damnation. Buñuel's bedrock charge against the bourgeoisie of

Swan song of a surrealist: Buñuel shooting his last film

complacency may well derive, furthermore, from his own origins in one of the smuggest, cruellest, and most narrow-minded of upper classes in Western Europe. 'Do you forgive your enemies?' a nineteenth-century Duke of Valencia was asked on his deathbed. 'I have no enemies,' he replied, 'I've had them all shot.'[7]

The works of *auteurs* always suggest a few archetypal images of their creators. Buñuel conjures up a café or bar where good wine (or a few dry martinis) has been drunk, brandy is served, and Buñuel is in form and holds forth, as roguish a raconteur as ever. Buñuel in fact confounds Emil Benveniste's claim that cinema is closer to *histoire* (the type of speech typical of an impersonal nineteenth-century novel) than *discours* (exemplified by a conversation implicating both speaker and listener).[8] With Buñuel, however, *histoire* continually cedes to *discours* partly through the constant use of digression, the force of personal obsessions reminding us of Buñuel's presence behind the film, his delight in parody, and an inimitable calculation of spectators' reactions.[9]

Tristana illustrates this last point beautifully. Don Lope invites Tristana into his bedroom; she kisses him and giggles, the dog waddles after her and the door closes. The camera retreats to the side of the bedroom and we are shown its interior by an amusingly hackneyed through-the-wall shot. But then Don Lope sees the dog. 'What are you doing here?' he asks. The dog is thrown out, and the bedroom door shut in the camera's face. The spectator, slyly looking forward to the scene (whatever his judgment of Don Lope's morality), is caught out by Buñuel and left with his tail between his legs in a delightful denial of (here visual) omniscience typical of the oral ironist. Flann O'Brien might have directed this scene. Buñuel's 'discourse' reflects an instinctive delight in ribbing any convention. Yet this second-natured satire was surely sharpened by a social life whose centre is the restaurant (as in Paris) or the café and bar (as in the poorer Madrid).[9]

Buñuel himself was quite sure of the importance of his Spanish influences. 'The critics talk about Goya,' he once said, 'because they ignore all the rest: Quevedo, St. Therese of Avila, the Spanish heterodoxes, the Spanish picaresque novel, Galdós, Valle-Inclán.'[10] The common strain connecting these writers is an urgent desire to disabuse Spaniards of illusions, whether carnal or material interests (the *desengaño* theme of the religious writers), pretensions of Golden Age Spaniards to grandeur, religiousness and wealth (the picaresque), *petit bourgeois* and provincial hypocrisy (Galdós), or more or less any pretence at all (Valle-Inclán). From the seventeenth century bathos, satire, sarcasm, parody and scorn become the dominant modes of Spain's best artists, influenced, no doubt, by the failure of Spain's greatest venture: its worldwide Empire.

Satire is not of course limited to Spain. What does seem more particular is the continuing ability of a country of limited economic and social capacities to generate illusions. During the Napoleonic Wars the Mayor of Móstoles, a village near Madrid, personally declared war on France. Young right-wing ultras in the 80s still dream of Spanish-led pan-Hispanic empires. During the 1982 football World Cup finals a (Spanish?) computer predicted that Spain would meet Brazil in the final; the national team only just scraped through the first round. 'Though every country has its Sanchos,' Jan Morris comments, 'Quixote could only be Spanish.'[11]

And so with Buñuel. The familiar dichotomy underlying his films is very often what should be, opposed to what is, though Buñuel turns the opposition on its head by identifying 'what should be' with spurious social pretensions. 'What is' becomes a few evident truths: man's carnal desire, his frequent cruelty, his paradoxical capacity for love, his greed. In *Viridiana*, for example, during their dinner the beggars freeze for a mock photograph in attitudes which parody Leonardo's *Last Supper*. The scene is not just meant to shock, but also to point the immense gulf between religious representations of human possibilities (embodied in Christ and his disciples) and the more frequent reality (embodied in the lecherous, murderous, blind and crippled beggars).

Buñuel's portrayal of the poor and the oppressed marks most clearly perhaps his Spanish temperament. Most northern European liberals would think such classes worthy of compassion. Not so Buñuel: a purely tragic rendering of suffering would smack too much of idealism. So the blind beggar in *Los olvidados* (1950) is seen unsentimentally as cruel and vindictive, slashing at his young assailants with a stick with a sharp nail at its end. The obvious literary precedent, as many critics have observed, is the blind man in the sixteenth-century picaresque novella *Lazarillo de Tormes*, who is similarly pictured as a rogue, miser, and religious hypocrite.

The basis of the 'Spanishness' in Buñuel's most national of films – *Viridiana* – may once more be its *esperpento*. The beggars come near to Valle-Inclán's view of man as marionette at the beck and call of base passion. When Don Jaime commits suicide, little Rita plays in the garden oblivious to his feet dangling heavily above her. And Don Jaime's expression of a sincere if frustrated love for his wife – dressing his niece in the bridal gown so as to consummate his marriage by proxy – is too adulterated with absurdity to be purely tragic. Tragedy in Buñuel and other Spanish film-makers so often seems tragicomic perhaps because it relates so obviously to a larger Spanish 'malaise' of centuries-old frustrations, oppressions and disappointments so appalling as to seem absurd. 'Spain is an absurd country,' wrote the turn-of-the-century essayist Ganivet. 'Absurdity is her nerve and mainstay. Her turn to prudence will denote her end.'[12]

Finally, perhaps the almost automatic transference from particular to general pointed by Buñuel's films, which usually seems representative of larger social situations, may in itself be a Spanish trait reflecting centuries of dictatorial government. A lack of privacy and constraints on individualism in Spain have meant that it is very difficult for Spanish characters in films realistically to suggest purely personal predicaments. An Englishman's home is his castle, the perversions he practices there usually his own business; a Spaniard's home is an arena, according to Buñuel or Saura, for oppressive social practices, and his perversions are signs of more general social ills.

How this ready leap to the general operates in Spanish films may be seen in *That Obscure Object of Desire* (1977), Buñuel's only post-Franco film, a Spanish-French co-production and Spain's 1978 candidate for the Best Foreign Film Oscar.[13] In Buñuel's last film a middle-aged bourgeois, Mathieu, explains to his travelling companions, all bound for Paris, why he threw a bucket of water over a girl who appeared on the platform in Seville to try to persuade him not to leave her. The girl, Concha, works briefly as his chambermaid, and then he meets her by chance in Switzerland. He begins to visit her in Paris, but Concha's attitude remains contradictory: she sits on Mathieu's knee but won't let him caress her; she accepts presents but then accuses Mathieu of buying her; she agrees to sleep with him, but gets into bed wearing a chastity belt. Finally, in desperation, Mathieu buys Concha a chalet which she uses to make love to a friend before Mathieu's eyes. The next morning Concha explains that the love-making was only make-believe. Mathieu strikes her in fury. 'Now, now I know you love me,'

That Obscure Object of Desire

Concha says, smiling. Mathieu has just finished his story when Concha appears in the train bucket in hand and douches him. The couple are last seen in Paris. Mathieu watches fascinated as a seamstress sews up some bloodied garments. Concha wanders off, Mathieu turns to follow her, but she pushes him away. A bomb explosion suddenly fills the screen with smoke and the film abruptly ends.

In an essay on the film, Katherine Kovács shows how it is a faithful adaptation of Pierre Louÿs' *La femme et le pantin* ('The Woman and the Puppet', 1898) in plot, character, incident and dialogue.[14] One might add that *all* Buñuel's additions – the train, the central theme of desire, the role of chance, the terrorist sub-plot, even the burlap bag – can be traced back to surrealist concerns of Buñuel's youth. Buñuel's 'Spanishness' merely gives his surrealism special emphases, which reappear in other Spanish films such as Saura's *Peppermint frappé* and Berlanga's *Tamaño natural* ('Life Size', 1973).[15] Both Saura and Buñuel draw a perverse connection between sexual frustration and desire. In *Peppermint frappé* Julián, a doctor living in the repressive provincial environment of Cuenca, thinks he has found his ideal woman in Elena, the chic, Nordic-featured wife of his best friend. When Elena rejects his advances, Julián tries to turn his deferential brunette assistant Ana into a second Elena by completely changing the way she looks. Julián then murders Elena in an ending of elegant ambiguities: Ana witnesses Elena's death, so establishing a latent tyranny over Julián, but how long will she conform to Julián's fantasies? Threatened in the future, Julián remains eternally frustrated by the past, for he has killed his true object of desire and so guaranteed that he will never possess her. And yet this very obstacle to satisfying his desire will keep that desire alive, a rationale equally reflected by *That Obscure Object of Desire*, where Concha's alternation of flirtation and rebuff maintains Mathieu's interest, creating an exquisite sense of frustration.

The narrative logic of *That Obscure Object of Desire* makes more than a nod to the surrealists. In *L'Amour fou*, André Breton claimed there was only a difference in degree between the emotion provoked by 'aesthetic' phenomena and erotic pleasure. Mathieu takes his story-telling seriously: 'You're sure I'm not boring you?' he asks his fellow travellers, and he keeps a check on his tale's propriety. Buñuel himself argued that the most important narrative appeal was suspense, and so Mathieu's propriety and sexual suspense reflect part of a story-telling game which recognises a natural fact: once Mathieu has deflowered Concha our interest in their story will flag.[16]

Yet beyond Mathieu's covert surrealism lies the weight of Catholic culture. The masochistic pleasure offered by sexual frustration in *That Obscure Object of Desire* will best be understood in Catholic countries, where there exists a constant attempt to turn negative prohibitions to positive account, to glimpse, for example, tensed sexual ecstasy in a martyr's torment or a religious statue's frozen paroxysm of devotion. Second, there is a residual supposition in Spanish society, as perhaps in any conservative country, that sex for a woman somehow debases her. Virgin cults still survive in the more backward parts of Spain, and any Spaniard brought up under Franco will be familiar with two dichotomies: a woman is a virgin or a whore; love and sex are completely separate.[17] 'Women stopped interesting him when they stopped being virgins,' the posters for Fons' *De profesión polígamo* ('Polygamous by Profession', 1975) proclaimed. Julián in *Peppermint frappé* tries to breach the gap between the sensual and the spiritual by blending the body of the virginal Ana with the appearance of the foreign (and so supposedly liberated) Elena.

Berlanga's *Tamaño natural* follows a similar course. Michel, a Parisian dentist, buys a lifesize plastic doll to substitute for his wife. But when his landlady's husband rapes the doll, Michel is appalled by what he sees as a sign of the doll's desiring sexuality, despite its obvious passivity in the affair. For Michel the doll has sinned. So she is made to confess in a scene which aligns but never synthesises Michel's twin conceptions of her as beloved and whore. 'I am listening, my daughter,' says Michel, pretending to be a priest. 'Filthy tart!' he then blurts out. Mathieu's tale in *That Obscure Object of Desire* is similarly designed to balance insinuations of Concha's liberation and her virginity, arriving at the climactic paradox of Concha apparently making love with a man but remaining a virgin.

Spanish films reflect, however, not only the perverse sexual delights of a repressed society but also its sexual fears. The commonest fear, which Buñuel's direction insists upon in *That Obscure Object of Desire*, is the castration complex. When Mathieu discovers that Concha has left Paris, for example, we hear the sound of an electric saw and cut (a film pun?) to a restaurant with plush, almost uniformly red decor. In symbolic terms Concha threatens castration: she pulls leaves off trees and hairs off Mathieu's chest, and threatens to shave off his beard. Manservant Martin catches a mouse in a trap; a jumbo jet is reported exploding – castration symbols are legion.[18]

Buñuel's films, like those of many later Spanish film-makers, draw significantly on Freudian theory. Freud argued that fears of castration were disavowed through fetishism. Buñuel's films are famous for forefronting their fetishes, which may be attributed to his characters (as when Mathieu ogles the bloodied garment at the end of *That Obscure Object of Desire*) or to Buñuel himself. The camerawork in his last film effectively 'fetishises' its tourist locations, reducing them to emblematic components – the Giralda, palm trees, religious processions, gypsy beggars and flamenco for Seville, for example – which construct an exotic tourist parallel to the elusive object of erotic interest. One surrealist achievement of Buñuel's film is indeed to present a sexual gloss on tourism.

According to Freud, fear of castration remains because Oedipal attachments remain, because children fail to develop away from their parents, or challenge them, which once more risks punishment, or suffer guilt complexes and fear or yearn for reprobation. The essential point, however, is the dominance of the parent figure, which ensures that even when a child grows up he or she will model his or her adult relationships on the intimate hierarchies of power suggested by father-daughter and mother-child relations. The protean personal politics of Buñuel's *Tristana* are a case in point. Don Lope welcomes a beautiful orphan to his home as his ward, uses his authority to convert her into his mistress, and threatens her patriarchally when she begins to show her independence: 'I'm your father and your husband. And I'll be one or the other as is convenient to me.' When Tristana loses her leg she also loses, she thinks, her sexual attraction and reverts in her own eyes to the non-sexual role of Don Lope's daughter. Don Lope exploits his renewed authority over Tristana to claim her as his wife. She replies in kind by seizing on Don Lope's increasing senility to become a domestic matriarch, stomping round their house on her wooden leg, as Gwynne Edwards observes, like a grotesque version of Lorca's tyrant Bernarda Alba. *Tristana* deals, like *Cría cuervos*, with the substitution of relations founded on affection by those founded on power.

Completely missing from *Peppermint frappé*, *Tamaño natural* and *That Obscure Object of Desire* is a sense of female individuality. In all three the woman is an embodiment of a social role or a projection of male desire, an idealised construct in a world where, as the misogynist Nietzsche wrote, 'Ultimately one loves one's desires and not that which is desired.' Underlying this attempt at dominance may be fears or threats other than castration. Isabel Escudero claims that the doll in Berlanga's *Tamaño natural* conjures up for Michel the 'emptiness of the feminine', its lack of signification. Michel's games, when he dresses the doll, takes it on holiday, even marries it, attempt to 'make "femininity" representable, to materialise and manipulate that indefinite phenomenon which worries him (as a man) and in some way has endowed him with the terrible responsibility of becoming the *subject* of History.'[19] Yet the only inkling of 'femininity' which Michel seems to gain from the doll, Escudero argues, is of its sexuality, which makes him suffer 'the masculine terror of approaching the inexhaustible and infinite, which men equate with the desire and pleasure of women.' Significantly, when his doll is raped Michel reacts with phallic aggression before this hint of sexuality, poking her in the face with a finger, sawing away her vagina, plunging a needle into her stomach. Antonio in *Carmen* similarly plunges a knife into Carmen, while Julián in *Peppermint frappé* throws Elena from a cliff. The traumatised love seen in Spanish films goes beyond the repression of women. It often entails their disavowal, a complete obliviousness to their independent existence which, if challenged, may prompt the woman's sublimation, and her total annihilation.

A farewell to arms: from a political to a personal cinema, 1977–1981

Un cero de la izquierda (Gabriel Iglesias) opens with two slogans: 'Suárez, traitor, you once sang "Cara al sol"', and 'Democracy brings insecurity'. A photograph shows Suárez as a young man dressed in Falangist uniform, hand raised in fascist salute. Then in a dramatised scene a mugger slips out from behind a stone sporting a slogan on liberty to assault a passer-by who has stopped to read the graffiti. At the end of the film a caterwauling baby is made to listen to 'Cara al sol' and soon calms down.

Made in 1980, *Un cero de la izquierda* attests to a Francoist cinema surviving the break-up of Francoism. The late 1970s in fact show very clearly that cinema evolves in a different manner and at a different pace from society, so that the changes in Spanish films following the change to democracy came far more sluggishly than might have been expected. Attempts at a testimonial cinema in 1977 fell down partly on the time-lapse between their conception and their making. Once irreverent films came to seem increasingly irrelevant. A case in point is *Las truchas* ('The Trout', 1977), José Luis García Sánchez's witty parable about an angling club banquet where the diners are served with the champion angler's trout which he has in fact fished out of a sewer. Protests at the trout's putrefaction are soon qualified since, as one member puts it, 'The honour of a

Las truchas

companion is at stake and the honour of one companion is the honour of everyone.' So the diners eat the trout and, despite sundry mortalities, demand more.

Scripted in the early 70s by García Sánchez, Gutiérrez Aragón and Luis Megino, *Las truchas* provides a hilarious portrait of the violence, immobilism and suicidal *esprit de corps* which had baffled any attempts at political reform under Carrero Blanco and Arias. Yet if the transition had demonstrated anything in 1976, it was the surprising capacity of the more progressive sectors of the Francoist establishment to evolve. The relevance of *Las truchas* to 1977 was in fact more industrial than thematic. Its massive cast and crew represented an endeavour to enrol as many film professionals as possible in an early project of Arandano, a company envisaged as a platform for independent film-making at a time when the break-up of the old government film unions was leading to a reshaping of the Spanish film industry.[20]

Whole tendencies of late-70s Spanish cinema respond to earlier initiatives. The several significant documentaries of the time mark a logical conclusion to the increasing movement towards a 'direct' cinema evident from the early 70s. They were also a reaction to the mystification of the NO–DO newsreels which, although since 1976 no longer obligatory, still survived in cinemas because of the nearly prohibitive costs of making short

171

features to replace them. The N O–D O and the Spanish television reportage which largely took over its functions from the 1960s tended, for example, in their emphasis on banquets, premieres and top-level meetings, to exclude the people from the responsibility for making history. In contrast, radical film-makers associated usually with Spain's Communist Party – Andrés Linares, José Luis García Sánchez, Miguel Hermoso, Roberto Bodegas and Juan Antonio Bardem – began filming popular action such as the strike at Victoria in March 1976 in which five workers died when the police opened fire on a crowd. Such material had no immediate chance of commercial distribution but, as Bardem put it, it was like 'creating a memory for the future'.[21] The absence of private television in Spain after the transition meant that there was still a need for film-makers to supply alternatives to the official versions of key historical figures, periods or events. Linares and García Sánchez interviewed La Pasionaria in *Dolores* (1980); Imanol Uribe reconstructed the celebrated 1970 trial of E T A activists in *El proceso de Burgos* ('The Burgos Trial', 1979); and Cecilia and José J. Bartolomé's uneven two-part *Después de …* ('After …', 1981) records events in Spain from May 1979 to mid-1980 to explain in particular the political apathy of the late 70s.

N O–D O sidestepped the unsettling. Gonzalo Herralde's *El asesino de Pedralbes* ('The Pedralbes Murderer', 1978) allows a murderer to explain in painstaking detail how he raped seven-year-old children; *Cada ver es* ('Each to His Own'/'Corpses', Angel del Val, 1981) films a day in the life of a mortuary attendant; Mañuel Coronado and Carlos Rodríguez Sanz's camera in their memorable *Animación en la sala de espera* ('Animation in the Waiting Room') focuses on the lost faces of patients in a psychiatric ward, the film's formal disorder perhaps a faint reflection of the disorientation of its subjects. Above all Spanish documentaries reacted against the frequent mystification of N O–D O by pointing to the frequent (and inevitable) incursion into documentary of techniques associated with fiction film. Portabella's *Informe general* ('General Report', 1977) played up the visual rhetoric of the political interview by placing the aged, pear-shaped Gil Robles in an armchair to match his patrician status but siting Communist intellectual Tamames in a 'university office to confirm, Portabella explained, his 'theoretical context'.[22] Setting becomes less a 'real' background than part of the *mise en scène*.

Gonzalo Herralde's *Raza, el espíritu de Franco* ('Race, the Spirit of Franco', 1977) also brings fiction formats – primarily a sense of narrative – to his documentary material, here interviews with Franco's loopy sister Pilar and the shrewd lead in *Raza*, Alfredo Mayo. In the counterpoint of interview and clips from Sáenz de Heredia's original film, fiction (the narrative chronology of *Raza*) structures 'facts' (the interviewees' observations ordered to contrast with the film extracts). Herralde makes a fine

172

structural comment on the impact of fictions on Franco himself who, however much a pragmatist, still saw himself, as Herralde makes clear, in the image of *Raza*'s hero figure José Churruca.

La vieja memoria ('The Old Memory', Jaime Camino, 1977) perhaps exploits the techniques of fiction to greatest effect. Camino interviews surviving figures from the Civil War. One, the writer José Luis de Villalonga, recalls how his Nationalist commandant would invite the local gentry to watch executions over lunch. Others are far less candid since far more compromised by events. Camino skilfully uses medium shots to observe his subjects' theatricality and eloquent reticence. At what Camino sees as the most significant moment in the film, for example, La Pasionaria, now in her eighties, has been leaning forward to describe the Spanish Cortes on the eve of Civil War, how the Deputies insulted and threatened one another . . . but she suddenly stops, leans back in her chair in a physical act of self-censorship, and declares that all this happened a long time ago and is 'the fog of the past which counts for very little in our lives'. Yet this break-up of parliamentary democracy was a crucial event in the lead-up to the Civil War.[23]

'I did not want to describe the truth of what happened during the Civil War,' Camino said of *La vieja memoria*, 'only to register memories of it.' The survival of indirect modes in Spanish film-making after the transition was another factor making for continuity in the Spanish cinema. Some cases, such as Camino's obliqueness, may be put down to discretion. The simplifications of a church education or state propaganda still left many Spanish directors, moreover, with an instinctive distrust of supposed clarities. The powerful economic reasons for using a family to describe wider historical realities still remained. Above all, perhaps, the continued making of 'oblique' films was a response to the limitations of its testimonial alternative. A testimonial cinema could not keep up with events in 1976–8, and interest in it inevitably declined with the passing of those events. Garci's films for example, though immediately popular, date fast. A testimonial cinema which went against mainstream opinion could rarely hope to be mainstream cinema. It is perhaps no coincidence, then, that the films which dissent most radically from contemporary optimism over the transition to democracy nevertheless show a degree of fictional autonomy which allows them to stand on their own. Their interest is not exhausted by their possible allegorical references.

Several charges were made against the transition. One was that the mentalities of older Spaniards at least had not changed. Vicente Aranda's fascinating *La muchacha de las bragas de oro* ('The Girl with the Golden Panties', 1980), based on Juan Marsé's prize-winning novel, features, for instance, a supposedly reformed ex-Falangist now writing his memoirs with the aid of his niece Mariana. Everything he narrates is pictured by the camera and yet many past scenes beg credence. Forrest's fraudulence is also suggested by his unremittingly chaotic and fallacious present. As José Luis Guarner points out, Forrest's life is one long *mise en scène*: he strolls by the beach perorating theatrically, his photograph in a magazine is tricked, and the male photographer who comes to stay turns out to be a girl.[24] Forrest, it is implied, is inveterately weak-willed and, in his Falangist past as much as his present, ignores what is going on around him. In a recidivist act of ignorance and capitulation to pressure, he allows himself to be seduced by Mariana as he once was similarly seduced (even to the sound of the same music) by Mariana's mother, though Forrest has forgotten this fact. Forrest ends up discovering that he has just slept with his daughter.

Aranda's vision in the film seems sharp and mature. The past, though not known with absolute certainty, may be inferred from the present. The Falangist, rather than a fanatic or petty tyrant – a simplistic vision which some left-wing films, such as *Réquiem por un campesino español* ('Requiem for a Spanish Peasant', Francesc Betriu, 1985), unfortunately promote – fits far more Gerald Brenan's knowing portrait of 40s Falangists as 'government clerks, *nouveaux riches*, second-rate intellectuals, lawyers and doctors with all that tribe of needy and ambitious people who in every country (but especially in a poor one such as Spain) join parties which have jobs to offer.'[25]

Aranda's film goes further than any other in pointing the ironies of the transition. An old Falangist such as Forrest lives with impunity, the fortune he made from his connections unimpaired. He is even acclaimed for his concessions in the past rather than attacked for seeking a position of power which allowed him to make such concessions. In one scene, Forrest meets his old gardener, whom he shot in the hand for urinating against a wall. The gardener is genuinely thankful to Forrest for not having shot him in the stomach. Forrest and the gardener now vote for the same political party. The scene, to Aranda, suggests 'the strength of this unfortunate desire to forget a highly dramatic situation which the country went through not so long ago.... The scene ironises on our present-day situation where we are thanking Suárez and other components of the past for not having strangled us all.'[26] Few other Spanish film-makers achieve such lucidity.

A second objection to the transition, raised perhaps unconsciously, was about the indissoluble trammels of power itself: those with it, whatever their nature, would always oppress those without it. This was the rationale of Berlanga's *La escopeta nacional* ('National Shotgun', 1977), a black-humoured vision of a Francoist shooting party in the 60s. Berlanga's film was inspired by an event which ruffled the political world: Manuel Fraga accidentally shooting Franco's daughter in the rump at a hunt. The film also shows a step-up in salaciousness (a starlet indulges in Sadeian sex and a marquis collects women's pubic hair) and a blasphemous priest whose dialogue (he assails the Catalan monastery of Montserrat for 'fucking up' Spain) would not have passed censorship before 1976.

Yet *La escopeta nacional* shows how a Spanish director simply could not or would not abandon a seemingly inveterate style just because the opportunities for a more direct expression had become available. Berlanga remains essentially faithful to his themes and techniques of the past. In 1962, for instance, Berlanga demanded a cinema which was 'revulsive' and would 'worry and unsettle'.[27] So in 1977, when Catalonia was so in the news, Berlanga's hunt has a protagonist, the pomaded Canivell, who presents a grossly parodic vision of the money-minded Catalan. In 1957 Berlanga had defined his 'social outlook' as 'individualistic, volatile and sentimental'.[28] So in 1977 his film obviously takes the side of the grovelling Canivell, who accepts all kinds of indignities and compromises in order to sell his automatic door-locks. And the choral style which Berlanga patented in *Plácido* (1961) allows for that constant intrusion of one reality upon another seen in *El verdugo* (1963) and which acts like a metaphor for the protagonist's *esperpento*-like condition: just as Canivell thinks he has persuaded a Falangist minister to commercialise his locks, a Cabinet reshuffle replaces the minister with a leading light from Opus Dei. Canivell has to begin his inveiglement all over again.[29]

A last snook cocked at Spain's transition was that any political concessions granted by its ruling classes were not out of any sudden conversion to democracy but rather to protect essential political and economic interests. The Francoist Cortes, it was said, only approved Suárez's crucial 1976 Law of Political Reform because of under-the-desk promises of jobs in a democratic Suárez government. 'Large numbers of Francoist cadres remained in positions of power,' historian Paul Preston writes, 'by means of a simple transfer from the Movimiento to UCD. For them, the transition constituted less a fundamental change than a political re-adaptation of certain elite forces.'[30]

Such accusations may seem churlish given the actual achievement of democracy itself. The transition did, however, provide film-makers with a fecund opportunity to do what they had practised most under Franco: dissent. The Spanish film dealing most perceptively with a political transition was Antonio Drove's *La verdad sobre el caso Savolta* ('The Truth about the Savolta Case', 1978). It was first scripted in 1976 when Suárez was still only Minister for the Movement and, despite an arresting (and perhaps not totally coincidental) physical resemblance between Suárez and Charles Denner, the actor playing the unprincipled Lepprince, the film was never intended to make analogies with Spain's as yet hypothetical transition. Nevertheless, in the light of that event it makes fascinating reading.

La verdad sobre el caso Savolta is set in Barcelona between 1917 and

1923 when old paternalist methods of control – dismissal or a good drubbing – were giving way to hired assassins (*pistoleros*) employed by industrialists to try to contain the growing workers' movements. The interest of Drove's film lies in the ways it breaks with nearly all previous Spanish political cinema. Firstly, it was a film of political ideas, mostly drawn from Brecht and Lukács. Drove stylises characterisation to create not personality archetypes but different models for political action. Savolta, an arms industrialist, favours a paternalist treatment of his workers. Lepprince, his *arriviste* assistant, purportedly favours a more liberal policy but resorts to *pistoleros* when advisable. Pajarito de Soto, a squat, chaotic pamphleteer, is a romantic individualist who plans to expose Savolta's illegal business deals. Javier Miranda is an office clerk who dithers between friendship with Lepprince and de Soto.

Like other Spanish film-makers, Drove sees politics as theatre: 'Actors represent before a public, while politicians don't represent the people who have voted for them but represent before them.'[31] Gesture and action reveal true character in a world of deceptions where, in the film's best sequence, Lepprince has Savolta gunned down at a masked ball. Drove's film also goes against the grain of Spanish cinema in proposing that the historical events portrayed were resistible. Their avoidability is empha- sised by a Fritz Lang-like mechanism where events combine with a clockwork consequentiality, the contributions of all the character-clogs turning a historical mechanism nearer to the reign of political violence. Pajarito de Soto keeps his proofs of Lepprince's illegal shipment of arms to himself instead of entrusting them to fellow workers. It is a crucial mistake: the wheel turns slightly. Pajarito gives the proofs to the unreliable Miranda; Lepprince kills Savolta and Pajarito: the wheel turns more. Miranda hands the proofs over to Lepprince, capitulates to his charm, and ends up working for Lepprince, organising his backstreet assassinations. 'We are victims,' Drove comments, glossing Brecht, 'not because we are good, but because we are weak.'[32] One worrying aspect of much recent Spanish film-making has been its tendency to reverse this argument.[33]

Yet *La verdad sobre el caso Savolta* charts a process of false liberalisation which ended in Primo de Rivera's dictatorship. Spain's mid-70s transition comprised a period of effective liberalisation ending in a formal democracy which did bring some changes, however belated and qualified, to the Spanish cinema. A first was the abolition of censorship. According to the Royal Decree of 11 November 1977, a Spanish film automatically received its exhibition licence two months after presenta- tion of a finished copy at the Under Secretariat for Cinema unless (Article 3.5) 'the exhibition of the film could constitute a crime' – in which case the film was passed on to the Attorney General.

The consequences of final freedom of speech were confused by the continuing influence of previous prohibitions. Spanish film-makers have in general failed, for instance, to exploit the opportunity for an erotic cinema, partly because of their own ingrained inhibitions.[34] In contrast, Spanish films had already passed and would continue to surpass normal European levels in their violence, racy dialogue and prolific drugs consumption. Quite a number of recent Spanish films, such as Agustí Villaronga's *Tras el cristal* ('Behind the Glass Cage', 1986), about an ex-Nazi's child torture and murder, could not hope for general circulation in many other countries. The continuing brutality of Spanish cinema has, however, good historical explanations and is easily assimilated by Spanish audiences themselves. 'It seems obvious,' Juan Antonio Masoliver wrote about the excesses of post-Franco literature – and his comment stands for cinema – 'that if we have not found liberty we have certainly found libertinism (*libertinaje*). At least it is a step forward.'[35]

Debate on post-Franco freedoms usually turns on how much censorship still effectively remains. Certainly there are still economic limitations to free film expression. Many Spaniards still discourage too finicky a discussion of the past. Fernando Fernán Gómez once remarked that the destructiveness of the Francoist censor should be measured not only by the works it banned or cut but also by those which were never begun because they had no chance of getting made. How many works have been broached by post-Francoist film-makers and dismissed out of hand as dealing with issues still too sensitive to be stirred?

Throughout the late 70s, moreover, various extremist right-wing groups sought to impose their cinema tastes on the Spanish public by threats and thuggery. When La Pasionaria appeared on the screen in a showing of *Dolores* in Gijón ultra-rightists attacked the audience with chains and knives. Protests were aimed not just at clearly contentious films (such as *Camada negra*, which was greeted in 1977 by two Molotov cocktails) but at any film which attempted to explore the past: the cinema showing *La vieja memoria*, despite its wide political spectrum of interviewees, was smashed up and an attempt was made to steal the print. Though Spain still has 'probably the largest number of fascist and neo-fascist sympathisers in western Europe ... their number is on the decline,' writes Robert Graham; and this factor, combined with the consensus cinema increasingly produced in the 80s, means that cinema attacks have also been on the wane.

Spanish television continued to cut and tone down films, employing four censors for this job as late as 1980.[36] Above all there were clear indications that limits to freedom were dictated by the army. The *cause célèbre* of military censorship was Pilar Miró's *El crimen de Cuenca* ('The Cuenca Crime', 1979). Set between 1910 and 1926, the film tells how two shepherds are accused of murdering their companion. Brutally tortured by the Civil Guard, they confess and show where they have buried their victim. The grave is found to contain the body of a woman. The shepherds are nevertheless sentenced to eighteen years imprisonment. Two years after their release their companion turns up live and well. An investigation is held but, the film reports, most of those responsible are now dead.

Presented for its exhibition licence in November 1979, *El crimen de Cuenca* was retained at the instance of the Ministry of the Interior; and in February 1980 the original prints were seized by the police by order of the Military Tribunal, although the film was shown the same month at the Berlin Film Festival. International protests greeted the news in April 1980 that Miró had been granted provisional liberty pending prosecution.

The contentiousness of *El crimen de Cuenca* had several causes. In showing the 'social-political machinery' explaining the torture of the shepherds, Miró spares few right-wing agencies.[37] The church, the local magistrate and the gentry combine to bring a case against the shepherds, hide evidence that their victim still lives, authorise the torture, and deny that it has ever occurred. The film, moreover, was based on a true incident, which gave added weight to its accusations. Yet arguments about whether *El crimen de Cuenca* was historically accurate tended to ignore the fact that the film's main force derived from the presence of techniques usually associated with fiction cinema. Whether consciously intended or not, the pastel browns and yellows and artfully composed

Pilar Miró's *El crimen de Cuenca*

178

shots of rural scenes give Miró's film an air of Sunday supplement sadism. Miró also uses the technique of parallel montage to cross-cut from, say, a hook being driven into the mouth of one of the shepherds to the local magistrate delicately slicing an apple. Above all the torture scenes are brutally substantive, filmed in aggressive close-shot and with such standard images of torture as a fingernail being wrenched off.

The detention of *El crimen de Cuenca* reflected above all the attitudes and power of the army in immediate post-Franco Spain. As the film magazine *Contracampo* pointed out, Miró's film was not a criticism of the Civil Guard as an institution so much as an acknowledgment that it was open to abuse. Only those who insisted on the infallibility of the Civil Guard could have grounds for objection. Reform of military justice in 1980, which limited the jurisdiction of courts martial to the purely military sphere, placed the Civil Guard outside the concerns of military courts and led in 1981 to the ultimate release of *El crimen de Cuenca*, which became the biggest grossing film in Spanish cinema history. Its sheer popularity does suggest the increasing exception of censorship by the 1980s.[38]

A second force for change was a decrease in films of historical reconstruction. Even in those with historical co-ordinates, critic Esteve Riambau recorded, 'the political reference ... has acquired a secondary importance or even been totally left aside in psychological studies where an intimist context is replacing the previous collective dimension'.[39] 'Political' films quite simply ceased to do good business after the 1977 elections when Spaniards, the basic objective of democracy achieved, turned back towards more personal concerns. *Raza, el espíritu de Franco, Caudillo* and *La vieja memoria* all fared badly at the box-office. After 1977 we might have expected a 'socialist' cinema in Spain. From the 50s, after all, quality cinema had been a near monopoly of the opposition. In failing to move on to such a cinema Spanish film-makers to a certain extent showed their class. Many were *niños de derecha*, the well-to-do children of right-wing families. Working-class Spaniards could not afford the long years of university studies (for which there were no government grants), the Spanish Film School, and a low-paid professional apprenticeship. The Spanish cinema of today remains predictably a liberal 'middle-class' cinema opposing autocracy in a political or family context rather than fostering a 'proletarian' culture.[40]

The 'political boom' of the mid-70s was in itself something of a mirage caused by the exceptional popularity and occasional quality of some films, their absolute novelty for Spain, and the contentiousness of their references, especially to the Spanish Civil War. Yet many Spanish directors fought shy of this key issue out of principle. In this they showed their age. Born after 1939, they belonged to the 80 per cent of Spaniards in 1977 who had no direct experience of hostilities. Saura, and Berlanga (who in typical contrast served as a medical assistant for the Republic, then fought for the División Azul), on this count remain exceptions. Younger directors refused to deal with a theme of which they had no first-hand knowledge.

Alfonso Ungría is a case in point. He had not lived the war, he declared, but he could portray its consequences, the 'tremendous frustration' felt by those who lost it.[41] In a significant reversal, the pre-war period and the war itself as portrayed in *Soldados*, Ungría's drab adaptation of Max Aub's *Las buenas intenciones*, allegorise Spain's post-war years. The Republican retreat of 1939 and the pre-war lives of three of those in flight – an assassin, a prostitute, and a brow-beaten son in love with his stepmother – convey, partly through Ungría's off-centre photography, the separations, persecutions and dismal tedium of the post-war period.

It was the post-war period which was inevitably to characterise Spain's post-Franco cinema. By 1977, relieved of urgent political duties, Spanish directors were freer to make a more private cinema, or at least to deliver a more personal verdict on generational issues. There can be few more eloquent testimonies to the ineradicable impact of the *posguerra* and the monotony of individual experience which it offered than the essential narrowness of interests and community of obsessions revealed by so many Spanish film-makers. Their concrete complaints also testify to the less visible legacies of dictatorship: a frustrated desire for regeneration, a continued sense of a loss of liberty, an inveterate feeling of solitude. These, whether actively articulated or not, were, immediately at least, the grand themes of post-Franco cinema:

The difficulties of regeneration: The keynote is *volver a empezar* ('to begin again'). In *Los días del pasado* ('The Days of the Past', Mario Camus, 1977), schoolteacher Juana travels to the mountains of northern Spain to be reunited with boyfriend Antonio, an ex-Republican who has returned to Spain in 1945 to fight against Franco as a *maquis*. *Tigres de papel* ('Paper Tigers', 1977), Fernando Colomo's bitter-sweet comedy of manners, is set in the run-up to the 1977 elections; *Solos en la madrugada* ('Alone in the Early Hours', José Luis Garci, 1978) takes place at the dawn of democracy, Easter weekend 1977 when the PCE was legalised; Garci's Oscar-winning film, entitled *Volver a empezar* (1982), begins literally at dawn in verdant Asturias as a train carries expatriate and Nobel Prize poet Antonio Miguel Albajara back to his native town of Gijón and an old flame, Elena.

There are often *asignaturas pendientes* – pleasures denied by the past: Antonio and Juana have not seen each other for six years, Antonio Miguel and Elena since the Civil War began; Garci's protagonist in *Solos en la madrugada*, a radio commentator, tries to rekindle a marriage which has failed through a lack of communication; Colomo's characters – a mother, her separated *progre* husband and a would-be boyfriend – break past taboos in their dalliance with sex, soft drugs, new ideas and militant politics.

Yet the pursuit of curtailed pleasures fails, although there is a subtle change in emphases explaining why in films made from 1977. Camus' film draws for its title on a biblical passage: 'The sands in the sea, the drops in the rain, the days in the past ... Who can count them?' Time, as much as Francoism, now seems the real enemy. The real horror of the dictatorship, Spaniards appeared to conclude, was not just its repressions but its sheer longevity, which left them free too late. Historical films such as *Los días del pasado* scarcely hid beneath their protest a nostalgia – brought out in the minutiae of daily life – for a past which, dictatorship notwithstanding, still represented many Spaniards' youth.

The cry of 'too late' endows many films with their poignancy. In Camus' film Juana feels too old to wait any longer for Antonio to finish his fighting. They break up. Symbols of the passage of time – the ceaseless flow of rivers especially – run throughout the film. Garci's radio commentator achieves a better understanding with his wife, but she has already found another man and won't go back to him now. Colomo's characters realise the absurdities of old modes, like the assumption that marriages last for ever, yet cannot adapt comfortably to new customs such as their married partner being unfaithful to them. Antonio Miguel Albajara is writing an essay on the medieval Spanish poet Jorge Manrique who declared, in the most famous lines in Spanish verse, that 'Our lives are rivers/Which will flow into the sea/Which is to die'. Antonio Miguel is terminally ill when he returns to Gijón, which lies beside the sea. Antonio Miguel's nostalgia for the 30s, the baroque pop soundtrack of Pachelbel's 'Canon', and the plangent presence of the sea in every second scene contribute, as David Thompson says, to a 'sentimental obviousness' which Spanish audiences found irksome.[42]

The loss of freedom: Despite democracy, Spanish films never shrug off their fatalism. *Los días del pasado*, in many ways like a Western, uses natural landscape to develop theme. The *maquis* are racked by cold and rain, they ford rivers and are for ever running up hill (as in the crucial and magnificent cliff-top battle with the Civil Guard). The *maquis'* final defeat, it is insinuated, is that of men who even had nature against them.

The fatalism of post-Franco cinema has many explanations: it is a traditional Spanish attitude; in stressing historical inevitability the past becomes a tragedy for which no one is responsible, a comforting consensus opinion; conscious of the impossibility of changing the past, Spanish film-makers tend to portray it as if, even at the time, it was already determined. A sense of passivity was also perhaps encouraged by the transition. Above all, repressions on freedom, especially in the provinces and within the family, did not suddenly disappear, as *El nido* ('The Nest', 1980) makes clear. Jaime de Armiñan's best known film portrays, as John Hooper says, 'the power of love and the lure of the irrational'.[43] Thirteen-year-old Goyita and middle-aged Don Alejandro carry on an innocent romance. When the local sergeant lets Goyita's eagle loose and has Goyita bundled off to her aunt's, the girl orders Don Alejandro to shoot the sergeant to prove her love to him. No murderer, Don Alejandro shoots at the sergeant with blanks. Returning fire, the sergeant shoots Don Alejandro dead.

El nido has all Armiñan's distinguishing traits: 'rounded' characters prompting large performances from Hector Alterio and Ana Torrent, a polished visual gloss, an improbable application of a believable if somewhat academic thesis, here that pressures from family and state can contribute to an adolescent's Oedipal drama. As Marsha Kinder writes, in *El nido* 'Both the incestuous and patricidal desires of the precocious child are acted out with a vengeance.'[44] Don Alejandro's white horse casts him as a kind of chivalric prince, for instance; but his greying beard gives him patriarchal features. Goyita is probably attracted to both sides of him. Don Alejandro first discovers Goyita when she is playing Lady Macbeth in a school play rehearsal, and Marsha Kinder observes how Shakespeare's play ties in with Goyita's Oedipal drama.

Democratic Spain has seen a vast increase in personal freedom. It is a sign of the different evolution of its cinema, however, that Armiñan's verdict on freedom differs little from Buñuel's. On the one hand, people are chained by their passions: in a symbolic love exchange Don Alejandro gives Goyita his old Republican concentration camp tag to hang around her neck. On the other, human contact inevitably involves the oppressed (Goyita's mother) oppressing others (Goyita) who oppress the even weaker (Don Alejandro). The only escape is fantasy. If Don Alejandro resembles Don Quixote it is not only because of his gaunt appearance but also because of his habit of imposing his own mental fantasies on his environment, imagining, for instance, that he is conducting Haydn in the middle of a wood. Yet, despite such fantasies, until he meets Goyita he feels utterly alone. As in so many Spanish films the price of liberty is paid in the coinage of solitude.[45]

Solitude: The key to solitude in so many Spanish films is the breakdown in relations between men and women. In married couples the husband is often absent either literally (*Poachers, Dulces horas*) or emotionally (the husband who leaves his wife to bring up the children in Josefina Molina's *Función de noche* ('Night Performance', 1981). Or the husband lacks sufficient masculine qualities to satisfy his wife (*Camada negra, El nido*, Regueiro's *Duerme, duerme, mi amor*, 'Sleep, Sleep, My Love', 1974).

As Carmen Méndez observes, frustrated as a wife, lover or mother, the woman becomes a matriarch, harridan, or hysteric.[46] This was a common theme of film under Franco. Siblings (*El extraño viaje*) or the fiancé (*El pisito*) are treated like children, while family loyalties are reinforced to the detriment of individual identities. 'Are you married?' a husband-hunting nurse asks two young men with a mother complex in *La visita que no tocó el timbre* (Mario Camus, 1965). 'No,' one answers, head bowed, 'we're brothers.' Juanita's predicament in *Vida perra* ('Dog's Life', Javier Aguirre, 1981) is no different. She is a middle-aged daughter, a spinster who lives alone, has imaginary conversations with her dead parents, wears her mother's clothes, blames her mother for the harm she did her but declares that it's 'too late to sin!' Losing her mother's photograph, she realises that she will be left utterly alone. Actress Esperanza Roy's superbly sustained monologue and Aguirre's tortuously slow approach shots give the film a memorable sense of absolute stasis.

Sex was inevitably debased in a country whose many private schools were run by nuns and monks. Relationships can break down because of a lack of sexual candour, prompting role-playing and deception. In Molina's documentary drama *Función de noche*, for example, actress Lola Herrera receives a visit from her actor husband Daniel Dicenta. She has recently filed for divorce and his appearance upsets her. Trying to console her, Dicenta says that she is the best of all the women he has known, to which she replies that she never once had an orgasm throughout their marriage: she had been acting. Much of the fascinating ambiguity of Molina's film comes from the fact that we never know how much Herrera and Dicenta are still acting, even in this supposed truth session. Representation before others, as before the camera, becomes a mode of and a barrier to communication.

Love for women is replaced in men by fear and resentment. Men fear for their sexual performance; woman is seen as sexually voracious, and even compared to a she-wolf in *Poachers* and *Duerme, duerme, mi amor*.[47] Women survive, men do not. In *Tamaño natural* and *La sabina* the male hero commits suicide, the woman lives on. In numerous recent Spanish comedies (*Sal gorda*, 'Coarse Salt'/'Get Lost, Fatty', Fernando Trueba, 1984; *A la pálida luz de la luna*, 1985) husband and wife split up, the wife soon finds another lover, the husband, faithful to their love, does not.

With misogyny, *machismo*, sex in short supply and women repelling phallic aggression, relationships become battles of the sexes, a theme which José Luis Guarner traces through the always intriguing works of Vicente Aranda. 'Men and women can love or hate each other,' he concludes, 'but they attack each other always: with words, acts, if not blunt objects, not to mention knives and pistols.'[48] So in *La novia ensangrentada* ('The Bloody Bride', 1972) a young wife, recently deflowered, dreams of castrating her husband. And in *La muchacha de las bragas de oro* Mariana promises to slip a razor into her vagina, just to stop Forrest raping her in the night.

Life as a battle is the tacit assumption underlying Pilar Miró's *Gary Cooper que estás en los cielos* ('Gary Cooper Who Art in Heaven', 1980) and explaining its protagonist's otherwise rather bizarre behaviour. On the eve of an operation which she may not survive, TV director Andrea Soriano visits her journalist boyfriend, mother, friends, an old lover, but she doesn't tell most of them about her operation. Busy, ignorant of Andrea's condition, they remain indifferent to her. She enters hospital lamenting 'this deep solitude', with a crumpled photograph of Gary Cooper, her childhood fantasy companion, in her hand. Notwithstanding some sharp darts at *machismo* in work relations, the crux of Miró's film is Andrea's seemingly masochistic silence about her illness. It points out a feminine dilemma in a male-oriented world. Having abandoned the traditional female model of emotional and economic dependence on men, Andrea competes with them on their terms for worldly success, gaining a 'Special Prize' for her film work, competing in an auction for a Roman mortuary vase to hold, if she dies, her ashes. Andrea has to prove to herself – by recording the indifference of the people who should love her – that she was right to reject a life based on dependence. 'I don't want to need anyone so that no one can let me down,' she confesses. Her actual behaviour just turns this formula round: she wants everyone to let her down so as not to want to need anyone.[49]

One hub of discontent may be that no new forms have been evolved to replace old models of love in Spain or elsewhere. Borau took up this point in *La Sabina* (1979). Set in contemporary Andalusia, this big-budget co-production with the Swedish Film Institute, which was designed to break into the international market, produced a critique of romantic love appealing in its mood, as Roger Mortimore says, to 'the Andalusia of nineteenth-century travellers like George Borrow ... the Andalusia of legends and mystery'.[50] Michael, an English writer living in Andalusia to research a book on the disappearance there in the previous century of a minor romantic poet, Hyatt, soon adopts romantic modes in his relationship with his day-help Pepa. But Pepa rejects Michael, partly out of respect for Daisy, Michael's American girlfriend. Michael's wife and writing partner Philipp arrive. Hyatt, investigations suggest, threw himself down a cave, called La Sabina after a dragon, out of an unrequited love for a local girl. After Philipp has seduced Pepa, claiming that it is like making love to Michael by proxy, Michael takes him up to the Sabina, pushes him down it to his death, and follows. Flames from their broken lamps make it look as if La Sabina really has eaten the two men.

The ending of *La Sabina* confirms multiple myths or traditions: the prophecy (here the pattern set by Hyatt's death); the double (Philipp), traditionally a harbinger of death; La Sabina itself as a she-dragon who makes love to men then kills them; above all, the myth of Woman as a fount of romance but also as a cruel-hearted devourer and destroyer, an image encouraged ironically by Borau in his equation of the cave with a female and with Pepa: in the final shot of the film, Michael and Philipp presumably dead, Pepa is framed in the entrance to the cave (shaped, moreover, like the female genitals), wild Andalusia behind her. Yet the fulfilment of all these myths is highly ironic, and Borau's direction dwells on the social and individual forces determining the action: Philipp's rivalry with Michael which has already caused him to steal his wife; the clear class and cultural barriers between Michael and Pepa, reinforced by accents (such as Michael's sardonic ex-public school tone), by sexual politics (such as when Daisy orders Pepa's half-wit brother to show her his penis), or by the fact that Pepa's Spanish boyfriend works in London, but only as a waiter. 'Woman destroys man,' Borau commented, 'because he destroys them first. Women live in a world made by men ... Pepa knows that ... she has no future with Michael because he would never take a woman to England who didn't know, for example, who Virginia Woolf was.'[51] Given such barriers, Michael and Pepa's relationship inevitably breaks down.

Solitude may have other sources. John Hooper comments, for instance, on the legendary 'self-centredness of the Spaniards ... a legacy perhaps of the *reconquista*, a hang-over from the days when self-reliance was of the essence' and explains Spaniards' 'reluctance to sacrifice any part of their own interests to the common good and their intolerance of other people's views'.[52] Such attitudes are dying – Spain's recent governments, as Hooper records, have tried desperately to promote *convivencia*, coexistence. But Spanish cinema still produces some remarkably self-possessed characters. One is Max in *Las palabras de Max*, Querejeta's most experimental production to date, where scenes were shot and the script further elaborated from their results to achieve a low-key but haunting work. Max's loneliness makes him neurotic. In the opening sequence shot, whose protractedness increases a sense of neurosis, Max telephones a friend, a former girlfriend, and an old schoolteacher he hasn't seen for thirty years, just to have someone to talk to. Max 'creates his own solitude', as director Martínez-Lázaro puts it: he can't communicate, he can't sense other people's feelings, he pigeon-holes other people. A friend jumps out of an apartment block, a casual girlfriend leaves him, but Max talks on. The sheer normality of situations in the film – such as Max's hostility towards his daughter's boyfriend – and the unaffectedness of the central performances – Max is played by a sociologist, Ignacio

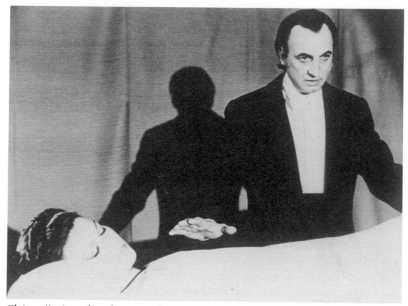

Chávarri's *A un dios desconocido*

Fernández de Castro, and his daughter by Querejeta's own daughter Gracia – gives the film a disturbing familiarity.[53]

If Spanish films made under Franco did not immediately abandon established themes, the attitudes towards them did evolve. An early sign of this is Jaime Chávarri's *A un dios desconocido* ('To an Unknown God', 1977), co-scripted by Querejeta and Chávarri only a few months after Querejeta had worked on the script of *Las palabras de Max* with Martínez-Lázaro. The film was made in Spring 1977, and marks the slight lift in optimism engendered by the imminence of democracy. In its portrait of a character emerging with good humour from a solitude of his own making, it has a grace rarely equalled in Spanish cinema.

A un dios desconocido begins in the garden of a prosperous family in Granada in the drowsy summer of 1936. At a distant window Federico García Lorca, the family's guest, can be heard imitating Chopin. José, the gardener's son, is seduced by Pedro, the family's son, but one of their night-time assignations is interrupted by men bursting into the garden and shooting José's father dead. Forty years later José works as a cabaret magician in Madrid. He returns to Granada to visit the house and garden where Pedro died from an illness soon after the Civil War began. But during tea with Pedro's surviving sister Soledad it is Lorca's photograph, not Pedro's, which José pockets surreptitiously to take back to Madrid,

186

and the rest of the film traces the subtle modulations in character which this decision symbolises.

A un dios desconocido was in many ways a fine reflection of its times. By 1977 films did not need to be strident as a few years earlier. Flushed by the immense box-office success of Saura's recent films, Querejeta could afford to experiment with a more elusive style. Comparing the film favourably to *La prima Angélica*, Marsha Kinder comments that while Saura 'explores the mental processes as they reconstruct past and present', Chávarri's central character remains far more 'complex, multi-faceted'.[54] One example of this is the sequence where José dries his sister Mercedes' hair as she sits bare-breasted in front of a mirror and describes what she feels when men make love to her. Her candour illustrates José's increasing contact with others as he abandons his isolating reverence for an idealised adolescence in Granada. Yet the scene also points to obstacles preventing a complete escape from the past or from solitude. Mercedes' description emphasises the solipsistic nature of physical pleasure which may be appreciated by others but never fully shared. Getting someone else to dry her hair reveals in Mercedes a dependence carried over from childhood. Chávarri's sustained medium close-up gives the scene almost a religious air, suggesting how lives are inevitably patterned by rite. The film is rich in such resonances.

A second indication of the time of the film's making is its treatment of Lorca. In July 1936 Lorca was arrested by the Nationalists and shot, no one knows where. 'His ill-explained death in Granada,' writes Robert Graham, 'came to symbolise the killing of a cultural renaissance in Spain under the Republic which had put Spanish artists in the European avant-garde.' It was 'shorthand for nationalist barbarism'.[55] Even by 1977 Lorca's death – more than his writing – was a sensitive subject. Chávarri does not film the death, although there is a clear echo in the murder of José's father. Lorca's poetry does, however, largely determine Chávarri's film. José listens to Lorca's *Ode to Walt Whitman* (from his surrealist collection *Poet in New York*) in a ritual repeated every night as he goes to bed. Key motifs of Lorca's poetry – carnations, the olive groves near Granada, traditional children's games, the flamenco *cante jondo* – appear in the film. Lorca's images often turn on oppositions of light and dark, day and night, the natural and the artificial. So does Chávarri's film: José in modern Madrid is seen mostly in dark interiors, lights are garish, and nature is confined to the flowers he buys or waters, or the convent garden he spies from his sister's flat, incongruous in its urban surroundings.

José also shares Lorca's moral sense as expressed in *Ode to Walt Whitman*. Lorca, while claiming a homosexual's right to sexual experience, relates Whitman's chaste homosexuality to 'a communion of innocence with the elemental life-force of nature', which Lorca contrasts with the homosexual demi-monde whose inhabitants try to corrupt the purity of Whitman's love.[56] While asserting his homosexuality, José also refuses to exploit the opportunity presented by a neighbour's son who, curious about the male visitors to José's flat, drops in one night in the hope of being seduced.

In general, José faces the problem posed by *Poet in New York*: the individual's struggle for spiritual survival in a dehumanised world. Lorca's poet finds solace in nature: José achieves a halting regeneration through, as Chávarri puts it, 'the destruction of a sentimental past and the assimilation of a historical and poetical past more relevant to the present'.[57] By stealing Lorca's photograph rather than Pedro's José takes his first step in this direction; a second comes when, after returning to Granada, he discovers that Pedro was unfaithful to him and, back in Madrid, burns Pedro's correspondence; a last is José's increasing candour with others, seen when he allows his boyfriend, a rising politician, to watch his bedtime ritual. When the taped voice reading the Lorca poem arrives at the lines 'Your tongue calls out for comrades to keep watch on your disembodied gazelle', José, now in bed, smiles faintly at his boyfriend. As much as the growing political consciousness implied by José's interest in Lorca, it is this sense of irony in an act of self-revelation which suggests that José has come to terms with an idealised and isolating past.

NEW DIRECTIONS

Manuel Gutiérrez Aragón and Victor Erice

When Hitler was informed that the image of Our Lady of Fuenciscla, kept in a Carmelite convent in Segovia, had been made a Nationalist Field-Marshal for her role in the city's defence, he swore that nothing on earth would induce him to visit Spain. Millions of subsequent tourists have proved more tractable. The social change engendered by tourism has, if anything, accelerated since the death of Franco. As Robert Graham has observed, things thought peculiar to Spain are now seen to reflect stages of historical growth common to many countries. Spain, a backward, austere country, the bastion of Catholic faith? By 1975 only 5 per cent of Spaniards in some cities were practising Catholics; in 1978 contraception was made available; and smoking marijuana is now decriminalised in Spain.

Spain still remains a babel of past and present whose contrary, even surreal, mix should not obscure the large achievements made under democracy: a democratic constitution in 1978; autonomy for Catalonia and, far less satisfactorily, for the Basque Provinces, in 1979; a divorce law in 1980; an education law passed by the socialists after their October 1982 election victory which gave greater popular access and control to private schools, previously the preserve of Spain's rich.[1] 'The loyalty of many centuries,' Jan Morris writes, 'does not wither in a generation.'[2] The ticket which allowed Felipe González's socialists to win a landslide in 1982 – an emphasis on the need for greater justice but a caution about radical change – has indeed placed the PSOE in a social democratic role which discourages dramatic new departures. Spain's entry into the Common Market in January 1986 will, however, open up the country to still greater foreign influence and do away with isolationism forever.

Observers talk about a 'New Spain'. Is there (again) a 'New Spanish Cinema'? One crucial factor would seem to discourage new initiatives: the absence since 1975 of a state-run film school to act as a focus for young talent. An overwhelming majority of leading Spanish directors in 1986

189

once belonged to the Madrid Independent Cinema, the last promotions of the Official Film School (such as supposedly 'new' directors of the 80s like Uribe and Pedro Costa), or the old 'New Spanish Cinema'. Their styles were formed by 1975.

Ironically, but in harmony with Spanish history, what has changed has not been the film directors so much as external circumstances. Political obligations, ill-focussed at the best of times, have yielded to economic necessities. The motor of change in cinema after Franco has come less from the film-makers themselves than from the moral and economic obligation to reach wider audiences, from the film industry crisis of the late 70s, and, when the state poured money into the film industry in the 80s, from the equal need to obtain state grants which allowed film-makers, ironically, largely to turn their backs on market forces.

Auteur analysis is thus even more inadequate a method of describing the modern Spanish cinema than it has proved for the cinema of most other countries. In talking of the films of the supposedly most individual of recent Spanish directors – Manuel Gutiérrez Aragón and Victor Erice – one has therefore to talk of 'Gutiérrez Aragón, Erice and their circumstances'.

Manuel Gutiérrez Aragón

'The only thing which continues to interest me passionately,' Gutiérrez said in 1979, 'is knowledge.'[3] The 'circumstances' which help to explain Gutiérrez, if only in terms of a reaction to them, is the assertive, absolutist, cut and dried manner in which knowledge is traditionally framed by both the right and the left in Spain. Gutiérrez's films respond less to themes than to an ordering temperament, a delight in contradiction, irony, and the subversion of expectations which derives from the fact that one film is rarely like the next: 'If there is anything worse than plagiarism,' Gutiérrez has said, 'it is self-plagiarism.' Gutiérrez clearly enjoyed making a fable with no moral (*Feroz*, 'Ferocious', 1984), embodying political reflections in stories which have an element of fairy tale or myth (in the backbone of his work – *Camada negra*, 'Black Brood', 1977; *Sonámbulos*, 'Sleepwalkers', 1977; *El corazón del bosque*, 'The Heart of the Forest', 1978), or making a so-called 'delinquent drama' – *Maravillas* (1980) – which mixed music, locations and characters and dwelt not on delinquency so much as human solitude. Part of the appeal of Saura's films under Franco was the ideological gratification offered to audiences who could identify not so much with the characters in the films as with the young, courageous anti-Francoist director who made the films. Though far more reflectively political, Gutiérrez's work denies such pleasures, and so has perhaps a more limited international appeal.

190

Gutiérrez's radical independence of spirit was seen immediately in his first feature, *Habla mudita* ('Speak, Mute Girl', 1973). At a time when other Spanish film-makers were becoming more contentious (if still obliquely), Gutiérrez set out to make a comedy of relativity which explored the power-play of education, the drawbacks of language, and the impossibility of human communication. An editor, Ramiro, holidaying in the northern Spanish mountains where he is studying the one surviving Spanish *carabo* (a variant of the tawny owl), one day gets lost, stumbles through the mist to a village tucked in a fold of the mountains, and chances upon a deaf-dumb girl whom he determines to teach to speak. From the beginning Ramiro remains sceptical about the ability of words to communicate rather than act as a vehicle for dominion. 'Say "field",' he reflects with the sententious melancholy of many Gutiérrez characters, 'and they'll put a fence round it, say "house" and they'll tell you to clean it, say "marvellous" and they'll try to sell you it, say "I want" and they'll say no.' Ramiro's classes are a predictable failure. When he is dragged back to civilisation by his scandalised family, the dumb girl is left to pass on the fruits of her education to her retarded brother, trying to make him vocalise an 'a'. A bathetic, gruff grunt resounds across the mountains. 'I think I'll read *Don Quixote* again,' Ramiro remarks as he is driven back to Madrid. Education, the communication of knowledge, seems, like Don Quixote's chivalry, a dignified but unrealisable ideal.

The foreign director who most influenced young Spanish Film School directors in the 60s was probably Antonioni. *Habla mudita* offers a kind of *esperpento* vision of non-communication, epitomised by the night that Ramiro and the dumb girl spend together shuddering from the cold, drenched to the skin, in the carcass of an old bus. In its harshness and its physical emphasis the sequence seems like a Spanish parody of *La notte*.

On its release *Habla mudita* was interpreted somewhat simplistically as an allegory of the intellectual's distance from the people.[4] Its political essence lies elsewhere, however, as Gutiérrez has suggested: 'Films operate directly on the spirit.... Their capacity for subversion is infinite.... A subversive cinema is always paradoxical ... multiplying contradictions and making sure it doesn't pact with anyone.'[5] Abandoning his original intention to make *Habla mudita* a fairly monotone disquisition on language, Gutiérrez constantly shifts styles to create formal paradoxes in the film. The opening presents a fairly hellish view of a middle-class Spanish family. Ramiro is alternately nagged and ignored, nobody responding to his elegant description of the lone *carabo*'s mating call as 'language without communication, or communication without language'; his grandson even asks him why, if he is old and bald, he doesn't die. To film such scenes Gutiérrez uses composed framing, balanced tonal photography creating a tension between subject and style which is echoed at the end of the film

A problem of communication: *Habla mudita*

when the enraged villagers' attempt to lynch Ramiro (whom they wrongly accuse of raping the deaf-dumb girl) acquires a festive, *sainete* tone.

Ironies abound in *Habla mudita*. Since Ramiro's desire for human contact is stronger than the mute girl's desire to learn, Ramiro has to pay her to be taught. Ramiro's interest in the *carabo* causes its destruction. Walking home one night, he stops to listen to the bird's call. The dumb girl thinks he wants to hunt the owl and throws a stone towards it. A flopping sound is heard nearby. 'Now,' Ramiro says sadly, '*carabos* exist only in Canada.' At the end, the retarded brother and the mute girl seem to abandon a relationship based on incest for one founded on the girl's classes. But it is unclear whether this exchange marks a step forward or just points to a new round in the personal power politics seen earlier.

Gutiérrez returns to somewhat similar ironies in *Feroz*, an arch parable about a boy, Pablo, who lives in the wooded north of Spain. The film's ironies centre on whether Pablo is an animal, as a local zoologist maintains, or a human being, as an upstanding psychologist, Fernando, maintains. Such categorical claims are undermined by events. At first the zoologist seems right: dogs yap at the human Pablo, his nails are claw-like, and, having spent the winter in a cave, he finally turns into a bear. Then the psychologist seems right as Fernando reclaims Pablo and lodges him in his bear form in his Madrid house, where he teaches him how to attend a tea and to work a computer. Yet though conceptually a man, Pablo remains emotionally a bear, dreaming about his favourite tree and pawing at

192

butterflies for play.[6] Even when Pablo reacquires human form he still eats leaves. Cut and dried distinctions seem impossible.

Comparisons between *Habla mudita* (1973) and *Feroz* (1984) show how Gutiérrez adopted a relatively similar style both under and after censorship. The real, artistic reasons for Gutiérrez's style, including its frequent obliqueness, and the dangers of allowing external factors to determine stylistic choices became clear with *Camada negra* (1977).[7] When the script was originally sketched out, before Franco's death, Gutiérrez and co-writer José Luis Borau drew back from showing clearly that the protagonist's brother, the leader of a fascist vigilante gang, was also a policeman. They merely envisaged a shot of him entering the notorious Dirección General de Seguridad, where political activists were often taken for interrogation. By late 1976, when he made the film, Gutiérrez felt secure enough to make the brother declare explicitly that he used to be a policeman. The fascist gang is shown committing outrages typical of the transition period: they attack a left-wing bookshop, slash paintings, attempt to break up a political dinner.

No other Spanish film underlines so unequivocally the violence of Spanish fascism. To join the fascist group the protagonist, fifteen-year-old Tatin, has to satisfy the three conditions laid down by its moral leader, his mother: 'Avenge the fallen brother, guard the sworn secret ... sacrifice the most sacred if the Fatherland should demand it.' To fulfil the last test, Tatin murders his girlfriend Rosa. Gutiérrez attempted to make this violence as appalling as possible: Rosa, played by Angela Molina, is the unmarried mother of a four-year-old son; Tatin kills her by smashing her skull with a boulder, accompanying each blow with a cry of 'Spain!'

The testimonial side to *Camada negra* may, however, have misfired. Initially banned, authorised after the 1977 elections, it finally opened, Borau recalls, to 'a terrible reaction – there were bombings, protests and threats. Even now, five years later, there are many towns and villages where the film is not shown.'[8] *Camada negra* was also widely misunderstood, being taken merely as an attack on Spanish fascism. Gutiérrez protested at such a limited interpretation: 'To say that fascists are evil ... that can be deduced from the newspapers. The real wager for knowledge is to make a film trying to understand a fascist ...'[9] *Camada negra* was intended in fact to portray 'the traits defining a fascist in any time, condition or party'.[10] And rather than evading censorship, Gutiérrez's oblique forms serve to generalise his observations.

A first oblique form is the family. Tatin, his brothers and other members of the fascist group are fed and housed by Tatin's mother, a fiery bigot called Blanca who champions 'holy anger' and accuses her sons of being namby-pambies when they regret having killed a waiter at a political dinner. Gutiérrez justifies his frequent use of the matriarch figure because of its historical accuracy: 'In *Camada negra* the mother expresses the concept of the vestal. The image of the father is far more diffuse in primitive societies. Our societies still retain relics from more primitive groups.'[11]

Gutiérrez also exploits the symbolic overtones of family structures. 'A film cannot portray a society, but a family can. And to a certain extent the family is a kind of microscopic state, a summary of the tensions and structures of the state.' In *Camada negra*, Blanca accommodates her fascist sons in an old state laboratory where she used to work; she buys them soap, tonic and sandals, cleans up after them and cooks their food. In return she regulates their habits (barring them from smoking and drinking) and imposes moral duties.[12] Once the family-state analogy has been established, events acquire richer connotations. On a political level, for instance, Tatin's murder reflects the abnegation of liberty from the Mother-State demanded by fascism. Psychologically it represents a still prevalent Oedipal complex. Sexually it signifies the denial of pleasure at the core of the fascist value-system. It is no coincidence that when Rosa is murdered she and Tatin, as Marsha Kinder points out, are on the verge of making love.[13]

A second obliqueness in *Camada negra* is its use of the fairy tale, echoed in the film-plot which has Tatin set several proofs of valour, leaving home to accomplish them, and meeting a kind of princess, Rosa, on one of the sorties. The fairy-tale echoes suggest a political reading: in following its guidelines Gutiérrez's characters respond to laws which are inherited and traditional rather than rational. Gutiérrez's films mimic in fact the narrowness of fairy tales where, as Vladimir Propp suggests in his classic analysis of the Russian folk-tale, characters, however varied, repeat essentially the same actions.[14]

Like Borau's *Poachers*, Gutiérrez's other films are, however, fallen fairy tales. In *Camada negra*, the final proof of the hero's valour is to kill the princess. A fictional perversion reflects back to a political perversion. The redirection of the hero's violence away from giants, ogres or other third parties does not obscure another suggestion, however: Tatin is identified with the hero figure of both fairy-tale romance and tragedy (via his support for a doomed cause, here Spanish fascism). The identification is hardly casual. Gutiérrez's use of a family to portray fascism suggests that in some ways a family may be innately fascistic; Tatin's confluence of the ethos of fascism and the modalities of a hero begs the question of whether heroes too are innately fascistic. A left-wing hero may be, this thought-provoking film suggests, a contradiction in terms.

Gutiérrez's resort to the fairy tale also forms part of a larger and immensely fertile strategy, as he has explained:

> There is something Marx says which I always like to use in my films. He stresses the need to make quotidian things seem strange and strange things quotidian. He refers to the fact that there are many quotidian

things which are accepted, such as there being rich and poor people, which should seem strange, and there are strange things, such as love, which should seem quotidian. In my films I try to make the most obvious things seem strange and the strangest things seem obvious.[15]

Feroz observes both sides of the coin. Pablo's strange metamorphosis acquires at least a degree of verisimilitude by echoing so many myths, such as the Moses story, about the birth of the hero: Fernando crashes his car, with the human Pablo in a trunk in the back, into a river; the trunk slides into the water, floats downstream, bathed in a shimmering light, comes to rest in a cave.[16]

On the other hand, as with any fictional transformation, Pablo's metamorphosis sheds fresh and memorable light on his original, human state. Pablo-the-bear's existence is really quite ordinary. He is not very photogenic, he is stuck in a body he would rather not have, he feels homesick even when growing up, and he likes to cuddle up to the girl-next-door figure of Fernando's friend Ana. If Pablo feels alienated, humiliated and alone, it's not just because he's a bear but because that is the human condition.

Gutiérrez developed this particular brand of magic realism in *Sonámbulos* ('Sleepwalkers', 1977). The dreamlike tenor of this remarkable film is caught at its beginning when our only narrative bearing is that the film is set during the widespread political unrest generated by the Burgos trials of 1970. A series of dissolves pictures Ana, a militant in a Communist cell in Madrid, asleep in a chair in a room of the National Library. Outside the library, silhouetted like Chinese shadow puppets beyond the huge glass window covering the whole of the wall behind Ana, demonstrators scuffle with the police. Suddenly, two horses come crashing through the glass window and scrabble on the library's wooden floor as their police riders flail at demonstrators with their batons. Ana sleeps on.

Sonámbulos is set around a performance of Strindberg's plays at which Ana's cell are preparing to drop leaflets and make a speech about the Burgos trials before the cream of Madrid society. Increasingly ill, Ana is told she is suffering from an incurable brain disease. Her small son discovers a book of fairy tales, in one of which a mortally wounded Princess is promised a book of guidance by a Magician if she in return kills the Queen. Ana realises that she in a way is the Princess. Her mother María Rosa, with whom she has never got on well, is also an activist who plans to take part in the theatre protest. Interrogated by the police, Ana betrays her mother.

The Strindberg cycle which we see being rehearsed and performed in the film forms a far from casual reference. Characters (Ana and her family's nurse-cum-housekeeper, Fatima), scenes (the ritual of a lentil lunch repeated by Ana's family for years, although it transpires that no one likes lentils), and even lines (María Rosa's lament that she has tried to sack

'I try to make the most obvious things seem strange and the strangest things seem obvious': *Sonámbulos*...

Fatima but the housekeeper won't leave), are based on or borrowed directly from Strindberg's work, especially *The Ghost Sonata*.[17] There are other similarities with Strindberg, in particular the way Gutiérrez weaves a narrative from multiple threads and his conclusion that we live in a world of illusion and folly.

Pursuing the theme of illusion, Gutiérrez brilliantly suggests analogies between various spheres of ideology, all dominated by ritualistic, false presentations of reality. There is, as Julio Pérez Perucha suggests, the myth of knowledge (the library where Ana works and where The Book of All Things, which includes her fairy story, is kept), 'the privileged space of representation' (the theatre), and a space of domestic ideology and political militancy (María Rosa's house to which Ana returns when ill, and which has an ETA hiding place).

In *Sonámbulos*, Gutiérrez achieves a director's dream: a theme which is a licence to invent images. Few Spanish films are so daring, none so justified in its inventiveness. Gutiérrez even reaches the stage of having an actress, Laly Soldevilla, suddenly appear in María Rosa's house as if it were a stage or her unexplained arrival part of a dream. The film ends framing a typical paradox: our personality is defined by habits which alienate or violate our true selves but whose absence connotes madness. And death denies real liberty and provides us with true knowledge. In a superbly shot finale Ana is taken to a happy home and is visited by her family (including María Rosa, who is due to go to prison next day – the unlikelihood of an ETA collaborator being allowed provisional liberty suggests that this sequence, like the rest of the film, may be a dream). They sit in the manicured gardens, where people in white coats drift by and sprinklers turn eternally. Ana makes notes in her diary: 'I love my mother and my favourite colour is...' But she can't remember. A librarian at the National Library, who acts throughout the film like a fairy godmother, brings Ana a Book of Knowledge which records the end of the fairy tale: 'Beware the Queen, for the Queen is death. Beware the magician, for the magician is madness. The Queen possesses the Book which only the magician can decipher.... If you want to know all answers to all questions you will destroy yourself. The Princess remained doubtful for several days during which time she wrote the story I am telling you.'

Sonámbulos represents one of the most intelligent reflections made about militancy under Franco. Though hardly seconding Ana's treachery (which he explains in part as motivated by family rivalry with María Rosa), Gutiérrez saw *Sonámbulos* as a 'farewell letter explaining the reasons for my abandonment of left-wing militancy'.[18] Seeing the Spanish Communist Party quite rightly as 'the only force to combat Franco', Gutiérrez had been a member since 1962, but resigned the day the PCE was legalised in 1977.

... Feroz

The PCE, Gutiérrez recalled, demanded 'a great sense of political and also ideological discipline.... This seems necessary to me at the same time as vitally and intellectually it bothers me. The role of an intellectual in a democratic society can be much more pluralistic than submission to a party programme.'[19]

Gutiérrez was to explore the abandonment of militancy in *El corazón del bosque* ('The Heart of the Forest', 1978), where various kinds of loose myth – political principles, the rural way of life, even a love affair – are all seen to be products of history, to be abandoned inevitably in time. The pathos of this realisation, and the paralleling of political allegiance and personal attachment, makes *El corazón del bosque* Gutiérrez's most sympathetic film.

The backbone of the film is its relationship between myth, especially political militancy, and Spanish history under Franco.[20] In a prologue set in 1942 myth and rural reality seem integrated. El Andarín, at the head of a hopeful *maquis* band in the woods of northern Spain, stands in front of the lamp of a lighthouse and projects a huge shadow over a nearby cliff. He arrives at a local dance, dances gallantly with the ladies and is watched admiringly by a young village girl, Amparo. By 1952 the PCE is abandoning the armed struggle and Juan P., Amparo's brother, is sent to the region from France to persuade El Andarín to lay down his arms. The harmony of myth and rural reality is now breaking down. El Andarín is pockmarked by a terrible skin disease, his men are sought out and shot by the Civil Guard, and the struggle against Franco is obviously passing to the cities. Juan P. slogs his way through the mud in the forest, gets lost, meets a former *maquis* who, like him, was born in the region, and comes down from the mountains.

At this point Juan P. nearly gives up his search for El Andarín. The crux of the film comes with his decision, when already leaving the area, to return, seek out El Andarín, and kill him. This decision goes beyond the fulfilling of a mission. Exploring the wood with his childhood acquaintance, Juan P. rediscovers his own rural roots: the way a goldfinch sings, the old anecdote about a cow which was given beer to increase its milk yield. Juan P. recognises that El Andarín belongs to the same world and seeks him out to kill him and so release a myth of his own rural world from the ravages of history. As he retreats downhill, the body of El Andarín is already fading into the landscape.

Love is equally time-laden. Amparo falls in love with El Andarín, but by 1952 can hardly bear to see him. When Juan P. appears at the local dance in 1952, an elegant interchange of glances between him and Amparo, mostly filmed in medium shot so that the two are continually separated by the crowd, establishes a complicity between them which goes beyond the fact that Juan P. is a member of an outlawed political party. The forest for Juan

198

P. represents the magical wood of childhood, with its ghosts, surprises (a jar of milk found on a hillside) and laws of its own. Searching for El Andarín through this leafy labyrinth, aided by Amparo (who lends him her boots) and a song which links various places in the forest, Juan P. re-enacts the Theseus legend, in which the killing of the minotaur is usually interpreted as a symbolic slaughter of its owner, King Minos, archetypal father figure of Greek myth. Gutiérrez integrates this suggestion into the killing of El Andarín. 'I've known you,' El Andarín says after Juan P. shoots him, 'from when you were that small.' Juan P. ends up living with Amparo in a kind of Hansel and Gretel cottage in the countryside, so affirming an elementary bond to a rural life and to each other, and the difficulty of evolving beyond first allegiances, whether personal or political. It is this sense of elementary attachment which Gutiérrez locates at the centre of his film's forest.[21]

El corazón del bosque launched Gutiérrez, playing for months at Madrid's prestigious Alphaville cinema, and establishing him as the leading figure among Spanish film-makers a half generation after Saura. Gutiérrez took a prominent part in the running debate which brought about a significant change in perspectives among Spain's more aware film-makers, finding echoes in Erice, García Sánchez, Berlanga and Viota, among others.[22] Speaking of the 'tension between the expressive and communicable', Gutiérrez turned against *Sonámbulos* as being 'expressive' but largely unintelligible. *Camada negra* had already persuaded him that 'journalism, the novel and also surely the theatre are much more capable than the cinema of producing a testimony about reality'.[23] Gutiérrez also voiced a fairly general disillusionment among Spanish film-makers with a self-reflexive film language. Up to *Sonámbulos* he had thought that cinema 'necessarily explored its own language as poetry and painting had done'. Now he saw the danger of films becoming 'art for cinephiles' when they should be a mass art.[24]

Aiming for greater communication, Gutiérrez's work in the early 80s has shown several developments. Save for *Feroz*, a Querejeta production, all his films since *El corazón del bosque* have been co-written and produced by Luis Megino, who now rivals Querejeta as Spain's foremost independent producer. Their films together employ more stars to good box-office effect: the double attraction of Angela Molina and actress-cum-pop singer Ana Belén in *Demonios en el jardín* ('Demons in the Garden') ensured its popular success in 1982. The ironies are less sophisticated, the possibilities for identification with the characters somewhat greater. The lattice-like narratives continue, but most of the films are made within a genre which orients the spectator: the thriller in *Maravillas* (1980), melodrama in *Demonios en el jardín*, the eighteenth-century comedy of romantic intrigue in Gutiérrez's last film to date, *La noche más hermosa* ('The Most Beautiful Night', 1984).

The new tenor of Gutiérrez's work is caught well by *Demonios en el jardín*. At first glance it seems direct, accessible, historical cinema. At a family wedding in a northern Spanish village in 1942 where Ana marries the ineffectual Oscar, his brother Juan seduces cousin Angela and, leaving her pregnant, goes to Madrid to occupy some unspecified position near to the Caudillo. Ten years pass: Angela is summoned by the domineering grandmother to bring her child Juanito to live with the family. 'Rarely,' Isidoro Fernández commented, 'has Spanish history been described with such acerbic accuracy.' In one sharp scene, for instance, the grandmother places Juanito beside her in the family grocery store (called 'El Jardín') and makes snide asides to him about her customers, especially those with a Republican past ('You've got to watch the till with these'). It is a mark of the grandmother's hypocrisy that the family fortune is founded on nightly black-marketeering.

The interest of *Demonios en el jardín* goes far beyond occasional historical satire. 'We must speak about the post-war,' Gutiérrez declared in 1982. But in doing so he went against pundits who proclaimed the post-war a dead issue, and also against the current practice of both right and left in Spanish politics to see the past in black and white terms. Gutiérrez refers obliquely to this habit in the film's title: primitive belief attributed evil or misfortune to the bad demon in a pair of brothers or twins. *Demonios en el jardín* gains its major moral interest from its attempt to explain the interior 'devils' inculcated in Juanito, especially his habitual falseness and the growth of his vaguely anti-Francoist consciousness. Gutiérrez uses the oppositions common to both primitive myth and the schematic interpretations usually given to the Spanish post-war. Oscar and Juan fight over Ana; Ana and Angela compete for Juanito's affections.

With characteristic scepticism Gutiérrez decries any simplifications. Nearly all the characters are false: Oscar feigns a triumphant nationalism ('Spanish chick-peas are the best in the world') to compensate for his own ineffectuality; Ana feigns respectability but hankers after the style of the manicured *femme fatale* she sees in films; Juanito feigns illness for most of the film. Angela, the daughter of Republicans, is not much more attractive as a character than Ana, and Juanito, constantly torn between love for his mother and nascent attraction for his aunt, ducks a clear choice between the two by demanding that both should pander to him.

Gutiérrez's use of genre is as pointedly cross-grained as his moral attitudes. His film, as Francisco Marinero observes, conflates fantasy (a bull bursts into the wedding ceremony), drama (post-war hunger exemplified in begging gypsies), melodrama and humour (anguished at her adulterous passion for Juan, Ana finally shoots him, though she only wounds him slightly), and political reflection, illustrated by Juanito's visit to Franco's cortege. Once more, family and national history combine. Juanito finds that his father is not a heroic soldier but just a waiter, and is then presented to Franco (kept off camera). Juanito's disillusionment is total. 'We didn't begin to be anti-Francoists,' comments Gutiérrez, 'because we were convinced that right and history made us anti-Francoists ... but out of disenchantment because we didn't like that short fat man with a piping voice who was El Caudillo.'[25]

The earlier *Maravillas* was if anything even more incisive. Its eponymous heroine takes part in a jewel robbery with Loles and Pirri, an endearing urchin delinquent whose slang, whistling through a gap in his teeth, provides many of the comic effects in the film. The priest they rob uncovers Maravillas' role in the crime and she is charged with retrieving the jewels or facing the consequences. But the stones have disappeared, and the fence who was given them is found murdered.

As with the fascists of *Camada negra* (who are petit bourgeois when Spanish fascism remains very much an upper class affair), Maravillas and the other delinquents are hardly typical of the Spanish phenomenon they represent. Pirri in fact rejects a facile sociological explanation for his crimes, offered by the priest: 'Perhaps you're not totally guilty ... society.' Pirri's unwittingly existential response closes the door on such reflections: 'No, no, I'm just very bad, very bad. If I'm not bad I'm nothing at all.' *Maravillas* is in fact an excellent example of a post-Franco trend in Spanish cinema: the subordination of sociological reflection to the renewal of cultural influences cut off or warped by the Francoist regime. Here the dominant influence is Cervantes, especially *Don Quixote*, as Gutiérrez has explained: 'Don Quixote rides through La Mancha, a geographical place known to everyone ... in which one can almost smell the mule trains and recognise the people, and yet where magical events take place.... This is characteristic of Spanish culture.'[26]

Gutiérrez's Madrid is equally real yet magic. Familiar locations are shot from fresh angles: seen from a patch of wasteland the Nuevos Ministerios skyscraper complex rises up like a land-bound Manhattan. From the top of La Torre de Madrid (where Buñuel used to stay) streets like the Gran Vía look like valleys or crevices, palatial buildings like wedding cakes. Gutiérrez's plot jumps in near cubist fashion from one enclave of fantasy to the next. We begin, for example, in a street arcade with Maravillas sprawled out asleep on the ground as nearby a black man jigs barefoot on glass to the rhythms of Nina Hagen's punk opera *African Reggae*. Maravillas returns home to remember her Jewish godparents sitting on her sun terrace, discussing the ingredients of date liqueurs and imitating the fog-horns of the ships entering a port in their Black Sea homeland.

Maravillas has a similar sense of comic inversion to that of *Don Quixote*. There a squire becomes a hermit, jilted women dress as men, and farm wench Dulcinea is regarded as a princess. In Gutiérrez's film, children

201

(Maravillas, Pirri) behave like adults and adults (Maravillas' unemployed father Fernando, to whom she occasionally lends money) behave like children. Women also take the lead in bed. Such inversions suggest, as in *Cría cuervos*, that relationships which should be based on love (between lovers, or parents and children) are actually founded on convention or power.

Cervantes' main concern, however, was to point to the lack of verisimilitude in most sixteenth-century chivalric literature by showing the absurdity of Don Quixote's attempts at comparable epic achievements in real life. At one point a priest and a barber rummage through Don Quixote's library and consign books lacking verisimilitude to the fire. Near the end of *Maravillas* a priest, a magistrate and a psychologist leaf through Fernando's pornography magazines (accused of creating the moral ambience which plunged his daughter into delinquency) and burn the most indecorous examples. Fernando (played superbly by Fernando Fernán Gómez) tries to keep one photograph. 'I have loved this woman greatly,' he protests. As ever in Fernán Gómez's delivery there is a slightly grandiose swirl about these lines. In *Maravillas* man's Quixotic dream is no longer for chivalric adventure but for mere human contact in a world of eternal solitude.[27]

Gutiérrez's film style discourages a sense of contact between characters and the spectator. Close-ups are rare. Not one medium or close shot in the opening sequences of *Maravillas* is seen from the point of view of another character, so merging his or her viewpoint with ours. Figures act before us but are not us. Even acts of intimacy seem darkly solipsistic, like Maravillas' love-making with a young friend.

Maravillas above all records the girl's initiation into the world. Here again the Spanish cinema reflects the harshness of Spanish life, the need for strength, independence and self-interest in a hard, lonely world. The film works once more like a jaundiced fairy tale. There is a treasure: the jewels. There is a labyrinthine wood of complexities: the film dwells on doors, parapets, passages, parlours, small rooms, arcades, steps, streets. There is a Prince, Chessman, a lanky youth from a reformatory with whom Maravillas falls in love. There is even an initiation ceremony as (in a reminiscence) Maravillas' godfather Salomón makes her, just after her First Communion, walk along a parapet high above Madrid. Yet though a golden late afternoon sun glints over this scene, giving Madrid's domes, parapets and towers the glow of fiction, the sequence is suffused with sadness. For Salomón's spell offers Maravillas no treasure, or promise, but a hard lesson in life: 'The fearful fall, the valiant vanquish.' Seven years later, to find out who has taken the jewels and killed the fence, Maravillas requests the aid of Salomón, now working as a cabaret magician. Salomón exposes Chessman. To save herself, Maravillas loses her lover. She ends the film like the other characters with a sense of exclusion, from their homeland (the Jewish godfathers), from a brilliant past (Fernando, erstwhile doyen of high society photographers), from their childhood, from love. At the end, nearly all the characters gather on Maravillas' terrace roof to burn Fernando's magazines. Fernando looks out over the Madrid skyline and declares, 'We live as we dream, alone.' The sun glows over evening Madrid. The scene is lit with the light of fiction, but shot through by the weight of irony.

Victor Erice

The distinctive voice of the Spanish cinema often seems made up in part by its moral accent. Whether patriotic alarums, sly satires or sheer hokum, the point of Spanish films still seems to be to make a point. The absolute divide under Franco between the sanest of popular pleasures and the moral values allowed by censorship indeed made even the most complacent of films seem morally contentious. Ideologically under Franco there could be no such thing as an escapist cinema.

Overshadowed by moral issues, stylistic concerns in Spanish films usually seem an afterthought or a question of practicalities. Lacking cheap studio facilities in the 1970s, directors have used natural interiors – such as rooms in the old Lycée Française in Madrid for *Dulces horas* and Fernando Trueba's *Opera prima* – which naturally cramp camera movement. Filming on a one-good-take-per-shot basis has cut down editing choices. Cranes are rarely used, so their use is rarely envisaged. Limited laboratory facilities and film-stock also curb innovation. Victor Erice and Luis Cuadrado in their more quixotic moments used to wonder what they could have made of *The Spirit of the Beehive* if they had been able to shoot it in Technicolor.[28]

'Every film is a unique experience,' Carlos Saura said, 'in which I face a series of narrative problems I never consider a priori.'[29] Few Spanish film-makers do. As Eugeni Bonet and Manuel Palacio point out, a Spanish film avant-garde has always been hobbled by the absence of both a sophisticated middle-class audience and a modern mainstream industry to advance beyond without falling laughably behind progressive movements abroad.[30] Innovative film-makers, such as the extraordinary film inventor and surrealist documentarist José Val del Omar (b. 1904), have normally worked in isolation. Film-makers of artistic ambition faced the dilemma in the 1970s of mainstream integration or emigration. Two strongly personal talents, Adolfo Arieta and Celestino Coronado, chose the second course.[31]

Victor Erice is one of Spain's few mainstream directors who invites a detailed study of style. Erice is loosely associated with the Madrid Independent Cinema, but his early career was more shaped by the zealous critical war sustained at the E O C, and carried over into the magazines *Nuestro Cine* and *Film Ideal*, between the advocates of neo-realism and the admirers of Hollywood cinema.[32] Erice co-founded *Nuestro Cine*, wrote for it, and made his industrial debut, the medium-feature episode in *Los desafíos* ('The Challenges'), in 1969.

An attempt to show 'the socio-cultural situation of Spain', Erice's sketch pictures two Spanish couples who arrive at a deserted village, swop partners, degenerate into violence because of the jealousies which this flirtation with modernity sparks. Though hardly inspired, the narrative has an intriguing mixture of Spanish cultural traits (theatricality, voyeurism, the slightly surreal touch of the pet monkey which accompanies the group) and superficial cultural grafts, mostly drawn from the spaghetti Western (one of the husbands declares free love in the village, challenges the other to a duel, and uses a dynamite trail to blow himself and his friends sky high). Rather than annulling Spanish violence, Spain's 'superficial modernisation' is seen as merely giving it slightly more contorted expressions.[33]

Producer Elías Querejeta was impressed enough by Erice's episode to pick up his idea of a film about Frankenstein's monster, a project made commercially viable by the early 70s horror film boom in Spain. Originally planning a political allegory, with the monster returning to a concentration camp Spain run by technocrats, Erice soon fell under the spell of a still from James Whale's *Frankenstein* which he kept on his table and which pictured a little girl kneeling with the monster beside a pool. Erice decided to focus on the meaning of the monster for the children of his generation. 'Perhaps the most important moment in any mythical experience is that which reveals the ghost, the initiation,' Erice has commented.[34] *The Spirit of the Beehive* charts the steps by which seven-year-old Ana, living in a sullen village on the wind-buffeted Castillian plateau around 1940, slowly conceives her personal myth of a real-life Frankenstein's monster.

Wide-eyed, receptive, Ana watches James Whale's *Frankenstein* at the local cinema. What she can't work out is why the monster kills the little girl and everybody kills the monster. Ana's slightly bigger sister Isabel explains at bedtime: nobody really dies in films. The monster, Isabel adds maliciously, is really a spirit who can take on human form. She has seen him in a cottage near the village; to call him you just have to close your eyes and say 'I'm Ana, I'm Ana'. Ana's next encounter with disembodied spirits is at school, where during an anatomy lesson the teacher treats a life-size doll as if it were human (Ana's task is to clip on his eyes). At the cottage, Ana finds the footprint of a man; at home, Isabel plays on Ana's growing interest in the monster by opening windows, screaming, falling down – echoing a scene in *Frankenstein* where the monster enters a room where Frankenstein's young wife is sleeping and attempts to throttle her. Isabel plays dead, then suddenly revives, once more denying Ana the idea of a definitive death. At a bonfire night (which, as E. C. Riley points out, recalls 'the Noche de San Juan, night of the spirits, with its firewalking rites',[35] and may also remind Ana of the giant fire in which the monster meets his death in

Whale's film) Ana decides to invoke the spirit. Next morning she discovers a Republican fugitive in the cottage. Identifying him as the monster's spirit, she brings him clothes. At night the fugitive is shot dead by the Civil Guard. But Ana knows that spirits don't die. Running off into the countryside, she hallucinates that she meets the monster beside a pool. She is found and taken home, but her belief is now complete. At night she goes to her bedroom window and whispers out into the darkness, 'I'm Ana, I'm Ana'.

Having, as Erice himself has said, 'a fundamentally lyrical structure', *The Spirit of the Beehive* brilliantly uses both camera viewpoint and editing to embody a myth as it is seen in a child's imagination.[36] Erice films key mythical sites – the village hall cinema, the film screen, Ana's house – straight on. The air of two-dimensionality endows these elements with a near totemic status, while also corresponding to the constructs of a young mind (think of the way small children draw houses). Editing ellipses produce an increasing atemporality. When the girls visit the cottage the first time, only the drift of clouds' shadows across the patchwork landscape, filmed in a series of dissolves, charts the time taken by the sisters to scamper from the ridge where we first see them down to the cottage below. Erice films the cottage in a medium shot. The children run out of the frame, but Erice holds the shot and Ana then re-enters the frame. But what is the time-lapse between Ana's visits? The film has entered the realms of myth where chronology and geography become blurred. It is the event, its symbolic setting and above all its relevance to the leading character which is all important.

Ana's story is open to psychological, cinematic and historical readings, all of which naturally overlap. The key to Ana's behaviour is in many ways her father Fernando. Seemingly deeply disturbed by the Civil War, in which he played an unspecified part, he retreats into study, writing a journal on beekeeping. For his family Fernando becomes literally at times a shadow, a point brought out with subtle economy, as many critics have noted, when Fernando undresses in his bedroom after a night of study. Erice films his shadow falling across his wife Teresa, who feigns sleep. Desiring protection and security, Ana sees the spirit as a kind of substitute father, giving the fugitive Fernando's clothes and his pocket-watch which, ordering his day, represents the hub of his domestic authority.[37]

Yet Fernando also figures in Ana's mind as a source of authority. She and Isabel interrupt a bedtime game of Chinese shadows when they hear Fernando approaching. 'Daddy's coming!' one whispers and they blow out the bedside candle. When Fernando goes off on a trip, home life becomes brighter: the children have pillow fights and play at shaving. Ana's final imagined meeting with the monster is modelled on the scene in Whale's *Frankenstein* where little Maria plays with the monster when her father has to go off to work.[38] Erice may be said to enrol Ana's attitudes towards both

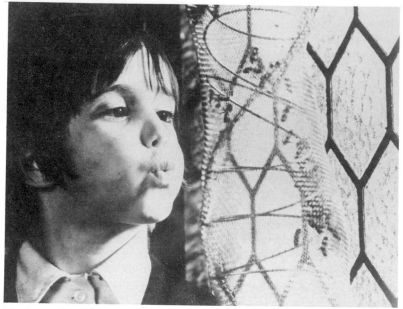

The Spirit of the Beehive

Fernando and the monster to comment on the normal ambivalences of a growing child's relationship to the outside world. To take two examples, the houses in the film, as Peter Evans observes, are both 'places of security and warmth' and 'structures of decay and imprisonment'.[39] And Ana is always seeking to run away from home, but to look for a figure very much like her father, the man most associated with her home.[40]

The one objection made to *The Spirit of the Beehive* is that Erice sometimes forces issues by details (such as the chance arrival of the fugitive at the cottage the very night that Ana invokes him) which correspond more to his thematic intentions than to Ana's lyrical consciousness of events. Such criticism overlooks the fact that the 'mythical experience' in *The Spirit of the Beehive* is not only Ana's monster fantasies but the mythical status and experience of film itself. Erice announces constantly that his film is a fiction and, in this sense, a myth. 'Once upon a time,' the film's opening caption reads. Superimposed over a child's drawing of a film screen, in which we see Whale's monster and little Maria beside him, the caption suggests the fictionality of both film and Ana's beliefs about the monster. Erice creates a parallel between the artificiality of film creation and the fabrication of the monster by cutting from a shot of a presenter in Whale's film who describes Frankenstein as 'a man of science who attempted to create a live being' to a shot of the projector in the cinema. On a poster outside the hall Whale's film is announced as 'Doctor Frankenstein, autor del monstruo'. And, as Vicente Molina Foix has observed, nearly all the family are pictured in creative activities, writing a journal (Fernando), letters (Teresa), or just pretending to type (Ana).

Our experience of Erice's film in fact compares with Ana's mythical experience. Both involve deduction (from Spanish history to Erice's film, from Isabel's explanations to Ana's own experience). Both work on analogy (for both the spectator and Ana primarily the links between Fernando, the monster and the fugitive). 'In film,' Ana's sister tells her condescendingly, 'everything is a lie.' But Ana is soon engrossed in the significance of *Frankenstein*. 'Once upon a time,' Erice warns us, but the spectator is soon engrossed in *The Spirit of the Beehive*. Erice's film not only portrays a mythical experience but embodies its structures and its fascination.

There is another fictional echo in the film's second caption: 'A place on the Castillian *meseta* around 1940.' *Don Quixote* begins: 'In a place in La Mancha, whose name I do not want to remember.' Like Cervantes, Erice is interested in balancing the general and the particular; and while his film deals in general issues – the ambivalence of the father-child relationship is one – he is careful to relate them to a particular historical background, which will explain their special emphases.

The Civil War and its consequences hover over Ana's family. A house in their village sports the yoke and five arrows of the Spanish Falange; at night Fernando listens to foreign news of the Second World War on his ham radio set; and at school a child recites a poem by Rosalía de Castro, originally written in Galician, now translated into Castillian Spanish, the language of Franco's regime. Rather than a realistic example or stylised symbol of the contemporary background, Erice's family seem more its consequence.[41] Fernando clearly embodies what Erice has called 'the emptiness of Spaniards who fought in the war ... an absence. They had died, gone abroad, or were left locked up in themselves radically deprived of the least elemental modes of expression ... defeated men who, independently of which side they fought on, lived the war without any clear idea of the reasons for their behaviour, acting simply to survive.'[42] Which side Fernando fought on is deliberately left vague, though Teresa writes letters to a Republican exile in France.[43] Abstracted by his beekeeping and his journal, Fernando's very fascination with the misspent energies of his bees ('Someone who saw these things,' he writes in his journal, 'quickly averted his gaze which showed a strange, sad terror') may well be an oblique reference to the febrile carnage of war. Fernando suggests well the consternation, impotence and silence of men who fought in the Civil War. As Roger Mortimore comments, dialogue is minimal (Fernando and Teresa never converse) and silence is broken only by the notes Teresa picks out on a piano or by the gun shots which end the fugitive's life – the sounds of boredom and death.[44]

207

Given the Civil War background, the monster acquires a special significance. In broad terms he is a part, as Peter Evans says, of 'the other', the mysterious world which children explore when growing and which gives them their sense of identity. This is underlined by Erice's remarkable lighting effects, consciously modelled on seventeenth-century Dutch painting. In an early sequence Teresa sits by a window writing. The lattice work on the windows, the silence, the yellow light filtering in, 'the quiet existence of a single figure within a mildly lit interior seen from close by' − all this suggests the paintings of Vermeer.[45] And as in Rembrandt's portraits, characters in the film often suggest a contemplative life, a loss of will, a receding into darkness in which light becomes an animating principle and a source of knowledge.

For Ana the key to knowledge is the mystery of death. An obsession with death, which Fernando shares, was only natural in a country where recriminations for the war were still being carried out and yet where mention of the subject of death was discouraged. The celebrated scene in Whale's film where the monster throws Maria into the pool is cut from the version of *Frankenstein* seen by Ana. Hence in part her curiosity about why the monster killed the girl. Far more than Mary Shelley's novel, Whale's film stresses that the monster is a patchwork creation of bodies from tombs and charnel-houses; its invocation by Ana forms part of that collective desire for resurrection which seeps into early 1940s Spanish culture.

Ana and Isabel constantly experiment with death. For Ana the local train represents not so much a symbol of escape as a guarantee of death to anyone it hits: she waits on the railway line until the last possible moment before jumping away as a train approaches. When Isabel nearly throttles the pet cat, Erice cuts significantly to a painting of St Jerome pointing at a skull. Later Ana imagines Isabel suspended on top of the bonfire which she and her friends are jumping over.

The monster combines associations of mortality with a fallen morality. Like Gutiérrez, Erice draws on manichean distinctions between good and bad 'demons'. In her room Ana has a painting of a good demon, an angel holding the hand of a child. In contrast the monster, according to Frankenstein's colleague in Whale's film, is 'a demon' and his brain 'that of a criminal'. Out mushroom-picking with Fernando, the girls play at guessing whether mushrooms are good or bad and discover a large one which Fernando calls 'an authentic demon ... If you try it you'll die instantly'.

Fernando's observation confirms Ana's final, imagined meeting with the monster as, from her viewpoint at least, a confrontation with death. Having disobeyed her father by running away, Ana imagines herself discovering the 'demon' mushroom, which she reaches out to touch; when the monster appears and sits down beside her, she closes her eyes to await her fate. She is discovered next morning beside a ruined wall reminiscent of an equally sinister structure seen at the beginning of *Frankenstein*. The round hole at the base of the wall, E. C. Riley suggests, indicates that Ana 'has come through the wall to the other side, with all the symbolic implication of this'.[46] Ana's final invocation of the monster is also an assertion of identity, an identification with a supposedly malevolent, death-dealing outcast which refers both to the side which lost the Civil War and to the early intimations of mortality to be found in any growing child.[47]

Awarded the First Prize at the 1973 San Sebastian Film Festival, *The Spirit of the Beehive* was heralded as the first film to portray the sadness and frustration attendant on Franco's victory and (erroneously) as the first Spanish film to be shot from the point of view of the war's losers. The film's importance for cinema after Franco, however, was that, with Gutiérrez's *Habla mudita* and the lone forerunner of Ungría's *El hombre oculto* (1970), it was the mainstream feature-length debut of one of the generation of film-makers after Saura who were to form the backbone of the post-Franco cinema. *The Spirit of the Beehive* set new standards for formal elaboration and helped inspire works by Chávarri (*Los viajes escolares*, 1974), Saura (*Cría cuervos*, 1975), Enrique Brasó (*In memoriam*, 1977), Ricardo Franco (*Los restos del naufragio*, 1978), Gutiérrez Aragón (*Demonios en el jardín*, 1982) and José Luis Guerín (*Los motivos de Berta*, 1984).[48]

A child's way of seeing: *The Spirit of the Beehive*

Erice used the interval between *The Spirit of the Beehive* and *The South* (*El sur*, 1983) to reflect on his own position as a director within the Spanish film industry. Rather than *The South*, Erice would have preferred to make something more self-reflexive, closer to 'the modern universe where one questions the act of speaking'. He had in fact sketched out a project for a film diary. Yet several factors made him pull back: a personal timidity, a childhood spent watching classical American cinema, market demands for him to return to the world of *The Spirit of the Beehive*, the fact that 'the Spanish cinema has not experienced several stages of growth' so that it was one thing to have received a theoretical education in modernist film-making but quite another, as a director, to attempt such a cinema.[49]

The South was consciously designed, Erice says, for 'major distribution channels' and has a stronger sense of narrative than his previous work. Set in a bare, bitter northern Spain between around 1950 and 1957, *The South* charts the relationship between an ex-Republican doctor and water diviner, Agustín, and his adoring daughter Estrella. At the age of eight Estrella enjoys a deep empathy with her father: he teaches her to divine; she goes with him on a dousing assignment; she waits for him to come home from work. Above all Estrella associates Agustín, who comes from Seville, with a warmer, more sensual, freer existence in the Spanish south.

On the eve of Estrella's First Communion, Agustín's dour mother and effervescent wet-nurse Milagros arrive from the South. At bedtime Milagros recounts how Agustín quarrelled with his reactionary father and left the South forever. Estrella and Agustín dance together like bride and bridegroom at the party held after the First Communion service. They are never again so close. Soon afterwards Estrella discovers sketches which Agustín has made of an actress called Irene Ríos. Estrella spies Agustín entering a cinema showing a film in which she acts, and later discovers him writing her a love letter. But Irene Ríos writes back rejecting a renewal of what seems an old relationship and Agustín, after an abortive attempt to travel to the South, withdraws into a sullen despair.

An ellipsis takes Estrella to the age of fifteen. Agustín remains withdrawn, locked up in his study. One day Agustín invites Estrella to lunch at a local hotel. Estrella fails to recognise the pasodoble played at a wedding reception in another room as the same tune she and Agustín danced to at her party, and in general rejects Agustín's attempts to renew their former complicity. That night Agustín shoots himself beside the local river. At the end of the film, Estrella prepares to travel to the South, find Irene Ríos, and discover the South's attraction for herself.

On one level, as Peter Evans and Robin Fiddian observe, *The South* is a fairly obvious Freudian drama. For Agustín, Estrella and Irene Ríos substitute each other: he stopped seeing the actress, their correspondence reveals, not when he got married but when Estrella was born; he starts writing to her after Estrella's First Communion, which marks the beginning of her growing up and inevitable independence from her father. For her part Estrella declares of her eight-year-old self that 'I just needed his presence at my side for everything else to stop worrying me.' *Mise en scène* during Estrella's First Communion develops the marriage undertones of the ceremony. In one graceful interior scene (reminiscent of Vermeer in its mellow blues, square-tiled floor, and picture of contained domestic activity) the women of the family bustle round Estrella with the happy nervousness normally associated with a wedding. Estrella, dressed in white, is the focus of attention.

Erice makes frequent connections between Estrella and Irene Ríos. Estrella means 'star'; Irene is a film star. The poster advertising Irene's film at the local cinema shows her face outlined against a background of stars in a blue night sky. The film is called *Flower in the Shadow*: both Estrella and Irene are 'stars' or flowers in Agustín's emotional night, a point brought out by Erice's frequent highlighting camerawork which picks out Estrella's face but hides the rest of a scene in semi-darkness. The film which Estrella imagines Agustín seeing has Irene Ríos shot dead by an old lover after she has failed to recognise a tune as 'our song'. As Evans and Fiddian suggest, this imagined scene may transfer on to Irene the guilt Estrella feels at having failed Agustín at their last lunch together.

Erice inscribes Estrella's childhood within more general patterns of growth, and describes this process with a tact, depth and sustained sensitivity which carries off one scene after another. A key scene is the one where Estrella learns to divine. Agustín's lesson takes place in his attic. Just as Estrella's life revolves around her father, so she literally walks, hand on his pendulum and guided by his instructions, around her father. Just as she is gaining a gradual independence from Agustín, so the scene begins with Agustín sitting centred in the frame and Ana in a subordinate position kneeling before him; but the scene ends with Ana standing frame-centre, watching enthralled as the pendulum begins to gyrate in her hands. And just as she associates her father's seemingly supernatural powers with his origins in the sensual, warm Spanish south, so the light which she remembers in the scene, bathing the sloping attic roof behind father and child, is of a sunny yellow which one would associate with the South.

The central sequence of the film, the First Communion party, is equally memorable. Beginning with a close-up of Estrella's gown, veil and bouquet deposited on a chair at the head of a table, sweeping down the table and out to Estrella and Agustín dancing together, tracking the two with great elan before returning to Estrella's First Communion attire, the sequence shot captures the panache of Estrella's particular joy but encloses it within a symbol of a social coming of age. Erice in general seems to view maturity as accession to a world of social symbols which distance people, annulling the

The South: Estrella and the pendulum

emotional spontaneity of youth or at least forcing emotion to be expressed by a fairly limited set of correlatives. Estrella's would-be boyfriend when she is fifteen complains that she gives all the signs of being attracted to him but then cold-shoulders him. Estrella as yet has not fully learnt the semiotics of love.

Maturity, however, is seen above all in *The South* as a partial renunciation of myth, and it is myth – its motives, images, and proper domain – which perhaps forms the film's major subject. Agustín mythicises Irene Ríos. Her real name is Laura, but he writes 'Irene Ríos' under his sketches of her, and when he writes to her after his cinema visit he is as much affected by her screen persona, as she points out, as by her real self. Estrella mythicises Agustín. Her first supposed memory, dramatised at the beginning of the film, is of Agustín using the pendulum to divine, while his wife Julia is still pregnant with Estrella, that the baby will be a girl. For Estrella the scene conveys 'a very intense image which I in reality invented'. Any scene or setting connected with Agustín is lit by sandy light or coloured yellow: Estrella's bedroom as she picks up the pendulum on the morning after Agustín's death; the provincial, sandstone hospital where Agustín works; the yellow walls of the family house. In a similar fashion the seagull weathervane on top of the house is always pictured against a clear blue sky. Lighting effects, such as in the attic divining lesson, are too sudden not to be

212

artificial, product of a fiction. Agustín becomes in effect a private religion for Estrella: the pendulum is her icon, his hospital is populated by nuns and, in one sequence, light streams from a window as Agustín walks down a corridor as if from the nave of a church. Estrella's view of Agustín's past conforms to religious myth. He is expelled by a Father from a Seville which, according to the postcards Estrella has of it, seems a kind of earthly paradise of gardens, fountains and happy, dancing people.

The origins of these myths are partly located in Spanish history. Agustín's past as a Republican who was jailed after the war would explain his difficulties in finding 'a fixed job' and, with his quarrels with his father, his need for a more settled existence which apparently led him to abandon Irene for the more placid Julia, and to spend Estrella's childhood 'moving from one place to the next' looking for stable employment. Estrella's abnormal closeness to her father also derives from this insecure early life. Yet *The South*, like *The Spirit of the Beehive*, transcends particular Spanish problems to relate myth to the universal desire for stability in a fleeting, dislocated existence. The artistic references in *The South – Wuthering Heights, Romeo and Juliet*, and Hitchcock's *Shadow of a Doubt* – generalise the film's implications by relating them to those of other fictions.[50] The reference used most – implicitly in the film's imagery of the South, explicitly in the final scenes of Erice's script, which were not filmed – is, however, Robert Louis Stevenson's travel journal *In the South Seas*.[51]

The script of *The South* begins with a quotation from Stevenson: 'The coral sprouts, the palm tree grows, but man goes away.' Irene Ríos touches an adjacent theme in her letter to Agustín, which we read with him: 'Time, Agustín, is the most implacable judge I have known, and although I'm now grown up, sometimes, above all at night, I'm afraid.' Running through *The South* is a variety of effects which connote the fleeting nature of life and the sense of a mapped-out destiny. Many scenes, for instance, flow into the next. When Agustín divines that Julia's baby will be a girl, the static camera begins to jog lightly, imitating the rocking of a train, and suddenly we are travelling across Spain in a train. At the end of the scene Agustín looks at the sleeping Estrella and a gleam of light crosses her face which is revealed in the next scene as the sunlight glinting over the river. Confirming this effect of flux are multiple images of diminishing perspectives: the lines of candles in the church during the First Communion, the long table at the party, the straight road down which Estrella cycles away from the camera at the age of eight and towards the camera (after a dissolve once more connoting the fleeting nature of time) when she is fifteen. A sense of time running out is conveyed by an almost classical image: Julia, distraught at Agustín's attempt to leave home for Andalusia, rapidly winding up a bundle of wool like some latter-day Parcae. And the characters' inevitable destiny is also suggested by the many repeated actions which Freud related to the death

213

instinct: Estrella rocking up and down on a swing; Agustín, brooding over Irene Ríos, banging his stick monotonously on the attic floor.

The South also studies the tenability of myths. Agustín makes two mistakes: he thinks that a temporal affair, Irene Ríos' love for him, should be everlasting; seeking perpetuation in Estrella, he takes her indifference to his nostalgia as a sign that he has no continuity in her.[52] Irene Ríos denies such paradisal myths as the South: 'I've travelled the world,' she writes to Agustín, 'but I've never found the place from which one never wants to return ... The past now doesn't move me as before ... I fear that, at last, I've grown up.'

The major pity about the unfilmed ending of *The South* is that in it Erice brings his subtle reflection on myth to a climax. Estrella essentially confirms Irene's experience. She travels to Seville, meets Laura and Octavio (Laura's fourteen-year-old son by Agustín), is able to place them and the South in a more realistic perspective, and returns matured. Myth finds a more proper domain in Octavio, who wants to be a writer. In the final scene in the script he stands in a field, Agustín's pendulum in hand (which he has learnt to operate, confirming the perpetuity which Agustín sought in his other child), closes his eyes and imagines that the fallow ground becomes corn, then sea speckled by islands. For Octavio, an avid reader of Stevenson, these islands are his own South. Some myths – the dream of knight gallantry, the yearning for a far off better land – may well create fictions, but they are none the less fascinating for that.

INTO THE FUTURE

By the 1970s Spain's economy was riding for a fall. 'The high degree of technological dependence,' writes Robert Graham on Spain's economic miracle, 'the heavy reliance on (still cheap) imported energy, the high level of protectionism for local industry, the cheap cost of credit, the exploitation of labour and the continued prosperity of north European economies were never really considered. Yet these were the pillars on which the miracle rested.'[1] When the world recession of the early 1970s caused these pillars to crumble, Spain's economy was bound to suffer. Arias and Suárez both attempted to buy goodwill by agreeing to wage increases during the transition. Suárez did finally react, arranging an incomes policy with the leading political parties and unions in October 1977. Otherwise he did too little too late, preferring to prop up loss-making businesses rather than attempt thoroughgoing industrial reconstruction. By 1983 2.2 million Spaniards, 17 per cent of the working population, were jobless. Nearly half of the jobless were young first-time job seekers who were not entitled to any social security.

A sense of disillusionment and impotence seeps into many turn-of-the-decade films. In the fittingly dowdy *Sus años dorados* ('Golden Years', 1980) Luis lives off his estranged wife, picks up money on the side collecting scrap, and meets a girl who has drifted equally aimlessly through a series of men. They act in a porno movie, spend a passionless night together, separate. In a perhaps forced finale Emilio Martínez-Lázaro counts the cost of such passivity. Luis wanders through a park, sees a friend who is a political activist in the distance and watches as a gunman walks up behind the friend. Luis panics and runs off while his friend is shot in the back, Luis' instinctive passivity costing him his life.[2]

Fernando Méndez-Leite's *El hombre de moda* ('The Fashionable Man', 1980) dealt more subtly with similar themes. In his literature classes school-teacher Pedro teaches Torrente Ballester's novel *Los gozos y las sombras*

215

whose hero Carlos Deza is 'liberal, abstentionist and sceptical, and never likes to get involved'. So too Pedro. He fails to help his father, who is increasingly disoriented by modern life, and shies away from a relationship with Aurora, an Argentinian exile who comes to him as a mature student. 'I wanted,' Méndez-Leite commented on his downbeat, elliptical film, 'to describe the bewilderment of a whole generation at this time.'[3] Pedro's attitudes are partly explained by late-70s Spanish *desencanto* – 'disenchantment'. Attributed by the far right to the alleged traumas of democracy – terrorism, street crime and recession – *desencanto* in fact stemmed from the *triumph* of democracy in 1977 which left erstwhile anti-Francoists feeling there was not much now to struggle for. Sustained by a tradition of protest, Spanish film-makers began to contest this apathy by showing the personal consequences of passivity or by suggesting, in a stance comparable with the dissidence of the 1960s and echoed in many transition films, that Spain in 1980 was failing to evolve.

In Jaime Chávarri's *Dedicatoria*, for instance, Juan, a rich, dilettante journalist, investigates the imprisonment of an old friend, Luis, and starts an affair with Luis' daughter, Carmen. Luis dies from an overdose in prison, leaving Juan a taped confession in which he suggests that it was Carmen who betrayed him to the authorities and who gave him the pills with which he killed himself. Carmen and Luis had been having an incestuous affair which she did not want to continue and he could not forget.

It is not the act of incest itself but the silence surrounding it which acts as a metaphor for larger historical realities. And obliqueness becomes not so much a censor-evading strategy as an assertion that such censorship still exists. So many things, the film implies, remain to be said. On a personal level, characters are separated symbolically by bars (as when Juan chats to Luis at the prison) or fences (Juan hands Carmen Luis' tapes through a fence). Characters simplify issues: for his readers Juan tags Luis as 'The Man With the Dogs', a whole personality squeezed into a subordinate phrase. Characters also skirt truths. 'Tell me about the first time,' Carmen whispers to Juan as they share a sleeper going back from the prison. But instead Juan starts a story which is a disguised version of how he met Carmen. As he jests with Carmen a shadow of sadness crosses his eyes (in one of the glancing inner observations which Chávarri handles so well). In this small act of retraction Juan recognises his essential solitude.

Above all Spain's past remains hidden in mystery. Background is left obscure (Juan, for instance, has a lovely flat but we never discover where he gets his money from). The same people enjoy influence and power under and after Franco – Juan's boss Paco, Carmen and Juan himself all attended high society hunts, now Paco runs an important news agency and Juan is one of his leading writers. Paco and Juan are engaged in filtering (i.e. censoring) information. Juan talks to an aristocrat's chauffeur; Luis at one

Chávarri's *Dedicatoria*

point offers to give Juan the names of people engaged in police torture.

In this key turn-of-the-decade film, love, pleasure and even communication remain reserved for moments of grace, marked out by a splendid musical score. One example is Luis' birthday party, celebrated in prison. Carmen and Juan bring him an accordion, an instrument he used to play as a young man. Luis is clearly touched and plays a *habanera*, creating an almost stubborn note of gaiety in the drab prison room. But behind the door, shadowed in the window frame, stands the figure of a prison guard, a splendid metaphor for the fact that authority, control and censorship in Spain may have been less intrusive by 1980 but still exercised a crucial behind-the-scenes influence.[4]

'The cinema,' Manuel Gutiérrez has said, 'is not the most appropriate medium for a testimony of reality because it is already testimonial in itself.'[5] The greatest indication of Spain's economic crisis given by its cinema was its own recession. The long-term origins of the film industry's crisis were a very small international market and declining national audiences. 'The money for a Spanish film,' producer Luis Megino has argued, 'should come ideally in equal parts from the home market, foreign sales, and government film-funding.' Yet, apart from the 30s, foreign sales have always paid a pittance, amounting in 1979 to 160m pesetas, as compared to domestic sales of 3,650m pesetas.

A series of developments from the 50s have put increasing pressure on Spain's home market. The Motion Picture Export Association's boycott on films to Spain from 1955 to 1958 transformed many Spanish distributors into effective North American subsidiaries, confirming permanently the multinational control on the distribution in Spain of both imports and the national product. Secondly, in the drab *posguerra* only the bulls, the church and football rivalled the cinema as entertainment and the government purposely kept cinema tickets down at so-called 'political prices'. Cinemas provided one of the only places where courting couples could enjoy some privacy. By the 60s, however, alternative entertainment, especially television, began to cut into cinema audiences, although Spanish cinemas still have one of the highest per capita attendance rates in Europe (141 million spectators in 1983). The most immediate effect of lifting censorship in 1977 was to authorise a spate of foreign films whose previous prohibition only increased their mystique. Drawn to *Last Tango in Paris*, *The Decameron* and sundry *Emmanuelles*, audiences for imports rose from 146 million (1977) to 168 million (1978) and 164 million (1979). Inflation (16 per cent by 1980), compounded by escalating production costs in part prompted by freer trade unions, meant that by the end of the decade a medium-budgeted Spanish film costing 30m pesetas (about £400,000) would have difficulty recouping costs from its only, national market. The alternative left to Spanish film-makers, producer José Sámano calculated, was either co-productions or cheap products aimed strictly at internal consumption. Hence the localism of many early-80s Spanish films.[6]

Minute foreign markets and diminishing home returns meant that by the late 70s government film-funding had become a life support system for the Spanish cinema. Suárez's UCD government effectively pulled the plugs. Suárez's own cultural ambitions went notoriously little further than a good hand in the card game *mous*. Under him the entire budget for the Ministry of Culture was less than that of the Pompidou Centre in Paris, and half of that was squandered by RTVE. By 1978 the Treasury was still defaulting on Protection Fund payments to producers, owing them a total of 1,500m pesetas. The UCD was also caught in its own ideological cross-fire, supporting in theory both cultural patronage and freer market economics, a contradiction causing the typically ill-contrived Decree of November 1977 which abolished the distribution quota along with censorship while lowering the screen quota to a 2:1 ratio.[7] With no mechanised box-office control the measure was impossible to enforce, and was satisfied in part by exhibitors unearthing old Spanish films. Finally, in July 1979 at the behest of the American-backed Federación de Empresarios, the Supreme Court abolished the screen quota, adjudging it to be unconstitutional.

Recession in the film industry brought several changes. First, films responded not to aesthetic movements or political programmes (both anyway

218

hardly traditions in the Spanish cinema) but to economy measures or production packages: 'to make a cheap film' (Fernando Colomo on *Tigres de papel*); 'as a means of getting into the industry' (debutant director Francisco Roma on his lightweight social satire *Tres en raya*, 'Three in a Row', 1978); 'market necessities' (Josep María Forn on why he chose the figure of Companys for his consciously Catalan late-70s production). Colomo used sequence shots, a minimal number of locations and young actors to keep the trend-setting *Tigres de papel* to a 9m pesetas budget; debutants Juan Miñon and Miguel Angel Trujillo arranged the sketches in their industrial calling card, *Kargus* (1980), so that the most elaborated episode – a truly nightmarish attempt to escape to France by sea during the Civil War, with leading actress Patricia Adriani – comes first.[8]

Secondly, rather than the exploitation of new freedoms by Spanish film-makers it was the economic crisis, forcing a disoriented and increasingly desperate industry to experiment with new industrial initiatives, which explains the increasing differentiation in Spanish films after 1977. 'The ideological struggle of the 60s,' wrote Francisco Marinero, 'has been diverted by the economic crisis into a struggle for survival and one scarcely notes a common global intention in the Spanish cinema.'[9]

The most obvious recipe for survival was a pornography industry; yet, despite assertions to the contrary, a sex cinema never really developed in Spain. Though the UCD government authorised hard-core films in theory, they never fully organised the establishment of the 'Special Cinemas' in which the 1977 Decree stipulated such films should be shown.[10] Cinemas did attempt sometimes to harden their soft-core material by strident publicity campaigns. ('Rapists!' the advertising slogan for one Spanish film read, 'the actresses will be attending the premiere!'[11]) Against this tendency more conservative distributors, fearing their films would be given a pornographic rating, often took censorship into their own hands: Pinocchio's wooden penis was carefully excised from all copies of Corey Allen's *Pinocchio*. The relatively low percentage of films achieving the normal soft-core rating – 16 per cent of Spanish productions from 1978 to mid-1983 – owed much to the sexual conservatism of Spanish directors. The sketches made by top Spanish directors in *Cuentos eróticos* ('Erotic Tales', 1979) could be witty (Colomo and Trueba's skit on Bergman, *Köñensonatten*), intellectually cogent (Augusto M. Torres' *Frac*, 'Dinner Jacket', which conceives of sex as a social rite for which two young girls dress up rather than undress), but only once, in Enrique Brasó's *La vida cotidiana* ('Daily Life') actually erotic.[12]

The Spanish sex film of most note is *Bilbao* (1978), José Bigas Luna's highly original portrayal of sexual desire embodied in an obsessive, Leo, who lives with his brow-beating wife María but secretly plots to possess the body of a vulgar prostitute called Bilbao. As Julio Pérez Perucha points out,

Leo's relation to reality is that of a hard-core pornography film to its object of desire. Leo spends the day wrapped up in his dreams, a condition caught by the self-obsessed monologue which runs through the film; he fragments, fetishises reality, insisting on minor physical detail. *Bilbao* charts the frustration of pornography. Leo attempts to possess Bilbao in every possible way: he buys a train ticket to the city of Bilbao, he tapes her voice, and finally he kidnaps her, ties her up, shaves her pubic hair. But an accidental bump on the head kills Bilbao, and Leo is left permanently frustrated, a symbolic fate for someone who views the world through the constructs of pornography.[13]

The industrial strategy practised with most success by Spanish film-makers, however, was the attempt to occupy some of the terrain of American cinema, particularly the genre film. Left-wing critics, struggling against a dull consensus cinema, advocated a genre cinema which would reflect a more conflictive reality. 'The Spanish state's political and economic transition,' wrote Julio Pérez Perucha in 1979, 'requires concordant fictions whose adventures and struggles will be developed with greatest narrative efficacy by formulae taken from the Western and the *film noir*.'[14] For want of a Film School, the basic training for many new Spanish directors was seeing films, not least American genre cinema. Genre films offered directors the benefits of a double familiarity: the possibility of combining stock film forms known to Spanish audiences of all kinds with an equally recognisable Spanish reality.

Spanish genre films did, however, present several problems. One was their ethos, the rugged individualism of, say, the adventure film hero which left-wing film-makers would condemn as a lack of class solidarity. Paulino Viota's enterprising *Con uñas y dientes* ('Tooth and Nail', 1978) confronted this problem by subverting genre. A trade union activist goes underground during a strike, keeping vital proofs of management corruption to himself. He is shot, the corruption is never exposed, the strike fails and the corrupt old boss is quietly replaced by a superficially more progressive management who end the film explaining to the factory floor the need for austerity measures. Viota's film was unusual in its exposure of the way that powerful economic interests sanctioned the transition, and in the emphasis it placed on the role of the masses in that transition. The film is part thriller, part detective story, part soft-core movie, but each of these modes is subverted.

Viota's film was too sophisticated in concept and too raw in execution. Rebuffed by Spanish critics, it was inadequately distributed. Straight *film noir*, insinuating hidden corruption in high places, offered a more attractive proposition. The Spanish law enforcement agencies provided easy targets. They were notoriously ineffective: Suárez once complained that two intelligence service captains had their jobs described on their visiting cards.[15] Nor

220

had they been thoroughly democratised: in 1978 the Minister of the Interior, Martín Villa, was quoted to the effect that he could only trust twenty police officers.

It was fear of serious acts of indiscipline which inhibited attempts at police reform under the U C D. A similar, strangely temporising tone is found in Spanish *film noir*. In Antonio Gonzalo's *Demasiado para Galvez* ('Too Much for Galvez', 1981) the witless eponymous journalist stumbles on a property speculation racket, but Gonzalo consistently deflates the brutal violence dealt out to the hero and his accomplices with comic bathos: a final bomb attempt on his life turns out, for example, to be an explosion on a film set. José Luis Garci's glum gumshoe, German Areta, traces the death of a client's daughter in *El crack* (1980) to a jet-setting industrialist associated with the Spanish establishment. But the fact that Areta follows the industrialist from Madrid to New York, where the climax of the film takes place, deflects the corruption from Spain to abroad. Garci also pulls his punches in *El Crack II* (1983), though the result is much sharper: besieged by death threats, Areta hesitates between further investigations and a long-prepared holiday with his girlfriend in Italy. He finally chooses the latter.

The most forthright Spanish *film noir* to date is José Antonio Zorrilla's promising debut *El arreglo* ('The Arrangement', 1983). 'A political reading of the transition,' Zorrilla commented, 'it is the first film to show state corruption from the inside.'[16] Cris (played by Eusebio Poncela, one of the outstanding young actors in Spain), a police inspector, returns to Security Headquarters after two years absence to find that, despite the transition, very little has changed. An old Francoist policeman dies symbolically at the beginning of the film; another, Leo, despite killing a student at headquarters under Franco, is about to become the youngest police superintendent in Spain. Cris follows a series of murders back to Leo, whom he shoots. The acid insinuation of *El arreglo* is that Cris' actions play into the hands of intriguing police authorities for whom Leo was proving an embarrassment.[17]

Such bated sarcasm was rare in the increasingly circumspect cinema of the 80s, a fact which makes the films of Eloy de la Iglesia even more refreshing. Under Franco, De la Iglesia made violent social protest films, including the outstanding *La semana del asesino* ('The Week of the Murderer', 1972) and *Una gota de sangre para morir amando* ('A Drop of Blood to Die Loving', 1973), favourably compared by José Luis Guarner to *A Clockwork Orange*. Since *Los placeres ocultos* ('Hidden Pleasures', 1976), De la Iglesia has tended towards a more realistic style, combining social melodrama with an increasing sophistication. *Los placeres ocultos*, *El diputado* ('The Deputy', 1978) and *Otra vuelta de tuerca* ('The Turn of the Screw', 1985) all turn on the main character's homosexuality. The first contrasts the fate of homosexuals from different social classes. The second

221

attacks the hypocrisy of a Spanish democracy which parades its liberties but rejects homosexuals. The last, and most ambitious, an elegant adaptation of the Henry James novel, changes James' governess to a governor, implies a latent homosexual attraction between him and his precocious male ward, and suggests that the ghosts the governor sees are really phantasma, the product, like the governor's horror at his own latent homosexuality, of a warped, repressive education in a seminary. Adopting the governor's viewpoint, picturing his hallucinations as if the ghosts really appear to him, De la Iglesia cleverly delays our recognition of his delusions.

De la Iglesia's family dramas also show increasing sophistication. In *Colegas* ('Mates', 1982) family hostility and unemployment push two young friends into delinquency. Hero José refuses to marry his girlfriend, even though she is pregnant and he loves her, and this is presented as a positive decision. *El pico* ('The Shoot', 1983) is more ambiguous. The family still makes for oppression. At his son's eighteenth birthday party a Civil Guard celebrates the boy's independence from one social institution (the family) by proposing his membership of another (the Civil Guard), getting him (by now, in a strident irony typical of De la Iglesia, a heroin addict) to dress up in his Civil Guard uniform and put on a moustache, emblem in Spain of right-wing authoritarianism. On the other hand, the film records the love which the family encourages between parents and children, and it is this ambivalence which makes its ending so excellent. The father, catching his son with heroin, drives him to the top of a cliff and throws the heroin, wrapped up in his Civil Guard's three-cornered hat, into the sea. His responsibility as a Civil Guard is subordinated not only to his love for his son but also to the survival of his family, arguably a stronger force for oppression. It is a salutary irony.

Eloy de la Iglesia's films also have a political cogency. *Navajeros* ('Knifefighters', 1980) is a rampant melodrama with stock characters (such as the Mexican whore with a golden heart with whom the protagonist has pointedly untraumatised sex for much of the film), simplistic moralising, scandal-mongering (policemen who are pimps, visit male prostitutes, and curse Spain's democracy[18]). And it takes an extreme case (the life of a celebrated Spanish delinquent, El Jaro) to an extreme end: the protagonist's corpse with shotgun wounds in head and face. Never has the new Spain been shown so brusquely.

De la Iglesia uses stylisation in *Navajeros* to assert the attraction of a youth culture which is ineradicably opposed to middle-class culture. To point up this separation, when Jaro and his gang rob pedestrians, raid phone boxes and smash windows, De la Iglesia accompanies the images with the graceful music of Tchaikovsky's *Sleeping Beauty*. In another pointed incongruity, as they escape from the police Jaro and his gang trample sniggering through a ballet class for the daughters of the rich. The attractiveness of the youth culture rests mostly with El Jaro himself. Disdaining realism, De la Iglesia plays to the strength of the melodrama hero, the way 'he greets every situation with an unwavering single impulse which absorbs his whole personality. If there is danger he is courageous ... untroubled by cowardice, weakness or doubt, self-interest or thought of self-preservation.'[19] Jaro dies while walking fearlessly, knife in hand, towards a middle-class housekeeper who holds a shotgun on him. The ending confirms both class enmity and that total absorption with the moment which made Spanish delinquents and the culture they embodied such attractive figures for Spaniards troubled by their past and the doubts of *desencanto*.

The popularity of the main Spanish film genre of the last ten years, the so-called New Spanish Comedy, may also be linked with its break with the past. Of its main figures – Fernando Colomo, Fernando Trueba, and Francesc Bellmunt – only the Catalan Bellmunt has made films under Franco. All, despite Colomo's *Tigres de papel*, appear optimistic about Spain's chance of burying the past. In Colomo's *¿Qué hace una chica como tú en un sitio como éste?* ('What's a Girl Like You Doing in a Place Like This', 1978), a housewife successfully makes the transition from a drudge married to a police informer into a groupie girlfriend of a punk-rock singer. In Bellmunt's *L'orgia* ('The Orgy', 1978), drama students get rid of sexual inhibitions simply by having an orgy together. These films cast fresh young acting talents in scripts which focus on the family not as an arena of repression so much as a setting for different approaches to life. In *L'orgia*, for example, while the parents go to Andorra to smuggle a few cut-price goods into Spain, a custom which survives from the *posguerra* years, their son goes off for an orgy. The New Spanish Comedy tried to break with past solemnities. In a patent reference to what young film-makers conceived as the portentous socially aware films produced by Querejeta, one of Bellmunt's orgiasts observes that there are two types of history: the official story of man's progress from bone to spaceship, and 'the history of normal people'. The New Spanish Comedy deals with the latter: students, people living drab lives who dream of making an easy killing (via a jewel robbery in *Siete calles*, 'Seven Streets', Javier Rebollo and Juan Ortuoste, 1981); a postman (the protagonist of *La reina del mate*, 'The Mate Queen', 1985) who is seduced by a *femme fatale* into drug smuggling; or conscripts off on a train to do their military service (*La quinta del porro*, 'The Stoned Conscripts', Bellmunt, 1980).

The film-makers usually associated with the New Spanish Comedy in fact show considerable versatility. After *Opera prima*, Trueba made *Mientras el cuerpo aguante* ('While the Body Lasts', 1982), an engagingly casual portrait of protest singer Chicho Sánchez Ferlosio in conversation and song. Colomo made *La línea del cielo* (1984), a comedy set in New York where the hero's pidgin English reduces him to something like the bumpkin status of protagonists in the Spanish Sex Comedy, and completely frustrates his plan to sell photographs to *Time* magazine.

The generation of Spaniards portrayed by the New Spanish Comedy is readily identifiable. Political militants perhaps in some distant past, they are now victims of the *desencanto*: out of work, out of luck, out of sympathy with any kind of politics, they live in hope that when they least expect it their normal, boring lives will take off into the fantasies of genre cinema. The New Spanish Comedies are genre-within-genre films, creating fictions which parallel the real world (often featuring the favourite haunts of Spanish youth) but in which almost anything may happen. If the fantasy is maintained, it will be at the cost of verisimilitude. In *La mano negra*, for example, Colomo's talent for bathetic irony transcends individual gags to question the reality of appearances. Manolo's typically dowdy life (dull parents, ramshackle car, frumpy girlfriend) is transformed when he meets Mariano, a school friend who is now a self-styled trouble-shooter and best-selling novelist under the name of Macguffin. Mariano seems genuine, but a mutual friend claims he is just a neurotic with the money to indulge his fantasies. Mariano soon plunges Manolo into a world of car chases, bomb attacks and murder. But like his *nom de plume* his final departure, sprinting towards a helicopter perched on a cliff, strains belief.

Fernando Trueba's *Opera prima* also attempts to sustain the magic of fantasy against the intrusion of the everyday. Matías, a part-time arts journalist, is reading a newspaper in the street when a pretty young girl walks up behind him, puts her hands over his eyes, and says, 'Guess who'. Matías reels off a whole list of girls' names with a quickfire wit which owes as much to Hollywood repartee as to Madrid manners. The magic of this meeting is sustained in a subsequent romance, and in Matías' conversation which, like Wilde's, tends to try to justify or oppose just about anything. Matías' world is also the stuff of fiction, being peopled by modern stock types: his motorbike macho friend, a nympho porn queen, a hard-swearing American novelist he interviews. Threatening this suspension of reality is Violeta's hippy violin teacher, who wants to take her off to Peru, Matías' wife, who wants to bar him from seeing their son, and Matías' own increasing tendency to jealousy. The ending accumulates ironies. Violeta packs her bags for Peru, Matías walks off, returns, just misses Violeta leaving for the airport. Violeta gets to the airport, repents, and sets off to return, just missing Matías arriving at the airport to apologise. Violeta and Matías are reunited, as chance and Trueba and Ladoire's stubbornly romantic script would have it, in their local square with a kiss on a warm blue night, as a saxophonist plays soulfully under the stars. Reality, we know, is not like this, but that may be the film's most serious point. The suspension of reality suspends belief. And although they are often attacked for their facetiousness, it is this very quality which gives the New Spanish Comedies much of their social point.[20]

Recuperation

By 1979 the crisis in the Spanish film industry was acute. Spanish films secured only 16 per cent of their home market, as opposed to almost 30 per cent two years before; and in June 1979, the month when the industry should have reached its yearly peak, only two films were being processed at Fotofilm, the leading Spanish laboratory.[21]

In January 1980 Suárez's UCD government re-established the screen quota at a 3:1 ratio and laid down a staggered distribution ratio calculated according to the success of a film's release. The law misfired: a pot-boiler released in twenty cities for one week qualified its distributor for three dubbed film distribution licences; a 'quality' box office success such as *El nido* qualified, by making more than 85m pesetas, for the maximum concession of five licences. The difference was not enough to encourage distributors to promote ambitious projects.[22] Like so much UCD legislation the 1980 law did not confront the major structural problems of the industry. The Spanish cinema's most serious stumbling block was finance. Film credit from the Banco de Crédito Industrial was tight, the Protection Fund budget had remained at 1,200m pesetas for years, box office fraud was rife, and special prizes were insufficient.[23]

Averse to market intervention, the UCD government attempted a back-door measure. In August 1979 RTVE announced that it would inject 1,300m pesetas into television serials or films suitable for prior theatrical release; projects based on the 'great works of Spanish literature' were to be preferred. This was a face-saving measure: by reallocating money from one beneficiary of its cultural budget to another, the UCD sought to prop up the reputation of Spanish Television at a time when the press were exposing serious corruption in its ranks.[24]

Despite such inauspicious origins, many of the projects produced were both competent and popular. The serial *Los gozos y las sombras* ('Pleasures and Shadows') was watched by more Spaniards each week than *Dallas*. Encouraged, RTVE were to put another 1,400m pesetas into films and series in 1983–4. A June 1981 decree also looked to the future by laying down a sliding scale of additional subventions calculated against both a film's budget and its subsequent box office performance.[25] A further decree attempted to facilitate medium-term credit for the cinema, which rose from 541m pesetas in 1980 to 953m pesetas in 1981.

Pilar Miró took up the position of Under Secretary for the Cinema under the Socialist government, promising 'a true revolution in the Spanish film industry'.[26] Yet most of Miró's measures have UCD antecedents. The difference is largely one of the commitment, both economic and vocal, with

225

which Miró pursued policies that the UCD government had stumbled towards. Abroad, Spanish Film Weeks were stepped up.[27] An exhibition law in 1983 finally determined conditions for Spain's 'X' cinemas, and twenty-two opened in March 1984.[28] An agreement between Spanish Television and independent producers in June 1983, pushed through by Miró, helped rationalise relations. Most important, the so-called 'Miró Law' of December 1983 substantially increased state funding and, crucially, channelled it into production investment rather than bonuses based on box office performance, thus assuaging the industry's perennial cash-flow problems. Under the new system the government could advance up to 50 per cent of a film's estimated budget, repayable only through amounts calculated against percentages of subsequent box office takings: 15 per cent for any Spanish film, 25 per cent more for 'Special Quality' films, another 25 per cent more for films with budgets over 55m pesetas.[29]

The co-financing deal with Spanish Television has now lapsed, but individual films are supported in 1986 for as much as 25m pesetas. With Spain's entry into the EEC in January 1986, Miró's successor, the Director of the newly named Spanish Film Institute (Instituto de Cine), Fernando Méndez-Leite, has established a 2:1 screen quota for the films of EEC countries (including Spain itself) against 'third' countries. A 4:1 distribution quota remains for Spanish films; EEC countries' films do not require dubbing licences.[30]

Film-funding since 1979 has changed the face of Spanish cinema. Though attempts have been made recently to vary the types of film funded, the tenor of mid-80s Spanish film-making is well reflected by Mario Camus' *Los santos inocentes* ('The Holy Innocents', 1984).[31] Set in a kind of neo-feudal Spanish countryside in 1966, the film is solidly middle-brow. The central characters are a peasant family whose social status finds a literal corollary in their physical position. As social outcasts Paco el Bajo and his family live in a tumbledown cottage on the heath, until they are invited to move to another cottage just outside the gates of the local Marchioness' country house. The overseer of the house wants Paco's son to work on the estate and his daughter to work as a maid. Though little more than a hut, the new home has an electric light: minor social advance is exchanged for social submission, and Paco's family only enter the big house's grounds in subservient roles. When one of the family kills the Marchioness' son, the *señorito*, for shooting his pet bird, Paco and his wife are sent back to the heath, while their children move to the city to try their luck in a less authoritarian world.

Los santos inocentes offers an acid portrayal of the Spanish authoritarian mind in the figure of the *señorito*. Hard-swearing and short-tempered, he assumes that his own feelings must always take precedence; so he shoots the bird out of frustration at a bad day's hunting. Paco's friendship with him is

226

based on his retrieving skills in the hunt, which allow the *señorito* to win high society shooting competitions. Even when his leg is broken, Paco is made to run around retrieving birds.

This sharp social criticism recalls the films of Bardem, whom Camus has acknowledged as a major influence.[32] In other ways, however, *Los santos inocentes* suggests another attempt to combine Spanish themes with American production values. In this it shares with other big-budget Spanish films of recent years the risk of contradictions. The film portrays a family living in squalor, but its polished camerawork creates an effect of picturesque poverty. One of the main justifications for state film-funding is that cinema is 'culture'; but unless film-makers can convince general audiences, at whom films like *Los santos inocentes* are aimed, that 'culture' is also about the ugly and the awkward, the tendency to be visually pleasing at any cost is likely to continue.

One possible solution to this problem is to justify a glossy vision of Spain's past by attributing it to a subjective consciousness. This happens in *The South*; and also in *Valentina* (Antonio J. Betancor, 1982), whose idyllic vision of a childhood in an Aragonese village in 1911 is justified as being the recollections of a Republican prisoner-of-war who is on the verge of death in a concentration camp in France. Childhood memories are a natural solace for a man for whom violence is no longer glorious and who is bewildered in defeat. And the film is given a retrospective pathos by the fact that we know from the start that the man dies in the camp.[33]

Los santos inocentes has no such clear viewpoint. It also ignores the Spanish film-making tradition of shooting an ugly reality in an ugly way. Carlos Saura tells a story of Bunuel shooting *Nazarín* with a cameraman who insisted on creating beautiful compositions. 'Luis told him to make a marvellous shot of Nazarín walking. In the distance was Popocatepetl wreathed in dawn mist, its summit under snow with an aureola of very "artistic" clouds. After the take, Luis made Figueroa turn the camera round and make the same shot against a dull, grey background: That's the shot *I* want, he said.'[34] The trouble with Spain's new glossier films is that, for Spanish audiences at least, rather than connoting improved production standards they merely suggest a glossier fictional reality, one which seems a lie.[35]

Recent Spanish films set in the immediate past often seem direct in their social criticism but vague about the relevance of that criticism to the present. The coda added by Camus to *Los santos inocentes*, showing the exodus of Paco's children from the countryside, sets the film's events in a past which Spain has put behind her. The use of well known actors diverts attention from the fictional world to such extra-fictional speculations as how Alfredo Landa, the hangdog lecher of the Spanish sex comedy, can impersonate the peasant Paco. One is struck by Landa's transformational skills as much as by the character he plays. Above all, the moral scales of *Los santos inocentes* lack the intertonal subtleties of Berlanga and Buñuel. The film comes near to creating what for years Spanish film-makers have fought so hard to avoid: historical myths.

What seems to be at stake in Spain in 1986 is the status of Spain's past itself. The outstanding film made in Spain in the 80s, it is sometimes claimed, was shot on the afternoon of 23 February 1981 when Colonel Tejero, recorded by a television camera, burst into the Cortes and held its deputies at gunpoint. King Juan Carlos earned Spaniards' eternal gratitude by opposing the coup; in his telephone conversations with Spain's regional commanders, the generals either endorsed democracy or at least refused to oppose their king. Next day Juan Carlos told the leaders of the major parliamentary groups that 'an open and tough reaction by the political parties against those who committed acts of subversion in the last few hours would be most inadvisable.' And he called on the political leaders to help foster 'the highest possible level of unity and concord in Spain'.[36]

The subsequent consensus politics pursued by the Spanish establishment, especially the P S O E, may be a sign of its political maturity or a symptom of the inordinate influence still exercised upon public affairs by an unelected minority, the Spanish military, an influence which plays into the hands of the Spanish right. One thing is certain: 'We have lived in a state of consensus,' said Vicente Aranda about Spain after 1975, 'and this is fatal for its cinema ... This is not a historical period which needs passionate descriptions. We have become our own censors and all we want to do is forget, be silent, not speak.'[37] When directors have spoken out, the result has been familiar. Pedro Costa's valiant *El caso Almería* ('The Almería Affair', 1984) recreates the trial and conviction for murder of three Civil Guards who had shot three men in cold blood, thinking them E T A terrorists. In 1984, a cinema showing the film in Granada was burnt down.

In such circumstances Spain's film industry remains cautious. 'I wrote a script about a year and a half ago,' Jaime Chávarri said in November 1982, 'but since it was about terrorism no exhibitor or distributor would touch it.'[38] Diverting attention from the present to the past allows directors to deal with seemingly important issues – the Civil War, violence, authoritarianism – their critical instincts disoriented by the fact that the present regime clearly enjoys a broad degree of support. 'It is no longer clear where the enemy is,' Berlanga asserts. Spaniards to the left of the Socialist Party would still see enemies.

The problem is that the past appears to have lost much of its interest. 'The 50th anniversary of the outbreak of the Spanish Civil War,' one foreign observer noted, 'is largely a non-event, and attracts only an occasional article in the press.'[39] For many Spanish minds the Spanish Civil War may possess the same status as the conquest of the West for Americans in the

1930s. Both were events much more exciting than the dull present; both affected the destiny of their nations and seemed to say something about national character, though perhaps that was all old hat; both offered a raw material for entertainment which needed to be processed for the popular imagination. The Western linked past and present via the metaphor of the cultivation of the West, part of America's civilising destiny. Many future Spanish Civil War films will, one suspects, link past and present by seeing the war as a frustration of Spain's European destiny, broached by the Republic and fulfilled by the democracy of the 80s. The fact that Spain has been drifting towards Europe since the 1950s may be forgotten.[40]

'We must speak about the *posguerra*,' Manuel Gutiérrez Aragón said in 1982, partly because other more logical witnesses to the times than Spanish cinema have kept markedly silent. In over twenty-five years of existence, notes Robert Graham, Spanish Television has made 'not one serious programme about the Basque country and ETA – precisely because it is one of the most sensitive issues facing Spain'.[41]

Financed by governments who tend towards the political centre, handled by cautious distributors, destined for a consensus public, Spanish films dealing with potentially contentious issues have naturally resorted to familiar film strategies of the 60s. In *La colmena* ('The Beehive', 1982), Mario Camus' solid adaptation of Cela's novel about the squalid lives of the clients of a Madrid café during the *posguerra*, a phrase or trait sums up a character, a single scene (a girl prostituting herself to buy medical care for her tubercular boyfriend) represents a human destiny. Repetitions – the constant return to the café, the monotonous tawdriness of the sets, the sober music – help generalise individual scenes.

Camus' obliqueness derives in part from Cela's original novel. Jaime Chávarri's *Las bicicletas son para el verano* ('Bicycles are for Summer', 1984), an adaptation of Fernando Fernán Gómez's award-winning post-Franco drama about the effects of the Civil War on an ordinary Madrid family, has a prologue added by Chávarri in which two boys play war-games on a wasteland in Madrid. The real gunfire on the soundtrack returns the spectator once more to the extra-fictional reality of the Civil War, which remains off-camera for the rest of the film, charted only in its consequences: news of a death at the front, air-raids and hunger, the constant postponement of the son's hope of getting a bicycle for the summer of 1936.

Another familiar strategy is the use of background symbolism. Manuel Gutiérrez Aragón's last film to date, *La noche más hermosa* ('The Most Beautiful Night', 1984), is a kind of alienation comedy set in the studios of Spanish Television and the never-never land of the chalets where Federico, a producer, and his boss Luis live. Characters in such a world all long for a truly authentic experience, something beyond their everyday lives – in Luis'

229

case to see a comet which passes over Madrid once every hundred years. The comedy of confusions set off by Federico's desire to test his wife's fidelity (he gets a friend to proposition her) illustrates how difficult it is to know what anybody else really thinks or feels. In this world, as in Saura's *Los ojos vendados*, symbolism becomes a way of expression. It also serves as social comment on a post-Franco Spain. Federico's office has models of an ancient temple, his home a neon lightning bolt. 'Nothing has happened,' he says, sitting on a crane which lifts him up to a mock-up of the heavens, just after Luis has capitulated to huge wage increases for the television workers. 'Television is a great family. The country functions!' To the sceptical Gutiérrez Aragón the state television and patriarchy are just two versions of the power hierarchies which have survived Franco's death. Spanish Television was once indeed called the last Winter Palace for democracy to storm.

'The administration is the administration,' a bureaucrat declares in Basilio M. Patino's *Los paraísos perdidos* ('The Lost Paradises', 1985). 'The only improvements possible will come from us, because here there's no more wax than that which burns.' More than at any time since the mid-60s Spanish film culture has become the patronage of the state. Directors freely admit that many large films just won't get made unless they receive a government advance and are bought by Spanish Television. The problems faced by the Instituto de Cine's Film Commission, which allots the first

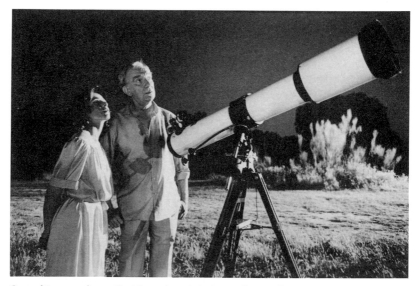

Something out there: Gutiérrez Aragón's *La noche más hermosa...*

230

... Ricardo Franco's *Los restos del naufragio*

grants, are common to many public-funding organisations. The members of the Commission are not required to answer for their decisions. No member will like to offend his caste by opposing concessions; his own back may need scratching later. With a finite budget to divide, there just isn't enough money to offer large sums to those with no say or influence in the industry.

The problem of new talent is now a large one in Spain. So far the main success of government film-funding has been to re-enlist directors from the New Spanish Cinema movement of the 1960s, like Basilio M. Patino and Gonzalo Suárez. Their recent work has much in common with their earlier films. Patino's *Los paraísos perdidos*, about the return to Spain of the daughter of an exiled Republican intellectual and her re-encounter with childhood friends, has the same lyrical lilt, subtle irony and social observation as his 1965 *Nueve cartas a Berta*. The reunion of two former writing partners in *Epílogo* ('Epilogue', 1984) serves notice, in a characteristically reflexive manner, of Gonzalo Suárez's return to his former literary preoccupations after some indifferent adaptations. The whole film turns out to be a story recounted by one of the writers, whose death during it undercuts its reality.[42]

The Spanish cinema is now faced with a generation gap. The average director is around forty-five and takes his inspiration from his childhood in the 40s and 50s and his experiences of the 60s. The average Spanish filmgoer is some twenty years younger and takes his cultural models largely from America in the 80s. Given the absence of a Spanish Film School, the directors most likely to cross this gap are figures from the New Spanish Comedy, or younger talents from the E O C and Madrid Independent Cinema, such as Ricardo Franco. His *Los restos del naufragio* ('The Remains from the Shipwreck', 1978) is an appealing mix of whimsy, romance and political undertow, featuring the friendship between Mateo (played by the director himself), a gardener at an old people's home, and Pombo (played by Fernando Fernán Gómez), a retired theatre director. Franco's film is about the capacity for illusion. Both Mateo and Pombo are 'washed up', Mateo by *desencanto* (we first see him throwing out his Bob Dylan records) and his girlfriend walking out on him, Pombo by an affair years before with a voluptuous Caribbean woman. Both relationships may be part fantasy: Mateo's early scenes at the home are shot straight on in squarish rooms, which makes them seem staged; both actors are over-theatrical in Pombo's Caribbean reminiscences. Franco's attitude towards illusion is delicately ambiguous: turning their memories to positive account, Mateo and Pombo stage a pirate play at the home and then go off treasure-seeking in the Caribbean. Yet this madcap adventure and the play itself draw on both high seas romance and the dreams of epic adventure which inspire fantasies of empire. The gallant in Pombo's play is played by Alfredo Mayo, the gallant of Francoist films. Dreams of love, adventure and empire emerge as comparably quixotic.[43]

Ivan Zulueta's *Arrebato* ('Rapture', 1979) explores neighbouring territory and achieved cult status in Spain. Described somewhat misleadingly as an avant-garde film, *Arrebato* really recasts stock horror genre elements. A hack horror movie director, José, receives a film with a taped commentary from a certain Pedro, whom he had once met at a rambling, oak-beamed house which might have come straight out of Poe's *William Wilson*. Pedro's story, told on the tape, also echoes Poe: he claims that when he is asleep his camera films him of its own accord; when he wakes, his face is bloodied and the film in the camera has turned red as if it had vampirised him. There is a further echo of Poe in the slightly turgid excitability with which Pedro's voice recounts these events. Zulueta builds tension with a crescendo of supernatural elements, blood-red imagery, and the suggestion that Pedro is José's double. As in Poe, the *doppelgänger* brings death. Pedro's camera finally absorbs him entirely, or so it seems; when José tries to repeat the experience, the camera shoots him dead.[44]

The character of Pedro is one of the most original creations in Spanish cinema; the character of José touches common concerns. 'José allows himself to be enraptured like a child or like Pedro,' Zulueta commented. Yet José is 'neither one nor the other, and for these things to happen it is not enough just to desire them'.[45] The last sequence of *Arrebato*, where José sits

232

blindfolded in front of the camera as it shoots him ever more quickly until it appears to shoot him dead, confirms José's alienation (his distance from his childhood self, and from others like the *doppelgänger*) and his frustrated attempt to escape an unsatisfactory reality.

Zulueta has not made a film since *Arrebato*. Another director, Imanol Uribe, has been more productive and has emerged as the central figure of a small but interesting Basque cinema.[46] The Basques are now thought by some to be the last survivors of Europe's original pre-Indo-European population,[47] and this sense of uniqueness has weighed heavily on film-makers working in the Basque provinces. The fall of Francoism offered an opportunity for a distinctive Basque cinema, but in the event production was nearly paralysed by arguments about what form this distinctiveness should take. Films which did get made, such as the series of *Ikuska* shorts, often gave a wholly anachronistic view of Basque culture, ignoring the social changes which have moved the centre of cultural life in the Basque provinces from the country to the towns. Uribe's *La canción vasca* ('Basque Song') is a refreshing contrast. It is filmed largely in a city, features pop groups as well as folk music, and is set against a contemporary background of economic depression. Outspoken as ever, Uribe suggests that no distinctive Basque music really exists.

Uribe's *El proceso de Burgos* (1979) had been the first Basque film to attract large audiences. His next project moved nearer to fiction, dramatis-ing Angel Amigo's book about the escape of thirty prisoners, mostly members of ETA, from a high security prison near Segovia in 1976. As an ex-Etarra, Amigo had taken part in the escape; and his co-scripting and producing of Uribe's *La fuga de Segovia* ('Escape from Segovia', 1981) and Alfonso Ungría's *La conquista de Albania* ('The Conquest of Albania', 1983) reflected the political movement of many Basque radicals from armed resistance under Franco to cultural militancy under democracy. 'I used to shoot 9mms,' Amigo once joked, 'Now I shoot in 35mm.'[48] Both Amigo and Uribe saw Basque films as engendering a modern Basque culture rather than resurrecting Basque folklore. For Amigo, 'Euskadi is still being built. The existence in the none too distant future of its own cinema is one more element in the process'.[49]

La fuga de Segovia shows the Amigo/Uribe policy in action. It deals with a Basque theme, but its cultural model is universal: the escape movie. In terms of the film's political rhetoric the format proved highly effective, establishing a real sense of complicity with the characters. Uribe and Amigo develop the downbeat appeal of the ETA escapers: the ingenuity with which they fox the prison guards, their sense of humour, their suffering. One prisoner, for instance, is married in prison, giving him a purely personal motive for escape. Audiences all over Spain found themselves sympathising with men who in real life they would happily have seen shot.

233

Having invested 10m pesetas in *La fuga de Segovia*, the autonomous Basque government instituted an enlightened film policy. In return for advances of up to a quarter of a film's budget, film-makers are required to shoot largely in the Basque provinces, to present a copy of their film in Basque (but not necessarily to shoot in Basque since some directors, such as Uribe, do not speak it), and as far as possible to use Basque actors and technicians. The first beneficiaries of this policy were Pedro Olea's *Akelarre* ('Witch's Sabbath', 1984), a rather pedestrian account of medieval witch-craft and torture, and Alfonso Ungría's *La conquista de Albania*. Ungría's film chronicles a little known Navarrese expedition to Albania in 1370. Part historical portrait, part boys' adventure, the film seems fractured, though it has a finely rendered battle sequence. It can also be seen as a cautionary tale about senseless acts of nationalist aggrandisement, in reference perhaps to the increasingly directionless violence of ETA.

The high point to date in Basque cinema remains Uribe's *La muerte de Mikel* ('Mikel's Death', 1984). The film describes how Mikel, a pharmacist and left-wing militant, gradually comes to terms with his homosexuality. Uribe avoids the self-righteousness of much nationalist cinema. His sarcasm, for example, covers the political spectrum. When Mikel openly goes round with his boyfriend, he is taken off his party's list of candidates for the Basque parliament. Basque left-wingers are not supposed to object to homosexuals; but they do. The police violently interrogate Mikel about his involvement with ETA under Franco. Under democracy Spanish police are barred from investigating terrorist crimes under Franco; but they do.

The power of *La muerte de Mikel* derives largely, however, from its teasing reticence. This is evident in Uribe's portrayal of Mikel's death. Released by the police, Mikel returns to the family home. We see him staring at the sea on a local promontory. His mother, who has bitterly opposed his honesty about being a homosexual, watches him through a window. The camera focusses on the family home at night: a light goes out in Mikel's bedroom. Next day a sequence shot keeps the mother in the foreground at the breakfast table as her other son walks down a corridor behind her, then comes slowly back to say that Mikel is dead. In the next scene, the funeral, the political party which previously ostracised him now declares Mikel a martyr of police torture. Editing and camerawork forefront the influences which induced Mikel's suicide: police, mother, politicians. It is left to the audience, however, to make the connections.

Also made in 1984, *Tasio* remains in geographic and economic terms on the fringes of the Basque cinema. The film is set in Navarre, was subsidised by both the central and autonomous governments, and was directed by the Basque based Montxo Armendáriz and produced by Elías Querejeta, a Basque established in Madrid. *Tasio* is an engaging fictionalised biography of a charcoal burner, played by three actors. We see a boyish Tasio playing

Tasio: environment as identity

truant in his village, an adolescent Tasio at a local dance, an adult Tasio playing *pelota*, courting, marrying, engaged in poaching pranks, an ageing Tasio refusing to abandon his charcoal heap to go and live with his daughter in the regional capital.

Querejeta called *Tasio* a 'hymn to liberty'. Such liberty is not seen as a total freedom but rather as a choice of destiny delimited by environment. The steps which define Tasio's destiny are precisely, almost fatefully, recorded. Deep-focus shots expose breathtaking views of the Navarrese hills and woods; recurring pans across the countryside also suggest symbolic spaces for individual action within a larger social context. And, as Vicente Molina Foix points out, Armendáriz 'isolates (fixes) a gesture of his characters with slow zooms which leaves them framed, alone in Nature ... underlining the inalienable *propiedad* of their world.'[50] As at a dance when the young Tasio compliments a girl on her dress and the camera draws closer to the couple, as absorbed in them as they are in each other.

One senses with *Tasio* that something in Spanish culture has changed. One of its key features, for example, is a sense of continuity, which in the anti-Francoist cinema would have connoted monotony, a lack of vistas. Now it becomes a source of charm as characters, conversations and vistas repeat themselves from one section of the film to the next. Under Franco the relation of environment to the individual was repressive; now it is far more symbiotic. Tasio feeds his charcoal heap and it provides him with a living. Its pyramid shape, its smoke, and its pervasive importance in Tasio's life gives it, as Molina Foix observes, a symbolic significance. Instead of repressing the individual, environment is a source of identity and security.

Other Spanish films also reveal a sense of radical change. In *Volver a empezar* ('Beginning Again', José Luis Garci, 1982), poet Albajara receives a telephone call from a jovial King Juan Carlos, who congratulates him on his Nobel Prize. Scripted soon after the attempted 1981 coup, Garci's film echoes most Spaniards sentiments by having Albajara tell his King: 'Sir, you are the man this country needs and with whom we should, elbow to elbow, carry Spain to the best.'[51] The King then says that next time Albajara is in Madrid he will take the poet to a nice little restaurant he knows. This 'buddiness' between culture and authority breaks with centuries of antagonism. And Albajara's uncomplicated affection for his home town would surely have been more problematic in the 70s (compare *A un díos desconocido*), the 60s (compare *Nueve cartas a Berta*) or the 50s (compare *Calle mayor*).

Most Spanish directors of interest inevitably respond in part to Spanish traditions. Growing up in a largely inward-looking culture during the 40s and 50s, Spaniards with any sensitivity would naturally assimilate some native influences. But can such traditions gell with modern attitudes and interest contemporary audiences? At least three options seem open to Spanish directors. One is to explore Spanish themes using accessible Spanish styles, such as that mixture of fantasy and reality which foreigners can interpret as a kind of Spanish surrealism. With films projected for 1986 on conquistador Lope de Aguirre and Federico García Lorca, Carlos Saura and Juan Antonio Bardem look set to follow this course.

An alternative is to work with styles such as the *sainete*, the *zarzuela*, and *esperpento*. One film-maker who does this is Fernando Fernán Gómez, whose comedy *Bruja, más que bruja* ('Witch, Nothing But a Witch', 1976) is an ingenious mix of *zarzuela* and modernist reflections on film itself. It is difficult to exaggerate the fascination which Fernán Gómez's personality still exercises on young directors through his films, his friendship and his acting style. His manner remains fully and consciously Spanish.[52] No other Spanish actor better embodies, for example, Spaniards' quixotism, their tenacious holding on to illusions through the most trying of circumstances.[53] Fernán Gómez's latest film, *Mambrú se fue a la guerra* ('Mambrú Went to War', 1986), represents something of a return to his earlier incisiveness. Using a superficially *sainete* style, it shows an old Republican's attempt to come out of hiding after Franco's death. His family oppose his re-emergence, mainly for financial reasons. In stressing the role played by economics during the transition and the immense mark left on Spain by its recent past, Fernán Gómez achieves a lucidity (some would say an honesty) which so many commentators on contemporary Spain seem to lack.

After two lacklustre sequels to *La escopeta nacional* Luis Berlanga made *La vaquilla* ('The Heifer', 1984), based with very few changes on a script Berlanga wrote with Azcona in 1957. Set during the Civil War, the film portrays the war as part of Spain's larger condition. The Nationalists on one side of a valley announce a bull-fight. The Republicans decide to steal the heifer to spoil the fiesta, and a hit-squad heads for the village where the heifer is guarded. As in *Plácido*, 'Characters move from one place to the next without really ever getting anywhere; they shout, insult, even attack one another', condemned to 'the most desolate collective solitude imaginable'.[54] The expedition's guide, who lived in the village before the war, takes everyone on a detour just to see some almond trees; the private who boasted of his bullfighting skills baulks when confronted by the heifer; the expedition's officer slips off to the local brothel. No other Spanish director takes such delight in recording the rumbustious self-centredness of the Spanish character, and its consequences. The expedition is a fiasco, the heifer runs off: the Nationalists lose their fiesta, the Republicans fail in their mission. Frustrated, soldiers start shooting at each other across the valley. *La vaquilla* repeatedly suggests the absurdity of war. In one scene, the members of the expedition are forced to bathe with some Nationalist soldiers; they paddle around quite happily together. But Berlanga's insistence on *esperpento* makes the outbreak of hostilities seem inevitable: the Civil War becomes a logical absurdity.

La vaquilla was Spain's box-office success of 1985. Of the first group of films sponsored under the terms of the Miró law and released together in 1985, the only one to succeed at the box-office was García Sánchez's *La corte del Faraon* ('Pharaoh's Court', 1985), about an amateur theatre company in the 1940s staging a saucy *zarzuela* set in Egypt. The popularity of these two films derives in part from their local references, like the song which closes *La vaquilla*, 'La hija de Juan Simón', which was sung by Angelillo in the Buñuel/Sáenz de Heredia film of 1935. Recognising the song and enjoying its romantic grandeur, Spanish audiences confirm both the survival of popular pleasures over the years and their own membership of that amorphous community, 'popular Spain'.[55]

The need to reaffirm a sense of continuity and community owes much to the fact that, like all Western Europeans, Spaniards now face a growing immersion in Europe as well as a technological revolution, prospects which threaten to change their lives irreversibly. If current Spanish films are anything to go by, then the epoch to which the 1980s compares most closely is the early nineteenth century, when much of Europe faced its first industrial revolution. Pilar Miró is now adapting Goethe's *The Sorrows of Young Werther*; Gonzalo Suárez is preparing a film on Mary Shelley.

237

The uncertainties of the age, with its new freedoms and its new anxieties, are evident in many of the films being made in Spain. Francisco Regueiro's *Padre nuestro* ('Our Father', 1985), for instance, could have been sketched out by Buñuel: a dying cardinal returns to his native Spanish village to arrange his family affairs and in doing so inadvertently sows death and destruction. Twenty years ago this would have been a thesis film; now part of its appeal is its very indeterminacy. It portrays the desolation of Castillian rural life. It has elements of *esperpento*: the Cardinal's illegitimate daughter has become a prostitute, styles herself 'La Cardenela' and always dresses in red. But Regueiro's aim is 'not to use fantasy to refer to an external reality but to transform the fantastic into reality'.[56] Many sequences may be comic, but they also have a wondrous air, as when the Cardinal's helicopter descends on the Castillian countryside, watched by a little girl, like a *deus ex machina*, landing on a plateau illuminated by a patch of sunlight.

José Luis Guerin's *Los motivos de Berta* ('Berta's Motives', 1984) also recasts traditional themes. In one way Guerin reflects Erice's concern for childhood myth in a rural setting. Lonely and impressionable, adolescent Berta latches on to a new neighbour, a romantic figure in a frock coat who makes her believe that his wife died in a car crash. Apparently driven by inconsolable love, the poet figure shoots himself as Berta watches. In other ways, however, Guerin's film differs from Erice's work. For one thing, Berta overcomes her trauma. At first she keeps the man's hat; but when his perfectly alive wife arrives to claim his belongings, she eventually hands it over. After so many films of brooding neurosis, Berta's acceptance of reality seems a refreshing change. And whereas in *The Spirit of the Beehive* the unknown world explored by Ana is seen as a product of Spanish history, the unknown world in Berta's experience is far less determinate. Guerin sets his film in Franco's Spain but avoids political reflections, concentrating rather on the fascination of individual objects and the uniqueness of individual moments. Above all, the open space beyond Berta is emphasised by the off-screen glances of the characters, by the way they repeatedly walk out of frame, and by the intrusion of objects from a more modern world (like an electric fan) and the intrusion of people into Berta's own world. Adolescence is cast as a receptivity to the open space of the imagination and the world at large.[57]

When they draw on their cultural heritage, it is Spain's artistic past rather than its Francoist history to which the country's younger directors seem to be turning. This distinction is particularly evident in the ebullient films of Pedro Almodóvar, who complained in 1983 that 'The attention of film-makers is fixed on the past, the post-war, but these are ghosts which half the country doesn't share.'[58] Almodóvar's own attitude to Spain's cultural past is in complete contrast. 'In the 50s and 60s Spain experienced a kind of

238

neo-realism which was far less sentimental than the Italian brand and far more ferocious and amusing. I'm talking about the films of Fernán Gómez (*La vida por delante, El mundo sigue*) and *El cochecito* and *El pisito*. It is a pity that the line has not been continued.'[59] Almodóvar has tried to do just this. The problems involved in a mix of tradition and modernity give his career its sense of evolution.

At first Almodóvar mixed old and new in a 'post-modernist' style, a witty art of the incongruous which played off various styles against each other. *Pepi, Luci, Bom y otras chicas del montón* ('Pepi, Luci, Bom and a Whole Lot of Other Girls', 1980) combines popular and modern culture to hilarious effect. As in the best traditions of Spanish sexploitation movies, Pepi (got up like a 50s adolescent in pigtails and flouncy dress) is summarily raped, by a policeman; but exaggerated close-ups and intercut titles make this sequence look like a page from a photo-novel. Pepi's friends, from a punk rock group, then dress up like characters from *La verbena de la Paloma*, sing *zarzuela* songs as they approach the policeman in the street, and launch into him with practised punk aggression.

Almodóvar's next films saw him experimenting with various moral positions, starting from the facetious amorality of *Laberinto de pasiones* ('Labyrinth of Passions', 1982), which is set in a glittering Madrid demimonde of transvestites, nymphomaniacs, punks, Iranian fundamentalists and so on; and continuing with the mock melodrama of *Entre tinieblas* ('In the Dark', 1983), where the nuns who run a home for fallen women take drugs, keep a tiger, and write best-selling novels.

Another direction is offered by *¿Qué he hecho yo para merecer esto?* ('What Have I Done to Deserve This?', 1984), in which Almodóvar constructs an exaggerated version of Spanish home life. The high-rise flat in the film contains a grandmother who hoards bottles of Vichy water and harps on about her village, a father still smitten by a woman he met during his emigrant days in Germany, one son who is a homosexual, another a drug addict. Next door is a prostitute (giving Almodóvar the chance to burlesque pornographic films); above a girl with supernatural powers (Almodóvar parodies the terror genre). The film has an innovatory camera style which gives an extra dimension to its often banal material. And Almodóvar's tongue-in-cheek parody now has a serious point. Gloria, the family's hard-pressed mother, shows the resourcefulness of the heroine of Hollywood melodrama. She drugs herself, she is forced into dire straits (selling one son to a homosexual dentist), she knows poverty (cleaning floors for a penniless writer), but her sufferings are not endured for romantic reasons but simply to make ends meet. For Spain's socially underprivileged, the film suggests, the modern world is a melodrama of survival.

¿Qué he hecho yo para merecer esto? obviously refers back to the Ferreri/Fernán Gómez style of neo-realism. *Matador* (1986) goes a step

further. A sense of Spanish tradition not only inspires scenes in the film but becomes its most intriguing subject. Driven by a guilt complex inculcated by his bigoted mother, an apprentice torero, Angel, confesses to a series of murders. The real murderers are his teacher, retired bullfighter Diego, and his defence lawyer María. Suspecting each other's guilt yet aroused by the idea of death, María and Diego finally meet, spread a huge torero's cape beside a log fire, make love, and kill each other in ecstasy.

Matador has a glittering surface, sleek clothes, dramatic camera angles, and its colour schemes are used thematically. The red of María's cape and lipstick echoes the red of Diego's torero cape (sex linked to death); and her black hair, wan face and black and white clothes, opposites exaggerated by lighting contrasts, set up a black and white symbolism which repeatedly suggests the irrational side of the human mind. Almodóvar's characters associate sex and death in a tradition which runs back through Buñuel's *The Criminal Life of Archibaldo de la Cruz* to Rafael Gil's 1943 film *Eloísa está debajo de un almendro*, where the heroine's fascination with the hero derives from her belief in his homicidal past. Spanish tradition is death-laden; the bullfighter and his murderous mistress in Almodóvar's film merely turn this to positive effect. The modernity of *Matador* is not its distance from the past, but its sensitivity to the legacy of the past.

A seasoned observer once compared the Spanish film industry to the last Moorish kingdom of Granada, absorbed in internal dissensions as the Catholic Kings closed in. In late 1985, as unprotected competition with EEC films beckoned, Spain's film potentates were once again embroiled. The first batch of films financed by the Miró Law had failed badly at the box-office. Critics accused Miró of over-financing, of favouritism, of backing such crass literary adaptations, José Luis Guarner wrote, that she and TVE between them had created a new genre: 'the Subsidised Assassination'.[60]

Pilar Miró's successor as Director of the Spanish Film Institute, Fernando Méndez-Leite, has shared subventions around more: between September 1985 and June 1986, 45 films divided 1,513m pesetas at an average of 33m pesetas (some £165,000). Projects underwritten also showed a greater variety. Such measures are, however, essentially running repairs. The two decisive factors which will shape the future of the Spanish film industry remain its dependence on the state and the increase in its films' budgets.

The factors are of course connected. With Spanish films spurned abroad and commanding less than 30 per cent of the home market (a dismal 22.5 per cent for the first eight months of 1985), only the Spanish state can afford to produce them. What some critics find particularly disturbing is the increasing equation of 'the state' with the interests of one political party,

Gutiérrez Aragón's *La mitad del cielo*

the PSOE. With Manuel Fraga's Alianza Popular still tarnished with the taint of Francoism, most Spaniards see no alternative to Felipe González's Socialists, who won a second term of office with a clear overall majority at the elections of June 1986. Unchallenged electorally at home and with little to prove abroad, González's government is unlikely to generate a film opposition, like the New Spanish Cinema in Franco's regime.[61] It would be naïve to expect any government to sponsor films which are inimical to its own interests. Many future Spanish films will steer clear of contemporary problems (with Spain's unemployment in 1986 at 20 per cent, the present is not good news), and will attack, somewhat superficially, the supposedly unequivocal target of Francoism in the past. These films will emphasise the role of the opposition in the transition to democracy and stress that under democracy (and especially under the Socialists) Spain has never had it so good. *Movida* films, on the upsurge in 1986, serve this last cause well.

The situation of the Spanish film-maker today suggests a scene from Gutiérrez's *Sonámbulos* in which some demonstrators are pursued by police into the National Library, where they pick up a painting by Goya and cower behind it: the police naturally hesitate about attacking. The motive for any state to back films is that they form a cultural heritage. Dissidents will be tolerated in the Spanish cinema quite simply because they are also often the culture-makers. Their culture becomes a shield. The largest advance in 1985–6 went to Gutiérrez's *La mitad del cielo* ('Half of Heaven').

There is no real contradiction that this showpiece of Spanish culture also proposes an unsettling view of the post-war for straight-jawed socialists, including, for instance, a kindly Falangist.

La mitad del cielo cost some 300m pesetas. Even Spanish state aid and home market receipts will hardly support such a higher-budget Spanish film. The pressure to capture foreign markets is now all the greater. One major problem confronting the Spanish Film Institute is how to convert the cultural kudos of worldwide Spanish Film Weeks and film festival prizes into more than a sporadic commercial clout. But while the Spanish Film Institute debates several options, individual producers and directors are taking matters into their own hands, attempting, particularly, to pre-condition foreign sales by a film's original packaging, especially its finance. Such strategies are likely to determine some of the axes along which the Spanish cinema will develop. Some more cosmopolitan directors (Herralde, Chávarri, Bigas Luna) may attempt to use foreign settings and international casts to treat what at first glance seem universal themes. Spain's relatively cheap labour, sun and rising production efficiency will probably attract more co-productions. Increased emphasis on international sales may also give the Catalan cinema a boost. Foreign audiences are largely indifferent to whether a subtitled film is spoken in Spanish or Catalan, and Catalonia still remains closer to the rest of Europe in its tastes than Castille.[62]

The vague but identifiable 'Spanishness' of films made in Spain is not likely to disappear. The assimilation of past film traditions may pay com-mercial dividends (as in *La vaquilla*) and create a sense of cultural bearing. In 1914, for instance, Manuel de Falla returned to Spain hoping to discover a genuinely universal musical style in Spanish national idioms and Spanish history. He wrote *El amor brujo*, which first gained international acclaim when it was danced in Paris in 1925 by Vicente Escudero. Sixty years later Antonio Gades, disciple of Escudero (as he admits in *Bodas de sangre*), danced the lead role in a film version of *El amor brujo* (1986) directed by Carlos Saura, whose intentions in the work closely echo Falla's own. Some sequences in *El amor brujo* are in turn inspired by the direction of a fellow Aragonese, Florián Rey, in *Morena Clara* (1936), whose lead actress, the great Imperio Argentina, has recently starred in José Luis Borau's *Tata mía* ('My Nanny', 1986). For all the move towards multi-national production, this sense of continuity may be important for the future of Spanish cinema.

Notes

Introduction
1. David Gilmour, *The Transformation of Spain*, London, Quartet, 1985, p. 141. The phrase was coined by Pío Cabanillas, the reformist Minister of Information whom Arias Navarro sacked in October 1974.
2. Ibid., p. 148. Up to his dismissal in July 1976 the beleaguered Arias Navarro's only (limited) achievement during the year was a restrictive Law of Assembly.
3. Raymond Carr, *Modern Spain, 1875–1980*, Oxford, Oxford University Press, 1980, p. 116.
4. The post-Franco cinema had, of course, other film precedents, and an important impulse in the radical opposition of the 'independent' sector of the Spanish film industry to the regime's film legislation and its continuing censorship. See pp. 63–71.
5. Juan Hernández Les and Miguel Gato, *El cine de autor en España*, Madrid, Castellote, 1978, p. 284.
6. Julio Pérez Perucha (ed.), *El cine de José Isbert*, El Ayuntamiento de Valencia, 1984, p. 207.
7. See pp. 213–14
8. See Robert Graham, *Spain, Change of a Nation*, London, Michael Joseph, 1984. A mass grave with 7,000 corpses was unearthed outside Saragossa as recently as 1981.

Roots and Reasons for Reaction
1. *My Last Breath*, London, Fontana, 1985, p. 8. According to philosopher José Ortega y Gasset, all that remained of Spain's imperial past was 'a cloud of dust left in the air when a great people went galloping down the high road of history' (quoted by Jan Morris in *Spain*, Harmondsworth, Penguin, 1982). Spain's decline was completed by its ignominious defeat at the hands of the United States and loss of Cuba in 1898. For an informative brief history of early 20th-century Spain see Raymond Carr, *Modern Spain, 1875–1980*, chs. 2–5.
2. For the birth and slow development of the Spanish cinema up to 1929 see Fernando Méndez-Leite Sr, *Historia del cine español*, Madrid, Rialp, 1965, and Juan Antonio Cabero, *Historia de la Cinematografía Española, 1896–1949*, Madrid, Gráficas Cinema, 1949.
3. Fructuoso Gelabert (1874–1955) was a prototype of the early Spanish film-maker. His father was a cabinet-maker (rather than from the upper classes); he worked in Barcelona (not in Madrid); he made money from cinema shows at fairs and in downtown districts (rather than from cinemas in fashionable areas). Gelabert made documentaries, special-effects films (*Choque de dos transatlánticos*, 1899), and popular comedies (*Cerveza gratis*, 1906). He never became rich, and at least once went bust. A career as actor, producer, director, emulsion print processor and studio founder suggests not only an indefatigable talent but something of the early Spanish cinema's industrial insecurities. See Carlos Fernández Cuenca, *Fructuoso Gelabert, fundador de la cinematografía españ-*

ola, Madrid, Filmoteca Nacional de España, 1957.

4. Few Spanish writers have so influenced their national cinema as Carlos Arniches (1866–1943), the major practitioner of the Madrid *sainete*. His best drama, *La señorita de Trevélez*, was adapted by Edgar Neville (in 1936), then by Bardem as *Calle mayor*. The *sainete* has influenced Buñuel, Berlanga, Fernán Gómez, and, less directly, the late-70s 'New Spanish Comedy'.

5. For a brief introduction see R. Alier, *La zarzuela*, Barcelona, Daimon, 1984.

6. G. G. Brown, *A Literary History of Spain: the Twentieth Century*, London, Ernest Benn, 1972, p. 10. The best scholarly overview of Spanish arts and history is *Spain, a Companion to Spanish Studies*, ed. P. E. Russell, London, Methuen, 1973.

7. For the plot and the *Lilian* affair see Cabero, *Historia de la Cinematografía Española, 1896–1949*, pp. 201–4.

8. In Max Aub's *Conversaciones con Buñuel*, Madrid, Aguilar, 1985, p. 114.

9. Cf. Carlos Fernández Cuenca, *El mundo del dibujo animado*, San Sebastian Film Festival, 1962. Most writers regard the first cartoon as Stuart Blackton's *Humorous Phases of Funny Faces* (1906); *El hotel eléctrico* may have been made as late as 1908.

10. Cinemas in Spain, 1925: Catalonia, Aragón and the Balearics: 622; Central Region (including Madrid) and Extremadura: 285. Figures from Cabero, *Historia de la Cinematografía Española, 1896–1945*, p. 247.

11. A small avant-garde cinema emerged in Spain with Manuel Noriega's *Madrid en el año 2000* (1925). Of most interest is Nemesio M. Sobrevila's *El sexto sentido* ('The Sixth Sense', 1926), a slightly cockeyed mixture of avant-garde and low-farce love plot. The *Gaceta Literaria*, Spain's leading avant-garde magazine (1927–32) ran a Cine-Club Español which attracted the 'Generation of 1927' (poets such as Lorca and Alberti) to the cinema. Of this generation only Buñuel and Neville went on to direct. For a cogent analysis see E. Bonet and M. Palacio's bi-lingual *Práctica fílmica y vanguardia artística en España/The Avant-Garde Film in Spain 1925–1981*, Madrid, Universidad Complutense, 1983.

12. Carr, *Modern Spain*, p. 109.

13. For the cinema of the Republic see M. Rotellar, *Cine español de la República*, San Sebastian Film Festival, 1977; R.Gubern, *El cine sonoro en la II República*, Barcelona, Lumen, 1977; J. M. Caparros Lera, *El cine Republicano español*, Barcelona, Dopesa, 1977, and the better *Arte y política en el cine de la República*, Barcelona, Universidad de Barcelona, 1981.

14. The outstanding Spanish film historian Emilio Sanz de Soto has a chapter, 'Hollywood', in *Cine español 1896–1983*, ed. A. M. Torres, Madrid, Ministerio de Cultura, 1984. See also *El cine*, a special edition (no. 22) of *Poesía*.

15. E. Sanz de Soto in Torres (ed.), *Cine español 1896–1983*, p. 54.

16. Gubern, *El cine sonoro en la II República*, p. 50.

17. *Poesía*, no. 22, p. 97. The inimitable Jardiel Poncela (1901–52) is unjustly overlooked by foreign critics. His *Celuloides rancios* ('Rancid Celluloid', 1933) provided commentaries for early silent films which 'deconstructed' the films by pointing their conventions. At its best, as in *Eloísa está debajo de un almendro* ('Eloisa is under the Almond Tree', adapted for the screen by Rafael Gil in

1943), Poncela's humour combines the absurdity of the Marx Brothers with the silk dressing-gown ethos of Noël Coward.

18. Carr, *Modern Spain*, p. 129.
19. For the film company Cifesa see Felix Fanés' exemplary *Cifesa, la antorcha de los éxitos*, Valencia, Institución Alfonso el Magnánimo, 1982, and Julio Pérez Perucha's programme notes for the Filmoteca Española, 1982–3. Together they provide the basis for any serious study of Spanish film 1935–50. For informative monographs on individual films see Fernando Méndez-Leite Jr's *Historia del Cine Español*, published weekly by the *Guía del ocio*, Madrid, from late 1985.
20. Florián Rey (1894–1962) deserves more attention. He was a reactionary whose visual flair has yet influenced the modern avant-garde, such as Lindsay Kemp's director Celestino Coronado.
21. Fanés, *Cifesa*, p. 124.
22. Cited by C. B. Morris in *This Loving Darkness*, Oxford, Oxford University Press, 1980.
23. Francisco Aranda, *Luis Buñuel*, London, Secker & Warburg, 1975.
24. From Buñuel's first (unpublished) autobiography, quoted by Virginia Higginbotham in *Luis Buñuel*, Boston, Twayne, 1979.
25. Quoted by Carlos Fuentes, 'The Discreet Charm of Luis Buñuel', in Joan Mellen (ed.), *The World of Luis Buñuel*, New York, Oxford University Press, 1978.
26. Aranda, *Luis Buñuel*, p. 102. See also Roger Mortimore, 'Buñuel, Sáenz de Heredia and Filmófono', *Sight and Sound*, vol. 44, no. 3, Summer 1975, and Manuel Rotellar, 'El cine español de Luis Buñuel', in *Aragón en el cine*, Ayuntamiento de Zaragoza, 1973.
27. *My Last Breath*, pp. 127–36.
28. Aranda, *Luis Buñuel*, pp. 110–11.
29. William Righter, *Myth and Literature*, London, Routledge & Kegan Paul, 1975.
30. K. K. Ruthven, *Myth*, London, Methuen, 1976, p. 82.
31. Carr, *Modern Spain*, p. 1.
32. *Homage to Catalonia*, Harmondsworth, Penguin, 1966, p. 141.
33. Ramón Sala and Rosa Alvarez Berciano, '1936–1939', in Torres (ed.), *Cine español 1896–1983*, p. 73. Sala and Alvarez point out that even the pro-Francoist Fernández Cuenca has to admit in his *La guerra de España y el cine* (Madrid, Editora Nacional, 1972, p. 244) that Franco's side had only enough film propaganda for a session of 'a little over two hours'.
34. Programme notes for the Filmoteca Española, June 1982.
35. For the Civil War cinema see also *Revisión histórica del cine documental español*, compiled by J. Pérez Perucha, Bilbao, Bilbao International Documentary Film Festival, 1979–1981. 'Guerra y franquismo en el cine', *Revista del Occidente*, no. 53, October 1985, includes some good essays and a short bibliography on Civil War cinema.
36. Cf. Tom Conley, 'Broken Blockage' in 'Guerra y franquismo en el cine', pp. 47–59.
37. Robert Graham, *Spain: Change of a Nation*, London, Michael Joseph, 1984, p. 35, an account of Spain under and after Franco. Other works on Spain since

1940 are: David Gilmour, *The Transformation of Spain*, London, Quartet, 1985; R. Carr and J. P. Fusi, *Spain: Dictatorship to Democracy*, London, Allen & Unwin, 1979; and John Hooper, *The Spaniards*, London, Viking, 1986.

38. For more details of the exodus see R. Gubern, *Cine español en el exilio*, Barcelona, Lumen, 1976. Gubern lists more than a hundred names.

39. Hugh Thomas, *The Spanish Civil War*, Harmondsworth, Penguin, 1977, and Gabriel Jackson, *A Concise History of the Spanish Civil War*, London, Thames and Hudson, 1974.

40. Juan Benet, *Una meditación*, Barcelona, Seix Barral, 1970.

41. Juan Benet, *En ciernes*, Madrid, Taurus, 1976, pp. 43–61. Benet relates such qualities to a writer's abandonment of scientific certainty. Their appearance in the work of so many post-war Spanish intellectuals – which Benet does not mention – is too insistent to be coincidental.

42. Juan Benet, *Volverás a Región*, Madrid, Alianza Editorial, 1974, p. 172. The novel is a brilliant portrayal of the emotional legacies of the Civil War.

43. Enrique Brasó, *Positif*, no. 162, October 1974, p. 33.

44. Thomas, *The Spanish Civil War*, p. 262.

45. Enrique Brasó, *Carlos Saura*, Madrid, Taller de Ediciones JB, 1974, a useful study with interviews covering Saura's career up to *Ana y los lobos* (1972).

46. Jackson, *A Concise History of the Spanish Civil War*, p. 175.

47. Thomas, *The Spanish Civil War*, p. 260. For a mesmerising account of the atrocities committed by both sides, see Larry Collins and Dominique Lapierre, *Or I'll Dress You in Mourning*, St Albans, Mayflower, 1970.

48. Thomas, *The Spanish Civil War*, p. 262. Thomas adds: 'Whether or not these particular atrocities occurred quite as has been alleged, there need be no doubt that many such events did happen up and down nationalist Spain.'

49. Augusto M. Torres, *Conversaciones con Manuel Gutiérrez Aragón*, Madrid, Editorial Fundamentos, 1985, an informative series of interviews.

50. All quotes from Gilmour, *The Transformation of Spain*, pp. 8 and 134.

51. Ibid., p. 105.

52. Ibid.

53. *Fotogramas*, no. 1560, 8 September 1978, p. 12.

54. Carr and Fusi, *Spain: Dictatorship to Democracy*, p. 17.

55. Ibid., p. 47.

56. Ibid., p. 17.

57. Graham, *Spain, Change of a Nation*, p. 53.

58. E. Sanz de Soto, 'Edgar Neville: un cineasta de la generación del '27', an unpublished article.

59. Orwell, *Homage to Catalonia*, pp. 233–4.

60. Gilmour, *The Transformation of Spain*, p. 53.

61. Ibid., p. 8.

62. See Herbert Rutledge Southworth's 'La Falange: un analisis de la herencia fascista española', in *España en crisis*, ed. Paul Preston, Madrid, Fondo de Cultura Económica, pp. 29–60. Southworth argues that the fascist Falange's programme was 'the formation of a movement' by '1) violence and direct action, 2) youth, and 3) ultra-nationalist propaganda' and then 'the take-over of the State'. The Falange differed from other rightwing groups by its desired

'transformation of the revolutionary impetus of the Spanish masses into an imperialist adventure'.

63. Cited in José Luis Guarner's *30 años de cine en España*, Barcelona, Kairos, 1971, p. 14.
64. *Fotogramas*, no. 191, 13 May 1977, p. 8.
65. 'Whatever else he was,' David Gilmour writes (*The Transformation of Spain*, p. 7), 'Franco was not a fascist.' Few serious historians would oppose this view. Franco adopted Falangist rhetoric when it suited him but told an ambassador that it was aimed to act as a cheerleader 'like a few people in a crowd who start clapping so that the others join in' (Gilmour, p. 15). Franco was a conservative authoritarian who never grasped even what a fascist vertical syndicate was.
66. Franco's 'elected warriors' are called 'the Almogáveres'; their closest ancestors were the Catalan *almogàvers*.
67. See Fanés, *Cifesa*, for similar consternation about *¡Harka!* (pp. 91–2).
68. J. Pérez Perucha in a programme note for the Filmoteca Española, January–February 1983.
69. Carr and Fusi, *Spain: Dictatorship to Democracy*, p. 47.
70. Ibid., p. 25.
71. Ibid., p. 27.
72. *Conversaciones con Manuel Gutiérrez Aragón*, pp. 161–2.
73. Fanés, *Cifesa*, pp. 131–53. This was an indicative event. It is too glib to dub Cifesa's directors as uniformly or unquestionably 'Francoist': Luis Lucía's father was sentenced to death by *both* sides in the Civil War; Orduña was a homosexual who claimed never to have made the film he wanted; Marquina attempted a personal cinema while holding sincere Establishment values; Sáenz de Heredia made *Raza* but also *Patricio miró a una estrella*, and attended the Salamanca Congress, an early act of collective protest against the regime (see pp. 57–8). Cinema under Franco was repressed and repressive; no 'revisionist' view must lose sight of that. But the mechanisms of repression – apart from the censor – were more disparate, pragmatic and contradictory than is usually alleged.
74. For Querejeta's admirable finessing of the censor's weaknesses, especially its sensitivity to foreign critics, see pp. 134–5.
75. See Victoriano López García's comments in S. Pozo, *La industria del cine en España*, Barcelona, Publicacions i Edicions de la Universitat de Barcelona, 1984. Compulsory dubbing fitted in, however, with the regime's demand for Castillian Spanish in public life.
76. Quoted in J. Pérez Perucha, *El cinema de Edgar Neville*, Valladolid, 27 Semana Internacional de Cine de Valladolid, 1982, p. 110. The concession of import licences entailed conformity but did little actively to encourage it. Rafael Gil and Sáenz de Heredia received fifteen import licences each for *El clavo* ('The Nail', 1944) and *El escándalo* ('The Scandal', 1943). But these films were among the film-makers' best; and *risqué*, being set in the nineteenth century (which Franco abhorred for its liberalism) and featuring, in the case of *El escándalo*, the first adultery in film under Franco. *¡A mí la legión!*, in contrast, got two licences.
77. Ibid.

78. Cf. Roger Mortimore, 'Spain: Out of the Past', *Sight and Sound*, vol. 43, no. 4, Autumn 1974.

79. See Jesús G. Requena's excellent analysis 'Malvaloca: melodrama latino y sacramental', paper read at the 1983 Valladolid Film Festival; and J. Pérez Perucha, *El cine de Luis Marquina*, Valladolid, 28 Semana Internacional de Cine de Valladolid, 1983.

80. Fanés, *Cifesa*, p. 129.

81. Neville's other outstanding film of the 40s was *La torre de los siete jorobados* ('The Tower of the Seven Hunchbacks', 1944) where, in *fin de siècle* Madrid, hero Basilio stumbles on a subterranean conspiracy of hunchbacks. Evil festering underground – what better metaphor for the nightmare of a nation still mesmerised by the sickly smell of corpses?

82. See J. Pérez Perucha, *Carlos Serrano de Osma*, Valladolid, 28 Semana Internacional de Cine de Valladolid, 1983. The surrealist flamenco of Lola Flores and Manolo Caracol in *Embrujo* ('Bewitched', 1947) is also quite remarkable.

83. Ferrán Alberich, who rediscovered *Vida en sombras*, has a short pamphlet and film on Llobet, *Bajo el signo de las sombras* ('Beneath the Sign of Shadows', Filmoteca Española, 1984); see also J. G. Requena's semiotic analysis, 'Vida en sombras', in *Revista de Occidente*. no. 53, October 1985, p. 76ff.

84. Fanés, *Cifesa*, p. 166.

85. S. Pozo, *La industria del cine en España*, p. 160.

86. However 'Francoist', Cifesa's films were part of a misguided commercial, not primarily political, strategy. See Fanés, *Cifesa*, pp. 156–7. Cifesa's initiative received no special government support. See Fanés (p. 206) for import licence concessions for the historical films. They are by no means extraordinary.

87. Franco liked to compare Spain's isolation from the rest of a hostile Europe to the siege of Numantia, a heroic resistance of Spanish inhabitants against the Roman armies in 134 B.C.

88. *Contracampo*, no. 32, January–February 1983, p. 83ff.

The Modern Spanish Cinema

1. For details of Spain's economic change see R. Carr and J. P. Fusi, *Spain: Dictatorship to Democracy*, London, Allen & Unwin, 1979, ch. 4, and Joan M. Esteban, 'La política económica del franquismo: una interpretación' in *España en crisis*, ed. Paul Preston, Madrid, Fondo de Cultura Económica, pp. 147–80. The quotation from Fusi in the following paragraph is from a BBC radio series on Spain broadcast in 1985.

2. Robert Graham, *Spain: Change of a Nation*, London, Michael Joseph, 1984, p. 34.

3. Carr and Fusi, *Spain: Dictatorship to Democracy*, p. 67.

4. Ibid., p. 79.

5. Equipo 'Cartelera Turia', *Cine español, cine de subgéneros*, Valencia, Fernando Torres, 1974, p. 158. In another 60s film, *Sor citroen* ('Sister Citroen'), a scatty nun learns to drive (acceptable modernity) but is sent back to her father in the country (so separated from progress) for taking too quasi-maternal an interest in two orphans.

6. A giant step in Spain's slow journey towards sexual candour was taken in Orduña's *El último cuplé* ('The Last Song', 1957), whose immense success proved the apotheosis of Sara Montiel as Spain's stellar sex symbol. Producers, Paquita Rico says, used to feed up their actresses to improve their bust measurements. For Montiel see R. Gubern, '*El último cuplé*', *Les Cahiers de la Cinémathèque*, no. 38–9, Winter 1984.

7. A. Castro, *El cine español en el banquillo*, Valencia, Fernando Torres, 1974, p. 279.

8. The director Nieves Conde, cited in Castro, *El cine español en el banquillo*, p. 264. Another vein of popularist cinema in the early 50s was Cold War melodrama, which was sometimes mixed with religious sentiment. In *La señora de Fátima* (R. Gil, 1951) the Virgin appears to declare that there will be another world war if men do not pray 'for Russia to convert'. For popular cinema in the 50s see D. Galán, '1950–1961', in *Cine español*, pp. 146–56.

9. Cf. Terenci Moix, 'El filón de "Osú"', *Nuevas Fotogramas*, 10 May 1974.

10. *Contracampo*, no. 35, pp. 18–21. The issue has an excellent interview with Fernán Gómez. Though better known as an actor (in at least 138 films by 1984, including as the father in *Spirit of the Beehive*), Fernán Gómez is also a director of unequal but sometimes magnificent achievement. He was an occasionally scathing critic of Francoist Spain; he was formally inventive, as when the stuttering Pepe Isbert's eye-witness report of an accident in *La vida por delante* is mimicked visually by a stop-go montage; he has absorbed more Spanish literary and theatrical influences than any other film-maker. His masterpiece, *El mundo sigue* ('Life Goes On', 1963), rates with *El verdugo* and *Viridiana*. See M. Hidalgo, *Fernando Fernán Gómez*, Huelva, Festival de cine iberoamericano, 1981.

11. J. C. Frugone, *Oficio de gente humilde ... Mario Camus*, Valladolid, 29 Semana de Cine, 1984, p. 53.

12. D. Grant, *Realism*, London, Methuen, 1982, p. 60.

13. *Cahiers du cinéma*, no. 94, April 1959, p. 6.

14. F. Llinàs, 'Edgar Neville, Última Etapa', a paper read at the 1982 Valladolid Film Festival. A Neville script, *Quince años*, was adapted by Berlanga for *Novio a la vista* ('Boyfriend in Sight', 1953), so completing Neville's bridge-building between the generation of Buñuel and that of Berlanga.

15. Carr and Fusi, *Spain: Dictatorship to Democracy*, p. 54.

16. García Escudero in *La historia del cine español en cien palabras*. Escudero's emphasis on *Surcos* to the detriment of earlier films with neo-realist overtones such as *El último caballo* or even *La calle sin sol* (R. Gil, 1948) owed much to his granting of the advantageous 'National Interest' status to *Surcos* when he was Under Secretary for the Cinema from September 1951 to February 1952. An award he pointedly refused for the para-governmental production *Alba de América*.

17. A *hedillista* was a supporter of Manuel Hedilla, leader of the Falange after Primo de Rivera's execution in November 1936 and imprisoned and ostracised when Franco took over the party.

18. Berlanga, in *El último austro-húngaro: conversaciones con Berlanga*, J. Hernández Les and M. Hidalgo, Barcelona, Anagrama, 1981, pp. 32–3.

249

19. Gilmour, *The Transformation of Spain*, p. 29.
20. In Fernando Lara's useful introduction, 'El mundo de Rafael Azcona', *Dirigido por*, no. 13, May 1974, pp. 26–31. Berlanga has always stressed Ferreri's influence via Azcona. Cf. *Casablanca*, no. 4, April 1981, pp. 23–9.
21. Lara, 'El mundo de Rafael Azcona', p. 28.
22. Recorded by Ricardo Muñoz Suay, *Dirigido por*, no. 15, July/August 1974, p. 17.
23. Ullastres travelled extensively within Europe negotiating closer trading contacts with the EEC with a view to Spain's ultimate entry into the EEC. But for the Francoist regime economic liberalism was one thing, political liberalism quite another.
24. A. Zahareas, *Luces de Bohemia*, Edinburgh University Press, 1976, p. 7.
25. *Contracampo*, no. 35, p. 66. The fact that the major influences on so many Spanish film-makers were literary rather than cinematic reflects another consequence of censorship: key foreign films were just not seen in Spain.
26. *El cine de José Isbert*, ed. J. Pérez Perucha, Valencia, Ayuntamiento de Valencia, 1984.
27. *El verdugo* is not strictly à condemnation of the death penalty; or at least it takes such a condemnation as read. The film, Berlanga explains, is about 'the ease with which a man loses his liberty, his capacity for self-decision ... the enormous quantity of subtle, interlocking factors which integrate us in a society' (in Castro, *El cine español en el banquillo*, p. 78).
28. Llinàs in '"El verdugo": algunos aspectos de la puesta en escena berlanguina', one of an excellent series of papers, and Berlanga's own articles in *En torno a Berlanga*, ed. J. Pérez Perucha, Valencia, Ayuntamiento de Valencia, Vol. I, 1980; Vol. II, 1981. For Berlanga see also D. Galán, 'Carta abierta a Berlanga', Huelva, Semana de Cine Iberoamericano, 1978.
29. J. Pérez Perucha, *Contracampo*, no. 24, p. 21.
30. An umbrella company backed by the Spanish Communist Party, UNINCI's associates included Buñuel, Ferreri, Azcona, Berlanga, Bardem, Fernán Gómez, Saura, Portabella, Querejeta, Picazo, and even a young Gutiérrez Aragón.
31. Fraga Iribarne's bullish politics since 1976 should not obscure this possibility.
32. *Stills*, September–October 1983, p. 34.
33. The Protection Fund was financed by a levy on the dubbing of foreign films, permits for subtitling and exhibiting original-version films, and a *tráfico de empresas* tax, imposed on exhibitors. Cf. Marta Hernández, *El aparato cinematográfico español*, Madrid, Akal, 74, 1976, p. 53.
34. The distribution quota obliged Spanish distributors to buy one Spanish film for every four dubbed foreign films on their list; the exhibition quota obliged exhibitors to screen one day of Spanish cinema for every four days of dubbed foreign imports.
35. Santiago Pozo, *La industria del cine en España* (Barcelona, 1984), has a fairly full transcript of this complex legislation (pp. 170–4).
36. *Nuestro cine*, no. 52, 1966, p. 10.
37. J. M. García Escudero, *La primera apertura: Diario de un director general*, Barcelona, Planeta, 1978. A fascinating self-portrait.
38. Cited by Pozo, *La industria del cine en España*, p. 62.

39. García Escudero also subordinated considerations of a film's quality to whether it possessed a 'European' air. Lamenting the narrow realism of so many 'new' films, he wrote in his diary: 'Despite everything, boring as this cinema may be, it's another type of film, no better or worse but different, one which will allow us to travel abroad, if only as modest apprentices.' So García Escudero gave low subventions to films in a particular Spanish tradition, such as *El extraño viaje*. Discouraged, Fernán Gómez abandoned quality film-making. It is ironic that when the Francoist regime finally intervened to promote a Spanish cinema, it attempted to make it more 'progressive' and, in doing so, destroyed one of its richest creative lines.

40. A. M. Torres, *Cine español, años sesenta*, Barcelona, Anagrama, 1973, p. 43.

41. Ibid. Torres places *Cada vez que . . .*, the most popular of the Barcelona School films, at no. 921 out of the 1,843 Spanish films exhibited between 1965 and 1969.

42. Carr and Fusi, *Spain: Dictatorship to Democracy*, p. 95.

43. Quoted by Pozo, *La industria del cine en España*, p. 149. When Picazo and Saura demanded to be allowed to speak out, the Under Secretary before García Escudero said, 'If you do that we'll be shooting at each other in the streets again.' (Quoted in *Nuestro cine*, no. 88, August 1969, p. 30).

44. Cited by García Escudero, *La primera apertura*, p. 54.

45. See Román Gubern, *La censura*, Barcelona, Península, 1981, for more cuts. *El verdugo* lost 4½ minutes, including all mention of José Luis wanting to work in Germany. Again, the Under Secretary was demanding serious social themes but not allowing even their mention.

46. The psychology of *La caza* is based on Sartre's concept of 'shame'. While Sartrian 'anxiety' shapes much of the political cinema in the 60s, other intellectual influences included Albert Camus, the Christian reformist Aranguren, Gramsci, and the Frankfurt School. For the patchwork culture and appalling university education of a post-Franco film-maker see Gutiérrez Aragón's account in Torres, *Conversaciones con Manuel Gutiérrez Aragón*, pp. 13–30.

47. Cf. Alvaro del Amo's excellent introduction to the script in *Nueve cartas a Berta*, Madrid, Ciencia nueva, 1968.

48. Ibid., p. 150.

49. Vicente Molina Foix, *New Cinema in Spain*, London, British Film Institute, 1977.

50. J. C. Frugone, *Oficio de gente humilde*, p. 61. Camus returned to more serious cinema in *Volver a vivir* ('Living Again', 1966) and *Los pájaros de Baden-Baden* ('The Birds of Baden-Baden', 1974).

51. For the wildly ambitious programme of the Barcelona School see Molina Foix, *New Cinema in Spain*, p. 23. For a candid view of the School as a publicity measure see Durán in Castro, *El cine español en el banquillo*, pp. 133–44. *Nuestro cine* served as a platform for the School. See particularly issues 54, 61, 82, 83, 90 and 91.

52. Durán in Castro, *El cine español en el banquillo*, p. 144.

53. *Dirigido por*, no. 21, 1975, pp. 36–40.

54. The 'underground' status of the Madrid group was something of a publicity device to get the films known and shown. See *Fotogramas*, no. 1501, 22 July 1977.

55. Cf. Noël Burch, *To the Distant Observer*, London, Scolar Press, 1979, p. 161, on the 'critical, aggressive effect' of the absence of human beings from the screen in *Contactos*.'

56. See A. Ungría, *Los hombres ocultos*, Barcelona, Tusquets, 1972, for the script and other documented cases of 'hidden men'.

57. Ibid., p. 21. A comparable film is Pedro Olea's *El bosque del lobo* ('The Wolf Forest', 1970), where the protagonist's lycanthropy is never explicitly motivated, though Olea leaves many clues in an ambience dominated by poverty, brutality and an omnipresent church. To avoid censorship, Olea claimed in *Nuestro cine*, criticism had to be 'more indirect, subterranean, more through the tone of the films than the concrete situations they reflect'.

58. Cited in *7 trabajos de base sobre el cine español*, Valencia, Fernando Torres, 1975, p. 250.

59. Cited in E. Brasó, *Carlos Saura*, Madrid, Taller de Ediciones JB, 1974, p. 250.

60. Román Gubern, *Carlos Saura*, Huelva, Festival de Cine Iberoamericano, 1979, p. 27.

61. Ibid., p. 29.

62. Torres, *Cine español, años sesenta*, p. 28.

63. *Stills*, September–October 1983, p. 34.

64. García Escudero, *La primera apertura*, p. 172. The connection is important: the censor under García Escudero allowed Querejeta's productions extra liberties because they brought the Spanish cinema so much prestige abroad. What hurt the regime was that all Saura's films were seen abroad as critiques of Francoism. Querejeta was once summoned by the government and asked to stop critics in Chicago from attacking Franco.

65. Castro, *El cine en el banquillo*, p. 419.

66. Hernández Les and Hidalgo, *El último austro-húngaro*, p. 73.

Saying a Long Goodbye to Mother

1. Robert Graham's telling phrase in *Spain: Change of a Nation*, London, Michael Joseph, 1984, p. 21.

2. Cited in R. Carr and J. P. Fusi, *Spain: Dictatorship to Democracy*, London, Allen & Unwin, 1979, p. 180. Franco showed no inclination to stand down. His phlebitis forced a temporary retirement for six weeks in 1974. His doctor made him walk round his study singing old Spanish Legion songs.

3. Ibid., p. 193. For a perceptive overview of the media during the transition see Nissa Torrents, 'Cinema and the Media after the Death of Franco' in *Conditional Democracy*, ed. Christopher Abel and Nissa Torrents, London, Croom Helm, 1984, pp. 100–14.

4. Quotations from J. Hernández Les and M. Gato, *El cine de autor en España*, Madrid, Castellote, 1978, p. 280, and *Contracampo*, no. 30, 1982.

5. Marta Hernández, *El aparato cinematográfico español*, pp. 59–67.

6. In his essay 'La provincia española y el cine' (in *7 trabajos de base sobre el cine español*, pp. 189–218) Juan Antonio Pérez Millán estimates that Madrid, Barcelona and Spain's other most urbanised provinces of Vizcaya, Valencia, Saragossa, Seville and Malaga together accounted for only 51.48 per cent of

cinema audiences in 1973. Provincial audiences supported Spain's last entirely indigenous film genre, the Spanish sex comedy.

7. See R. Gubern, *La censura*, Barcelona, Península, 1981, pp. 219–24.
8. Ibid., p. 266.
9. Hernández, *El aparato cinematográfico español*, p. 54.
10. There is an excellent essay on the Spanish horror film by Juan M. Company, 'El rito de la sangre', in *Cine español, cine de subgéneros*, Valencia, Equipo Cartelera Turia, 1974, pp. 17–76.
11. *Comedia cinematográfica española*, Madrid, Cuadernos para el diálogo, 1975.
12. Quotations from Gubern, *La censura*, p. 255, and *Cine español, cine de subgéneros*, p. 255.
13. For Dibildos see 'Dibildos: un cine español en desarrollo' in Hernández, *El aparato cinematográfico*, pp. 237–40. Querejeta was forced by the prohibition for seven months of *El jardín de las delicias* to become an executive producer on foreign films for the whole of 1971. Even in 1973 he was still working on, along with his Spanish productions, co-productions such as Wim Wenders' *The Scarlet Letter*.
14. In *Revista de Occidente*, November 1985, p. 117.
15. Graham, *Spain: Change of a Nation*, p. 7.
16. Quoted by Marcel Oms in *Carlos Saura*, Paris, Edilig, 1981, p. 58.
17. A crucial belief, expressed to A. Castro in *Dirigido por*, no. 69, December 1979, p. 50. For the script of *La prima Angélica* see C. Saura and R. Azcona, *La prima Angélica*, Madrid, Elías Querejeta Publications, 1976.
18. To E. Brasó in *Positif*, no. 159, May 1974. Saura points out that Luis tries to escape, 'to leave the town ... but he cannot. A splitting has taken place, and in that other image of the past, in that image of himself in his past, is the key to what he is in the present.'
19. Ibid.
20. Quoted by Marsha Kinder, 'The Children of Franco', *Quarterly Review of Film Studies*, vol. 8, no. 2, Spring 1983, p. 63.
21. Cited by Diego Galán, *Venturas y desventuras de la prima Angélica*, Valencia, Fernando Torres, 1974, pp. 61–2.
22. *Positif*, no. 159.
23. Galán, *Venturas y desventuras de la prima Angélica*, p. 119.
24. Ibid., p. 65.
25. Ibid., p. 39.
26. Cited by Carr and Fusi, *Spain: Dictatorship to Democracy*, p. 197.
27. Kinder, 'The Children of Franco'.
28. Gutiérrez Aragón, *Fotogramas*, no. 1474, January 1977. Ozores and Lazaga were (Ozores still is) prolific commercial directors.
29. Another is Manuel Summers, who capitalised on Spain's growing liberties in *Ya soy mujer* ('Now I'm a Woman', 1975) and *La primera experiencia* ('The First Time', 1976).
30. 'La prostitución en España', *Hechos y dichos*, July 1974, pp. 8–11, cited by A. Pérez Gomez in *Cine para leer*, Bilbao, Mensajero, 1974, p. 32.
31. Drove in an illuminating interview, *Contracampo*, no. 12, May, 1980, p. 23.
32. P. Esteve and Juan M. Company, 'Tercera vía, La vía muerta del cine español',

Dirigido por, no. 22, April 1975, p. 21.

33. Cited in Gubern, *La censura,* p. 272.
34. Fernando Méndez-Leite Jr, 'El cine español de la transición' in *Cine español, 1975–1984,* Primera Semana de Cine Español, Murcia, 1984.
35. Cited by Roger Mortimore, *International Film Guide,* London, Tantivy, 1978, p. 284.
36. Kinder, 'The Children of Franco', p. 58.
37. Vicente Molina Foix, *New Cinema in Spain,* London, British Film Institute, 1977, pp. 30–1. For Borau's early career see Miguel Marías, 'José Luis Borau: El francotirador responsable' in *Dirigido por,* no. 25, September 1975. For a brief bibliography on Borau see *Cine español, 1975–1984,* p. 108.
38. Drove interviewed in *Dirigido por,* no. 20, February 1975, pp. 22–7.
39. Javier Maqua and Pérez Merinero, *Cine español, ida y vuelta,* Valencia, Fernando Torres, 1976, p. 43.
40. Roger Mortimore, *Sight and Sound,* vol. 45, no. 1, Winter 1975–6, p. 15.
41. *Cinema 2002,* no. 9, November 1975, pp. 36–9.
42. Quoted by Carr and Fusi.
43. Quoted by Kinder, 'The Children of Franco', p. 71.
44. *Cinema 2002,* no. 9, November 1975, p. 37.
45. Mario Vargas Llosa, 'Furtivos', *Quarterly Review of Film Studies,* Spring 1983, pp. 77–83.
46. Cited by Carr and Fusi, *Spain: Dictatorship to Democracy,* p. 205.
47. The script of *Furtivos* expanded a Gutiérrez Aragón storyline, in its turn based on a real incident about a poacher turned gamekeeper. See A. M. Torres, *Conversaciones con Manuel Gutiérrez Aragón,* Madrid, Editorial Fundamentos, 1985, p. 62.
48. In *Dirigido por,* no. 25, August 1975, p. 36.
49. Kinder, 'The Children of Franco', p. 73.
50. Ibid. Luis Cuadrado died in 1980, of an illness which left him blind. His last film was not *Poachers* (as Kinder suggests) but *Emilia ... parada y fonda* (Angelino Fons, 1976), which he had to abandon.

Dictatorship to Democracy, 1975–1977

1. Vázquez Montalbán, *Crónica sentimental de la transición,* IX, published by *El País semanal,* 1985.
2. Cited in R. Carr and J. P. Fusi, *Spain: Dictatorship to Democracy,* London, Allen & Unwin, 1979, p. 221. Deciphered, this meant that the armed forces would allow reform from above but not a democratic 'break'. The opposition's abandonment of 'ruptura' tactics was, given this, unavoidable.
3. A third factor in the military's toleration of reform was their immense allegiance to Juan Carlos. He was brought up to be a soldier king, and his first act after being crowned was to fly to the Sahara to express his support for the army stationed there.
4. For instance, Carlos Saura: 'I was very pessimistic, I almost expected a hecatomb, that the change-over wouldn't be as bad as a civil war, but still very dramatic with people being shot in the streets.' Sol Alameda, 'Saura, trece y

254

medio', *El País semanal*, 11 November 1979. Saura did, however, believe that Francoism was doomed even before Franco's death (see the chapter on Saura).

5. 'El primer Gobierno de la Monarquía y la reforma Suárez' in *Revista de Occidente*, no. 54, November 1985, pp. 5–21.

6. Ibid., p. 143.

7. Carr and Fusi, *Spain: Dictatorship to Democracy*, p. 225.

8. David Gilmour, *The Transformation of Spain*, London, Quartet, 1985, p. 160.

9. *Fotogramas*, no. 1593, April 1979.

10. Antonio Castro has a book on Bardem forthcoming. L. Egido has an appreciative study, *Juan Antonio Bardem*, Huelva, Festival de cine iberoamericano, 1983.

11. Nissa Torrents, 'Cinema and the Media after the Death of Franco' in *Conditional Democracy*, ed. Christopher Abel and Nissa Torrents, London, Croom Helm, 1984, p. 103.

12. Equally important is a film-maker's confidence in his own abilities. In Bardem's case this may well have been shaken by the late 1970s. Critics have overlooked Bardem's earlier achievements such as the impressive provincial drama *Nunca pasa nada* ('Nothing Ever Happens', 1963).

13. *Dirigido por*, no. 58, 1978, pp. 8–14. Monterde's view is fairly representative of the Spanish Left's position on transition cinema.

14. *Fotogramas*, no. 1498, 1 July 1977.

15. Torrents, 'Cinema and the Media after the Death of Franco', p. 112.

16. *Fotogramas*, no. 1700, September 1984. See also no. 1533, 3 March 1978, where Garci recalls the 'marvellous refrigerators' and 'marvellous women' of Hollywood films.

17. C. Santos Fontenla, 'Amor y desamor, sexo, antierotismo y represión en el cine español' in *7 trabajos de base sobre el cine español*, Valencia, Fernando Torres, 1975, pp. 109–38.

18. Vicente Molina Foix, *New Cinema in Spain*, London, British Film Institute, 1977, p. 37.

19. J. Hernández Les and M. Gato, *El cine de autor en España*, Madrid, Castellote, 1978, p. 352.

20. Ibid., p. 380. The other women directors of feature films are Margarita Aleixandre (two co-directed films in the 50s), Pilar Távora (*Nanas de espinas*, 1984), and Cecilia Bartolomé (*Vámonos, Bárbara*, 1977, and *Después de ...*, 1981). Apart from Bartolomé's first feature and some short films, a consciously feminist cinema has yet to appear in Spain. See catalogue to the *Segunda muestra de cine realizado por mujeres*, Ayuntamiento de Madrid, 1986.

21. Hernández Les and Gato, *El cine de autor en España*, p. 358. Miró's observations are from the same source.

22. For the contemporary Catalan cinema see *Dirigido por*, no. 47, 1977, pp. 18–23, and *Cinema 2002*, no. 38, April 1978, pp. 9 and 28–80.

23. Carr and Fusi, *Spain: Dictatorship to Democracy*, p. 11.

24. Cf. Molina Foix, *New Cinema in Spain*, p. 27, for the ICC's full programme.

25. *Cinema 2002*, no. 38, April 1978, p. 37.

26. 'Variaciones sobre un oso de juguete', *Contracampo*, no. 30, 1982.

27. Ibid.

28. Ibid.
29. In the published script (Madrid 1976), which includes an introduction by Jorge Semprún, comments by the Paneros, and observations by Chávarri which reveal interesting details about Querejeta's production strategy for 1974–5.
30. Ibid.
31. Quoted in a perceptive study on the role of memory in Saura's films: Jean Tena, 'Carlos Saura et la mémoire du temps escamoté' in *Le cinéma de Carlos Saura*, Presses Universitaires de Bordeaux, 1984.
32. Reliably reported in David Serafin, *Saturday of Glory*, London, Collins, 1979, pp. 137 and 147–7. Serafin's detective novels on post-Franco Spain offer excellent insights into the period.
33. A. Castro, *El cine español en el banquillo*, Valencia, Fernando Torres, 1974, p. 313.
34. Antonio Lara in *Revista de Occidente*, no. 53, October 1985, p. 98.
35. *Dirigido por*, no. 55, 1978, pp. 10–15.
36. Molina Foix, *New Cinema in Spain*, pp. 39–40.
37. Hernández Les and Gato, *El cine de autor en España*, p. 202. There is a published script (Madrid, 1976) with comments by Querejeta.
38. Ibid., p. 202.
39. *Fotogramas*, no. 1419, December 1975.
40. Leopoldo María Panero in *Fotogramas*, no. 1475, January 1977.
41. Quoted by Gilmour, *The Transformation of Spain*, p. 20.
42. Carr and Fusi, *Spain: Dictatorship to Democracy*, p. 82.
43. R. D. Laing, *Self and Others*, London, Tavistock, 1969, p. 40.
44. Ibid., p. 41.
45. A. M. Torres, *Conversaciones con Manuel Gutiérrez Aragón*, Madrid, Editorial Fundamentos, 1985, p. 160.
46. Hernández Les and Gato, *El cine de autor de España*, p. 134.

Carlos Saura

1. Quoted in Enrique Brasó, *Carlos Saura*, Madrid, Taller de Ediciones JB, 1974, p. 319. This does not mean that Saura worked in absolute freedom. Rather, he tried to take account of the limits on that freedom, and determined, after *Llanto por un bandido*, 'not to make any more films which I couldn't really control totally' (Brasó, p. 97).
2. For example: 'I won't make literary adaptations. That way I force myself to think up a film's driving idea. That's a kind of obligation for a director who considers himself to be an "auteur".' Brasó, *Carlos Saura*, p. 72.
3. 'Sometimes,' said Bardem, 'I think that you should demand that anyone attempting a film career should have a large personal fortune, especially in this country.' A. Castro, *El cine español en el banquillo*, Valencia, Fernando Torres, 1974, p. 67.
4. Ibid., p. 350. Another valuable source of income was Stanley Kubrick, who insisted on Saura directing the dubbing of his films into Spanish.
5. *Hablemos de cine*, no. 72, November 1980, p. 63. Saura continues: 'That often helped to free a film blocked by the censor. Nothing scared the Francoist regime

more than what was said of it outside Spain.' Good reviews at the 1970 New York Film Festival persuaded the censor to approve *El jardín de las delicias* with relatively minor cuts. The finished version of *Ana y los lobos* was first banned totally, then approved totally. Rumour had it that Franco saw and passed the film, thinking it nonsense.

6. V. Hernández in *Le cinéma de Carlos Saura*, Bordeaux, Presses Universitaires de Bordeaux, 1984.

7. *Dirigido por*, no. 31, May 1976, p. 17.

8. Brasó, *Carlos Saura*, p. 243.

9. *Thousand Eyes Magazine*, vol. 2, no. 2, October 1976, p. 10.

10. Brasó, *Carlos Saura*, p. 40.

11. Ibid., p. 140.

12. Marsha Kinder, 'The Children of Franco', *Quarterly Review of Film Studies*, Spring 1983, p. 65.

13. In conversation with the author.

14. Quoted by Jean Tena in *Le cinéma de Carlos Saura*, p. 27.

15. Azcona and Saura had 'fairly violent arguments' while writing together. One source of disagreement was their different notions about women: Azcona's misogyny is notorious.

16. R. Carr and J. P. Fusi, *Spain: Dictatorship to Democracy*, London, Allen & Unwin, 1979, p. 82.

17. The hidden trauma suggested in Irene's dream generalises Ana's condition. Similarly, when Ana enters school she is just one of a depersonalised group.

18. Peter W. Evans, 'Cría Cuervos and the Daughters of Fascism', *Vida Hispánica*, vol. 33, Spring 1984, pp. 17–22.

19. Vicente Molina Foix, 'El cine de la distancia' in the published script of *Cría cuervos* (Madrid, 1975).

20. Rosa shows Ana her gargantuan breasts; Rosa and Ana fold sheets together and Ana learns to sew; the house has a madonna; and Isabel cuts pictures of scantily clad girls from a magazine.

21. Kinder, 'The Children of Franco', p. 65.

22. Some details in *Cría cuervos*, as in Buñuel's films, defy exhaustive explanation. One such is the frozen chicken legs seen three times by Ana in the fridge. Explanations: a) an image of death; b) in Aragón, where Saura was born, chicken legs symbolise bad luck; c) animals' feet in Spanish are 'patas', and the chicken legs are included to 'épater' the critic or spectator who thinks a film should be wholly comprehensible.

23. *Fotogramas*, no. 1457, 17 September 1976, p. 4.

24. For a standard critique of *El gran teatro de este mundo* see A. A. Parker, *The Allegorical Drama of Calderón*, Oxford, Dolphin, 1968.

25. For this important writer see P. E. Russell (ed.), *Spain, a Companion to Spanish Studies*, London, Methuen, 1973, pp. 341–6. For the influence of Gracián on *Elisa, vida mía*, as well as the film's formal techniques, see Emmanuel Larraz, 'Elisa et l'Androgyne' in *Le cinéma de Carlos Saura*, pp. 211–31.

26. Larraz, 'Elisa et l'Androgyne'.

27. What Saura says in interviews should be balanced by the evidence of his films: he is far less self-conscious a film-maker than he is often considered, and in any

case he quickly loses interest in his films once made.

28. '¿Quién me dijera, Elisa, vida mía,/cuando en aqueste valle al fresco viento/ andábamos cogiendo tiernas flores,/que habia de ver, con largo apartamiento,/ venir el triste y solitario día/que diese amargo fin a mis amores' (Eclogue I). This Eclogue by one of Spain's finest poets, Garcilaso de la Vega (1501–36), clearly influences *Elisa, vida mía* in its contrast of a beautiful natural backdrop to the individual's sorrows, and its sense of time and nature continuing their course impervious to human suffering.

29. *Cinestudio*, no. 119, April 1973, p. 24.

30. In the opening sequence, for example, we automatically match voice-over and image, assuming that one of the occupants of the car approaching the camera is describing a marital crisis. The male voice-over but female identity of the 'I' throws us. The voice-over is in fact one of Luis' texts, as its minor discrepancies with reality might suggest.

31. Raul Beceyro, 'Lectura de *Elisa, vida mía*' in *Le cinéma de Carlos Saura*, pp. 87–113.

32. Quoted in Román Gubern, *Carlos Saura*, Huelva, Festival de Cine Iberoamericano, 1979, p. 44. Saura had been appalled by the Atocha murders, and his sixteen-year-old son had been attacked by neo-fascist youths.

33. Marcel Oms, *Carlos Saura*, Paris, Edilig, 1981, p. 74.

34. Quoted by Marsha Kinder in 'The Political Development of Individual Consciousness', *Quarterly Review of Film Studies*, vol. 32, no. 3, February 1979.

35. *Los ojos vendados* also portrays regeneration in an explicitly post-Franco age. A wall poster glimpsed briefly in the film announces a demonstration for the Francoist faithful on the first anniversary of Franco's death; Emilia begs Luis, 'Let's start from zero.' Their regeneration depends on a mutual representation of who they are and who they were.

36. To José Luis Guerin, 'El cumpleaños de Saura', *Cinema 2002*, no. 56, January 1980, p. 61.

37. Susan Tate, 'Spain and Mama Turns One Hundred', *Cinema Papers*, no. 37, April 1982.

38. Cf. Carr and Fusi, *Spain: Dictatorship to Democracy*, p. 86.

39. Such changes in style may have been influenced by the substitution of Luis Cuadrado by Teo Escamilla as a cameraman. 'Luis is more Castillian, Teo is Andalusian. His work is "happier" than Luis', which has been more profound at times, but Teo has more advantages because he is more imaginative, quicker and willing to take risks' (Saura to José Luis Guerin, 'El cumpleaños de Saura'). Escamilla has shot all Saura's films from *Cría cuervos*. Agustín Sánchez Vidal has pointed out to me that Castillian families are normally patriarchal, Aragonese families matriarchal. This fact, plus the disproportionate time mothers spend with their children while the father is out to work, would help explain the importance of the mother-figure in Saura's work, especially when he stops satirising the Francoist family (as in the Castillian *Ana y los lobos*) and, drawing on the celebrated Aragonese sense of humour, portrays a matriarchy.

40. *Contracampo*, no. 6, October–November, 1979, p. 71.

41. Cited by Oms, *Carlos Saura*, p. 81.

42. *Télérama*, no. 1556, 10–16 November 1979.

43. In the re-enactment of the miracle of Elche a model of God, an angel or the Virgin is let down from the church roof. The film's music, which includes *sevillanas* and Chueca's Military March, creates for Saura 'a farcical tone which is very Spanish'. Saura's plot recalls the *zarzuela*.

44. 'At Easter, Passion plays were staged throughout Spain. Rambal did a beautiful one in Huesca. The figures were completely motionless, but the effects – lightning, thunder, winds, etc. – were marvellous.' Saura quoted by Antonio Castro in *Dirigido por*, no. 69, December 1979, p. 48.

45. Another example is Saura's use of traditional religious motifs – the supernatural voice and beam of light streaming down from the heavens – to describe Mama's supernatural communication with others. Saura's idea was to portray 'the mysterious relations mothers have with their children' (*Télérama*, 10–16 November 1979).

46. Quotations from Esteve Riambau in *Dirigido por* and Carlos Boyero in *La guía del ocio*. The radical Left in *Contracampo* accused Saura of not knowing how to shoot his films formally.

47. *Deprisa, deprisa* was made after Saura had separated from Geraldine Chaplin and moved to a flat in an old working-class part of Madrid. The real delinquent selected to play Pablo was shot dead by the police a few weeks before shooting began.

48. Despite its documentary intercuts, non-professional actors and colloquial language, *Los golfos* is closer to a current of social realism in the contemporary Spanish novel than to Italian neo-realism. See Jean Tena, 'Carlos Saura et la mémoire du temps escamoté' in *Le cinéma de Carlos Saura*, pp. 11–29.

49. The Cerro de los Angeles, the geographical centre of Spain, was the scene of a celebrated act of sacrilege during the Civil War when a group of Republican militia 'executed' its statue of Christ. Buñuel (of course) was much struck by the episode; Saura's delinquents clearly have not heard of it.

50. Quoted by C. B. Morris in a useful critical guide, *Bodas de sangre*, London, Grant and Cutler, 1980.

51. Another transcription is of Lorca's Andalusian background. Gades uses stylised props, and the dancers look like gypsies; Saura eavesdrops on the Andalusian twang of the musicians as they chat in the make-up room.

52. *Cine cubano*, no. 104, 1983, p. 40.

53. Carlos Saura, 'Historia de nuestra película' in *Carmen*, Barcelona, Círculo/ Folio, 1984, p. 54. The book has Mérimée's novella, statements by Gades, and a history of screen Carmens.

54. Just how unacceptable Carmen's independence was to traditionalist morality is suggested by Florián Rey's *Carmen, la de Triana* (1938), made in Germany with Imperio Argentina. Rey's conservatism diminishes Carmen, and Don José dies while performing his military duties.

55. In pointing out its own possible fictionality, *Carmen* echoes the style of Jorge Luis Borges, whose influence Saura has acknowledged.

56. Alcohol for Borges, and perhaps for Saura, is a sign of a fantasising mind creating fictions. Antonio and Carmen drink sherry like their fictional counterparts in Mérimée. During the staged card game there is a half-empty bottle of Rioja on the table.

57. *Carmen*, p. 64. Saura admired Mérimée's novella but thought the libretto to Bizet's opera a 'betrayal'. Classical ballet is too 'mannered' for tragedies, Saura commented, but 'flamenco ballet can express their violence and capture their passion'. *Image et son*, no. 386, September 1983, p. 24.

58. Vicente Molina Foix, 'Música maestra', *Fotogramas*, no. 1687, June 1983, pp. 83–4.

59. Before dancing this scene Gades asks for a ladder (symbol of hierarchy?) to be removed from the stage.

60. *Elisa, vida mía*, Recherches Ibériques Strasbourg I, 1983, p. 18.

61. This point is established when Juan takes Berta for a picnic to the same riverside spot where he was taken by his parents as a child. He now sits next to the wife/mother figure, taking his father's place. The boy actor playing his childhood self runs up and kisses both 'parents'. Here as a child Juan had attempted to break up the couple by pulling his mother away.

62. One subtlety of *Dulces horas* is to find the mother's smothering love as traumatising as repression. Guilt at his love for his mother causes Juan to remember her approaching him with scissors, and his father hitting him with an axe, which he interprets as an accident. Juan sublimates his guilt by attributing to himself a role in his mother's suicide.

63. 'What I would like to do is tell the same story over the years because new elements will certainly appear and the perspective will change. . . . If I don't do it any more it's because the critics attack me . . . and don't let me work.' *Elisa, vida mía*, Recherches Ibériques Strasbourg I, p. 18.

64. Saura himself claimed he went to Mexico to make *Antonieta* 'to get away from myself'. He thought Antonieta overrated as a writer and her idea that culture diminished violence rather absurd.

65. For *Los zancos* see the interview with Julián Marcos and Esteve Riambau in *Dirigido por*, no. 119, November 1984. Here we discover a forward-looking Saura: 'Up to now we've been in the pre-history of the cinema. With video we can talk of something quite different.'

Stocktaking: 1977–1981

1. *Fotogramas*, no. 1458, September 1976, p. 15.

2. Luis Buñuel, *My Last Breath*, London, Fontana, 1985, p. 170.

3. For more details of the Cannes meeting see Francisco Aranda, *Luis Buñuel*, London, Secker & Warburg, 1975, pp. 190–3. The fact that some of the most 'national' films in Spanish film history were being made at this time by Ferreri, Berlanga and Fernán Gómez merely illustrates the chronic disregard shown by every generation of Spanish film-makers towards its immediate predecessors.

4. *Quarterly Review of Film Studies*, Spring 1983, p. 97.

5. Shots of a whale-processing factory deflate a romantic scene in Camus' *La joven casada* (1975); similar background bathos is supplied by a pig being slaughtered in Buñuel's *Wuthering Heights* (1953).

6. Don Quixote, for example, completely lacked *discreción*.

7. Quoted by Jan Morris in *Spain*, Harmondsworth, Penguin, 1982, p. 47. As the leisured son of rich parents, Buñuel still retained some upper-class mannerisms

even into the 30s. One of these, perhaps, was a contempt for popular film-making. For Buñuel at that time popular films could only be made for fun.

8. Cf. especially Benveniste's *Problems of General Linguistics*, University of Miami Press, 1971.

9. Buñuel's humour obviously owes an immense debt to Ramón Gómez de la Serna, 'the man who influenced our generation more than anyone else' (Max Aub, *Conversaciones con Buñuel*, Madrid, Aguilar, 1985, p. 109). Comparisons with other film-maker members of that generation – Eduardo Ugarte, José López Rubio, Edgar Neville, Jardiel Poncela – reveal startling resemblances.

10. The liberal and anticlerical Benito Pérez Galdós (1843–1920) was Spain's greatest realist novelist. *Nazarín* and *Tristana* are based on novels by him; *Viridiana* draws on his *Halma*.

11. Morris, *Spain*, p. 143.

12. Ibid.

13. The film had only one-fifth Spanish capital, but this, plus its settings and actors, has warranted its inclusion in most surveys of post-Franco cinema.

14. 'Luis Buñuel and Pierre Louÿs: Two Visions of Obscure Objects', *Cinema Journal*, vol. 19, no. 1, 1979, pp. 87–98.

15. Filmed in France and so free of censorship restrictions, the Spanish–French co-production *Tamaño natural* is, to this extent, Berlanga's first 'post-Franco' film.

16. In *L'Age d'or*, as Linda Williams points out in *Figures of Desire* (Urbana, University of Illinois Press, 1981, p. 133), 'the possibility of finally satisfying the lover's desire has the paradoxical effect of dampening it'.

17. Buñuel's best study of the virgin/whore dichotomy is *Belle de Jour* (1967). Séverine loves her husband but cannot have sex with him and derives her bodily pleasures from working as a daytime prostitute.

18. In the film's first sequence an advertising hoarding sports the phrase 'Puros Preciados' ('Valuable Cigars'), cut off by camera framing to leave just '. . . dos' ('two').

19. 'Del amor y la caza en el cine de Berlanga', *Berlanga II*, Valencia Film Festival, 1980, pp. 45–6.

20. For Arandano which, under Luis Megino, went on to produce Gutiérrez's films, see *Fotogramas*, no. 1530, February 1978. For García Sánchez, see *Dirigido por*, May 1976, pp. 46–7 (on *Colorín colorado*), *Fotogramas*, no. 1531, and *El cine de autor en España*.

21. Interview with Peter Evans and the author, April 1986.

22. *Fotogramas*, no. 1498, June 1977. The unequal *Informe general* was Portabella's last film before he became a Senator representing the Catalan left.

23. Camino also chose camera placements so that speakers in different interviews appeared to be replying to each other. See *Fotogramas*, no. 1570, November 1978.

24. Cf. José Luis Guarner and Peter Besas, *El inquietante cine de Vicente Aranda*, Madrid, Imagfic, 1985, a succinct portrait.

25. Brenan was talking about the Falangist New Shirts, those who joined the party after February 1936 when they saw its star rising. See *The Spanish Labyrinth*, Cambridge University Press, 1943, p. 330.

26. Aranda in *Dirigido por*, no. 8, 1980.
27. *Nuestro cine*, no. 6–7, December–January 1962.
28. *Film Ideal*, no. 12, October 1957.
29. Ungría's 'dwarf spectacle' *Gulliver* (1976) makes much the same point. An entertainment company of dwarfs take in a fugitive, who is first persecuted, then takes control; finally the dwarfs rise up against him. Power changes hands, but oppression remains. See *El cine de autor en España*, and an interview with Ungría and Fernán Gómez (who helped script the film and played the fugitive) in *Fotogramas*, no. 1447, July 1976.
30. Cf. Paul Preston, *The Triumph of Democracy in Spain*, London, Methuen, 1986, p. 120. More enlightened big business interests in Spain generally supported a move towards democracy in order to avoid possibly cataclysmic social confrontation.
31. *Contracampo*, no. 12, pp. 11–33, an illuminating interview.
32. Ibid., p. 29.
33. As for instance, in *Réquiem por un campesino español* (1985).
34. See below, pp. 219–20.
35. 'The Spanish Novel from 1972–1982: A Mirage of Freedom', in *Conditional Democracy*, ed. Christopher Abel and Nissa Torrents, London, Croom Helm, 1984, pp. 115–24. Masoliver's analysis of the novel confirms the difficulties Spanish culture has had in its attempt to evolve beyond its Francoist past.
36. See John Hooper, *The Spaniards*, London, Viking, 1986, p. 136. *Splendour in the Grass* was shown in 1982 with a full ten minutes cut. Berlanga complained in 1981 that a recent transmission of *Esa pareja feliz* had had all its (anyway incidental) references to the monarchy excised.
37. Miró's phrase. For *El crimen de Cuenca*, both film and affair, see *Fotogramas*, nos. 1612, 1625, 1643 and 1666; *Cineinforme*, 11 April 1981, pp. 3–4; Roger Mortimore, 'Reporting from Madrid', *Sight and Sound*, vol. 49, no. 3, Summer 1980; *Casablanca*, no. 9, September 1981, p. 55.
38. Though not its absolute disappearance. In 1981, *Rocío* (Fernando Ruiz), a basic documentary exposing economic interests behind the Andalusian religious procession and implicating a co-founder of the Brotherhood of Rocío in Nationalist atrocities, was prohibited from exhibition in south-west Spain, which is rather like a film accusing a Leeds man being banned in Yorkshire. *Rocío* only went on general release, with two cuts, in 1985.
39. 'Cine Español, 78/80' in *Dirigido por*, no. 77, p. 31ff.
40. The biographical details in *El cine de autor en España* show time and again the same syndrome: a strict, often religious, middle-class education; abandonment of professional studies; incomprehension and hostility from parents who, nevertheless, support the would-be film-maker through Film School.
41. *Dirigido por*, no. 60, 1979, pp. 38–45 for interview with Ungría. Reacting against the apparent failure of a 'committed' cinema in the 50s and 60s, some directors (Berlanga, Javier Aguirre) had little faith in a political cinema in the 70s.
42. See David Thompson's review in *Time Out*, 7 June 1984.
43. Hooper, *The Spaniards*, p. 152.
44. 'The Children of Franco', *Quarterly Review of Film Studies*, Spring 1983, p. 66.

45. Buñuel thought freedom should be used to acquire commitments. 'Only crypto-Fascists pretend they are ideologically free,' he once said, and illustrated the point in one of his most beautiful films, *Cela s'appelle l'aurore* (1956).
46. In conversation with the author.
47. Regueiro's later *Las bodas de Blanca* ('Blanca's Weddings', 1975) is similarly a black-humoured anthology of Spanish phobias.
48. Guarner and Besas, *El inquietante cine de Vicente Aranda*, p. 12. The sexual connotations of guns, arms and warfare provide Spanish films with a long tradition of unintended psychological undertones.
49. After *Gary Cooper que estás en los cielos*, Pilar Miró made the fractured but haunting *Hablamos esta noche*, a downbeat portrait of male behaviour.
50. 'Reporting from Madrid', *Sight and Sound*, vol. 49, no. 3, Summer 1980.
51. *Contracampo*, no. 8, January 1980, p. 7. For the late-70s career of this enterprising film-maker see also *Fotogramas*, no. 1622, November 1979; Katherine S. Kovács, 'Nuevo cine español: José Luis Borau', *Suplemento Cultural de la Opinión*, 30 March 1980; José María Carreño, 'Entrevista con José Luis Borau', *Casablanca*, no. 30, June 1983; Miguel Marías, 'Borau en la frontera', in *Cine español, 1975–1984*.
52. Hooper, *The Spaniards*, p. 266.
53. For *Las palabras de Max* see Juan Carlos Rentero's interview in *Dirigido por*, no. 54, 1978, pp. 54–7, and *Fotogramas*, nos. 1523, 1532, 1535.
54. Kinder, 'The Children of Franco', p. 68.
55. Robert Graham, *Spain, Change of a Nation*, London, Michael Joseph, 1984, p. 33.
56. Quotations from Derek Harris' analysis in *Poeta en Nueva York*, London, Grant and Cutler, 1978.
57. See Chávarri's declarations in *Fotogramas*, no. 1512, October 1977, p. 28.

New Directions: Manuel Gutiérrez Aragón and Victor Erice

1. See John Hooper, *The Spaniards*, London, Viking, 1986.
2. *Spain*, Harmondsworth, Penguin, 1982, p. 122. Like many foreign observers Morris slightly regrets the passing of the old Spain. Most Spaniards, however, are only too pleased to have a Spain with less donkeys and more television sets.
3. In an extended interview published in *Contracampo*, no. 7, December 1979.
4. See Diego Galán and Fernando Lara, 'Manuel Gutiérrez: ¿hasta qué punto comunican las palabras?', *Triunfo*, 9 March 1974. Gutiérrez rejected this.
5. In one of Gutiérrez's most revealing interviews, with José Carlos Arévalo, in *Lui*, no. 23, November 1978. Gutiérrez, like Saura, has always stressed that his opposition to Franco, as his indirectness, was far more visceral, far less intellectualised, than is normally asserted: 'We didn't have any option but to break with the dominant cinema. There was nothing heroic about it. It was a necessity.' The dissidence in Gutiérrez's films is as much a matter of style as of constructs such as allegory.
6. Gutiérrez would acknowledge the parallel with the state of Gregor Samsa in Kafka's *Metamorphosis*: he directed Peter Weiss' version of *The Trial* for the stage in 1979.

263

7. Gutiérrez has always rejected the idea of his obliqueness being just a censor-evading strategy: 'People were saying that with censorship gone we should speak clearly. But ... neither my cinema nor Saura's style was a question of camouflage.' (*Lui*, November 1978, p. 6.)

8. Marsha Kinder, 'The Children of Franco', *Quarterly Review of Film Studies*, Spring 1983, p. 70.

9. See also *Fotogramas*, no. 1474, January 1977, where Gutiérrez considers *Camada negra* with reference to the politics of heroism.

10. In *Contracampo*, no. 7, December 1979, p. 30.

11. Cited in Miguel Juan Payán and José Luis López, *Manuel Gutiérrez Aragón*, Madrid, Ediciones JC, 1985.

12. These comments draw on Vicente Molina Foix's review of *Demonios en el jardín* in *Fotogramas*, no. 1680, November 1982.

13. Kinder, 'The Children of Franco', p. 70.

14. Cf. Vladimir Propp's *Morphology of the Folktale*. Propp saw the folktale as made up of stock narrative units repeated from one tale to the next. Gutiérrez's technique is to structure his plot around some of the more common of these units such as (using Propp's descriptions) 'An interdiction is addressed to the hero', and 'The hero is tested, interrogated, attacked, etc. which prepares the way for his receiving either a magical agent or helper.' Propp might have been describing *Maravillas*.

15. Augusto M. Torres, *Conversaciones con Manuel Gutiérrez Aragón*, Madrid, Editorial Fundamentos, 1985, p. 80.

16. The very fantasy of the scene makes it seem realistic; the very humdrum life of Pablo as a bear makes his situation seem, on reflection, all the more fantastic. A characteristic Spanish irony.

17. Conversely, characters in Strindberg plays often make observations which could be referring to Gutiérrez's films.

18. Cited by Vicente Molina Foix in his unpublished essay, 'Manuel Gutiérrez Aragón and the resurgence of Spanish cinema', p. 4.

19. Torres, *Conversaciones con Manuel Gutiérrez Aragón*, p. 84.

20. See Julio Pérez Perucha, 'Dos observaciones sobre el itinerario de Manuel Gutiérrez Aragón', *Contracampo*, no. 7, 1979.

21. See *Fotogramas*, no. 1624, 19 December 1979.

22. Cf. Juan Hernández Les and Miguel Gato, *El cine de autor en España*, Madrid, Castellote, 1978, p. 278, and Torres, *Conversaciones con Manuel Gutiérrez Aragón*, pp. 72 and 97.

23. Ibid.

24. The success of mid-70s films such as *Cría cuervos* and *Furtivos* persuaded producers like Querejeta and Ricardo Muñoz Suay (who produced *Sonámbulos*) to back more 'difficult' films. Their release coincided with the advent of democracy. Their poor box-office performance perhaps contributed to their makers' desire for a more popular cinema.

25. Interview with Pachín Marinero, *Casablanca*, no. 23, 1982.

26. Torres, *Conversaciones con Manuel Gutiérrez Aragón*, p. 135. Franco's regime could only accommodate *Don Quixote* because a) it was a classic, and b) hardly anyone read it. Its satire of military illusions did, however, produce discomfort.

In its supposed ideals, at least, Francoism was quixotic; perhaps the Don would have been a Francoist.

27. 'The only adventure possible is solitude,' Gutiérrez said. 'We are Robinsons from the traffic, tourism and the television.' (Quoted by Vicente Molina Foix in his introduction to *Conversaciones con Manuel Gutiérrez Aragón*.)

28. For the technical resources available to film-makers see Luis Cuadrado in *Contracampo*, no. 11–12, March–April 1980, pp. 13–30, and Teo Escamilla in *Casablanca*, no. 9, September 1981, pp. 31–8.

29. Enrique Brasó, *Carlos Saura*, Madrid, Taller de Ediciones, 1974, p. 177.

30. Cf. Eugeni Bonet and Manuel Palacio, *Práctica fílmica y vanguardia artística en España, 1925–1981*, Madrid, Universidad Complutense, 1983, pp. 11–12.

31. For the intriguing films of Arieta see Vicente Molina Foix, *New Cinema in Spain*, British Film Institute, 1977, p. 29. Coronado made a series of 16mm films in London between 1973 and 1976, and in 1984 the feature *A Midsummer Night's Dream*.

32. The magazines' polemics were strident, and somewhat invalidated by the fact that, because of the censor, critics had not always seen the films they cited.

33. For *Los desafíos* see interview with the directors in *Nuestro cine*, 1969.

34. From a rare interview with Erice in the published script of *El espíritu de la colmena*, Madrid, Ediciones Elías Querejeta, 1976.

35. E. C. Riley, 'The Story of Ana in *El espíritu de la colmena*', *Bulletin of Hispanic Studies*, LXI, 1984, p. 494.

36. Cited by Pablo López, 'Las mejores películas de la historia del cine: El espíritu de la colmena', *Fotogramas*, no. 1689, September 1983, pp. 45–52.

37. There are numerous other parallels between Fernando and the spirit. See Riley, 'The Story of Ana', and Peter Evans, 'El Espíritu de la Colmena: The Monster, the Place of the Father, and Growing Up in the Dictatorship', *Vida Hispánica*, Autumn 1982, vol. XXXI, no. 3.

38. In 'The Children of Franco' Kinder points out how Whale's film multiplies patriarchal figures, all of whom are opposed to the monster. Ana may well empathise with the monster's rejection.

39. Evans, 'El Espíritu de la Colmena', p. 13.

40. So, viewed from the ridge, the countryside around the fugitive's cottage takes on exactly the same green and yellow tones as the light in the family's house.

41. For a symbolic reading of Ana's story see Kinder, op. cit., who equates 'The Children of Franco' and 'the children of Frankenstein'.

42. *El espíritu de la colmena* (published script), p. 144.

43. Almost certainly in a concentration camp, otherwise Teresa's plea for him to write back if he is still alive would seem over-dramatic. Molina Foix argues that Fernando was a Republican. See his essay 'La guerra detrás de la ventana', *Revista de occidente*, no. 53, October 1985.

44. See Roger Mortimore's report on the film in *Sight and Sound*, vol. 43, no. 4, Autumn 1974, p. 199.

45. Erice showed Luis Cuadrado copies of paintings by Rembrandt and Vermeer before he shot the film. But whereas Vermeer's characters are happily absorbed in his domestic scenes, Erice's characters constantly turn their thoughts beyond their home.

46. Riley, 'The Story of Ana', p. 495.
47. When Ana looks into the pool (in an action suggesting a search for identity), her face dissolves into that of the monster: Ana recognises the death within her.
48. See Ricardo Franco's comments in *El cine de autor en España*, and Enrique Brasó, interviewed in *Fotogramas*, no. 1499, July 1977.
49. Vicente Molina Foix, 'Victor Erice: El cine de los supervivientes', *Mayo*, no. 12, September 1983. There is another version of the interview in *Fotogramas*, no. 1688, July 1983, pp. 12–17.
50. Such as *Tess of the d'Urbervilles*, where Hardy shows how different environments affect Tess' sensibility.
51. Producer Elías Querejeta stopped shooting on the film when apparently it ran into financial problems. For Erice's own account see 'Los males de *El Sur*' in *Cambio 16*, no. 601, 6 June 1983. Co-scriptwriter Angel Fernández Santos recorded what was left out from the script in '33 preguntas eruditas sobre *El Sur*' in *Casablanca*, nos. 31–2, July–August 1983, pp. 55–8.
52. Estrella almost says as much when she tells Agustín that 'you can't compare' how she was as a child and how she is as a fifteen-year-old.

Into the Future
1. *Spain, Change of a Nation*, London, Michael Joseph, 1984, p. 86. John Hooper outlines Spain's still deficient welfare state in *The Spaniards*, London, Viking, 1986, pp. 103–7.
2. Other Spanish films express more *desencanto* with the course of modern civilisation. Cf. Josep Salgot's atmospheric *Mater amatísima*, about a mother living with an autistic child.
3. Son of veteran film historian Fernando Méndez-Leite von Hafe, ex-EOC student, critic, and director of films for TVE, Méndez-Leite went on to direct and front the popular weekly Spanish film series, *La noche del cine español*.
4. For *Dedicatoria* see review and interview in *Contracampo*, no. 17, December 1980.
5. Augusto M. Torres, *Conversaciones con Manuel Gutiérrez Aragón*, Madrid, Editorial Fundamentos, 1985, p. 72.
6. See *Cineinforme*, no. 7, 1 April 1979.
7. The more devolved nature of UCD cultural policies did allow, however, for individual initiatives such as the research into Spanish film history sponsored by the Filmoteca and various festivals between 1979 and 1983. As yet no comparable scholarship has been produced under the Socialist government.
8. For an analysis of the industrial strategies understandably employed in *Kargus* see Ignasi Bosch, *Contracampo*, no. 23, September 1981, pp. 66–7.
9. 'Tres años de cine español', *Casablanca*, no. 34, October 1983, pp. 14–18.
10. Private viewing was another matter: in the mid-70s, John Hooper reports (*The Spaniards*, p. 185), 'hard-core one-reelers were being churned out by the dozen by an outfit called Pubis Films'.
11. For more information see Julio Pérez Perucha, 'El porno aquí y ahora: miscelánea', *Contracampo*, no. 5, pp. 9–12.
12. Spaniards may still have thought foreigners sexier. The most accomplished 'S'

film actress was the Chilean Raquel Guevara, who appeared as 'Rachel Evans'. But neither she nor any Spanish actress would perform in hard-core films and they denied that they were making pornography. See '¿Qué es la pornografía, me preguntas?', *Fotogramas*, no. 1572, December 1978, p. 17.

13. For Perucha's analysis see *Contracampo*, no. 5, September 1979, p. 34.
14.. See *Contracampo*, no. 4, July–August 1979, p. 11.
15. See Paul Preston, *The Triumph of Democracy in Spain*, London, Methuen, 1986.
16. 'El arreglo', *Fotogramas*, no. 1700, September 1984.
17. An ex-diplomat, José Antonio Zorrilla (b. Bilbao, 1945) had previously directed a short film and a medium-length film (*Argeles*, 1978), both in the context of a nascent Andalusian cinema.
18. The background to many De la Iglesia films, as well as to *Deprisa, deprisa* and *Maravillas*, is the sharp rise in the crime rate which began before the death of Franco. Rather than a product of the licence of democracy, as the Spanish right argued, delinquency drew on the emergence of a new social class, the disaffected urban youth.
19. James L. Smith, *Melodrama*, London, Methuen, 1973, pp. 7–8.
20. The *desencanto* background implicit in the New Spanish Comedy meant that by 1982 it had had its heyday. From then on directors such as Trueba gave up the genre; bigger budgets popularised literary adaptations; and the Madrid background changed steadily from the *desencanto* to the *movida*.
21. Cf. José Luis Guarner in the *International Film Guide*, London, Tantivy, 1980, p. 277.
22. See Angel Fernández Santos, 'El cine español se debate entre la expansión y la bancarrota', *El País*, 18 May 1982.
23. Special prizes stood at 1½m pesetas, which amounted to very little after it had been distributed among the cast and crew of a film.
24. An audit of RTVE in 1978 revealed 'a degree of inefficiency and dishonesty that at times beggars belief' (John Hooper, *The Spaniards*, p. 138).
25. The relationship of film budget to subvention (calculated as a sum equivalent to a percentage of box-office takings) was: 35m pesetas – an extra 10 per cent; 45m pesetas – 12.5 per cent; 50m pesetas – 15 per cent.
26. *Cineinforme*, no. 98, 11 January 1983. For Miró's aims see also no. 1682, January 1984, and *Casablanca*, no. 25, January 1983, pp. 12–16.
27. Such as a Film Week in New York in 1984, and panoramas of Spanish cinema in Paris and London (1986).
28. They are now in financial trouble, in part because of a 46 per cent levy on takings at 'X' cinemas (now reduced to 33 per cent). Audiences have decreased by as much as 70 per cent between 1984 and 1986. See *Fotogramas*, no. 1718, April 1986.
29. See Angel A. Pérez Gómez, 'Un año de cine en España' in *Cine para leer*, 1984, pp. 9–33, for the figures for *Tasio*.
30. See *Fotogramas*, no. 1721, July–August 1986, p. 18. The 10:1 RTVE screen quota for Spanish films, compared with a 4:1 quota in 1983, shows just how much relations between RTVE and Spanish cinema have deteriorated.
31. Homages (at the Valladolid Film Festival in 1984), the National Prize for

Cinematography in 1985, and Pilar Miró's own admiration for Camus' work have tended to establish Camus as a model to follow. See *Casablanca*, no. 25, January 1983, p. 16.

32. At the Valladolid Film Festival in 1984, where Camus made the distinction still common among ex-I I E C students that they are basically disciples of Buñuel (i.e. Saura), Berlanga (i.e. Regueiro) or Bardem (i.e. Camus).

33. Ex-E O C student, assistant to Camus and T V director, Betancor (b. 1942) made a competent sequel, *1919, Crónica del alba* (1983).

34. Carlos Saura, 'Le retour à Espagne' in Marcel Oms, *Carlos Saura*, Paris, Edilig, 1981, p. 115.

35. See José Luis Guarner's review of Betriu's *Réquiem por un campesino español*, *Fotogramas*, no. 1712, October 1985, p. 6.

36. Cited by Preston, *The Triumph of Democracy in Spain*, pp. 203–4.

37. José Luis Guarner and Peter Besas, *El inquietante cine de Vicente Aranda*, p. 39. Exploited by many vested interests in Spain, the general desire for moderation is also a reaction against the extremism which is commonly held to have destroyed Spain's last experiment in democracy under the Republic of 1931–6.

38. In an interview in *Fotogramas*, no. 1680, November 1982.

39. Peter Kemp in the *Daily Telegraph*.

40. The attitudes of Spaniards towards the Civil War remain contradictory. A large number (one in four, perhaps) had relatives killed in the war. But though many Spaniards acknowledge that the war had consequences for the present, they still regard it as 'in the past'.

41. *Spain, Change of a Nation*, p. 239. A new charter in 1977 has ensured that the ruling party in Spain always has more representatives than the opposition on the governing body of R T V E. The primary source of information for two-thirds of the population (according to opinion polls) has thus become an effective organ of the party in power.

42. *Parranda* ('Binge', 1977) proved uncharacteristic, *Reina zanahoria* ('Queen Carrot', 1978) somewhat laboured. There is an interview with Suárez in *Casablanca*, no. 39, March 1984, pp. 22–9.

43. For *Los restos del naufragio* see *Fotogramas*, no. 1501, July 1977.

44. Pedro acts as a Zulueta *alter ego*. Like Zulueta's shorts, the film he sends to José uses refilmed, speeded-up Super-8 film and atmospheric music to picture hallucinatory visions which, for Pedro, approach the experience of an *arrebato*.

45. *Fotogramas*, January 1980, p. 55. For Zulueta, see Juan Bufill's 'Entrevista con Ivan Zulueta', *Dirigido por*, no. 75, 1980, pp. 38–41; Julio's Pérez Perucha's review of *Arrebato* in *Contracampo*, no. 16, p. 61; Eugeni Bonet and Manuel Palacio, *Práctica fílmica y vanguardia artística en España, 1925–1981*, pp. 46–9 and 109.

46. For a brief introduction to the Basque Cinema see José María Unsain, *Hacia un cine vasco*, San Sebastian, Filmoteca Vasca, 1985.

47. See Hooper, *The Spaniards*, Ch. 18, pp. 211–27. The major evidence comes from skull shapes, blood tests, and the Basque language.

48. In an interview with the author, June 1983.

49. Cf. '¿Por qué un cine vasco?' in 'Disidencias', *Diario 16*, 24 June 1983. Imanol Uribe made a similar point in his introduction to Basque film-making, 'Dejadle

respirar al feto', *Boletín del XXX Festival Internacional de Cine de San Sebastián*, no. 3, 19 September 1982. Uribe and Amigo give an interview together in *Contracampo*'s panorama on the Basque Cinema in no. 27, 1982.

50. In his *Fotogramas* review; *'propiedad'* means 'appropriateness', 'property', 'propiety' and 'naturalness'.

51. Many Spaniards found Garci's belief that he could script the speeches of a Nobel Prize winner the height of pretentiousness. When R T V E annulled a (verbal) promise to buy *Sesión continua* ('Double Feature', 1984) the picqued Garci announced his retirement from direction.

52. The Italian director Rafael Matarazzo once told Fernán Gómez that he was too influenced in his acting style by American films and that he should be 'more Spanish' – advice which Fernán Gómez said in a television interview he has always attempted to follow.

53. Equally characteristic are Fernán Gómez's consciously disruptive changes in pace and tone.

54. José Luis Guarner on *Plácido* in 'Notas sobre el concepto de espacio en el cine de Berlanga', *En torno a Berlanga I*, p. 44. For the post-Franco Berlanga see 'Saura y Berlanga atacan de nuevo' in *El País Semanal*, 21 September 1980, and an interview with Enrique Alberich, 'La vaquilla, Berlanga, otra vez' in *Dirigido por*, no. 124, April 1985, pp. 50–7.

55. *A la pálida luz de la luna* ('By the Pale Light of the Moon', José María González Sinde, 1985) exercises exactly the same appeal.

56. In an interview with the author. *Fotogramas*, no. 1709, June 1985, has an interview with Regueiro.

57. Born in Barcelona in 1960, Guerin already had a substantial short and sub-format career behind him.
    By the 1980s full-length features with any sense of experiment were becoming increasingly rare. Two such were Alvaro del Amo's *Dos* ('Two', 1980) and Paulino Viota's *Cuerpo a cuerpo. Contracampo*, no. 36, has reviews and interviews with Guerin and Viota.

58. *Dirigido por*, no. 111, January 1984, p. 13.

59. *Fotogramas*, no. 1705, February 1985, p. 53. For Almodóvar see also *Contracampo*, no. 23, September 1981; *Dirigido por*, no. 117, 1984; *Fotogramas*, no. 1674, May 1982.

60. In his review of *Réquiem por un campesino español*, *Fotogramas*, no. 1712.

61. There is also concern about the influence exercised by one political party over the media. González's Socialists effectively control R T V E; Spain's most prestigious daily, *El País*, is traditionally close to P S O E interests; the group controlling *El País* have also bought Cadina Ser, Spain's largest radio network, and are leading contenders to launch Spain's only 'independent' T V channel, provisionally in 1988.

62. Catalan films may now be picking up. While they accounted for only 8 per cent of government advances in 1984, an Evaluation Commission was created in 1986 to administer Spanish Film Institute financing of the Catalan industry.

DICTIONARY OF POST-FRANCO FILM-MAKERS

ALMODOVAR, Pedro
b. Calzada de Calatrava (Ciudad Real), 1949. Actor in avant-garde companies. Super-8 films from 1974, including the short films *Dos putas, o Historià de amor que termina en boda* ('Two Whores, or Love Story Ending in Marriage', 1974), *La caída de Sodoma* ('The Fall of Sodom', 1974), *El sueño* ('The Dream', 1975), and mock trailers and publicity in *Complementos* (1977), and the feature *Folle, Folle, Folleme, Tim* ('Fuck Me, Fuck Me, Fuck Me Tim'/'Feulletim', 1978). In 1985 he made *Trayler para amantes de lo prohibido* ('Trailer for Lovers of the Forbidden'), a medium-length film for television. Also a novelist, and columnist in the Madrid magazine *La Luna*.

FILMS: *Salomé* (16mm, short, 1978); *Pepi, Luci, Bom y otras chicas del montón* ('Pepi, Luci, Bom and a Whole Lot of Other Girls', 1980); *Laberinto de pasiones* ('Labyrinth of Passions', 1982); *Entre tinieblas* ('In the Dark', 1983); *¿Qué he hecho yo para merecer esto?* ('What Have I Done to Deserve This?', 1984); *Matador* ('Killer'/'Torero'/'Golden Hair', 1986).

ARANDA, Vicente
b. Barcelona, 1926. Lived in Venezuela, 1952–9. Formed his own production company in Barcelona in 1964. A central, if unconvinced, member of the 'Barcelona School'. From *Cambio de sexo*, has worked in close collaboration with Carlos Durán.

FILMS: *Brillante porvenir* ('Brilliant Future', with Román Gubern, 1964); *Fata Morgana* (1966); *Las crueles* ('The Cruel Women', 1969); *La novia ensangrentada* ('The Bloody Bride', 1972); *Clara es el precio* ('Clara is the Price', 1974); *Cambio de sexo* ('Sex Change', 1977); *La muchacha de las bragas de oro* ('The Girl with the Golden Panties', 1980); *Asesinato en el comité central* ('Murder in the Central Committee', 1982); *Fanny Pelopaja* ('Fanny Straw Top', 1984); *Tiempo de silencio* ('Time of Silence', 1986).

270

ARMENDARIZ, Montxo
b. Olleta (Navarra), 1949. Professor of Electronics at the Pamplona Polytechnic. Short films on Navarrese themes, e.g. *Rivera navarra* ('Navarrese Riverside', released as Ikuska 11), *Nafarrako Ikazkinak* ('Navarrese Charcoal Burners', 1984). Has recently worked in close collaboration with producer Elías Querejeta.

FILMS: *Tasio* (1984); *27 horas* ('27 hours', in production).

ARMIÑAN, Jaime de
b. Madrid, 1927. From a well-known family of writers and politicians. Prolific television director and scriptwriter. Screenplays include *El secreto de Mónica* ('Monica's Secret', José María Forqué, 1961), *La becerrada* ('The Fight with the Yearling Bulls', Forqué, 1962), *Sólo para dos* ('Just for Two', Luis Lucía, 1968), and *El Bengador Gusticiero y su pastelera madre* ('The Vengeful Avenger and His Pastrycook Mother', Forges, 1976).

FILMS: *Carola de día, Carola de noche* ('Carola by Day, Carola by Night', 1969); *La Lola dicen que no vive sola* ('They Say Lola Doesn't Live Alone', 1970); *Mi querida señorita* ('My Dearest Señorita', 1971); *Un casto varón español* ('The Chaste Spanish Male', 1973); *El amor del capitán Brando* ('The Love of Captain Brando', 1974); *¡Jo, papá!* ('Oh, Daddy!', 1975); *Nunca es tarde* ('It's Never Too Late', 1977); *Al servicio de la mujer española* ('At the Service of Spanish Womanhood', 1978); *El nido* ('The Nest', 1980); *En septiembre* ('In September', 1981); *Stico* (1984); *La hora bruja* ('The Witching Hour', 1985).

BARDEM, Juan Antonio
b. Madrid, 1922. Son of actor Rafael Bardem and actress Matilde Muñoz Sampedro. Member of the Spanish Communist Party from 1943. Arrested repeatedly and finally jailed in 1976. Entered the IIEC in 1947. A moving spirit behind the Salamanca Congress. President of UNINCI. President of the Spanish Directors Union, ASDREC. After an indifferent critical reception for *Siete días de enero* Bardem was unable to place a project with any Spanish producer and was forced to work abroad. Returned to the forefront of Spanish film-making when he directed an acclaimed episode in the TVE series *La huella de un crimen* ('Clue to a Crime', 1985). Now shooting a long cherished project, *Lorca, muerte de un poeta* ('Lorca, Death of a Poet').

FILMS: *Esa pareja feliz* ('That Happy Couple', with Berlanga, 1951); *Cómicos* ('Comedians', 1953); *Felices pascuas* ('Happy Christmas', 1954); *Muerte de un ciclista* ('Death of a Cyclist', 1955); *Calle Mayor* ('Main Street', 1956); *La venganza* ('Revenge', 1957); *Sonatas* (1959); *A las cinco de la tarde* ('At Five in the Afternoon', 1960); *Los inocentes* ('The Innocents', 1962); *Nunca pasa nada* ('Nothing Ever Happens', 1963); *Los pianos mecánicos* ('Player Pianos', 1965); *El último día de la guerra* ('The Last Day of the War', 1968); *Varietés* (1970); *La isla misteriosa* ('The Mysterious Island', 1971); *La corrupción de Chris Miller* ('The Corruption of Chris Miller', 1972); *El poder del deseo* ('The Power of Desire', 1975); *El puente* ('The Long Weekend', 1976); *Siete días de enero* ('Seven Days in January', 1978); *La advertencia* ('The Warning', 1982, made in Bulgaria).

271

BELLMUNT, Francesc

b. Sabadell (Barcelona), 1947. Directed shorts in an isolated Barcelona response to the Madrid Independent Cinema: *Catherine* (1970), *Semejante a Pedro* ('Like Pedro', 1971) and *La mano de Belgrado* ('Belgrado's Hand', 1971). Filmed *La Torna* (1977), a recording of a theatre performance by Los Joglars, videos, industrial shorts, and four Noticiari de Barcelona: *C.O.P.E.L. presos en lluita* ('C.O.P.E.L., a Prisoners' Fight', 1977), *Les festes de la Merce, Vaga de Gasoliners* ('The Service Station Conflict', 1978) and *Port de pescadors de Barcelona* ('Barcelona Fishermen's Port', 1979).

FILMS: *Pastel de sangre* ('Blood Cake', 1972, one episode); *Robin Hood nunca muere* ('Robin Hood Never Dies', 1974); *La Nova Cançó* ('The "New Song"', 1976); *Canet Rock* (1976); *L'orgia* ('The Orgy', 1978); *Salut i força al canut* ('Health, Lust and Fun', 1979); *La quinta del porro* ('The Stoned Conscripts', 1980); *Pa d'angel* ('Angel Bread', 1984); *Un par de huevos* ('A Pair of Balls', 1985); *La radio folla* ('Radio Screwball', 1986).

BERLANGA, Luis

b. Valencia, 1921. Medical assistant in the Republican rearguard in the Civil War and volunteer for the División Azul. Student at the IIEC 1947–50. Collaborated with Bardem (scripts of *Esa pareja feliz* and *Bienvenido Mr. Marshall*), Miguel Mihura, Edgar Neville and Rafael Azcona (from 1959 when they scripted *Se vende un tranvía*, 'Tram For Sale', a medium-length feature which Berlanga effectively co-directed). Professor at the EOC. President of the National Film Library, a lucid authority on film-making under Franco, and from *La escopeta nacional* the most consistently popular director in Spain. Editor of an erotic literary collection, *La sonrisa vertical*, and co-presenter of a radio advice service on erotica.

FILMS: *Esa pareja feliz* (with Bardem, 1951); *Bienvenido, Mr. Marshall* ('Welcome Mr. Marshall', 1952); *Novio a la vista* ('Boyfriend in Sight', 1953); *Calabuch* (1956); *Los jueves, milagro* ('Miracles on Thursdays', 1957); *Plácido* (1961); *Las cuatro verdades* ('The Four Truths', episode: 'Death and the Woodcutter', 1962); *El verdugo* ('The Executioner', 1964); *La boutique* (in Argentina, 1967); *¡Vivan los novios!* ('Long live the Bride and Groom', 1969); *Tamaño natural* ('Life Size', shot in France, 1973); *La escopeta nacional* ('The National Shotgun', 1977); *Patrimonio nacional* ('National Patrimony', 1980); *Nacional III* (1982); *La vaquilla* ('The Heifer', 1985).

BETRIU, Francesc

b. Orgaño (Lérida), 1940. Worked as theatre director during military service in North Africa. EOC student. Numerous aborted projects, including film (prohibited by Fraga) of the Beatles' visit to Spain. Prime mover of Inscram production company, whose fiction shorts included Drove's *¿Qué se puede hacer con una chica?* (1969), Gutiérrez's *El último día de la humanidad* (1969), Carlos Morales' *Gente de metro* and *Gente de baile*, and Betriu's own *Gente de mesón* ('The Tavern Crowd', 1969). Betriu's short *Bolero de amor* ('A Love Bolero', 1970) was originally an Inscram project. Worked on the editorial staff of the Noticiari de Barcelona.

Produced *Los fieles sirvientes* in the co-operative Cop-Nou.

FILMS: *Corazón solitario* ('Lonely Heart', 1972); *Furia española* ('Spanish Fury', 1974); *La viuda andaluza* ('The Andalusian Widow', 1976); *Los fieles sirvientes* ('The Faithful Servants', 1980); *La Plaça del Diamant* ('Diamond Square', 1982); *Réquiem por un campesino español* ('Requiem for a Spanish Peasant', 1985).

BIGAS LUNA, José Juan

b. Barcelona, 1946. Worked in graphic design until 1970. Many short films, 1972–6. Fiction writer, *Bilbao* and *Caniche* being based on his own stories. President of the Col-legi de Directors de Cinema de Catalunya.

FILMS: *Tatuaje* ('Tattoo', 1976); *Bilbao* (1978); *Caniche* ('Poodle', 1979); *Renacer* ('Reborn', made in USA, 1981); *Lola* (1985).

BODEGAS, Roberto

b. Madrid, 1933. Early career as assistant director in France. Scripted Christian de Chalonge's *O salto* (1969). Producer (*Picasso* by Rossif, *Siete días de enero* by Bardem). PCE militant. Assistant director on Garci's Oscar-winning *Volver a empezar*. Now preparing *La sombra del ciprés alargada* ('The Lengthened Shadow From the Cypress Tree').

FILMS: *Españolas en París* ('Spanish Women in Paris', 1970); *Vida conyugal sana* ('A Healthy Married Life', 1973); *Los nuevos españoles* ('The New Spaniards', 1974); *La adúltera* ('The Adulteress', 1975); *Libertad provisional* ('Provisional Liberty', 1976); *Corazón de papel* ('Paper Heart', 1982).

BORAU, José Luis

b. Saragossa, 1929. Film critic, *El Heraldo de Aragón*. Student at the IIEC 1957–60; graduated with *En el río* ('On the River', 1960). Professor at the EOC. Produced films by Zulueta, Chávarri, Armiñan, Gutiérrez (*Camada negra*) and the Puerto Rican Ray Rivas (*El monosabio*, 'The Trained Monkey', 1977).

FILMS: *Brandy* (1964); *Crimen de doble filo* ('Double-edged Crime', 1965); *Hay que matar a B.* ('B Must Die', 1974); *Furtivos* ('Poachers', 1975); *La Sabina* (1979); *Río abajo/On the Line* (made in USA, 1984); *Tata mía* ('My Nanny', in production).

BUÑUEL, Luis

b. Calanda (Teruel), 1900, d. 1983. Moved to Paris 1925–30; Hollywood 1930–1; Spain 1931–3; Paris 1933–4; Spain from 1934, where he dubbed films for Warner Bros and worked as Head Producer at Filmófono; Paris 1936–7 (worked for the Republic); USA 1938–46. From 1946 made his permanent home in Mexico. Visited Spain frequently from the 1960s. After *Cet obscur objet du désir*, scripted *Agon* or *Haga la guerra y no el amor* ('Make War, not Love'), planned as a French–Spanish co-production but postponed because of Buñuel's declining health.

FILMS IN SPAIN: *Las Hurdes* ('Land Without Bread', 1932); *Don Quintín el amargao* ('Embittered Don Quintín', 1935; at least co-direction with Luis Mar-

273

quina); *La hija de Juan Simón* ('Juan Simón's Daughter', 1935; effectively directed); *¡Centinela alerta!* ('Look Out, Sentry', 1935; directed some scenes); *Viridiana* (1961); *Tristana* (1970); *Cet obscur objet du désir* ('That Obscure Object of Desire', 1977, minority Spain–France co-production).

CAMUS, Mario

b. Santander, 1935. IIEC student 1957–62, graduating with *El borracho* ('The Drunkard'); with Saura worked on the scripts of *Los golfos*, *Llanto por un bandido*, and his own *Muere una mujer*. From 1968 TV director. Co-scripted Miró's forthcoming *Werther*.

FILMS: *Los farsantes* ('The Actors', 1963); *Young Sánchez* (1963); *Muere una mujer* ('A Woman Dies', 1964); *La visita que no tocó el timbre* ('The Visitor Who Did Not Ring The Doorbell', 1965); *Con el viento solano* ('With the East Wind', 1965); *Cuando tú no estás* ('When You Aren't There', 1966); *Volver a vivir* ('Living Again', 1966); *Al ponerse el sol* ('When the Sun Sets'); *Digan lo que digan* ('No Matter What They Say', 1968); *Esa mujer* ('That Woman', 1969); *La cólera del viento* ('The Wind's Wrath', 1970); *Los pájaros de Baden-Baden* ('The Birds of Baden Baden', 1975); *La joven casada* ('The Young Married Woman', 1975); *Los días del pasado* ('The Days of the Past', 1977); *La colmena* ('The Beehive', 1982); *Los santos inocentes* ('The Holy Innocents', 1984); *La vieja música* ('That Old Music', 1985).

CHAVARRI, Jaime

b. Madrid, 1943. EOC 1968–70. Short films include *Blanche Perkins o vida atormentada* ('Blanche Perkins or A Tormented Life', 1964), *El cuarto sobre el jardín* ('The Room Overlooking the Garden', 1966) and *Estado de sitio* ('State of Siege', 1970). Super-8 features include: *Run, Blancanieves, Run* ('Run, Snow-White, Run', 1968) and *Ginebra en los infiernos* ('Guinevere in Hell', 1970). Critic (*Film Ideal*), set designer (e.g. *The Spirit of the Beehive*), assistant director (Regueiro's *Me enveneno de azules*), and TV director, working on adaptations of Carroll and Wilde, and the 16mm feature *Luis y Virginia* (1982). Also actor, notably in *¿Qué he hecho yo para merecer esto?*

FILMS: *Pastel de sangre* ('A Blood Cake', 1971, one episode); *Los viajes escolares* ('School Trips', 1973); *El desencanto* ('Disenchantment', 1976); *A un dios desconocido* ('To an Unknown God', 1977); *Cuentos eróticos* ('Erotic Tales', one episode: 'The Small Planet', 1979); *Cuentos para una escapada* ('Stories for an Escapade', one episode: 'The Deaf Woman', 1979); *Dedicatoria* ('A Dedication', 1980); *Bearn o la sala de las muñecas* ('Bearn or The Dolls Room', 1983); *Las bicicletas son para el verano* ('Bicycles Are for Summer', 1984); *El río de oro* ('Golden River', 1986).

COLOMO, Fernando

b. Madrid, 1946. The last EOC student, graduating in set design. Producer (the short *Lola, Paz y yo*, Miguel Angel Díaz, 1974), co-scriptwriter (*De fresa, limón y menta*, 'Strawberry, Lemon and Spearmint', Díaz, 1977), and director (of the shorts *En un París imaginario*, 'In an Imaginary Paris', 1975, and *Pomporrutas imperiales*,

1976). Founder of La Salamandra film company, producer of Trueba's *Opera prima*.

FILMS: *Tigres de papel* ('Paper Tigers', 1977); *¿Qué hace una chica como tú en un sitio como éste?* ('What's a Girl Like You Doing in a Place Like This?', 1978); *Cuentos eróticos* (episode: 'Köñensonatten', 1979); *La mano negra* ('The Black Hand', 1980); *Estoy en crisis* ('I'm in Crisis', 1982); *La línea del cielo* ('Skyline', 1983); *El caballero del dragón* ('The Knight of the Dragon', 1985).

DROVE, Antonio

b. Madrid, 1942. Graduated from the EOC with the banned *La caza de brujas* ('Witch Hunt', 1968). Medium-length feature, *¿Qué se puede hacer con una chica?* ('What Can You Do With a Girl?', 1969). Scripted Mario Camus' TV production *La leyenda del Alcalde de Zalamea* (1972); co-scriptwriter of Borau's *Hay que matar a B.* (1974). Has also directed TV drama.

FILMS: *Tocata y fuga de Lolita* ('Lolita's Toccata and Fugue', 1974); *Mi mujer es muy decente dentro lo que cabe* ('My Wife is Decent as Far as That's Possible', 1974); *Nosotros que fuimos tan felices* ('We Who Were So Happy', 1976); *La verdad sobre el caso Savolta* ('The Truth about the Savolta Case', 1978).

ERICE, Victor

b. San Sebastián, 1940. In 1960 entered IIEC, where he made 16mm short films: *En la terraza* ('On the Terrace', 1961), *Entrevías* ('Gauges', 1961) and *Páginas de un diario* ('Pages from a Diary', 1962). Graduated in 1963 with *Los días perdidos* ('The Lost Days', 35mm). Contributed to magazines *Cuadernos de Arte y Pensamiento* and *Nuestro cine*; co-scripted Antón Eceiza's *El próximo otoño* ('Next Autumn', 1963) and Miguel Picazo's *Oscuros sueños de agosto* ('Obscure August Dreams', 1967). In the 70s worked in advertising. Since *El sur* (1983) has adapted a series of Borges stories for TVE and co-written a book on Nicholas Ray.

FILMS: *Los desafíos* ('The Challenges', 1969, one episode); *El espíritu de la colmena* ('The Spirit of the Beehive', 1973); *El sur* ('The South', 1983).

FERNAN GOMEZ, Fernando

b. Lima, Peru, 1921. In Spain from the age of three. The Civil War interrupted his studies and he turned to acting. By 1984 had acted in at least 138 films, winning the Best Actor Award at Berlin for *El anacoreta* ('The Anchorite', Juan Estelrich, 1976) and *Stico* (Jaime de Armiñan, 1984). Novelist (*El vendedor de naranjas* offers a satire on the Spanish film business), dramatist (his play *Las bicicletas son para el verano* took the Lope de Vega prize in 1977), theatre director, poet, columnist and TV director.

FILMS (as director): *Manicomio* ('Insane Asylum', 1952, with L. M. Delgado); *El mensaje* ('The Message', 1953); *El malvado Carabel* ('The Wicked Carabel', 1955); *La vida por delante* ('Your Life Before You', 1958); *La vida alrededor* ('Your Life Around You', 1959); *Sólo para hombres* ('For Men Only', 1960); *La venganza de don Mendo* ('Don Mendo's Revenge', 1961); *El mundo sigue* ('Life Goes On',

1963); *El extraño viaje* ('The Strange Journey', 1964); *Los palomos* ('The Pigeons/ Idiots', 1964); *Ninette y un señor de Murcia* ('Ninette and a Gentleman from Murcia', 1965); *Mayores sin reparos* ('Adults without Consideration', 1966); *Cómo casarse en 7 días* ('How to Get Married in 7 Days', 1969); *Crimen imperfecto* ('Imperfect Crime', 1970); *Yo la vi primero* ('I Saw Her First', 1974); *La querida* ('The Mistress', 1975); *Bruja, más que bruja* ('Witch, Nothing but a Witch', 1976); *Mi hija Hildegart* ('My Daughter Hildegart', 1977); *Cinco tenedores* ('Five Stars', 1979); *Mambrú se fue a la guerra* ('Mambru Went to War', 1986); *Viaje a ninguna parte* ('Journey to Nowhere', in production).

FRANCO, Ricardo

b. Madrid, 1949. Worked as assistant director to his uncle Jesús Franco. In 1969 formed Buho Films which produced several shorts by Martínez-Lázaro and Franco himself. First Prize for his short *Gospel* (1969) at the Benalmádena Film Festival; jailed after a political incident at the same festival the following year. Spent much of the early 80s developing the uncompleted project *El sueño de Tangers* ('The Dream of Tangiers'). Has directed for TV.

FILMS: *El desastre de Annual* ('The Massacre at Annual', 1970); *Los crimenes de la Tía María* ('The Murders of Aunt Maria', unfinished, 1972); *El increíble aumento del costo de la vida* ('The Incredible Rise in the Cost of Living', short, 1974); *Pascual Duarte* (1975); *Los restos del naufragio* ('The Remains from the Shipwreck', 1978); *San Judas de la Frontera* (made in Mexico, 1984).

GARCI, José Luis

b. Madrid, 1944. Film critic for *Signo, Aún*, and *Cinestudio*; editor-in-chief of *Reseña* and *Revista SP*. Author (*Ray Bradbury, humanista del futuro, Cine de ciencia-ficción*, and *La Giaconda está triste*). From 1970 scriptwriter for the producer José Luis Dibildos. Scripted Antonio Mercero's celebrated TV short film *La cabina* ('The Telephone Booth', 1972), which won an Emmy. Shorts: *Al fútbol* ('Let's See Football!'), *Mi Marilyn* ('My Marilyn'), and *Tiempo de gente acobardada* ('Time for Discouraged People'), all made in 1975. In 1983 Garci's *Volver a empezar* won the Oscar for the Best Foreign Film.

FILMS: *Asignatura pendiente* ('Pending Exam', 1977); *Solos en la madrugada* ('Alone in the Early Hours', 1978); *Las verdes praderas* ('Green Pastures', 1979); *El crack* ('The Crack', 1980); *Volver a empezar* ('Starting Over', 1982); *El crack II* ('Crack II', 1983); *Sesión continua* ('Double Feature', 1984).

GARCIA SANCHEZ, José Luis

b. Salamanca, 1941. EOC student and PCE militant. Worked in Inscram and assisted Patino on *Canciones para después de una guerra*. Co-scriptwriter of Betriu's *Corazón solitario* and *Furia española*, Gutiérrez's *Habla mudita*, and Patino's *Queredísimos verdugos*. A prolific children's writer, and author of screenplays for television. *Las truchas* shared the Golden Bear prize at the 1978 Berlin Film Festival.

276

FILMS: *El love feroz* ('The Fierce Love/Wolf', 1972); *Colorín colorado* ('They All Lived Happily Ever After', 1976); *Las truchas* ('The Trout', 1977); *Cuentos para una escapada* (one episode: 'A Multi-coloured Gift', 1979); *Dolores* (1980); *La corte de Faraon* ('Pharaoh's Court', 1985).

GUTIERREZ ARAGON, Manuel

b. Torrelavega (Santander), 1942. PCE militant 1962–77. EOC student 1962–70. Graduated with *Hansel y Gretel* (1970), having already made *El último día de la humanidad* ('The Last Day of Humanity', 1969) for Inscram. Co-scripted García Sánchez's *El love feroz*, Betriu's *Corazón solitario*, Borau's *Furtivos*, Camino's *Las largas vacaciones del '36*, García Sánchez's *Las truchas*, and the TVE serial *Los pazos de Ulloa* (Gonzalo Suárez, 1985). From *El corazón del bosque* has worked with producer/co-scriptwriter Luis Megino (except *Feroz*, co-scripted and produced by Elías Querejeta). Numerous international awards include Directors Prize for *Camada negra* at the 1979 Berlin Film Festival.

FILMS: *Habla, mudita* ('Speak, Mute Girl', 1973); *Camada negra* ('Black Brood', 1977); *Sonámbulos* ('Sleep Walkers', 1977); *El corazón del bosque* ('The Heart of the Forest', 1978); *Cuentos para una escapada* (episode: 'Test for Children', 1979); *Maravillas* (1980); *Demonios en el jardín* ('Demons in the Garden', 1982); *Feroz* ('Wild', 1984); *La noche más hermosa* ('The Most Beautiful Night', 1984); *La mitad del cielo* ('Half of Heaven', 1986).

HERRALDE, Gonzalo

b. Barcelona, 1949. After drama studies, made his first short *El cartel* ('The Poster', 1970), and produced a series of short films.

FILMS: *La muerte del escorpión* ('Death of a Scorpion', 1975); *Raza, el espíritu de Franco* ('Raza, the Spirit of Franco', 1977); *El asesino de Pedralbes* ('The Pedralbes Murderer'); *Vértigo en Manhattan/Jet Lag* (made in USA, 1980); *Ultimas tardes con Teresa* ('Last Afternoons With Teresa', 1984).

DE LA IGLESIA, Eloy

b. Zarauz (Guipúzcoa), 1944. Directed the Teatro Popular Infantil before working in TVE on a series of films on children's books. PCE member.

FILMS: *Fantasía ... 3* ('Fantasy ... 3', 1966); *Algo amargo en la boca* ('Something Bitter-tasting', 1967); *Cuadrilátero* ('Quadrilateral', 1969); *El techo de cristal* ('The Glass Ceiling', 1971); *La semana del asesino* ('The Week of the Murderer', 1972); *Nadie oyó gritar* ('No One Heard the Scream', 1972); *Una gota de sangre para morir amando* ('A Drop of Blood to Die Loving', 1973); *La otra alcoba* ('The Other Alcove', 1975); *Los placeres ocultos* ('Hidden Pleasures', 1976); *La criatura* ('The Creature', 1977); *El sacerdote* ('The Priest', 1977); *El diputado* ('The Deputy', 1978); *Miedo a salir de noche* ('Fearing to go out at Night', 1979); *Navajeros* ('Knife Fighters', 1980); *La mujer del ministro* ('The Minister's Wife', 1981); *Colegas* ('Mates', 1982); *El pico* ('The Shoot', 1983); *El pico II* (1984); *Otra vuelta de tuerca* ('The Turn of the Screw', 1985).

MARTINEZ-LAZARO, Emilio

b. Madrid, 1945. Film critic for *Griffith* and *Nuestro cine*. As a member of the Madrid Independent Cinema he shot the 16mm short *El camino al cielo* ('The Way to Heaven') and the 16mm medium-length feature *Amo mi cama rica* ('I Love My Rich Bed'). Co-scriptwriter of *Pascual Duarte*. From 1976 has combined a versatile film career with extensive television work, including a full-length feature for television *Todo va mal* ('Everything's Going Badly', 1984). *Las palabras de Max* shared the Berlin Golden Bear for 1978.

FILMS: *Pastel de sangre* (episode: 'Victor Frankenstein', 1971); *Las palabras de Max* ('Max's Words', 1976); *Sus años dorados* ('Golden Years', 1980); *Lulu de noche* ('Lulu by Night', 1985).

MIRA, Carles

b. Valencia, 1947. E O C student. Assistant to José Luis Gómez on various theatrical productions. His short films include the ecological documentary *Biotopo* (1974), *Michana* (1974), and *Viure sense viure*.

FILMS: *La portentosa vida del padre Vicente* ('The Miraculous Life of Father Vicente', 1978); *Cuentos para una escapada* (episode: 'Memories of the Sea', 1979); *Con el culo al aire* ('Caught With Your Pants Down', 1980); *Jalea real* ('Royal Jelly', 1981); *Que nos quiten lo bailao* ('No One Can Take Away Our Good Times Together', 1983); *Karnabal* (1985).

MIRO, Pilar

b. Madrid, 1940. Worked in Spanish Television since 1960 and T V E's first woman director with *Revista de mujer* in 1963. Subsequently a prolific T V director, specialising in dramas and literary adaptations. Graduated from the E O C in 1968 with a diploma in scriptwriting, which she later taught at the Film School. Her own screenplays include co-authorship of Manuel Summers' *La niña de luto* ('The Girl in Mourning', 1964) and *El juego de la oca* ('Snakes and Ladders', 1964). Under Secretary for the Cinema (Director General at the Dirección General de Cine) between 1982 and January 1986; resigned the post to prepare a feature based on Goethe's *Werther*.

FILMS: *La petición* ('The Engagement Party', 1976); *El crimen de Cuenca* ('The Cuenca Crime', 1979); *Gary Cooper que estás en los cielos* ('Gary Cooper Who Art in Heaven', 1980); *Hablamos esta noche* ('Let's Talk Tonight', 1982).

MOLINA, Josefina

b. Cordoba, 1936. First woman to graduate with a diploma in direction from the E O C. Directed much T V drama, notably the serial *Teresa de Jesús* (1984). Also theatre director.

FILMS: *Vera . . . un cuento cruel* ('Vera . . . a Cruel Story', 1973); *Cuentos eróticos* (episode: 'The Linden-blossom Tea', 1979); *Función de noche* ('Night Performance', 1981).

278

OLEA, Pedro
b. Bilbao, 1938. EOC student, graduating with *Anabel* (1964). Critic for *Nuestro cine*; worked in advertising; for TVE has made documentaries on Spanish regions (e.g. *La ría de Bilbao*) and drama and pop programmes (*Ultimo grito*). Producer of some of his own films.

FILMS: *Días de viejo color* ('Days in Old Colour', 1967); *Juan y Junior en un mundo diferente* ('Juan and Junior in a Different World', 1969); *El bosque del lobo* ('The Wolf's Forest', 1970); *La casa sin fronteras* ('The House Without Frontiers', 1972); *No es bueno que el hombre esté solo* ('A Man Shouldn't Be Alone', 1973); *Tormento* ('Torment', 1974); *Pim, pam, pum ... fuego!* ('Ready, Aim ... Fire!', 1975); *La Corea* (1976); *Un hombre llamado "Flor de otono"* ('A Man Called "Autumn Flower"', 1977); *Akelarre* ('Witch's Sabbath', 1984).

PATINO, Basilio M.
b. Lumbrales (Salamanca), 1930. Founder of the Salamanca University Film Club which helped organise the Salamanca Film Congress. Film criticism in *Cinema Universitario*. Graduated from the IIEC in 1961 with *Tarde de domingo* ('Sunday Afternoon'); made commercials and two documentary shorts, *El noveno* ('The Ninth One') and *Torerillos* ('Young Bullfighters'). His only television work, an adaptation of *Rinconete y Cortadillo*, was embargoed for political motives. From 1975 has worked in advertising and made video documentaries.

FILMS: *Nueve cartas a Berta* ('Nine Letters to Berta', 1965); *Del amor y otras soledades* ('On Love and Other Solitudes', 1969); *Canciones para después de una guerra* ('Songs for After a War', 1971); *Queridísimos verdugos* ('Dearest Hangmen', 1973); *Caudillo* (1975); *Los paraísos perdidos* ('The Lost Paradises', 1985).

REGUEIRO, Francisco
b. Valladolid, 1934. Football player, journalist, cartoonist, writer. Graduated from the IIEC with *Sor Angelina, virgen* (1961). Television work includes *La niña que se convirtió en rata*. From 1975 his projects were repeatedly rejected by producers; he continued to write scripts, and painted.

FILMS: *El buen amor* ('The Good Love', 1963); *Amador* ('Lover', 1965); *Si volvemos a vernos* ('Smashing Up', 1967); *Me enveneno de azules* ('I'm Poisoning Myself with the Blues', 1969); *Carta de amor de un asesino* ('Love Letter from an Assassin', 1973); *Duerme, duerme, mi amor* ('Sleep, Sleep, My Love', 1974); *Las bodas de Blanca* ('Blanca's Weddings', 1975); *Padre nuestro* ('Our Father', 1985).

RIBAS, Antoni
b. Barcelona, 1935. Worked as script boy and assistant director, 1959–64, for Isasi, Torado, Gil, Lucía and Amadori. A member of the Institut de Cinema Catalá. Made documentary, *Catalans universals* (1978), for TVE. Vice-President of the Col-legi de Directors de Cinema de Catalunya.

FILMS: *Las salvajes en Puente San Gil* ('The Wild Women on San Gil Bridge', 1966); *Tren de madrugada* (1968, disowned by Ribas); *Medias y calcetines* ('Stockings and Socks', 1969); *La otra imagen* ('The Other Image', 1972); *La ciutat cremada* ('The Burnt City', 1976); *Victoria! La gran aventura d'un poble* ('Victory! The Great Adventure of a People', 1983); *Victoria! II. La disbauxa del 17* (1983); *Victoria! III. El seny i la rauxa* (1984); *El primer torero porno* ('The First Porno Bullfighter', 1985).

SAURA, Carlos

b. Huesca (Aragón), 1932. Professional photographer 1950–3. Entered IIEC, 1953. Assistant director on the uncompleted *Carta de Sanabria* (Eduardo Ducay, 1955); made short films *El tiovivo, Pax, El pequeño río Manzanares*, and graduated in 1957 with *La tarde del domingo* ('Sunday Afternoon'). Actor (as a spectator in *Los golfos*, as a priest in *El cochecito*, as himself in *Nueve cartas a Berta*). IIEC Professor 1957–64. Author of various abortive scripts with Mario Camus, as well as *Muere una mujer*, which Camus directed. Numerous international awards, including Golden Bear at the 1981 Berlin Film Festival for *Deprisa, deprisa* and a Special Award from the American Academy in 1986 for the whole of his work.

FILMS: *Cuenca* (medium-length documentary, 1958); *Los golfos* ('The Hooligans', 1959); *Llanto por un bandido* ('Lament for a Bandit', 1963); *La caza* ('The Hunt', 1965); *Peppermint frappé* (1967); *Stress es tres, tres* ('Stress is Three', 1968); *La madriguera* ('The Den', 1969); *El jardín de las delicias* ('The Garden of Delights', 1970); *Ana y los lobos* ('Ana and the Wolves', 1972); *La prima Angélica* ('Cousin Angelica', 1973); *Cría cuervos...* ('Raise Ravens...', 1975); *Elisa, vida mía* ('Elisa, My Love', 1977); *Los ojos vendados* ('Blindfolded', 1978); *Mamá cumple cien años* ('Mama Turns a Hundred', 1979); *Deprisa, deprisa* ('Fast, Fast', 1980); *Bodas de sangre* ('Blood Wedding', 1980); *Dulces horas* ('Sweet Hours', 1981); *Antonieta* (1982); *Carmen* (1983); *Los zancos* ('The Stilts', 1984); *El amor brujo* ('A Love Bewitched', 1986).

SUAREZ, Gonzalo

b. Oviedo, 1934. Has worked as actor and sports journalist. Novelist and short story writer. Made commercials and shorts during the film industry crisis of the late 70s (*Una leyenda asturiana*, 'An Asturian Legend', 1980) and worked in television.

FILMS: *Ditirambo vela por nosotros* ('Ditirambo is Watching Over Us') and *El horible ser nunca visto* ('The Horrible Unseen Being'), 16mm shorts, 1966; *Ditirambo* (1967); *El extraño caso del doctor Fausto* ('The Strange Case of Dr Faustus', 1969); *Aoom* (1970, unreleased, later destroyed); *Morbo* ('Disease', 1971); *Al diablo con amor* ('To the Devil with Love', 1972); *La loba y la paloma* ('The Wolf and the Dove', 1973); *La regenta* ('The Regent', 1974); *Beatriz* (1976); *Parranda* ('Binge', 1977); *Reina zanahoria* ('Queen Carrot', 1978); *Cuentos para una escapada* (episode: 'Miniman and Super-wolf', 1979); *Epílogo* ('Epilogue', 1984).

TRUEBA, Fernando

b. Madrid, 1955. Film criticism in *El País, La guía del ocio* and *Casablanca*. Short films, usually co-scripted with Oscar Ladoire: *Oscar y Carlos* (1974), *Urculo, En legítima defensa* ('In Self-defence', 1978); *El león enamorado* ('The Amorous Lion',

1979), *Homenaje a trois* ('Menage à trois'), and *Oscar y Carlos 82* (1982). Best Actor award to Ladoire at Venice Festival for his lead role in *Opera prima*. Co-scripted Colomo's *La mano negra* and *Köñensonatten*, Ladoire's *A contratiempo*, and Sánchez Valdés' *De tripas corazón*, which he also produced.

FILMS: *Opera prima* ('A Cousin in Opera/First Work', 1980); *Mientras el cuerpo aguante* ('While the Body Lasts', 1982); *Sal gorda* ('Coarse Salt'/'Get Lost, Fatty', 1984); *Sé infiel y no mires con quién* ('Move Over, Mrs Markham', 1985).

UNGRIA, Alfonso
b. Madrid, 1946. 16mm medium-length feature, *Querido Abraham* ('Dear Abraham', 1968). Prolific NO-DO newsreel director, sacked after his controversial medium-length *La vida en los teleclubs* ('Life in the Tele-Clubs', 1969); TV director from 1971.

FILMS: *El hombre oculto* ('The Hidden Man', 1970); *Tirarse al monte* ('Take to the Hills', 1971); *Gulliver* (1976); *Soldados* ('Soldiers', 1978); *Cuentos eróticos* (episode: 'Love is Marvellous', 1979); *La conquista de Albania* ('The Conquest of Albania', 1983.)

URIBE, Imanol
b. San Salvador (El Salvador), 1950. Lived in Spain from an early age; graduated EOC in 1974. With Fernando Colomo and Miguel Angel Díaz founded Zeppo films; made two short films, *Off* (1976) and *Ez* (1977), and co-scripted and produced Díaz's *De fresa, limón y menta* (1977). A leading figure in the Basque film industry, Uribe made the short *La canción vasca* ('Basque Song', Ikuska short no. 13) and produced *Fuego eterno* ('Eternal Fire', José Angel Rebolledo, 1984).

FILMS: *El proceso de Burgos* ('The Burgos Trial', 1979); *La fuga de Segovia* ('The Segovia Escape', 1981); *La muerte de Mikel* ('Mikel's Death', 1984); *Adios, pequeña* ('Farewell, Little Girl', in production).

VIOTA, Paulino
b. Santander, 1948. Film criticism for Radio Popular and *El Diario Montañes*. Made three medium-length Super-8 features, 1966–7, and then *Fin de invierno* ('Winter's End', 1968). Madrid-based from 1969, Viota has consistently worked with the actress Guadalupe G. Güemes.

FILMS: *Contactos* ('Contacts', 1970); *Jaula de todos* ('Cage for Everybody', 1975); *Con uñas y dientes* ('Tooth and Nail', 1978); *Cuerpo a cuerpo* ('Hand-to-Hand', 1982).

ZULUETA, Ivan
b. San Sebastián, 1943. EOC student. Worked on *Ultimo grito*, a television pop programme, with Drove and Chávarri; designed record covers and film posters (e.g. for *Furtivos*, *El corazón del bosque*, and *Laberinto de pasiones*). Has made many short and Super-8 films, including *Masaje* (35mm), *Frank Stein* (35mm), *Souvenir*

(Super-8), *Babia* (Super-8), *Mi ego está en Babia* (feature, Super-8), *Acuarium* (Super-8), *Kin Kon* (Super-8), *Marilyn* (Super-8), *Will More seduciendo a Taylor Mead* (Super-8), *Leo es pardo* (16mm, 1976), *A Mal Gam A* (medium-length, Super-8), *En la ciudad* (1977, fragment of collective film).

FILMS: *Un, dos, tres ... al escondite inglés* ('Hide and Seek', 1969); *Arrebato* ('Rapture', 1979).

SELECT BIBLIOGRAPHY

Individual sources are referred to in the Notes. The following books and articles provide an introduction to the major themes and figures of Spanish cinema.

Max Aub, *Conversaciones con Buñuel*, Madrid, Aguilar, 1985.

Luis Berlanga, 'El cine español de posguerra', *Contracampo*, no. 24, October 1981.

Enrique Brasó, *Carlos Saura*, Madrid, Taller de Ediciones, 1974.

Luis Buñuel, *My Last Breath*, London, Fontana, 1985.

Antonio Castro, *El cine español en el banquillo*, Valencia, Fernando Torres, 1974.

Jean Delmas, 'Cinéastes espagnols de l'après-franquisme', *Jeune Cinéma*, 118, April–May 1979.

Gwynne Edwards, *The Discreet Art of Luis Buñuel*, London, Marion Boyars, 1982.

José Luis Egea, 'Buñuel is written with a tilde and is seventy years old' in Joan Mellen (ed.), *The World of Luis Buñuel*, New York, Oxford University Press, 1978.

Equipo reseña, *Cine para leer*, Bilbao, Mensajero, annually from 1972.

Felix Fanés, *Cifesa, la antorcha de los éxitos*, Valencia, Institución Alfonso el Magnánimo, 1982.

Emilio C. García Fernández, *Historia ilustrada del cine español*, Madrid, Planeta, 1985.

Antonio García Rayo, 'La década de los 70 en el cinematógrafo español', *Cinema 2002*, nos. 61–2, March–April 1980.

José Luis Guarner, 'Apuntes sobre la primera década prodigiosa, 1975–1985', *Fotogramas*, no. 1714, December 1985.

José Luis Guarner and Peter Besas, *El inquietante cine de Vicente Aranda*, Madrid, Imagfic 85, 1985.

Román Gubern, *La censura: Función política y ordenamiento jurídico bajo el franquismo, 1936–1975*, Barcelona, Ediciones Península, 1981.

Juan Hernández Les and Miguel Gato, *El cine de autor en España*, Madrid, Miguel Castellote, 1978.

Juan Hernández Les and Manuel Hidalgo, *El último austro–húngaro: conversaciones con Berlanga*, Barcelona, Anagrama, 1981.

Marta Hernández, *El aparato cinematográfico español*, Barcelona, Akal, 1976.

Virginia Higginbotham, *Luis Buñuel*, Boston, Twayne, 1979.

283

John Hopewell, 'The Art of the Possible', *Stills*, no. 5, 1982.
Annette Insdorf, 'Spain Also Rises', *Film Comment*, vol. 16, no. 4, July–August 1980.
Katherine S. Kovacs (ed.), 'New Spanish Cinema', *Quarterly Review of Film Studies*, vol. 8, no. 2, Spring 1983.
Francesc Llinàs and Julio Pérez Perucha, 'Nunca estuvimos en el río Mississippi: entrevista con Antonio Drove', *Contracampo*, no. 12, May 1980.
Francesc Llinàs, José Luis Téllez and M. Vidal Estévez, 'El viaje del comediante (Conversación con Fernando Fernán Gómez)', *Contracampo*, no. 35, Spring 1984.
J. M. Marti-Rom and Jacqueline Lajeunesse, 'Le cinéma espagnol après Franco: de la politisation au désenchantement', *La Revue du Cinéma*, no. 301, May 1981.
Vicente Molina Foix, *New Cinema in Spain*, London, British Film Institute, 1977.
'Victor Erice: El cine de los supervivientes', *Mayo*, no. 12, September 1983.
Marcel Oms, *Carlos Saura*, Paris, Edilig, 1981.
Marcel Oms and Pierre Roura (eds.), *Les Cahiers de la Cinémathèque*, no. 38–9, Winter 1984.
P. A. Paranagua, 'Espagne: desencanto', *Positif*, no. 240, March 1981.
Jesús Pérez Besada and José Antonio Ventoso Mariño, 'El erotismo y la mujer española en el cine durante el franquismo', *Cinema 2002*, nos. 29–30, July–August 1977.
Julio Pérez Perucha (ed.), *En torno a Berlanga*, I and II, Publicaciones del Archivo Municipal del Ayuntamiento de Valencia, 1980, 1981.
Santiago Pozo, *La industria del cine en España*, Publicacions i Edicions de la Universitat de Barcelona, 1984.
María José Rague Arias, 'La imagen de la mujer en el cine español', *Cinema 2002*, nos. 29–30, July–August 1977.
Nick Roddick, 'Raising Ravens', *Stills*, September–October 1983.
Agustín Sánchez Vidal, *Vida y opiniones de Luis Buñuel*, Teruel, Instituto de Estudios Turolenses, 1985.
Emilio Sanz de Soto, 'Edgar Neville: Un cineasta de la generación del 27', in the transcripts of the symposium on Neville at the 1982 Valladolid Film Festival.
Carlos Saura and Antonio Gades, *Carmen, el sueño del amor absoluto*, Barcelona, Círculo/Folio, 1984.
Nissa Torrents, 'Cinema and the Media after the Death of Franco', in Nissa Torrents and Christopher Abel (eds.), *Spain: Conditional Democracy*, London, Croom Helm, 1984.
Augusto M. Torres, *Conversaciones con Manuel Gutiérrez Aragón*, Madrid, Editorial Fundamentos, 1985.
Augusto M. Torres (ed.), *Spanish Cinema 1896–1983*, Madrid, Ministerio de Cultura, Instituto de Cine, 1986.
Universidad de Murcia, *Cine español 1975–1984*, Murcia, 1984.
Fernando Vizcaíno Casas, *Historia y anécdota del cine español*, Madrid, Ediciones Adra, 1976.

INDEX

Note: Spanish surnames often include both a patronymic and a matronymic. This index follows the usual (though not invariable) Spanish practice of indexing names under the patronymic surname: for example, Manuel Gutiérrez Aragón is indexed under G.